Stockholm 26/7-95

To Emmy W.

with appreciation
and gratitude

Eggert W.

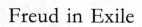

Freud in Exile

Freud in the year of his death.

Freud in Exile
Psychoanalysis and its Vicissitudes

edited by
Edward Timms and Naomi Segal

Yale University Press
New Haven and London
1988

Set in Monophoto Garamond
at the Alden Press, Oxford

Library of Congress Cataloging-in-Publication Data

Freud in exile.

Bibliography: p.
Includes index.
1. Psychoanalysis – History – Congresses.   2. Freud,
Sigmund, 1856–1939 – Congresses.   3. Freud, Sigmund,
1856–1939 – Exile, 1938–1939 – Congresses.
4. Psychoanalysis – Translating – Congresses.
I. Timms, Edward.   II. Segal, Naomi.
BF173.F856 1988   150.19′52   87-37236
ISBN 0-300-04226-4

Contents

Illustrations

Acknowledgements: Permission to reproduce illustrations is gratefully acknowledged as follows: The Freud Museum, London (Nos 7, 9, 20); André Deutsche Ltd (13, 17); The Hogarth Press Ltd (10, 11, 15, 19); Sigmund Freud Copyrights (frontispiece, 1, 3, 4, 6, 8, 12, 22); Routledge & Kegan Paul Ltd (5); The Melanie Klein Trust (14); Archivi Alinari S.p.A. (16); The British Library Newspaper Library, Colindale (2).

List of Abbreviations

works by or about Sigmund Freud:

Sigmund Freud, *Gesammelte Werke*, ed. Anna Freud *et al.*, 18 vols. (London 1940–[1952])   *GW*

—— *Standard Edition of the Complete Psychological Works*, trans. and ed. James Strachey *et al.*, 24 vols. (London 1953–74)   *SE*

—— *Letters, 1873–1939*, ed. Ernst L. Freud, trans. James and Tania Stern (London 1960)   *Letters*

Ernest Jones, *Sigmund Freud: Life and Work*, 3 vols. (London 1953–7)   Jones

other abbreviations and short forms used:

American Psychoanalytic Association   APA
International Journal of Psycho-Analysis   *Int'l Jn Psych*
International Psycho-Analytical Association   IPA
International Review of Psycho-Analysis   *Int'l Rev Psych*
Internationale Zeitschrift für [ärztliche] Psychoanalyse   *Int'l Z Psych*
Internationaler Psychoanalytischer Verlag   Verlag
Journal of the American Psychoanalytic Association   *Jn APA*
Psychoanalytic Study of the Child   *Psych Study of Child*

Introduction

The Dynamics of Exile

The arrival of Freud and his family in London in June 1938 can be seen as a symbolic event. Five years earlier, at the book-burning in Berlin, the Nazis had placed his writings high on the list of works to be destroyed: 'Against the soul-destroying overvaluation of sexual life! For the nobility of the human soul! I consign to the flames the writings of Sigmund Freud', the Nazi herald proclaimed. This book-burning was the signal that sent a whole generation of Jewish writers, scholars and scientists into exile. And yet many of them were to make a far greater impact abroad, particularly in the English-speaking world, than they had in their country of origin. The aim of this book, published to mark the fiftieth anniversary of Freud's arrival in London, is to pay tribute to that generation by focusing on the paradoxical concomitants of exile – both for individuals and for their ideas.

The irony of history is that the psychoanalytic exodus, far from extinguishing Freud's endeavours, actually accelerated the worldwide dissemination of his ideas. Looking back over the developments of the past fifty years, Ernest Gellner writes: 'Of the various belief systems that have emerged in the modern world, psychoanalysis is by far the most successful. . . How was this astonishing conquest of our thought and language accomplished, in a period well under half a century, and unaided by special resources?' It is on this question that our book focuses, from a variety of angles, drawing on the research of more than a score of scholars who assembled in London in October 1986 to contribute to a symposium entitled 'Freud in London – Psychoanalysis in Transition'.[1] Revised for publication in book form, these contributors' papers trace the evolution of psychoanalysis through some of its principal phases: its origins in the culture of Vienna at the turn of the century; its reception in the English-speaking world and the tribulations of its practitioners in exile; the problems which have arisen as a result of ideas originally formulated in Freud's idiosyncratically expressive German being disseminated worldwide in a 'Standard' English translation; and finally some of the more recent developments and debates, not least among the feminists, which testify to the continuing vitality of psychoanalysis and open up perspectives for the future.

The story begins with the 'Origins' of psychoanalysis, which are explored in Part One in a sequence of interrelated papers. In his account of the struggle of psychiatry with psychoanalysis, Sander L. Gilman draws attention to the difficulties encountered by Jews wishing to enter the medical profession in late nineteenth-century Vienna. It was through specializing in such 'marginal' areas as psychopathology and sexuality that Freud (like his friend Fliess) was able to aspire to academic status. But their early enquiries became enmeshed in a network of associations linking Jewishness with sexuality, noses with genitalia. The problem of the status of the psychoanalyst was to recur in the 1920s in the debates about 'lay analysis', and again in the United States twenty years later.

The question of the Jewish origins of psychoanalysis is taken up in the following paper by Ivar Oxaal, who reviews a wide range of publications devoted to this theme. Oxaal offers a demographic answer to the question why early psychoanalysis in Vienna was 'exclusively Jewish', emphasizing the preponderance of Jewish graduates among those who gained access to higher education.

Origins of a different kind are explored in subsequent chapters, which draw attention to some of the intellectual sources of Freudian theory. Uwe Henrik Peters traces the antecedents of psychoanalysis in German Romanticism. The close links which he establishes make the loss to German intellectual life resulting from the subsequent psychoanalytic exodus all the more poignant. Edward Timms takes as his starting-point certain books in the library which Freud brought with him into exile (now preserved at the Freud Museum in London). Annotations in Freud's own hand show that he did not merely read for relaxation, but also engaged in the systematic study of literary texts. The pioneering discoveries of psychoanalysis are attributable to his 'syncretic imagination', which enabled him to synthesize an extraordinary range of divergent material.

The theme of exile recurs in a displaced form in Ritchie Robertson's analysis of Freud's 'testament' – *Moses and Monotheism*. Robertson shows that this book, completed during Freud's final period in London, should be read more as an imaginative than as a scholarly work – and that it can be taken as an implicit statement about Freud's identity as a Jew. The practical problems with which Freud had to cope during the years before he was forced into exile are examined by Murray G. Hall in his account of the fate of the Internationaler Psychoanalytischer Verlag. The Vienna-based publishing house came under political as well as economic pressure after the Nazi seizure of power in Germany;

but the story of its demise after the German occupation of Austria is more complex than has generally been realized. And the fact that Freud was able to bring with him to London such a large part of his personal library, as well as antiquities and furnishings, proves to have been due to the practical support of the Nazi official entrusted with the liquidation of the Verlag.

Part Two, 'Reception and Exile', begins with an account of the role of Ernest Jones in the reception of psychoanalysis in the English-speaking world. Drawing for the first time on the full range of the Jones–Freud correspondence, R. Andrew Paskauskas shows that Jones's own account of his early attitude to psychoanalysis is in certain respects misleading. Unpublished letters also reveal for the first time certain aspects of Jones's involvement: Freud's sensitive handling of the break-up of Jones's relationship with his common-law wife in 1913; Jones's behind-the-scenes activities as a member of the 'Secret Committee', particularly during the rivalry with Jung; and Jones's leading role in the project of translating Freud's writings into English. It becomes clear that the close personal bond between Jones and Freud, which endured from their first meeting in 1908 until Freud's death in 1939, was one of the crucial factors in the history of the psychoanalytic movement.

The early divergences between the Psycho-Analytical Societies of London and Vienna provide the theme of the paper by Pearl King, Honorary Archivist of the British Psycho-Analytical Society. Her account of the rapid development of psychoanalysis in London emphasizes the fruitful co-operation between Vienna and London, as well as the divergences. The British Society, unlike that in Vienna, had very few Jewish members; but it included a number of 'gentleman scholars' who were fascinated by the possibility of applying the new theories to a wide range of social and cultural issues. The most striking divergences became apparent after the arrival of Melanie Klein in London in 1925. Klein's contributions encountered criticism because of her use of phantasy, her interpretation of the death instinct and the early date she assigned to the development of the super-ego. To shed light on the ensuing controversy, Ernest Jones arranged in 1935–6 a series of 'Exchange Lectures' with the Vienna Society. After the German occupation of Austria, the British Society extended a welcome to a significant number of analysts exiled from Vienna, including Freud himself and his daughter Anna. The regular scientific meetings of the Society, although still enlivened by controversy, provided moral support for those having to cope with the deprivations of exile.

A further aspect of the British assimilation of psychoanalysis is explored in the paper on the aesthetic criticism of Adrian Stokes. In this the art historian Stephen Bann singles out Stokes for special attention

because he was the first English critic of note unreservedly to accept the
relevance of psychoanalytic method, particularly the ideas of Melanie
Klein, to his work. A careful analysis of Stokes's writings (including
unpublished notebooks) shows however that there was no abrupt
conversion to a new aesthetic theory. Instead, his response to painting
and sculpture, in particular to the work of Italian masters like
Giorgione, underwent a subtle transformation through which aesthetic
discourse in the manner of Ruskin became enriched by vivid psychoanalytic insights.

Even before the psychoanalytic exodus from Central Europe, the
ideas of Freud and his followers were being enthusiastically assimilated
in the English-speaking world. This creative interaction acquired a new
dynamic as a result of the experience of exile, which is explored from
different angles in the papers by Frederick Wyatt, Ernst Federn and
Martin Stanton. Wyatt, himself a refugee analyst who spent thirty-five
years in the United States, draws attention to the alienating effects of
exile on a person who has to cope with a language barrier and to accept
diminished professional status. More subtle forms of deprivation
resulted from the loss of the cultural matrix within which psychoanalytic theory had evolved, and the need to adapt, in the United States, to
the dominance of medical psychiatry. The rise of ego psychology was
a further distorting factor. To be set against these, however, were the
important gains which resulted from the interaction between European
analysts and their American colleagues, leading to a rapid expansion of
psychoanalysis in new directions.

A less sanguine view of American experience is taken in the paper by
Ernst Federn, whose father Paul Federn was one of the first generation
of psychoanalytic exiles, and who later himself spent a number of years
in the States. Federn deplores the fate of psychoanalysis as a 'science in
exile', which he attributes partly to the divergence between the
empirical Anglo-Saxon concept of 'science' and the very different
epistemological assumptions underlying Freud's conception of 'Wissenschaft'. The 'tragedy' which befell psychoanalysis in exile Federn
attributes to the loss of its original language as well as its cultural
bearings. The 'Americanization' of psychoanalysis, with its pragmatic
emphasis on treatment rather than on theoretical understanding, is seen
as a serious distortion. By contrast, the developments in England,
particularly those associated with the work of Anna Freud and Melanie
Klein, are viewed more favourably.

For refugee analysts in England too the experience of exile could be
traumatic. This is made clear in the account by Martin Stanton of the
last years of Freud's erstwhile collaborator, Wilhelm Stekel, who
committed suicide in London in June 1940. The question unravelled in
Stanton's paper is whether Stekel's death, as well as the earlier suicides

of other prominent members of the psychoanalytic movement, should be taken as a sign of inherent instability within the group. Through a careful reconstruction of the outlines of Stekel's career and of the difficulties he faced in exile, the paper suggests that his suicide should rather be seen as a logical reaction to exceptionally adverse circumstances.

The most subtle form of deprivation resulting from exile was the loss of the original language of psychoanalysis – that uniquely resonant German in which Freud's insights were first formulated. Part Three, on 'Problems of Translation', thus raises fundamental questions – both for historians interested in the evolution of psychoanalysis and for practitioners concerned with its future development. Malcolm Pines, chairman of the Publications Committee of the Institute of Psycho-Analysis, identifies two factors which give a special urgency to this debate – the growing dissatisfaction with Strachey's 'Standard Edition', and the impending expiry of the Freud copyright – which provide incentives for new translations. In his paper, tracing the process by which the term 'standard' came to be applied to the first English translations of Freud, Riccardo Steiner casts back to the very earliest attempts, by Jones, Brill and Putnam, to find English equivalents for key technical terms. These equivalents, designed to enhance the status of psychoanalysis in the eyes of the British and American medical profession, replaced Freud's homely and richly variable metaphors with elements of jargon (often with a Greek or Latin base) in terms like 'cathexis' and 'parapraxis', the 'ego' and the 'id'. These technical terms were consolidated in official 'glossaries', so that when James Strachey set about producing his Standard Edition, he found himself working within parameters already established under the authority of Ernest Jones. Admittedly Freud expressed his approval both of Strachey as a translator and of many of the technical terms he used; but the English Standard Edition has nevertheless had the effect of imposing a sort of Anglo-American 'Newspeak' on psychoanalysis.

The limitations of the Standard Edition are explored from a different angle in the paper by Darius Gray Ornston, who contrasts Freud's flexible and imaginative style with Strachey's reliance on a narrower range of fixed categories. Working within a more rigid paradigm of scientific method, Jones and Strachey replaced Freud's variegated idiom with a technical terminology devoid of feeling. Ornston's argument is reinforced by two shorter papers by analysts with recent experience of both English and German therapeutic practice. Alex Holder urges that the task of retranslating Freud should be undertaken without delay, since the distortions of the Strachey edition tend to destroy the associative links essential to Freud's idiom. Helmut Junker makes the paradoxical observation that for a German with a good reading knowledge of English the Standard Edition is actually easier to understand – and can even seem theoretically more 'correct' – than the German original. Indeed the German edition most often used by students incorporates Strachey's footnotes to Freud's text, translated into German. The result is a complex set of distortions which makes the task of retranslation both urgently necessary and almost insuperably difficult. The associations of Freud's style have receded, even for German readers, with the passage of time. Language, knowledge and reading experience are all subject to organic processes of growth and mutation which make the quest for a more 'correct' English translation elusive.

The vigorous developments of psychoanalytic theory since Freud's death are reflected in the final part of the book, 'Perspectives for the Future'. Ernest Gellner approaches the subject from the position of an anthropologist, identifying certain features in Western society which have made it especially receptive to Freudian theory: the lack of integrated social structures, coherent hierarchies and rituals of salvation; the unintelligibility of experience in a scientific age which separates personal beliefs from the practicalities of daily life; and the primacy of human relationships. Psychoanalysis squares the circle by providing a theory of man which is both firmly grounded in biology and intricately structured in its analysis of emotional life. Through its theory of the unconscious, the realm in which 'dark drives encounter complex meanings', it offers a system of belief which does not depend on any kind of transcendence. Psychotherapy offers a promise of salvation in a secular world and a paradigm for the pastoral services which our society so desperately requires.

John Bowlby, doyen of British child psychologists, adds a further dimension to the complex picture. His paper on changing theories of childhood lays particular emphasis on the 'attachment theory' which he pioneered. His review of the wide-ranging field work which this theory has generated confirms the importance for the growth of personality of the very earliest experiences of 'attachment' and 'deprivation'. The child's experience of mothering is assigned central importance in a significantly modified model of psychoanalysis.

The traditional Freudian assumptions are challenged from a feminist perspective in two papers. In the first Naomi Segal, reacting against the tendency in traditional psychoanalysis to make women 'the object, not the subject, of language', surveys the feminist critique of psychoanalysis from Simone de Beauvoir through to the present. The polemics of Kate Millett and Germaine Greer are contrasted with the more differentiated approach of critics like Juliet Mitchell who argue for a return to Freud, not a repudiation of him. Psychoanalysis (in Mitchell's suggestive definition) is 'not a recommendation *for* a patriarchal society, but an analysis *of* one'. That Freud's conception of femininity was highly tendentious is clear, nevertheless, above all from recent debates about the case history of 'Dora'.

The complexities of the feminist position are further elaborated in a paper by Teresa Brennan, which establishes surprising connections between Lacanian-influenced feminism of the 1980s and the 'Controversial Discussions', provoked by the work of Melanie Klein, at the British Psycho-Analytical Society in the 1940s. The argument hinges on the distinctions between 'psychical reality' and social conditioning, Klein's concept of the infant's unconscious phantasies about the breast being contrasted with the Freudian emphasis on penis envy as the determinant of emotional development. The Lacanian distinction between the 'imaginary' and the 'symbolic' is invoked to clarify and resolve the issue. The problem remains that although Lacan's theory supports the view that femininity is 'constructed', not 'biologically given', he still follows Freud in assigning to the penis / phallus a central symbolic role.

The implications of psychoanalysis are explored on a more practical plane in Walter Toman's account of Freud's influence on other forms of psychotherapy. After an introduction dealing with the relations between philosophy and psychotherapy, the author constructs a model of the classical procedures of Freudian psychotherapy, in which the therapist adopts an attentive, benevolent and relatively passive role. Toman then reviews the rich proliferation of alternative therapies which have been evolved from the classical model, showing how they adapt or accentuate particular features of the original method. Even therapeutic strategies evolved in explicit opposition to Freud, like Eysenck's 'behaviour therapy' and Rogers's 'client-centred therapy', prove on closer inspection to have important features in common with the classical model. Toman concludes with an optimistic prognosis, in which the different schools of psychotherapy, acknowledging how much they have in common, develop a greater readiness to consult with and learn from each other.

The final session of the symposium on 'Freud in London' was held at the newly opened Freud Museum in Maresfield Gardens, Hampstead. It is thus appropriate that this collection of papers should end with an account of the contents and importance of the Freud Museum by its first Curator, David Newlands. The Museum is not intended as a shrine, but as a centre for research. In addition to the library, antiquities and furnishings (including the famous couch) which Freud brought with him from Vienna, the Museum has a collection of documents, photographs and letters. The work of Anna Freud, who spent so much of her working life in Maresfield Gardens, is also commemorated in the

Museum. David Newlands sketches the legal, financial and organizational background to the opening of the Museum, including the negotiations which took place in 1969 with the Sigmund Freud Society in Vienna. The aim of the Museum is to reflect the unique contribution which Freud made to our culture and the continuing debate about his ideas. In a wider sense the Museum may also be regarded as a memorial to the Jews who found refuge in Britain, and to those who lost their lives in the Holocaust.

Freud in Exile, as its subtitle indicates, is a study of the vicissitudes which have shaped the psychoanalytic movement.[2] It examines the diverse ways in which a system of ideas, transplanted from its original Austrian setting into the English-speaking cultures of Britain and the United States, has been adapted to new environments. However traumatic the experience of exile may have been for those directly involved, it is clear that it contributed to the worldwide dissemination of psychoanalysis (although with certain distortions). Indeed, Freud's coming to London in 1938 must be seen not as a defeat, but as a token of the growing prestige of the movement which he had pioneered.

This was evident in the intense diplomatic activity which led the Nazi authorities to grant exit visas to Freud and his family, after the German occupation of Vienna. The American Consul in Vienna took a personal interest in Freud's predicament and sent urgent messages to the US State Department in Washington. President Roosevelt himself instructed his Secretary of State to make forceful representations through the American Ambassador in Berlin. Meanwhile Ernest Jones was using his influence with senior members of the British government to obtain permission for Freud and his family to come to London. And William Bullitt, American Ambassador in Paris, was making arrangements for the Freuds to be welcomed to France.

While waiting for the visas that would enable him to leave Vienna, Freud wrote a moving letter to his son Ernst in London, expressing – in a phrase written in English – his wish 'to die in freedom'. He was granted a visa to enter France, and it was even suggested that he and his family might settle in the United States. The fact that he chose London as the place to spend the final eighteen months of his life reflects not only his sense of personal affinity with England, but also his great respect for all that had been done by his English adherents to establish psychoanalysis in the English-speaking world. 'The events of the past years', he noted in a letter to Ernest Jones in March 1939, 'have brought it about that London has become the main site and centre of the psycho-analytic movement'.

On his arrival with his family in London, Freud was welcomed as an honoured guest. And he was gratified to receive a visit from the

1. Sigmund Freud with his daughter Anna, on their way into exile, June 1938.

2. Report of Freud's arrival in London: *Daily Mail*, 7 June 1938.

Freud Comes to London Poor and a Refugee

"ALL HE HAD HAS BEEN TAKEN AWA

'HERE I CAN END MY LIFE-WORK IN PEACE'

By F. G. PRINCE-WHITE

PROFESSOR Sigmund Freud, world-famous founder of the science of psycho-analysis, came to London yesterday to join the company of exiles from Austria—and went straight to bed.

He is 82, and very frail—though still strong in spirit, with a keen glint in his dark eyes, and a pugnacious way of thrusting out his trim white beard.

"I have come to England for peace," he said, tremulously, when he got out of the train at Victoria leaning on the arms of his daughter, Dr. Anna Freud, and his son, Ernst, an architect practising in London. With him also were his wife and other son, Martin, a lawyer.

"England is a country I have always loved," he added, "and it is a great joy to me to be here, and to be able to finish my life's work in quiet."

He could bring with him only a few trifles from his personal possessions—but he was not parted from his favourite dog Lun, a Chow.

Ordered to Sleep

A home had been prepared for Dr. Freud at St. John's Wood, N.W. His

Professor Freud photographed at his new home with his eldest daughter, Mrs. Hollitschek, and Dr. Ernest Jones, who met him at Victoria.

Glider Freezes 2 Miles Up

A box containing a height recording barograph will be left at the Royal Aero Club in Piccadilly to-day by Mr. Philip A. Wills, of Berkhamsted, to establish his claim to the British gliding altitude record.

The barograph was fixed to the German sailplane in which he climbed

Famous Mare Fights for Life—at 20

From Daily Mail Correspondent

3. Freud at his desk in London, July 1938, with the manuscript of *An Outline of Psycho-Analysis*.

4. Freud with Anna at 20 Maresfield Gardens, London.

secretaries of the Royal Society, who brought the official Charter Book of the Society for him to sign. But amid all these greetings and honours he was especially pleased to receive what he described as 'something special for England, numerous letters from strangers who only wish to say how happy they are that we have come to England and that we are in safety and peace'. This detail too belongs in an account of psychoanalysis and its vicissitudes. But the final word may be given to *The Lancet*, a journal which had earlier provided a forum for Freud's opponents but which in 1938 welcomed his arrival in London with the following tribute: 'His teachings have in their time aroused controversy more acute and antagonism more bitter than any since the days of Darwin. Now, in his old age, there are few psychologists of any school who do not admit their debt to him. Some of the conceptions he formulated clearly for the first time have crept into current philosophy against the stream of wilful incredulity which he himself recognized as man's natural reaction to unbearable truth'.[3]

EDWARD TIMMS
NAOMI SEGAL

Cambridge, June 1987

Notes

[1] The editors, who were also the organizers of the symposium 'Freud in London – Psychoanalysis in Transition', on which this book is based, wish to thank the following institutions which generously sponsored and acted as hosts to the symposium: the Austrian Institute in London (and its Directors, Dr Bernhard Stillfried and Dr Ernst Menhofer); the Institute of Germanic Studies, University of London (and its Honorary Directors, Professors J.P. Stern and R.A. Wisbey); and the Freud Museum in London, its Trustees and its first Curator, Mr David Newlands. The papers delivered at the symposium have not only been revised for publication in book form, but are placed in a new sequence. Two of the papers were unfortunately not available for publication here: 'Child Psychology in Vienna – Psychoanalysis in London' by Ilse Hellman, and 'Psychoanalysis in the British Universities: An Unhappy Childhood' by Brett Kahr.

[2] Our subtitle contains an allusion to the phrase chosen by James Strachey as English title for one of Freud's essays, 'Triebe und Triebschicksale': 'Instincts and their Vicissitudes', *SE* XIV. 109.

[3] The quotation from *The Lancet*, 11 June 1938, together with other details about the circumstances of Freud's arrival in London, are based on Jones, III. 233–65, and Ronald W. Clark, *Freud: The Man and the Cause* (London 1980), 502–30.

PART ONE

ORIGINS

1

Constructing the Image of the Appropriate Therapist

The Struggle of Psychiatry with Psychoanalysis

Sander L. Gilman

The historical background

What if Wittgenstein and Popper were right after all? What if psychoanalysis is not 'scientific', not scientific by any contemporary definition – including Adolf Grünbaum's – but what if it works all the same?[1] What if psychoanalysis is all right in practice, but the theory isn't scientific? Indeed, what if 'science' is defined ideologically rather than philosophically? If we so redefine 'science', it is not to dismiss psychoanalysis but to understand its origin and impact, to follow the ideological dialectic between the history of psychiatry, its developing as a medical 'science', and the evolving self-definition of psychoanalysis which parallels this history.

We know that Freud divided psychoanalysis into three quite discrete areas – first, a theory, a 'scientific structure'; second, a method of enquiry, a means of exploring and ordering information; and last, but certainly not least, a mode of treatment. Let us, for the moment, follow the actual course of history, at least the course of a history which can be described by sorting out the interrelationship between psychoanalysis and psychiatry, and assume that we can heuristically view the mode of treatment as relatively independent of the other two aspects of psychoanalysis. What if the very claims for a 'scientific' basis for psychoanalytic treatment, and by extension the role of the psychoanalyst as promulgated by Freud and his early followers, were rooted in an ideologically charged historical interpretation of the positivist nature of science and the definition of the social role of the scientist? This may seem an odd premise with which to begin an essay on the mutual influence of psychoanalysis and psychiatry, but it is no stranger than the actual historical practice.

Psychoanalysis originated not in the psychiatric clinic but in the laboratories of neurology in Vienna and Paris.[2] Its point of origin was

not nineteenth-century psychiatry but rather nineteenth-century
neurology. That origin points to a major difference between the traditional practice of nineteenth-century psychiatry and modern clinical
psychiatry in our post-positivistic age. Psychiatry in nineteenth-century
Europe, in Vienna as well as in Paris, was an adjunct to the world of
the asylum. Indeed, the second great battle (after Pinel's restructuring
of the asylum) which nineteenth-century psychiatry waged was the
creation of the 'alienist' as a new medical speciality. The alienist was the
medical doctor in administrative charge of the asylum, rather than
serving as a medical adjunct to the lay asylum director as had earlier,
in the age of 'moral treatment', been the practice.

The medicalization of psychiatry was, by the closing decades of the
nineteenth century, successful. Its success, however, was due to
political factors.[3] In Britain, a series of parliamentary commissions
began, in the first decade of the century, to examine the abuses of the
asylum, abuses which seemed to provide a rationale for the medicalization of such institutions. This view was not based on the actual benefit
which medicine had to offer the mentally ill; rather, it was an attempt
to place the asylum within the growing sphere of medicine as science.
But it also continued to treat psychiatry as a separate mode of treatment,
undertaken in asylums rather than in general hospitals. Moral
treatment, coming as it did out of a religious (the Tukes and Quaker)
tradition or a more radical, revolutionary tradition (Pinel and the
'freeing' of the insane), was seen as scientifically 'old-fashioned' and / or
politically 'dangerous'. The development of the asylum out of the early
nineteenth-century 'reformed' British asylums with their lay directors
relied on a new scientistic definition of the nature of psychiatry. It ran
on a track parallel to but clearly different from the development of the
general medical hospital. 'Reform' was simply not enough; medicalization was needed. For 'madness' came to be seen as 'mental illness' in
what was understood as a natural extension of the general model of
somatic pathology. The new science of psychiatry had been imbued
with the status of science, but it was placed in its own ghetto, the
asylum, which still isolated it from all the other medical specialities
being practised in the general hospital.

Psychiatry was a rather unique case in other ways, too. For in
accepting the power of the state to control directly the actions of a
group labelled as 'different' and 'diseased', psychiatrists straddled the
worlds of politics and science, much like the police doctors, whose area
of control, public health, was the inspection of prostitutes. While they
laid claim to the status of scientists through the introduction of the
medical model of madness, the psychiatrists were still perceived in their
older, non-scientific function as the administrators of institutions of
control. This function lowered the prestige of the alienists. It was the

search for a higher status within medicine, and thus within the academy, which drove the psychiatrist to seek the standing implicitly accorded those in the anatomically based areas of medicine. But it was also the relatively lower status of psychiatry which enabled individuals viewed as marginal, such as Jews, to enter this new medical speciality.

The German and Austrian situation (if one can generalize over a wide range of experience and a large number of national variations) was likewise the result of a gradual professionalization of medicine, and an extension of this medicalization into those areas of health-care delivery, from the running of lying-in hospitals to the direction of the asylums, which were not traditionally seen as part of 'medicine'.[4] This made itself especially evident in the creation, in the mid-nineteenth century, of the huge centralized state asylum at Bielefeld with its professional staff. But the central focus of all these movements was the medicalization of the office of asylum director, and the concomitant rise in the status of this role. Psychiatry in Germany and Austria was as much the administration of the asylum as the treatment of the insane. Neurology, on the other hand, was often seen as a 'pure' medical science, using the positivistic model of late nineteenth-century science, and was seen as quite independent of any 'applied' function (at least to the degree that psychiatry had claimed for itself).

After the mid-nineteenth century, however, neurology and psychiatry shared a set of scientific presumptions which were heavily laced with nineteenth-century racist ideology. Their basis was, indeed, first articulated in the academic forum by Kant in his essay of 1764 on the nature of illness of the head.[5] There he mocks the view that mental illness could have its roots in the emotions, seeing that form of illness as inherently somatic. Kant undertook to apply to the area of mental illness the increasingly influential new French biology, which attempted to explain all aspects of human nature (such as racial differences) through the biological model. It was an effort to move the understanding of mental illness away from what Kant perceived to be the moralizing tendency of religion, which had labelled madness the result of the stigma of sinfulness. Madness was a disease and, like all diseases in the age of Jenner, was understood to be somatic. (It was not the wrath of God which caused illness, but the failure of the corporeal machine.) But it is vital to understand that views such as those espoused by Kant had inherent in them the racist premises of eighteenth-century French biology and anthropology: the 'great chain of being', with its implicit hierarchy among the various races, as well as the polygenetic origin of those races. Kant, in his own anthropology, commented that the Jews are a unique group in the West, marked by their own sign – for him the corruption of their discourse – which sets them apart from all other groups.[6]

Kant's view was clearly in the avant-garde of the eighteenth century. But the general view after the mid-nineteenth century was, following Wilhelm Griesinger's standard textbook of 1845, that 'mind illness' was 'brain illness', and much attention was given to the description and localization of neurological pathologies.[7] Between Kant and Griesinger, however, lay an epoch which stressed the independent existence of mental illness, illness rooted in the mechanics of the emotions and their repression. J.G. Langermann in his 1797 dissertation on mental illness cast these views into their most representative form.[8] Langermann presented a theory of the origin of mental illness that not only dismissed the origin of psychopathologies as anomalies of the brain, but also stressed the origin of psychopathology in the 'spirit'. He abandoned the mind–body dichotomy completely. But even more important, Langermann presented a case study of a 'psychological' cure. He was not alone. Later 'Romantic' psychiatrists such as Ideler, Heinroth, Carus, Kieser, and the widely translated Belgian asylum director Guislain stressed the centrality of psychological mechanisms in the manifestation of mental illness.

Such a view was dynamic in that it denied the primacy of human biology in shaping the human psyche and assumed a certain flexibility of human emotions. It was also implicitly racist. Indeed, the most widely read popularization of this view, Christian Heinrich Spiess's *Biographies of the Mentally Ill* (1795–6), had as one of its centrepieces the tale of the 'beautiful Jewess' Esther L— and her collapse into madness.[9] Spiess's views are typical of the tendency to see mental illness as the result of psychological rather than physical disease. Spiess uses Esther L— as his exemplary case of 'love madness', erotomania, stressing above all the sexual nature of the Jew and the relationship of this psychological weakness to psychopathology. Thus both biological and Romantic psychopathology were strongly formed by contemporaneous attitudes towards race.

The domination of the biological model over the psychological was in point of fact the presumptive success of the 'scientific' over the 'religious', or at least that is how the nineteenth century perceived it. The position which late nineteenth-century clinical psychiatry took was not merely in line with the sense of the status of medicine as it existed after the mid-century, but also in opposition to what Emil Kraepelin as late as 1918 felt compelled to dismiss as 'natural–philosophical specula-tion'. Kraepelin's views, however, were not aimed at the 'Romantic' psychiatrists of the early nineteenth century, but at the resurrection of their position in the works of Sigmund Freud.[10]

The predicament of Freud and Fliess

Sigmund Freud's early work in the laboratories of Theodor Meynert centred on the neurological description of primitive vertebrates, with the hope that such analysis would lead to an understanding of the mechanisms and structures which are also present in human neurological development. His work was aimed at a purely mechanistic description of the nature of human psychology. When he came into contact with Jean-Martin Charcot in Paris, he maintained his attitude towards the nature and value of such a scientific undertaking, an undertaking which was 'pure' science. For Meynert and Charcot shared in the patriarchal status of the new scientific medicine, following Claude Bernard's lead. Or so the legend created by Freud is supposed to be read.[11] As I have shown elsewhere, in the tradition of French, as well as German, anthropological psychiatry Jews were labelled at high risk for specific forms of mental illness.[12] But neurology, in which modern psychoanalytic thought originated, was itself not free from such perversions. And it was in Freud's relationship with one individual, the Berlin ear, nose and throat specialist, Wilhelm Fliess, that the racist overtones of 'scientific' medicine were articulated and distanced.

In Freud's correspondence with Fliess, the nature of the scientific undertaking of psychiatry and neurology and the definition of the medical practitioner were drawn into question.[13] Traditionally Fliess is represented as a marginal figure in the history of medicine. He is seen as the mute sounding board for Freud's views. Everyone (up to but not including Peter Swales, who is now writing Fliess's biography) has wondered how Freud, as bright and insightful as he evidently was, could have got himself associated with this Berlin quack. It has been accepted that Fliess was a quack – he put forth absolutely mad views, such as the intimate relationship between the nasal passages and the genitalia, or the idea that male as well as female physiology reflected rigid periodic cycles. But quackery implies a misappropriation of the status of scientific medicine, and it is the implication of this misappropriation which can help us understand Freud's gradual redefinition of the science of medicine.

Fliess in fact acted on his theories, carrying out surgical intervention on the nose to relieve sexual problems. His ineptitude almost killed Freud's patient Emma Eckstein, when he left a wad of surgical dressing in the nasal cavity which caused massive bleeding and infection. He also operated on Freud's nose, during the stay in Vienna in which he undertook the Eckstein operation. This action, as Max Schur stated when he first revealed the material, must have had a negative influence on Freud's understanding of the implications for science, both in the ineptitude it revealed and the fact that Fliess had been placed by Freud on an intellectual plane that clearly paralleled the level which he himself

wished to attain.[14] Fliess's assumed role as a 'surgeon', the highest of
the medical specialities, was only disguised by his label as a 'nose'
doctor. His actions were those of medical practitioners whose status
was clearly higher than that permitted him by the society in which he
lived. The denial was based on Fliess's racial identity.

And it is no accident that all of Fliess's patients, Freud included, were
Jewish. The isolation still felt by the Jewish health-care practitioner
formed both Freud and Fliess. Both saw in the social status of medicine
a chance to establish themselves in a society which rejected Jews but
acclaimed academic physicians. Freud and Fliess both sought out specialities which were open to Jews, but they restructured these areas
conceptually to reflect the higher status of other medical specialities.[15]
Sexual questions were dealt with by the psychiatrist in the role of
forensic specialist on deviant behaviour as well as by the syphilologist,
who, as a dermatologist, occupied the lowest rung in Viennese
medicine. Indeed, when Ferdinand Hebra assumed the chair of dermatology (a field nicknamed 'Judenhaut [Jewskin]' in Vienna), he was
able to recruit only Jewish assistants. And psychiatry, with its transitional status between administration and practice, had an equally
heavy and early Jewish representation. Thus Freud and Fliess sought
out two areas, psychopathology and sexuality, where Jews were
permitted to function on the level of the academician. Their meetings,
which they dubbed 'congresses', were mock academic events. And their
desire was to move the study of psycho- and sexual pathologies into a
new area – that of neurology.

Freud and Fliess both needed the status of the higher academic
specialities. Both sought this status in the area of neurology and
addressed their need for status by attempting to ask questions about
sexuality and psychopathology that were (in Viennese medicine) traditionally 'Jewish' through the higher-status sub-speciality of neurology.
For Wilhelm Fliess, it was a movement from a concentration on the ear,
nose and throat to the interconnection of all human experience by
means of the nervous system. Now Fliess was clearly marginal in the
Berlin medical community, as was Freud in that of Vienna. But to be
'marginal' means to have direct relation to the centre. Both Freud and
Fliess oriented themselves towards the centre of German medicine;
both sought (and Freud obtained) the status of the medical academic.
Both functioned in relation to a discourse, that of medicine, that was
critical of marginality – and that defined marginality in racial terms.

Fliess's theories, based on the best of late nineteenth-century endo-
crinological and neurological theory, appear to us as more than slightly
mad.[16] But they fulfilled a function for Fliess, as well as for Freud, in
creating a sense of the new pathway which medicine, stripped of its
openly racist overtones, could take. Let us look at two of Fliess's 'mad'

ideas – the relationship between the nose and the genitalia, and his 'proof' of male periodicity – in the light of the science of medicine, with all its racist overtones in late nineteenth-century Germany and Austria. It was precisely the implications of even the higher medical specialities, such as neurology, which coloured Freud's and Fliess's sense of the status of medicine and the medical practitioner.

The idea that the nasal cavities were anatomically parallel to the genitalia grew out of the study of human embryology during the nineteenth century. As early as 1835, in G. Valentin's handbook of human development, the parallels in the development of soft-tissue areas and cavities of the foetus had been noted. By the time of the publication of the standard atlas of human embryological development by Wilhelm His, in 1885, the assumption of such parallels was at the centre of European embryology.[17] But the history of embryology, and His's very creation of 'standard developmental stages', is rooted in the ideology of recapitulation. Nineteenth-century biologists believed that they could see in the development of the human foetus the 'highest' form of life, the repetition of all the evolutionary stages. Central to this biological reworking of the 'great chain of being' was the innate superiority of the human as the end of the teleological development of evolution. Biology placed humanity at the acme of this development and saw in Ernst Haeckel's commonplace that 'ontogeny recapitulates phylogeny' the statement of human superiority.[18] But in late nineteenth-century Germany some humans were better than other humans. And it is the implied sense of the hierarchy which is present in German embryology.

Hierarchy in late nineteenth-century German and Austrian science implied a hidden analogy to the science of race – and the key figures in this hierarchy were the Jews. Christianity saw in the Jews a stage through which modern humans had progressed. Hegel labelled the Jews as an atavistic structure in Western history. For, once having played a role in history, like other ancient peoples, they should have vanished. Their presence in the society of the West was a sign of how much further modern humans had come. If indeed 'ontogeny re-capitulates phylogeny', then the Jew was on a lower rung in the hierarchy of the human races. This view was so powerful that it was shared even by Ferdinand Ratzel, the originator of modern geographical anthropology, when he looked at the Jews of Western Europe.[19]

But embryology also proved that the development of the nasal passages and the incipient genitalia was very early in the development of the foetus. Fliess, by making this association overt, showed that the 'head', as the source of the rational, and the 'genitalia', as the source of the irrational, were related on an atavistic level and that the manipulation of one could affect the other. The assumption of a primitive relationship between sexuality and the nose is not only bad embryology but bad medicine. It points, however, to a necessary preoccupation by two Jewish scientists of *fin-de-siècle* Europe with the significance of this relationship between the nose and the genitalia. For Fliess and Freud it served as a sign of universal development rather than as a specific sign of an 'inferior' racial identity.

The association between the Jewish nose and the circumcised penis was made in the crudest and most revolting manner during the 1880s, when, in the streets of Berlin and Vienna, in penny papers or on the newly installed *Litfassäulen* (advertising pillars), caricatures of Jews could be seen.[20] These extraordinary caricatures stressed one central aspect of the physiognomy of the Jewish male, his nose, which stood for the hidden sign of his sexual difference, his circumcised penis. For it was the Jews' sign of sexual difference, their sexual selectiveness as an indicator of their identity, which became, as Nietzsche strikingly observed in *Beyond Good and Evil*, the focus of the Germans' sense of insecurity about their recently created national identity.[21] This fear was represented in the caricatures by the elongated nose. (The traditional folkloric association between the size of the nose and that of the male genitalia was made a pathological sign.[22]) When Fliess attempted to alter the pathology of the genitalia by operating on the nose (in this age before plastic surgery), he was drawing on an accepted sense of the implication of human development joined to the association of the nose and the genitalia in the German biology of race.

The nose and the genitalia were associated not merely in the popular mind. The central sign of male periodicity for Fliess (and for Freud) is male menstruation. And its representation, according to Freud in a letter of 20 July 1897 to Fliess, is an 'occasional bloody nasal secretion'. Later, in a letter of 15 October 1897, Freud traces the implications of male menstruation for himself as well as (one assumes) for Fliess:

My self-analysis is in fact the most essential thing I have at present and promises to become of the greatest value to me if it reaches its end. In the middle of it, it suddenly ceased for three days, during which I had the feeling of being tied up inside (which patients complain of so much), and I was really disconsolate until I found that these same three days (twenty-eight days ago) were the bearers of identical somatic phenomena. Actually only two bad days with a remission in between. From this one should draw the conclusion that the female period is not conducive to work. Punctually on the fourth day, it started again. Naturally, the pause also had another determinant − the resistance to something surprisingly new. Since then I have been once again intensely preoccupied [with it], mentally fresh, though afflicted with all sorts of minor disturbances that come from the content of the analysis.[23]

The editor of the new edition of the Freud / Fliess letters, Jeffrey Masson, comments on Fliess's observations on male menstruation that it is 'highly unlikely that these communications to Freud played any role in Freud's research at the time'. Quite to the contrary – had Masson researched a bit into the history of the concept of male menstruation he would have found a lively nineteenth-century medical literature on this topic, by writers such as F.A. Forel and W.D. Halliburton, as well as a fascination with the question in regard to the problem of herm-aphroditism as a sign of bisexuality as prominent in the nineteenth century as it had been in the Middle Ages. With the rise of modern sexology at the close of the nineteenth century, especially in the writings of Magnus Hirschfeld, male menstruation came to hold a very special place in the 'proofs' of the continuum between male and female sexuality.[24] The hermaphrodite, the male who menstruated, became one of the central focuses of Hirschfeld's work. But all of this new 'science' which used the existence of male menstruation still drew on the image of the marginality of those males who menstruated and thus pointed towards a much more ancient tradition.

The idea of male menstruation is part of a Christian tradition of seeing the Jew as inherently, biologically different. Thomas de Cantimpré, the thirteenth-century anatomist, presented the first 'scientific' statement of this phenomenon (calling upon St. Augustine as his authority). Male Jews menstruated as a mark of the 'Father's curse', their pathological difference. This image of the Jewish male as female was introduced to link the Jew with the corrupt nature of the woman (both marked as different by the same sign) and to stress the intransigence of the Jews. Thomas de Cantimpré recounts the nature of the Jews' attempt to cure themselves. They are told by one of their prophets that they would be rid of this curse by 'Christiano sanguine', the blood of a Christian, when in fact it was 'Christi sanguine', the blood of Christ in the sacrament, which was required. Thus the libel of blood guilt, the charge that Jews sacrifice Christian children to obtain their blood, is the result of the Jews' intransigence in rejecting the truth of Christianity, and is intimately tied to the sign of Jewish male menstruation. The persistence of menstruation among Jewish males is thus not only a sign of the initial 'curse of the Father' but of the inherent inability of the Jews to hear the truth of the Son. For it is the intrinsic 'deafness' of the Jews which does not let them hear the truth which will cure them. The belief in Jewish male menstruation continued through the seventeenth century. Heinrich Kornmann repeated it in Germany in 1614, as did Thomas Calvert in England in 1649.[25]

Franco da Piacenza, a Jewish convert to Christianity, repeated this view in his catalogue of 'Jewish maladies', published in 1630 and translated into German by 1634. He claimed that the males (as well as the females) of the tribe of Simeon menstruated four days a year. These charges continued throughout the age of Enlightenment in slightly altered form. In F.L. de la Fontaine's survey of the health of the Polish Jews, published in 1792, their sexual pathology is stressed.[26] Jews show their inherent difference through their damaged sexuality, and the sign of that is, in the popular mind, the fact that their males menstruate. Freud's contemporary, the arch-racist Theodor Fritsch – whose 'Anti-Semite's Catechism', published in 1887, was the encyclopaedia of German anti-Semitism – saw the sexuality of the Jew as inherently different from that of the German: 'The Jew has a different sexuality than the Teuton; he will not and cannot understand it. And if he attempts to understand it, then the destruction of the German soul can result'.[27] The hidden sign, the link between the homosexual, the woman and the Jew, is the menstruation of the Jewish male.[28]

Freud and Fliess attempt to move this sign from being one of difference to one of universality. Just as Franco da Piacenza tried to remove himself from the 'curse of Eve' by claiming that only ancient Jews (and those from one of the 'Ten Lost Tribes' at that) menstruated – not of course da Piacenza himself and his contemporaries – so, too, do Freud and Fliess distance this charge from the Jews by making it universal. The public sign of Jewish identity (from the standpoint of the anti-Semitic society in which they lived) was the nose that 'men-struates'. But its significance for Freud and Fliess, who were desperately trying to escape classification as 'Jews' in the racial sense and therefore as inferior and different, was as a universal sign, a sign of the universal law of male periodicity which links all human beings, male and female.

The implicit charge of pathological bisexuality had traditionally been lodged against the Jews. (Male Jews were like women in that, among other things, they too menstruate as a sign of their pathological difference.) Freud and Fliess turned this into a universal sign of human nature in a successful form of resistance to the racist substructure of European medicine. Fliess was not simply a quack; his 'quackery' was accepted by Freud, since it provided an alternative to the pathological image of the Jew in conventional medicine.

The basic nature of the medical sciences during the late nineteenth century was racist. And this was true whether the speciality was a 'Jewish one', such as syphilology, or a 'non-Jewish' one, such as surgery. Freud's attempt to distance the racism of medicine through his identification with Fliess's neurological theories was an effort to use the status of science to overcome the stigma of race. Freud could not, nor did he wish to, abandon the status which he needed to define himself as a full member of his own community. But using the model of medicine and accepting the role of the medical practitioner, whether in psychiatry or neurology, meant that he had to deal with the racist attitudes of that community towards the Jews.[29]

The changing concept of the practitioner

Sigmund Freud was forced to decide among a series of poisoned alternatives: psychiatry (like dermatology / syphilology) had implicit police functions and a relatively low status; neurology, like psychiatry, was damaged by the racist implications. But of course psychiatry and sexology (in the guise of syphilology) were medical specialities open to Jews, as was neurology, though only with great difficulty and as long as it remained on the level of laboratory science rather than clinical practice. What we see in the early history of psychoanalysis is the desire of the psychoanalyst for the higher status of specific medical specialities competing with his innate understanding that medicine condemns (by labelling as pathological) those groups which it perceives as marginal. Thus medicine is poisoned initially for the Jewish physician, whose marginality is linked to racial identity and who is therefore labelled as part of a group at risk. Jews can be patients, but can they be doctors? But it is also poisoned, in the pre-World War I period, for the psychoanalyst, for whom this definition of marginality was part of the new definition of the psychotherapist. The sense of marginality is rooted in the Jewish identity of the early psychoanalysts.

Freud's desire to recruit non-Jewish psychoanalysts, such as C.G. Jung and Lou Andreas-Salomé, was based on his need to overcome the sense of marginality implicit in the parallel positions of the Jew and the psychoanalyst in the intellectual world of *fin-de-siècle* Viennese medicine.[30] However, the psychoanalyst, whether Jew or non-Jew, was to the medical profession what the Jew was to society at large – a frightening outsider. Thus Freud's 'myths' (to use Frank Sulloway's highly suspect term) about isolation and anti-Semitism had a real basis in the perception of reality shared by nineteenth-century Jewish medical practitioners. In Freud's history of the psychoanalytic movement, there is a tendency to perceive as absolute the opposition to the equal access of Jews (and therefore psychoanalysts) to medicine. This sense of the monolithic nature of the medical profession (whether true in detail or not) shaped Freud's relationship to medicine, and medicine's perception of psychoanalysis.

What Freud had come to understand by the 1920s was that the status granted him as a medical doctor was not sufficient to counter the hesitancy and animosity directed at him as an outsider – both as a Jew (given the increase of public anti-Semitism in Vienna and Freud's own increased visibility) and as a psychoanalyst. During World War I he began to dismiss the various conceptual categories, beginning with those of anthropology, which had given psychiatry its status in the nineteenth century.[31] This was not difficult, for by this period the presence of anthropology in psychiatry was viewed as slightly old-fashioned, as well as decidedly 'French' – two categories which, in *fin-de-*

siècle Vienna with its stress on the modern and the Teutonic, were quite easily dismissed. Freud assigned to the anthropologist a negative role, as the creator of the idea of degeneration. (In this, of course, he was right – Morel had introduced this concept into psychiatry as a means of labelling entire groups perceived as marginal. Among those groups were the Jews.)

But Freud also began to doubt whether the status that medicine had grudgingly granted to psychoanalysis was a positive factor, especially since he saw psychiatry as being much under the state control which he feared elsewhere. Psychoanalysis was to be its own master. Thus in 1926, in a court case brought against Theodor Reik, one of Freud's most orthodox supporters, for quackery, the question of the relationship of psychoanalysis to the status of medicine was raised for the first time within the structures of power which Freud had always associated with medicine. Reik, whose Ph.D. was in German and French literature, had been accused of practising medicine without a license. Freud, along with a number of his supporters in the Viennese Psycho-Analytical Society, undertook Reik's defence with the argument that it was not necessary to be a medical practitioner in order to be a psychoanalyst.

While the charges against Reik were eventually dropped, Freud used them as the occasion, in a memoir written in support of his colleague, for examining the relationship between the expanding status of psychoanalysis and the more evident racism of medicine. He states his position quite directly: 'Doctors have no historical claim to the sole possession of analysis'.[32] He continues by defining (or actually redefining) what a quack is by dismissing the need for state control ('possessing a state diploma to prove he is a doctor') and stressing the 'knowledge and capacities necessary' to undertake treatment. The shadow of Fliess stretches over this view of the primacy of 'knowledge' over certification. 'Knowledge' is, however, not to be understood as the knowledge of the 'science' of medicine. It is precisely this type of 'knowledge' which Freud dismisses, rejecting the 'doctor' as the ideal practitioner, just as he had rejected the anthropologist.

His (the doctor's) interest is not aroused in the mental side of vital phenomena; medicine is not concerned with the study of the higher intellectual functions, which lies in the sphere of another faculty. Only psychiatry is supposed to deal with the disturbances of mental functions; but we know in what manner and with what aims it does so. It looks for the somatic determinants of mental disorders and treats them like other causes of illness.[33] Psychiatry is but medicine; medicine is but biological science; and (we can add) biological science is racist.

But Freud could not cavalierly abandon the status of science which he had so painstakingly acquired for psychoanalysis. He continued his argument with the (in recent years) oft-quoted passage: 'In view of the intimate connection between the things that we distinguish as physical and mental, we may look forward to a day when paths of knowledge and, let us hope, of influence will be opened up, leading from organic biology and chemistry to the field of neurotic phenomena'.[34] This future time also will mark the period when purified science no longer needs to label the marginal as diseased.

In the micro-autobiography cum mini-history of the psychoanalytic movement which he appends as a Postcript of 1927 to the publication of his essay on lay analysis, Freud outlines this sense of marginality within science without giving actual voice to its racist implications:

In my youth I felt an overpowering need to understand something of the riddles of the world in which we live and perhaps even to contribute something to their solution. The most hopeful means of achieving this end seemed to be to enrol myself in the medical faculty; but even after that I experimented – unsuccessfully – with zoology and chemistry, till at last, under the influence of Brücke, who carried more weight with me than anyone else in my whole life, I settled down to physiology, though in those days it was too narrowly restricted to histology. By that time I had already passed all my medical examinations; but I took no interest in anything to do with medicine till the teacher whom I so deeply respected warned me that in view of my impoverished material circumstances I could not possibly take up a theoretical career. Thus I passed from the histology of the nervous system to neuropathology and then, prompted by fresh influences, I began to be concerned with the neuroses. I scarcely think, however, that my lack of a genuine medical temperament has done much damage to my patients.   (*SE* xx. 253–4)

Implicit in his statement is the fact that in Vienna Jews could attain status in the academy within the laboratory sciences, whereas their ability to acquire academic appointments in the medical faculty was much more limited. While a private practice was possible, such a practice did not give the individual status unless it was at least tangentially connected with the University – which was, of course, merely an extension of the 'imperial and royal' state of Austria-Hungary.

Freud's Postscript to his critique of the medicalization of psychoanalysis concludes with a passage casting an eye towards the American scene. He condemns the American psychoanalytic community's rejection of lay analysts (spearheaded by A.A. Brill) while acknowledging that 'local conditions' may alter the reputation of the lay analyst, as was the case with Fliess in Berlin. Nevertheless, Freud maintains his newly articulated position, rejecting the medicalization of psychoanalysis. The status of psychoanalysis in Vienna by 1926 was grounded in public as well as academic opinion.[35] Freud had been granted his academic position at the University of Vienna, and he had acquired a number of important academic disciples, among them Eugen Bleuler. Training institutes had sprung up throughout Europe – all of them created after the pattern of academic institutions. Freud saw that psychoanalysis no longer depended on the status of medicine. Indeed, the inability of the 'brain mythologists' of the 1890s to localize the anatomical lesions purported to lead to most forms of mental illnesses had brought their work into some disrepute by the 1920s. (The more recent work by Kurt Goldstein on aphasia avoids any discussion of mental processes other than strictly observable ones, such as the disruption of speech and movement.) Freud no longer needed the status of medicine, even though he still did not feel himself free to abandon its protection completely.

There is a hidden, private dimension to the question of lay analysis, one which was rarely mentioned in public during the late 1920s. This involved the redefinition of the analyst, as part of Freud's search for his eventual successor as head of the psychoanalytic movement, as his intellectual heir. Freud had initially sought a potential heir from within the medical establishment, preferably the Christian medical establishment (e.g. Jung). But none of the medical psychoanalysts considered proved a reliable candidate to succeed him. Between 1918 and 1921 Freud twice analysed his youngest child, Anna, whose professional credentials were minimal, except for her interest in pedagogy.[36] Anna Freud's analysis by her father was not, on the surface, that unusual. Many of the early analysts undertook prophylactic analyses of their own children. Without a doubt the best-known such analyses were those by Anna Freud's later chief rival, Melanie Klein.[37] But Klein's children were very young at the time of their analysis; Anna Freud was a grown-up young woman. And Freud's analysis of his daughter was a training analysis, a passing on of the ability to treat patients.

Sigmund Freud, unlike the others who analysed their own children, had a secondary interest in his daughter's analysis. He began to see her, at least in the 1920s, as his heir apparent. But she would be an heir without any pretentions to medical training, without the imprimatur of state and profession. To no little degree, it was the thought of Anna Freud as potential heir to the leadership of the psychoanalytic movement which made it imperative that lay analysis be the wave of the future.

A further aspect to Anna Freud's position in relation to the question of lay analysis must be the implications of her own analysis. It is clear that Melanie Klein's analysis of her children was conducted in the light of her clinical interest in early childhood development. It was in line with earlier attempts to record (and analyse) childhood changes, the earliest being Charles Darwin's detailed account of his oldest child's development. But the analysis of an adult female by a father who must – given Freud's own theoretical position – loom so large in her own fantasy life, was clearly much more problematic. And this was in the context of basic problems such as transference with a beloved parent. What is implied is a type of psychological incest, a doubling of roles in a socially unacceptable manner. The charge is one which cannot be taken lightly, at least not by a Viennese Jew who knows that one of the labels he wears is that of an individual at risk from mental collapse as a result of his incestuous inbreeding.[38] For Freud, the charge must at least have been lurking in the background of his analysis of his daughter. For Jews were believed to commit incest, and this act to lead to their degeneracy and madness, to lead from the religious origin of the sexual selectivity to their inherent difference. This association would have left the idea of lay analysis charged with a great deal of covert political tension.

It is evident that Anna Freud, given her complex relationship with her father, her gender as well as her sexual identity, needed to find a female analyst, and that, at least by proxy, she did with Lou Andreas-Salomé. But by then the role of heiress had become part of her identity. Her own ambiguity concerning the question of lay analysis can be judged by her careful political behaviour once she moved to Great Britain in 1938. She never challenged the second-class status of lay analysis which permitted her to practise (like all lay analysts in Great Britain) only under medical supervision. She quickly became the ally of Ernest Jones, an MD, who wished to see this dual definition of competency maintained within the profession of psychoanalysis in Britain. Better the ability to practise legally with fetters than not to practise at all, as in the United States. Such a position, given Anna Freud's own role in defining the nature of lay analysis, is not unexpected. But it did point to her awareness that her role was in conflict with a masculine world which defined its power in terms of its professional, i.e. medical, standards. The irony is that her medical supervisor in London, Willi Hofer, became in many ways her surrogate, even presiding over the International Psycho-Analytical Society. He became an extension of the power which Anna Freud had assumed as her father's designated successor, just as she was assumed to be an extension of Hofer's medical status. The implications of lay analysis in Great Britain were quite different from those in Vienna and in the United States, but were still rooted in complex definitions of difference.

The American dimension

In 1933 Theodor Reik fled the Nazis, from his position in the psychoanalytic institute in Berlin, first to The Hague and then, in 1938, to New York. In that year, the question of lay analysis was again raised before the American Psychoanalytic Society's 'council on professional training'. A 'majority resolution' was proposed 'against the future training of laymen for the therapeutic use of psychoanalysis', which definitively banned the training of lay analysts except for 'non-thera-peutic purposes' such as 'research and investigation in such non-medical fields as anthropology, sociology, criminology, psychology, and education, etc.'. (This excluded Theodor Reik, among others, from ever becoming a full-fledged member of the American Psychoanalytic Association.)

From that moment, what had been a general policy became a specific rule which exists today. But this was not sufficient. In February 1939 Sándor Radó proposed to the same committee a *'numerus clausus'* on the admission of analytic candidates to the American Psychoanalytic As-sociation. The extraordinary move of limiting the number of qualified medical practitioners admitted to candidacy, following the exclusion of the non-medical practitioners, bears examination. It documents the high status of the 'new' science of psychoanalysis within the medical profession. For the 3 fellowships at the Boston Institute in 1938, there were 75 enquiries and 25 actual applications from qualified persons. But who were the individuals whom Radó wished to exclude – and why?

The minutes of the 26 February 1939 meeting, chaired by Franz Alexander, the director of the Chicago training institute, summarized Radó's proposal: 'Advisability of a date as a limitation of registration for students in each institute each year. For frank attention to the problem of social and financial deterioration of any professional medical group. Necessitates a limitation of students on social, intellec-tual and economic grounds.' Bertram Lewin saw this as a problem specifically in the New York Psychoanalytic Institute: 'They [the students in New York] work under exceptional economic pressure. They are primarily interested in earning a living and not in academic or scientific work. They hold meetings like county medical politicians.'[39] This is an extraordinary statement given the influx of Viennese-trained Jewish psychotherapists into the United States. Lewin stresses the image of the psychoanalyst as scientist, but as a scientist in a mode both attractive to as well as clearly rejected by Freud. For inherent in the image, as Freud made clear in his Postscript, is the notion of the scientist as a well-to-do individual taking up science as an extension of a *haute bourgeois* identity. The analyst as money-grubbing practitioner is thus contrasted with the pure scientist, pure in a number of senses of the word – pure as unsullied by filthy lucre, pure in devotion to an abstract science.

But Lewin had picked up the thread of racism present in Freud's rejection of science. Theodor Billroth, one of Freud's teachers, had put the case against the admission of Jews to the Viennese medical faculty most directly (and most publicly) in his survey of medical education in the German-speaking countries:

Young men, mostly Jews, come to Vienna from Galicia and Hungary, who have absolutely nothing, and who have conceived the insane idea that they can earn money in Vienna by teaching, through small jobs at the stock exchange, by peddling matches, or by taking employment as post office or telegraph clerks in Vienna or elsewhere, and at the same time study medicine. These people, who present to anyone not acquainted with Viennese conditions a most puzzling problem, who are not seldom inherently queer, but whose numbers are fortunately diminishing year by year, could hardly exist anywhere else.... So this outcast [the Jewish medical student] in the Viennese world must first of all look for pupils, but he finds that the lesson hours conflict with the lectures. Still, he must live before he can study; the private lessons that he is to give cannot be postponed; he must accept them, and therefore cannot attend his classes.[40]

The image of the student as Jew and its extension, the urban psychoanalytic candidate as Jew, is thus part of the idea of the Jew as incapable of *Bildung*, the type of culture represented by abstract science in nineteenth-century and early twentieth-century Vienna. For Lewin in 1939, the urban Jew corresponds to the conceptual category of 'money-grubbing Jew' in European anti-Semitic rhetoric. The rejection of this image assigns status to the idea of pure science – an idea that was in many ways, for the Jews involved, corrupted by racism.

During the succeeding decades psychoanalysis was removed from the sphere of anti-Semitic European science to the United States, where the racism of science had another, more accessible object, the black. The status of the Jewish psychoanalyst was tied to the status of European science, and Freud's attempt to loosen these bonds ran counter to the needs of the exiled or emigrant psychoanalysts who had to draw on the status of European science to establish themselves within the closed world of American medicine. The spectre of racism, which had haunted psychoanalysis because of its questionable reliance on the status of Viennese medicine, undermined the status of the psychoanalyst. In the European perspective, especially that of Germany and Austria of the 1930s and '40s, the psychoanalyst no longer had the status of medical practitioner; rather, the very term 'psychoanalyst' came to stand for quackery.

In the United States the case was quite different. Jewish medical practitioners, once they were certified to practise in the United States, entered a world where medicine not only had a high status, but where continental medicine was ranked even higher. And one of the medical specialities most representative of continental medicine was psychoanalysis. The psychoanalyst was free, at least momentarily, from the blemish of race, but of course, as we have seen, that blemish remained within his sense of himself and his profession. Moreover, the status of medicine in the United States was still tied to the biological definition of medicine and to an acceptance of the medical model in defining medical practice. Psychoanalysis furthered this attitude in part during the 1940s and '50s with its enthusiasm for 'general medicine' in the form of psychosomatics. As Robert Michels cogently observed: 'In fact, for a time, one of the appeals of psychoanalysis to psychiatry was that it seemed to offer a chance for psychiatry to join the mainstream of medicine. Surprising though this may seem today [1981], psychoanalytic ideas concerning psychosomatic illness marked the first legitimatization of the return of the alienist-psychiatrist to the general hospital and the medical community – in many ways playing the same sociological role in the 1940s that neurobiology and psychopharmacology played in the '70s.'[41] With the introduction of psychotropic drugs in the 1960s, the centuries-old division between psychiatry defined as the treatment of the brain versus its definition as the treatment of the mind reappeared, and at that point the status of psychoanalysis became ever more tenuous.

Even with the perceived decline in the status of psychoanalysis in the 1970s and '80s, the debate about who was to be given the title of psychoanalyst continued. The American Psychoanalytic Society set up a series of committees – on professional standards, on the feasibility and desirability of the training of lay analysts. And this debate marked another turning-point in the relationship between the now firmly entrenched biological psychiatrist and the ever more isolated psychoanalyst. The status of 'medicine' during the 1970s and '80s had become that of the biological model of medicine. One marker of this sense of dissolution and separation was Robert Michels's address, referred to above, at the fiftieth anniversary celebration of the Washington Psychoanalytic Institute in December 1980. Michels, chairman of the Department of Psychiatry at Cornell Medical College, speaking on 'Psychoanalysis and Psychiatry – the End of the Affair', saw the pressure for lay analysts as a potential watershed marking the dissolution of the relationship between psychiatry and psychoanalysis. Contemporary psychoanalysis (represented by Klein, Schafer, Ricoeur and Lacan) had, he observed, consciously moved away from the older, 'biologically rooted' psychoanalytic model towards 'the study of language, symbols, and meaning'. Michels thus saw a parallel to the movement away from psychiatry in the movement towards the humanities and the social sciences, with the older model of 'Naturwissenschaften' being replaced by the antithetical model of 'Geisteswissenschaften'. This was understood as a movement from science to its antithesis. And the movement was taking place, he said, even though 'psychoanalysis continues to be the dominant paradigm organizing the way that psychiatrists think about patients and treatment'. Michels saw in this 'end of the affair' a turning of the two fields 'to a more open, less monogamous, but more honest, relationship', and in his belief a far more promising future as a result'.[42]

The separation of practice from theory has become absolute. Freud saw the need to distance himself from the corruption inherent in the medical model, with its image of domination (and the racist implications of the model of control). But the risk he took was in distancing himself, at least tenuously, from the status of medicine. The debates that this position caused centred around the newly undermined position of psychotherapy and the need, at least within American medicine (Freud's *bête noire*), to undermine it. To address the question of who is or is not to be considered a psychoanalyst would be to write a history of modern American psychoanalysis. The innumerable committees set up by the American Psychoanalytic Association as well as study groups in the various institutes of psychoanalysis have chronicled the growing sense of defensiveness brought about by the redefinition of the status of psychoanalysis in the age of the re-Kraepelinization of American psychiatry.

The objections which grew out of its altered status before World War II have not been accepted by the profession, but for quite different reasons. As recently as 1985 the debate about who is or is not a psychotherapist continued to rage within the psychiatric and psychoanalytic communities. But the imperatives of status are now quite different. Within the psychoanalytic institutes the small number of MDs applying for training reveals the diminished attraction of psychoanalysis for the medical practitioner. The institutes are now turning to other areas, such as social work, to recruit their students. Yet the opposition is loud and shrill. A letter published in the *New York Times* in May 1985 from Seymour C. Post, Associate Clinical Professor of Psychiatry in the Columbia University College of Physicians and Surgeons, bemoans the coming age of the 'barefoot psychoanalyst'. Post objects to the introduction into psychiatry of 'lay psychotherapy', which 'threatens to denude the country of its only wholly qualified line of defense against mental and emotional illness: the physician trained both in biological and psychodynamic psychiatry'. For Post, the villains are clear – the professionals, but especially the psychoanalysts: 'And Freud was the first psychiatrist, but not the last, to train a member of his family (his daughter Anna) to do psychotherapy or psychoanalysis. Conflict of interest makes it difficult to speak frankly. Absence of criticism has emboldened lay therapists.'[43] Here again echo the veiled charges of perversion, present in the 1920s, reviving the sense of difference implicit in the question of lay analysis.

We have now come full circle. Medicine, represented by clinical psychiatry, first accepted psychoanalysis in order to purge itself of the last vestiges of the stigma of political control, and moved it back into the general hospital. Rejected by Freud because of its inherent racism, of its need to marginalize the mentally ill, medicine continued to draw on the new science of psychoanalysis, to the degree that psychoanalytic-

ally oriented psychotherapy became the norm even for those practitioners who rejected psychoanalysis. With the introduction of psychotropic drugs in the 1960s, medicine began to loose itself from the
theory of psychoanalysis, while maintaining the model of treatment.
Psychoanalysis wished to rid itself of medicine and its pretensions. But
psychoanalysis, now firmly established (like osteopathy) as part of
Western medicine, has worked to preserve its sense of centrality by
retaining a pre-Freudian definition of the appropriate (or competent)
psychotherapist. Thus the question of whether Freud's theories are
scientific or not may well rest on a definition of 'science' quite different
from that debated by the philosophers of science – it may well rest on
the sociology of status (and its relationship to definitions of centrality
and marginality) within the greater culture.

Notes

This paper is an expanded version of an article first published in *Critical Inquiry*, xiii,
no. 2 (Winter 1987), 292–313. Permission to reprint the sections concerned is gratefully
acknowledged.

[1] The debate about the scientific status of psychoanalysis is summarized in A.
Grünbaum, *The Foundations of Psychoanalysis: A Philosophical Critique* (Berkeley 1984).
On Grünbaum see Barbara von Eckardt, 'Adolf Grünbaum: Psychoanalytic Episte-
mology', in *Beyond Freud: A Study of Modern Psychoanalytic Theorists*, ed. J. Reppen
(Hillsdale, N.J., 1985), 353–403. A brief historical overview of the nature of
psychotherapeutic treatment is given by Sol L. Garfield, 'Psychotherapy: A 40-Year
Appraisal', *American Psychologist*, xxxvi (1981), 174–83.

[2] The historical background is outlined by Peter Amacher, *Freud's Neurological
Education and Its Influence on Psychoanalytic Theory* (New York 1965); Kenneth Levin,
Freud's Early Psychology of the Neurosis: A Historical Perspective (Pittsburgh 1978); and
polemically in Frank J. Sulloway, *Freud, Biologist of the Mind: Beyond the Psychoanalytic
Legend* (New York 1979).

[3] On the history of psychiatry as a mode of control, see Michel Foucault, *Histoire de
la folie à l'age classique* (Paris 1972), and, more recently, *Madhouses, Mad-Doctors, and
Madmen: The Social History of Psychiatry in the Victorian Era*, ed. Andrew Scull
(Philadelphia 1981).

[4] On the history of the psychiatric hospital, see Dieter Jetter, *Grundzüge der Geschichte
des Irrenhauses* (Darmstadt 1981).

[5] Immanuel Kant, *Werke*, ed. Wilhelm Weischedel, 6 vols. (Wiesbaden 1956–64), i.
887–906.

[6] William Bynum, 'Time's Noblest Offspring: The Problem of Man in British Natural
Historical Sciences' (diss., Cambridge 1974). Kant, *Werke*, vi. 517–18.

[7] On the general background of this debate, see Henri Ellenberger, *The Discovery of the
Unconscious: The History and Evolution of Dynamic Psychiatry* (New York 1970); Gerlof
Verwey, *Psychiatry in an Anthropological and Biomedical Context: Philosophical Presup-
positions and Implications of German Psychiatry, 1820–1870* (Dordrecht 1985); and U.H.
Peters, 'Die Situation der deutschen Psychiatrie bei Beginn der psychiatrischen
Emigrationsbewegung 1933', in *Zusammenhang: Festschrift für Marielene Putscher*, ed.
Otto Baur and Otto Glandien (Cologne 1984), 837–64.

[8] J.G. Langermann, *De methodo cognoscendi curandique animi morbos stabilienda* (diss., Jena
1797).

[9] C.H. Spiess, *Biographien der Wahnsinnigen*, ed. Wolfgang Promies (Cologne 1966).

[10] E. Kraepelin, 'Hundert Jahr Psychiatrie', *Zeitschrift für die Neurologie und Psychiatrie*, XXXVIII (1919), 161–275.

[11] Sulloway (see n. 2) claims that Freud's perception of anti-Semitism, and his sense of the marginality of his own views, were 'myths'. If indeed Sulloway is right, and there is little doubt about the force of this argument and the materials he has mustered to prove it, we must ask the evident next question: Why did Freud perceive the world in the manner in which he reported? It is the reconstruction of fantasies about the world rather than the assumption that there are 'realities' in history to be 'discovered' that is the central undertaking, especially of the historian of psychoanalysis.

[12] See Sander L. Gilman, 'Jews and Mental Illness: Medical Metaphors, Anti-Semitism and the Jewish Response', *Journal of the History of the Behavioral Sciences*, XX (1984), 150–9.

[13] See Hannah S. Decker, *Freud in Germany: Revolution and Reaction in Science, 1893–1907* (New York 1977).

[14] Max Schur, 'Some Additional "Day Residues" of the Specimen Dream of Psychoanalysis', in *Psychoanalysis, a General Psychology: Essays in Honor of Heinz Hartmann*, ed. Rudolph M. Löwenstein *et al.* (New York 1966), 45–85.

[15] Monika Richarz, *Der Eintritt der Juden in die akademischen Berufe* (Tübingen 1974), 28–43, and Erna Lesky, *Die Wiener medizinische Schule im 19. Jahrhundert* (Graz 1978).

[16] See the introduction by Jeffrey Moussaieff Masson to his edition of *The Complete Letters of Sigmund Freud to Wilhelm Fliess, 1887–1904* (Cambridge, Mass., 1985), 1–14. See also Peter Heller, 'A Quarrel over Bisexuality', in *The Turn of the Century: German Literature and Art, 1890–1915*, ed. Hans H. Schulte (Bonn 1978), 87–116.

[17] G. Valentin, *Handbuch der Entwickelungsgeschichte der Menschen* (Berlin 1835); Wilhelm His, *Anatomie menschlicher Embryonen*, 3 vols. (Leipzig 1880–5).

[18] Ernst Mayr, *The Growth of Biological Thought: Diversity, Evolution and Inheritance* (Cambridge, Mass., 1982).

[19] See Jacob Katz, *From Prejudice to Destruction: Anti-Semitism, 1700–1933* (Cambridge, Mass., 1980).

[20] Judith Vogt, *Historien om et Image: Antisemitisme og Antizionisme i Karikaturer* (Copenhagen 1978).

[21] Friedrich Nietzsche, *Beyond Good and Evil*, trans. Marianne Cowan (Chicago 1955), 184–8. Compare this with Jacques Derrida's discussion of the Jews and circumcision in *Spurs: Nietzsche's Styles*, trans. Barbara Harlow (Chicago 1978), 69.

[22] *Handwörterbuch des deutschen Aberglaubens*, ed. Hanns Bächtold-Stäubli, vol. XI (Berlin and Leipzig 1934–5), 'Nase', 970–9.

[23] *Complete Letters Freud to Fliess*, ed. Masson, 256, 270.

[24] Ibid., 199. On male menstruation see, for example, F.A. Forel, 'Cas de menstruation chez un homme', *Bulletin de la Société medicale de la Suisse romande* (Lausanne), 1869, 53–61, and W.D. Halliburton, 'A Peculiar Case', *Weekly Medical Review and Journal of Obstetrics* (St. Louis, Mo.), 1885, 392. M. Hirschfeld, *Sexualpathologie*, 2 vols. (Bonn 1917–18), II. 1–92.

[25] Thomas de Cantimpré, *Miraculorum et exemplorum memorabilium sui temporis libro duo* (Duaci 1605), 305–6. H. Kornmann, *Opera curiosa I: Miracula vivorum* (Frankfurt 1694 [1st edn. 1614]), 128–9; Thomas Calvert, *The Blessed Jew of Marocco; or, A Blackmoor Made White Being a Demonstration of the True Messias out of the Law and Prophets by Rabbi Samuel* (York 1649), 20–1.

[26] On Franco da Piacenza see Leon Poliakov, *The History of Anti-Semitism*, trans. Richard Howard, 3 vols. (New York 1965–75), I. 143n. F.L. de la Fontaine, *Chirurgisch-Medicinische Abhandlungen verschiedenen Inhalts Polen betreffend* (Breslau 1792). See also J.A. Elie de la Poterie, *Questo medica. An vivis lex eadem quä mulieribus, periodicas evacuationes pati?* (diss., Paris 1764).

[27] T. Fritsch, *Handbuch der Judenfrage* (Leipzig 1935), 409 (with a further discourse on psychoanalysis as a sign of Jewish degeneracy).

[28] E.P. Eckholm, *The Picture of Health: Environmental Sources of Disease* (New York 1977). The irony is that the image of male menstruation among the Jews probably has a pathological origin. Even today in parts of Africa 'male menstruation', in the form of urethral bleeding, seems to be an indicator of 'sexual maturation'. What actually happens is that, for reasons not completely understood, a parasite, *Schistosoma haematoboum*, which lives in the veins surrounding the bladder, becomes active during the early teenage years. One can imagine that Jews infected with schistosomiasis, giving the appearance of menstruation, would have reified the sense of difference of which the Northern European, not prone to this snail-borne parasite, was aware. On the symbolic value of this manifestation, see Herbert Ian Hogbin, *The Island of Menstruating Men; Religion in Wogeo, New Guinea* (Scranton, Pa., 1970).

[29] On the implications of the attitudes of Christian Vienna towards the new 'Jewish' science of psychoanalysis, see Dennis B. Klein, *Jewish Origins of the Psychoanalytic Movement* (New York 1981). Freud's ambiguous quest for status in science was paralleled by his fascination with Christianity. Just as the society he lived in never permitted him to become a full-fledged academic, at least in his own eyes, it also tantalized him with the promise of acceptance based on conversion. As with the temptation of science, Freud remained on the outside in terms of his relationship to structures of power such as the Church – although, in the case of the latter, clearly fascinated by it. See Paul C. Vitz, 'Sigmund Freud's Attraction to Christianity: Biographical Evidence', *Psychoanalysis and Contemporary Thought*, VI (1983), 73–183.

[30] See the discussion in Robert S. Steele, *Freud and Jung: Conflicts of Interpretation* (London 1982).

[31] See Sander L. Gilman, 'Sexology, Psychoanalysis and Degeneration: From a Theory of Race to a Race to Theory', in *Degeneration: The Dark Side of Progress*, ed. J.E. Chamberlin and S.L. Gilman (New York 1985), 72–96.

[32] S. Freud, 'The Question of Lay Analysis: Conversations with an Impartial Person', *SE* xx. 177–258.

[33] Ibid., 230.

[34] Ibid., 231.

[35] See the debate between Josef and Renée Gicklhorn, *Sigmund Freuds akademische Laufbahn im Lichte der Dokumente* (Vienna 1960), and Kurt R. Eissler, *Sigmund Freud und die Wiener Universität: Über die Pseudo-Wissenschaftlichkeit der jüngste Wiener Freud-Biographik* (Bern 1966). On the debate in the United States see Norman S. Greenfield and Gener M. Abroms, 'The Role and Status of the Non-Medical Psychotherapist in the United States', *Human Context*, v (1973), 657–8.

[36] Uwe Henrik Peters, *Anna Freud: Ein Leben für das Kind* (Munich 1979), 61–4.

[37] Phyllis Grosskurth, *Melanie Klein: Her World and Her Work* (New York 1986).

[38] Sander L. Gilman, *Difference and Pathology: Stereotypes of Sexuality, Race, and Madness* (Ithaca, N.Y., 1986), 155–7.

[39] All the material cited here is from the archives of the American Psychoanalytic Society, now housed in the Archives of Psychiatry, Cornell Medical College, Ithaca, N.Y. See also Hendrick M. Ruitenbeek, *Freud and America* (New York 1966).

[40] Theodor Billroth, *The Medical Sciences in the German Universities: A Study in the History of Civilization*, trans. William H. Welch (New York 1924), 106–8.

[41] Robert Michels, 'Psychoanalysis and Psychiatry – the End of the Affair', *Academy Forum*, xxv (1981), 7–8. See also Michels's more detailed discussion in *The Evolution of Psychodynamic Psychotherapy* (Philadelphia 1985), as well as I.F. Knight, 'Paradigms and Crises in Psychoanalysis', *Psychoanalytic Quarterly*, LIV (1985), 597–614.

[42] Michels, *Academy Forum*, 8–10.

[43] *New York Times*, 19 May 1985, p. 20.

2

The Jewish Origins of Psychoanalysis Reconsidered

Ivar Oxaal

Origins of the problem

Few ethnic groups have aroused such widespread curiosity among scholars as the Jews of pre-1914 Vienna. This interest has been stimulated chiefly by the fact that so many of the outstanding cultural innovators of the late Habsburg era came from families of Jewish origin. Cultural historians have found it difficult to write about Freud's or Kraus's or Wittgenstein's Vienna – the list can be expanded almost indefinitely – without at least a fugitive query about the influence of their Jewish backgrounds.[1] William M. Johnston, author of the encyclopaedic study *The Austrian Mind* (1972), notes that no other ethnic group produced so many thinkers of transcendent originality and that 'any study of intellectual life in Austria must single out the Jews for special attention'.[2]

The question of a relationship between Jewish culture, or more diffuse notions of a Jewish essence, and the origins of 'modernist' European culture has not been restricted to Vienna, nor has such a mode of enquiry in the past been prompted solely by scientific curiosity. The venomous polemical tradition running from Richard Wagner's essay 'Judaism in Music' to Hitler's *Mein Kampf* and the official ideology of the Third Reich, which ultimately forced Sigmund Freud and thousands of other Jewish thinkers and artists into exile, raised questions of a superficially similar kind.

There exists, of course, a crucial difference between the classic anti-Semitic theorist, with his dogmatic belief in the existence of an immutable Jewish racial essence, which cunningly penetrates Aryan culture to the latter's detriment and ultimate destruction, and the historian who rests his analysis on social, cultural and psychological hypotheses. These hypotheses have arisen not out of deterministic racial theory, but from the common-sense expectation that the process through which a previously distinctive, and typically segregated, ethnic group was partially absorbed into Central European civil society in the late nineteenth and early twentieth centuries left unique imprints on, and psychic residues within, those who experienced it. And, as an extension of this view, it has been held by some writers that as a consequence of this process, and the resistances encountered, those who underwent it could bring to their socially integrated adult occupational roles certain values and insights which conferred on them a unique advantage in those spheres of society in which creative achievements were valued and rewarded.

As has often been lamented, however, it is one thing to be attracted by an intriguing theory or set of hypotheses, but rather more difficult to substantiate them. Some students of the Austrian case will be quick to protest that the process of Jewish cultural absorption and adaptation had a different impact on various social classes, families and individuals, thus making generalizations about the consequences extremely hazardous. The process took place over several generations; its impact on later generations reared in strongly assimilationist bourgeois families would have been substantially different from its effects on their elders. In such instances, it might be asked, would not the reduction or near-total loss of a Jewish identity be accomplished without leaving a basic ethnic imprint or psychic residue? If there is to be a quest for the social origins of Viennese cultural achievements, should it not be within the wider framework of the Viennese bourgeoisie, many of whom just happened to have had Jewish ancestors? Did not the scientific, scholarly and artistic communities themselves place a premium on creative innovation, and dictate the 'state of play' in a given activity according to which the next paradigmatic leaps of inspiration, by Jew or non-Jew, could logically occur? These are clearly weighty objections against the application of a general sociological formula for interpreting the role of a Jewish ethnic background in shaping the content of Viennese bourgeois culture.

Despite these difficulties, specialists in the work of particular Viennese individuals and intellectual circles frequently suggest that at least some aspects of their creative activity, if not the spirit of the whole project, exhibit features which relate to some form of Jewish experience. Freud and the emergence of psychoanalysis are a classic case in point. But Kraus, Schnitzler, Schoenberg, Mahler, the Austro-Marxists, the Vienna Circle and a host of other figures and cultural groupings appear, at least to some students of their creative work, to have been significantly influenced by their status as an ethnic minority group.[3] The purpose of the present paper is, first, to provide an overview of the different modes of causal analysis which have been applied to the question of the origins of Viennese culture, especially psychoanalysis. I shall deal essentially with the question of whether the *content* of the

Hypothesized Relationships Between Jewish Ethnicity and
Intellectual–Artistic Achievement

---

1   Hypotheses concerning the effect of Jewish religion, solidarity, custom
and tradition (*sub-cultural influences*)
(a) the religious quest for righteousness
(b) the Jewish family as a source of psychological and motivational
support
(c) supportive ethnic peer groups (e.g. B'nai B'rith)
(d) historical role-models stimulating achievement-motivation (e.g.,
Moses, Joseph)
(e) elements in the Jewish heritage conferring special forms of
competence, e.g.,
    (i) Talmudic scholarship; Jewish philosophers; rabbinical wisdom
    (ii) Jewish lore and esoteric knowledge (e.g. cabbalah)
2   Hypotheses concerning the cognitive and psychological effects of
Jewish marginality and alienation (*situational influences – the
assimilation-problematic*)
(a) the positive effects of marginality and 'outsider' status, e.g.,
    (i) personal and group mobilization; intellectual ferment
    (ii) crises of personal and collective identity
    (iii) entrepreneurship; risk-taking; radicalism
    (iv) unique cognitive orientations: relativistic, perspectival styles of
thought; scepticism
    (v) linguistic preoccupations; irony; humor
(b) the personally painful effects (but potential spurs to creativity) of
social marginality, e.g.,
    (i) social isolation; sense of rejection
    (ii) self-hatred; generalized anxiety, neuroses; suicidal tendencies

---

Underlying the discussion of Jewish contributions to modern culture
is the issue of the causes of personal striving and of achievement itself,
independent of vocational sphere or productive content. It is argued
that Jewish religious and secular values, reinforced by a family-centred
system of instilling ambition, intellectual discipline and solidarity,
shaped the character of Sigmund Freud, and that of thousands of other
members of the Viennese middle class. These values are such a common
element in the lives of many later prominent Viennese that their
significance is often played down. Achievement-motivation was a pre-
condition of creative accomplishment and upward social mobility, and
the two were often inextricably linked, as the case of Freud perhaps
illustrates. Even well-born Jews could only gain recognition and
prestige within artistic and intellectual milieus through originality and
productivity. This says much for the quality of the late Habsburg
educational system and cultural standards, which were shared with
non-Jews. But interpretations of the Viennese situation, like more

general sociological accounts of Jewish culture, have sometimes identified a uniquely Jewish thrust in the drive for success. As William Johnston suggests: 'The dream of Freud's mother that her "golden Sigi" would become famous acted as a self-fulfilling prophecy: she did everything possible to further her son's education, even banishing his sister's piano when it annoyed the budding scholar'. The stereotyped notion of the Jewish mother's Messianic expectations and absorption in the destiny of a male offspring is not far removed from this account.[9]

A closely related notion, purporting to explain the near-universal phenomenon of above-average social mobility and achievement among Jews, argues that the heightened self-esteem which Jews experience as a consequence of their self-image as a Chosen People – whether as a religious belief or a secularized assumption – supplies an exceptional degree of motivational energy. Moreover, the emphasis in Judaism on the pursuit of righteousness as the ultimate value, and the link between this hallowed precept and the obligation to scholarship – while by no means universally observed – can be regarded as powerful enabling values for attainments in the secular sphere.[10] Mention has already been made of the importance attached, in discussions of Freud, to the great biblical role-models of Moses and Joseph – men of action and historical achievement. More concretely, there is no doubt that Freud highly valued his formal status as a Jew in a largely Roman Catholic society and was pleased to have access to the Jewish organization B'nai B'rith for the purpose of presenting some of his most important scientific papers. This has been fully documented by Dennis B. Klein, who shows how such ethnic peer-group solidarity helped to mitigate for Freud the sense of personal and professional isolation which his radical theories had engendered.

The foregoing factors all deal with the motivational, enabling functions of the Viennese Jewish subculture in producing persons of genius like Freud. But what of the actual structure and content of psychoanalytic theory and practice as it emerged? What was distinctively 'Jewish' about the purported scientific theory in the sense of direct or indirect, conscious or unconscious, ideational transferences from Jewish culture? It must be conceded that cultural innovation, even revolutionary transformations in a scientific paradigm, can occur independently of the degree of ethnic socialization and identification of the scientist or philosopher. Freud's achievement can be interpreted without recourse to his ethnic background. But the central question is: can that remarkable achievement be properly understood from a historical perspective without full regard for its origins in the Jewish subculture of Vienna? The religious reductionism of David Bakan's early study of psychoanalysis has tended perhaps to discredit, through overstatement, causal hypotheses of that sort – such as his interesting suggestion concerning parallels between Jewish Cabbalistic doctrine and psychoanalysis.[11]

This question is taken up in a more sceptical spirit in the account by Marthe Robert:

Immediately after the appearance of *The Interpretation of Dreams*, certain of Freud's students who were versed in Hebrew began searching ancient writings for parallels. For, amid the vast body of rabbinical literature, it is indeed possible to find precepts and maxims *that come curiously close to Freud's most daring ideas*. The rabbis attached great importance to the interpretation of dreams, to sexuality and day-to-day existence. Furthermore, parallels can be drawn between Freudian symbolism and the theories of words and numbers which were the principal instrument of rabbinical exegesis. [Emphasis added.]

Marthe Robert continues: 'All this, to be sure, makes it possible to draw ingenious correspondences, but amounts to little more than doubtful speculation, first of all because those who make much of such analogies based on approximate resemblances say nothing of the enormous gulf between Freud's purposes and those of the rabbis, and also because in all likelihood very similar and equally inconclusive parallels might be found in very different traditions.'[12] Freud himself, she adds, was amused by these friendly, in-group attempts to link psychoanalysis to traditions in Judaism, but took no active part in them since he felt no need to stress the local colour of the scientific discoveries for which he claimed a universal validity.

Two comments may be made about this passage: First, it seems that certain parallels between rabbinical writings and psychoanalysis were immediately apparent to those of Freud's followers who had had religious training. Second, it is hardly surprising that Freud the German-Viennese scientist would not be eager to acknowledge conscious or semi-conscious Jewish thought-models in psychoanalysis, since to do so would immediately risk having its claims to scientific status dismissed – not to mention playing into the hands of the anti-Semites who were already convinced all Jewish intellectual and artistic production was infused with a racial essence. 'Freud never really tried to define his exact place in contemporary Jewry,' states Marthe Robert, 'nor did he ever explain how it came about that psychoanalysis, though profoundly marked by Jewish origins, has something essential to say about mankind in general, quite apart from all ethnic, historic, cultural and social variables.'[13] The paradox this represents for the sociology of knowledge lies in the fact that a localized particular can give rise to something universal; a modern paradox which Ernest Gellner's account of the market for psychoanalysis in alienated Western societies can partially explain.

The significance of social marginality

The second major set of hypotheses about the effect of a Jewish identity
in Vienna on the work of Jewish intellectuals and artists refers to the
situational context of the groups in question. Leaving to one side for
the moment the objective status of the Jewish minority, it is evident
from countless contemporary sources that Viennese Jews often experienced an acute sense of marginality and alienation *vis-à-vis* the
politically and socially dominant Christian community. Conversion was
always an option, and several hundred Jews converted annually; but to
do so did not necessarily eliminate the sense of alienation and might,
indeed, intensify it. The causes of such pressures can be identified at
several levels, from the macro-structural tensions generated by pre-
monitions of the imminent collapse of the Habsburg Empire, which
had provided Jews with a relatively secure position within the multi-
ethnic state, to the persistent but unpredictable flare-up of anti-Semitic
incidents. Michael Pollak has traced the way in which fears about the
break-up of the Empire in the late nineteenth century led to political
mobilization along ethnic and religious lines, as each group attempted
to reposition itself. The rise of political anti-Semitism in Vienna in the
form of the Catholic Christian Social movement was one manifestation
of this crisis. Social status as defined by religious background acquired
a critical importance as the brief interlude of Austrian liberalism –
which had completed the emancipation of Jews in the Empire – came
to an end.

This was the crisis-laden atmosphere in which Freud was developing
his ideas in the closing years of the century. Pollak argues that the
political tensions had widespread cultural and psychological consequences, particularly for Jews:

One can observe basically two modes according to which stabilization of
identity is attempted. First, political involvement such as with Austro-Marx-
ism or Zionism provides alternative attachments for the declining identification with Austrian nationality or loyalty to the monarchy. Second, aesthetic
and psychological projects have the effect of stabilizing the self by altogether
displacing criteria of identity from the social and particular group level,
putting in their place a primary concern with the inner self and a crucial
awareness of the self.[14]

Seen in this context, the implicitly political character of early psychoanalysis as a 'movement', even as a Jewish sect, becomes more readily
explicable, and may help to explain some of Freud's basic attitudes: the
pessimism, the deep scepticism concerning external social agencies of
personal salvation.

The *locus classicus* of discussions of the effect of social marginality on
Jewish intellectual creativity is Thorstein Veblen's essay 'The Intellectual Pre-Eminence of the Jews in Modern Europe', written in response

to the Balfour Declaration. Veblen argued that the establishment of a Jewish state could destroy the social bases of contemporary Jewish intellectual creativity, to the extent that it reduced the need of Jews to question the basic assumptions of their diaspora societies. Marginality – the sense of neither identifying with one's minority ethnic group of origin nor being fully accepted by the majority – was a perfect location for developing radical and original perspectives, a major factor in the emergence of Jewish intellectual pre-eminence.[15] This basic idea, that alienation can be an important stimulus to certain types of cultural innovation, has acquired the status of a self-evident proposition, but can it plausibly be expanded into an explanation of the fundamental structure of a scientific paradigm? This is what John Murray Cuddihy attempts to do in his account of the social–psychological origins of Freud's vision of man in society.

Cuddihy argues that the marginality of a Jewish thinker like Freud must be viewed in the light of his internal psychic conflict – the 'ordeal of civility' occasioned, in Freud's case, by the fact that the founder of psychoanalysis was caught between two cultural universes, the crude, backward, uncouth world of the *shtetl* and the sophisticated, polite society of the élite German bourgeoisie. The contradiction in Freud's cultural background, as in that of Viennese Jews in general, was one which required them constantly to suppress the more uncouth side of their nature, associated with the Jewish ghettoes of Eastern Europe. This was the source of Freud's concept of the id, and formed a sharp contrast to the refinements and sublimations of the élite Gentile world to which they aspired – whence came his concept of the super-ego. Cuddihy maintains that Freud's theory of dreams and public discussions in the nineteenth century of the eligibility of Eastern European *shtetl* Jews, or *Ostjuden*, for admission to civil society – the so-called Jewish Emancipation problem – have the same inner structure, reflecting the fact that the Jew was a late-comer to the modernization process. 'No one realized this more than Freud,' Cuddihy claims, 'born in culturally peripheral Freiburg, Moravia, in 1856, but soon to move to the Pfeffergasse in the largely Jewish quarter of Vienna called Leopoldstadt.'[16] For the upwardly mobile Jewish professional man the stigmatized, latent, repressed backwoods Jewish identity was bound constantly to clash with an authoritative, internalized high culture.

Thus the struggle between id and super-ego was phenomenologically precisely congruent with Freud's own social situation and, equally to the point, with that of his Jewish followers and early private patients in Vienna as well – hence the potential of developing psychoanalysis as a social movement. The basic features of the Freudian paradigm were not, of course, a conscious invention to fit a particular intellectual situation; they evolved quite intuitively and unconsciously: the system which claimed to unmask psychic reality was itself a kind of mask shaped by deeper psychic needs.

Cuddihy's interpretation represents what appears to be a situational, ethnic parallel to the suggestion by Steven Marcus, quoted above, which identifies the origins of the conflict between the super-ego and the id with the late Victorian ethos.[17] Given the political salience attached to Jewish ethnicity in Vienna during this period, the mode of analysis attempted by Cuddihy – while clearly an example of the 'ingenious correspondences' queried by Marthe Robert – should not be dismissed out of hand. Although Cuddihy's notion of Freud's personal exposure to the culture of the *Ostjuden* is exaggerated, the presence of these Jews in Vienna was a constant source of anti-Semitic complaint. The fact that both his parents came from the province of Galicia may have had a particular significance for the young Freud, complicating his sense of Jewish identity through an ambivalent empathy with an intra-ethnic minority which was disliked by many assimilated Viennese Jews. This and related issues have been sensitively explored in historical depth in a major study by Sander L. Gilman, *Jewish Self-Hatred* (1986) – an analysis of Jewish, and anti-Jewish, forms of discourse, and the relationship between them. Freud had a certain admiration for Otto Weininger – usually characterized as the supreme Viennese example of intellectual misogyny and Jewish self-hatred. The following passages from Gilman's book place this relationship in a new perspective:

Freud read and used many of Weininger's views. One view that he seems to have accepted was the need to draw a distinction between the language of science used by him and the language attributed to the Jew. This hidden language, the language that Viennese society used to characterize the Jew, was the language of the outsider. It was part of the hostile labeling of the Jew as different. But Freud projects this universal labeling of the language of the Jews as different onto a subset of Jews. He characterizes the *mauscheln* of the Jew attempting to enter Austrian society from the East as the true sign of the different, hidden language of the Jew. It is a public indicator of the Jew's difference and of Freud's identification with the non-Jew rather than with the non-Jew's caricature of the Jew.

Freud wishes to stand outside the limited world view attributed by this caricature of the Jew. He wishes to speak a different language . . . the language of scientific discourse. Yet that discourse as it manifests itself in Weininger is itself contaminated. In this medium Freud creates a language for himself that is neither the language of women nor the language of Jews. The exercise of collecting and retelling Jewish jokes, of removing them from the daily world in which Freud must live to the higher plane of the new scientific discourse, that of psychoanalysis, enables Freud to purge himself of the insecurity felt in his role as a Jew in *fin-de-siècle* Vienna.[18]

This focus on linguistic insecurity, together with the emphasis on social marginality, also constitutes a form of Ethnic Maximalism. The approaches of these authors may, by their very hypothetical, speculative character, invite dismissal as fascinating conjectures and nothing more. Yet if one is prepared to accept that new systems of thought do not arise autonomously, then the significance of Jewish ethnic factors in the intellectual developments of *fin-de-siècle* Vienna cannot be discounted. The views of advocates of Ethnic Minimalism like Peter Gay and Allan Janik certainly deserve respect.[19] But the remainder of this paper will suggest reasons why, in addition to factors already alluded to, sociological analysis of the position of Jews in Vienna further supports the case for a strong ethnic dimension in interpretations of Viennese culture.

Why was early psychoanalysis exclusively Jewish?

As Dennis Klein has pointed out: 'Until March 6, 1907, when Carl Jung and another Swiss psychiatrist, Ludwig Binswanger, attended their first meeting in Vienna, every member of the circle – by this time there were about 20 – was Jewish. . . . Freud surrounded himself with fellow Jews in the psychoanalytic circle, in pursuit of his scientific ideas. His attraction to Jews was so strong that when non-Jews first entered the movement he responded with an uncomfortable feeling of "strangeness".'[20] Klein is here describing, of course, a group of highly educated, cosmopolitan, secularized bourgeois men engaged in scientific discussions with universal application – and yet they seem to flock together with a degree of ethnic exclusivity more appropriate to a devout, ghettoized existence; or to a society in which Jews were legally excluded from residential, educational, economic or social intercourse with non-Jews. But despite anti-Semitism, late Habsburg Vienna was in essential respects an ethnically integrated social and economic order. There were virtually no legal restrictions on the careers Jews might pursue, which of the excellent state schools they might attend, or where they might live. Assimilation beckoned, and by 1910, when legally registered Jews numbered around 175,000, or 9 per cent of the city's total population, there were probably an additional 20,000 ex-Jewish converts, or their offspring, in the city. These are social facts which support the image of the Viennese social structure provided by the influential cultural historian Carl Schorske, whose seminal essays over several decades have implicitly given support to what we have here dubbed the Ethnic Minimalist perspective.

Although Schorske does not address the issue of ethnic salience at length in the writings collected in *Fin-de-Siècle Vienna* (1980), his emphasis is entirely on viewing Viennese Jewry as incorporated into the city's bourgeoisie, with a corresponding absorption into high German culture:

In Austria, where higher culture was greatly prized as a mark of status by the liberal, urban middle class, the Jews of that class merely shared the prevalent values, holding them perhaps more intensely, because the taint of trade had stained their lives more deeply. . . . Assimilation through culture, as a second stage in Jewish assimilation, was but a special case of the middle class phaseology of upward mobility from economic to intellectual vocations.

In Schorske's view, the great trauma of Viennese society came with the failure of the liberal bourgeoisie as a whole to acquire a monopoly of power, leaving them as outsiders seeking integration with the aristocracy. 'The numerous and prospering Jewish element in Vienna,' he writes, 'with its strong assimilationist thrust, only strengthened this trend.'[21] Yet we know that, while psychoanalysis may have been a rather extreme case, other major intellectual circles in Vienna – even the leadership of the Social Democratic Party – were largely, if not exclusively, composed of men with some degree of Jewish background or ancestry. How did this come about if, as Schorske maintains, middle-class Jews were apparently incorporated into the activities and culture of the wider bourgeois class? The explanation rests on complex demographic factors, which can be presented here in précis form only.

Freud's home at Berggasse 19 was located in the 9th district, Alsergrund (see map). At the time of the meetings of his Wednesday Psychological Society the population of that district was about 79 per cent Christian and 21 per cent Jewish. His disciples came from many other areas of Vienna, some of which were more, some less, ethnically balanced. All were of mixed ethnic composition, although the 2nd district, Leopoldstadt, one-third Jewish, retained its character as a kind of home base for many Viennese Jews and new arrivals. About a quarter, or 40,000, of the Jews in Vienna in 1910 had been born in Galicia, the Polish–Ukrainian outpost of the Habsburg Empire from which many *shtetl* Jews had migrated to Vienna as well as overseas. The largest proportion of Viennese Jews had been born in the city itself or had migrated within the Empire from Jewish communities in Bohemia, Moravia and western Hungary – where they had had previous exposure to German, or 'western' culture.[22]

The Jewish migration to Vienna was not unique – it coincided with the large-scale influx of Czech and rural Austrian workers attracted by the wages and other perceived advantages of a sojourn in 'the City of Dreams'. But the social and economic differentiation of Jews from their Christian fellow migrants had begun even before they left the provinces. There the Jews had typically experienced a long history of segregated living, having been in varying degrees isolated or cross-pressured by the nationalist awakenings of the period. Cultural differences prevalent during the pre-migration phase were eroded by the more open market opportunities which the state attempted to promote

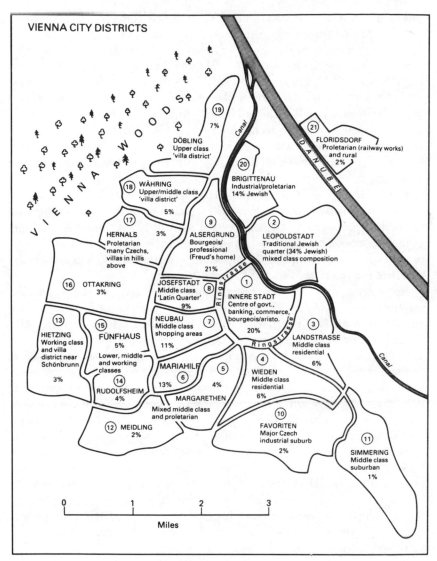

VIENNA CITY DISTRICTS

19 7%

DÖBLING
Upper class
'villa district'

21 FLORIDSDORF
Proletarian (railway works)
and rural
2%

18 WÄHRING
Upper/middle class
'villa district'
5%

20

BRIGITTENAU
Industrial/proletarian
14% Jewish

17

HERNALS
Proletarian
many Czechs,
villas in hills
above
3%

9 ALSERGRUND
Bourgeois/
professional
(Freud's home)
21%

2 LEOPOLDSTADT
Traditional Jewish
quarter (34% Jewish)
mixed class composition

16 OTTAKRING
3%

JOSEFSTADT
Middle class
'Latin Quarter'
9%
8

1 INNERE STADT
Centre of govt.,
banking, commerce,
bourgeois/aristo.
20%

13 HIETZING
Working class
and villa
district near
Schönbrunn
3%

15 FÜNFHAUS
5%
Lower, middle
and working
classes

NEUBAU
Middle class
shopping areas
11%
7

3 LANDSTRASSE
Middle class
residential
6%

14 RUDOLFSHEIM
4%

MARIAHILF
13%
6

5 4%

4 WIEDEN
Middle class
residential
6%

MARGARETHEN
Mixed middle class
and proletarian

12 MEIDLING
2%

10 FAVORITEN
Major Czech
industrial suburb
2%

11 SIMMERING
Middle class
suburban
1%

0   1   2   3

Miles

5. Vienna City Districts, 1910. Percentages indicate the proportion of Jews in the total population of each district.

in Vienna against the obstructionist protectionism of the Guilds; but historic differences between Jews and non-Jews in occupational specialization and preference also persisted.

Marsha Rozenblit exaggerates the degree of Jewish–Christian occupational differentiation in her *The Jews of Vienna* (1983) – claiming, for example, that Jews acquired a virtual monopoly over white-collar employment in the private sector.[23] But major differences did indeed exist and, most important, the overall economic profiles of Jews and Catholics showed a high degree of ethnic segmentation. By 1910 fully three-quarters of the half-million male members of the Viennese work force from a Catholic background were classified as wage-labourers, *Arbeiter*. Less than one-third of the Jewish male work force of 50,000 were *Arbeiter*. Two-thirds of Jewish men were classified as either self-employed or private-sector salaried employees. The proportion of Jews among the latter was much higher than of Catholic men, of whom less than 10 per cent were so engaged in the private sector; but the numerical base of the Catholics was so much larger than that of the Jewish work force – 10 to 1 – that even their much lower rate of white-collar employment generated a much higher number of Catholic salaried employees: 45,000, as opposed to only 17,000 Jews. Moreover, 1 Jewish man out of 7 was classified as an industrial worker. Thus occupational differentiation along ethnic religious lines, while substantial, was far from absolute in Freud's Vienna.[24]

But within Vienna's bourgeoisie, and particularly in that relatively small section of the middle classes which had acquired the higher education requisite for participation in German high culture, the *Bildungsbürgertum*, the differences both in relative proportions and in absolute numbers of Jews versus Catholics appears to have been nothing short of phenomenal. Steven Beller's investigation of the social composition of the Viennese *Gymnasien* during the late Habsburg era provides a major clue to the Jewish predominance in Viennese intellectual life. Two-thirds of all *Gymnasium* graduates surveyed, in a large sample spanning 1870 to 1910, who came from what are defined as liberal bourgeois backgrounds – i.e., students with fathers having occupations in commerce, finance, industry, the legal and medical professions, journalism, or enjoying a private income – were Jewish. Eighty per cent of the graduates with fathers in commerce, the largest single occupational group, were Jewish. And the proportion of Jewish graduates from liberal bourgeois backgrounds appears to have increased after the turn of the century.[25]

Beller's study directly challenges Carl Schorske's account of the Viennese bourgeoisie. It hardly seems appropriate, in the light of these data, to speak of the intellectual élite of that class as containing within it an assimilated Jewish minority; it appears, rather, that there was a strong majority of educated Jews among whom non-Jewish participants may perhaps have engaged in a degree of reciprocal acculturation. We have already touched on the probable motivational factors which help to account for the striking command of the cultural heights achieved by the sons of Jewish migrants who, like Jakob Freud in 1859, began the move from the provinces to the imperial capital.[26]

We can now see that there existed a very great statistical probability that Freud's circle would contain a high proportion of Jews, despite the absence of any gross forms of ethnic apartheid in Vienna. And it is not difficult to construct a model of the circumstances under which that group acquired an exclusively Jewish pedigree. The socially and inter-personally polarizing impact of a resurgent anti-Semitism in Vienna has already been stressed. Moreover, both Jews and Catholics were legally classified according to religion. Traditional theological and cultural pressures enforcing religious endogamy, reinforced by the legal pro-hibition of intermarriage between Jews and Catholics without prior conversion, placed powerful, although not insuperable, obstacles in the way of the breakdown of ethnic-based family networks and association-al life generally.[27] As Rozenblit has pointed out, in some of the lower schools in Jewish districts friendships would crystallize along ethnic lines, while the large representation of Jews in many of the *Gymnasien* would tend to structure interpersonal contacts on an ethnic basis – contacts which might later be reactivated in the formation of intellec-tual and artistic circles. Viennese Jews adapted to the secular culture of the Austro-German dominant group, but they tended to do so *together*. Herein lies the explanation for the apparent paradox that a minority group undergoing urbanization, social mobility and a cultural trans-formation fails to dissolve its in-group ties. The natural flow of recruit-ment to Freud's early circle in Vienna almost inevitably ran along the lines of sociometric choice based on personal contact and it presup-posed, within broad limits, similar sensibilities and shared experien-ces.[28]

In conclusion I would suggest that the case, or cases, for an important Jewish ethnic causation – cultural, situational, or the two combined – while perhaps not proven by the above considerations, nevertheless should serve, when marshalled as above, to concentrate the minds of all Ethnic Minimalists. The ready and eager acceptance of Freud's ideas in Bloomsbury, and other important reception centres outside Jewish Central Europe, demonstrates the trans-cultural power of his genius. But it in no way vitiates the central hypothesis of the foregoing discussion: that Freud's definition of his own identity, in response to the world he inhabited, was implicated in his analytical vision of human life in its more universal manifestations.[29]

Notes

I would like to express a long-standing personal debt to two scholars, Melvin Seeman and Kurt H. Wolff, whose seminars on the Jewish marginality problematic, and on the sociology of knowledge, at Ohio State University many years ago, were responsible for the underlying assumption of this essay: that empirical methodology and hermeneutics are not mutually exclusive forms of discourse.

[1] For a more comprehensive assessment of the role of Jews in Viennese intellectual life, see Steven Beller, 'Jews in Viennese Culture 1867–1938' (diss., Cambridge 1986, to be published in revised form by Cambridge University Press).

[2] W.M. Johnston, *The Austrian Mind: An Intellectual and Social History* (Berkeley 1972), contains a section headed 'The Intellectual Pre-eminence of the Jews: Its Roots in Tribal Tradition and Gentile Reaction', 23–9.

[3] For Kraus's problems in the area of Jewish identity, see Edward Timms, *Karl Kraus – Apocalyptic Satirist: Culture and Catastrophe in Habsburg Vienna* (New Haven and London 1986), 1–29, 237–49 *et passim*. See also Sigurd Paul Scheichl, 'Karl Kraus und die Politik, 1892–1919' (doctoral diss., Innsbruck 1971), 813–1074. Robert S. Wistrich has explored the possible effects of Jewish self-hatred on the ideology and politics of the Austro-Marxists in *Revolutionary Jews from Marx to Trotsky* (London 1976), and *Socialism and the Jews: The Dilemmas of Assimilation in Germany and Austria-Hungary* (London 1982).

[4] P. Gay, *Freud, Jews and Other Germans* (New York 1978), 33–4. Gay discusses Freud's Jewishness and psychoanalysis at great length, but with essentially the same minimalist conclusion, in *A Godless Jew* (New Haven and London 1987), 115–56.

[5] S. Marcus, *Freud and the Culture of Psychoanalysis* (Boston 1984), 189–90.

[6] E. Gellner, *The Psychoanalytic Movement: or, The Coming of Unreason* (London 1985), 22.

[7] W.J. McGrath, *Freud's Discovery of Psychoanalysis: The Politics of Hysteria* (Ithaca, N.Y., 1986), 26, 27. L. Shengold, 'Freud and Joseph', in *Freud and His Self-Analysis*, ed. Mark Kanzner and Jules Glen (New York 1979), 67–86; Martin S. Bergmann, 'Moses and the Evolution of Freud's Jewish Identity', *Israel Annals of Psychiatry and Related Disciplines*, xiv, Mar 1976, 3–26.

[8] M. Robert, *From Oedipus to Moses: Freud's Jewish Identity*, trans. R. Manheim (Garden City, N.Y., 1976), 3.

[9] Johnston, *The Austrian Mind*, 26. The extensive sociological literature that exists in the area of Jewish family studies, while dealing mainly with present-day Jewish families, is methodologically and conceptually relevant to historical studies; for example, Howard M. Schapiro's 'Perceived Family Structure as an Explanation of Jewish Intellectuality', *Sociological Quarterly*, xviii (1977), 461–72.

[10] E. Etzioni-Halevy and Z. Halevi, 'The Jewish Ethic and the Spirit of Achievement', *Jewish Journal of Sociology*, xix (1977). This article contains a useful review of the range of hypotheses which have been advanced to account for Jewish achievement-orientation. See also David McClelland, *The Achieving Society* (Toronto 1961), which argues that it was the forward-looking, hopeful Messianic strain in Judaism which, in contrast to the fatalism of Hinduism and Buddhism, provided the motivational bridge from Talmudic, rabbinical wisdom to the exercise of critical reason in worldly, secular roles.

[11] D. Bakan, *Sigmund Freud and the Jewish Mystical Tradition* (Princeton, N.J., 1958).

[12] Robert, *From Oedipus to Moses*, 6, 7.

[13] Ibid.

[14] M. Pollak, 'Cultural Innovation and Social Identity in *Fin-de-Siècle* Vienna', in *Jews, Antisemitism and Culture in Vienna*, ed. Ivar Oxaal, Michael Pollak and Gerhard Botz (London and New York 1987). See also Pollak's *Vienne 1900: Une identité blessée* (Paris 1984).

[15] Veblen's essay first appeared in the *Political Science Quarterly*, March 1919, and was republished in an abridged version in *The Portable Veblen* (New York 1953).

[16] J.M. Cuddihy, *The Ordeal of Civility: Freud, Marx, Lévi-Strauss, and the Jewish Struggle with Modernity* (New York 1974), 39.

[17] Cuddihy (19) cites Talcott Parsons as the originator of basic insights into the major relevance, for a general theory of society, of the Freudian paradigm: ' "Not only moral standards but *all the components of the common culture* are internalized as part of the personality structure", writes Talcott Parsons in crediting Freud with the discovery of "internalization" [Parsons's emphasis].' Indeed Freud's concept of the super-ego can be interpreted on three social levels: that of abstract scientific theory (Parsons), or in historicized accounts stressing either the ethos of a social class, the Victorian bourgeoisie (Marcus), or the social psychology of an ethnic minority (Cuddihy).

[18] S.L. Gilman, *Jewish Self-Hatred: Anti-Semitism and the Hidden Language of the Jews* (Baltimore 1986), 267–8.

[19] A leading Ethnic Minimalist has been Allan Janik, co-author with Stephen Toulmin of *Wittgenstein's Vienna* (London 1973). See Janik's critique of Peter Gay's description of Weininger as prototypical Jewish self-hating intellectual, 'Viennese Culture and the Jewish Self-Hatred Hypothesis', in *Jews, Antisemitism and Culture in Vienna*, ed. Oxaal *et al.*, also Janik's collected essays, *How Not To Interpret a Culture: Essays on the Problem of Method in Geisteswissenschaften* (Bergen: University of Bergen, Filosofisk Institutt [Stensilserie no. 73], 1986).

[20] D. Klein, *Jewish Origins of the Psychoanalytic Movement* (New York 1981), 93. In this context Klein also cites the well-known letter from Freud to Karl Abraham referring to 'the great inner resistances' which a non-Jew like Carl Jung must experience to his ideas. Freud, however, stressed the need to recruit non-Jews to the movement lest it retain the appearance of being a 'Jewish national' cause.

[21] C. Schorske, *Fin-de-Siècle Vienna: Politics and Culture* (New York 1980), 148–9.

[22] Further details of the sociological profile of Viennese Jews can be found in Ivar Oxaal and Walter R. Weitzmann, 'The Jews of Pre-1914 Vienna: An Exploration of Basic Sociological Dimensions', *Leo Baeck Institute Year Book*, xxx (1985), 395–432.

[23] M. Rozenblit, *The Jews of Vienna: Assimilation and Identity* (Albany, N.Y., 1983), 47–70.

[24] The implications of these data for the interpretation of Viennese anti-Semitism, and the failure of the Austro-Marxists to combat it, are discussed by I. Oxaal in 'The Jews of Young Hitler's Vienna', in *Jews, Antisemitism and Culture in Vienna*, ed. Oxaal *et al.*

[25] Beller's findings appear to substantiate earlier impressionistic claims by writers like Stefan Zweig, in *Die Welt von Gestern* (Stockholm 1944), that nine-tenths of Viennese culture depended on Jews. A first report of these findings is provided by S. Beller in 'Class, Culture and the Jews of Vienna', in *Jews, Antisemitism and Culture*, ed. Oxaal *et al.*

[26] See the fascinating account by Marianne Krüll, *Freud and His Father* (London 1987).

[27] Despite fundamental differences between the two cultures, the position of Jews in German society seems in Jacob Katz's characterization to be closely parallel to the situation of Viennese Jews: '. . . the experience of certain individuals nothwithstanding, the entrance of Jewry as a *collective* into the body of German society did not mean real integration into any part, stratum, or section of it. It meant, rather, the creation of a separate subgroup, which conformed to the German middle class in some of its characteristics.' See 'German Culture and the Jews', in *The Jewish Response to German Culture: From the Enlightenment to the Second World War*, ed. Jehuda Reinharz and Walter Schatzberg (Hanover, N.H., 1985), 85.

[28] Edward Timms has made a useful preliminary attempt at diagramming the overlapping membership of various Viennese intellectual and artistic circles in *Karl Kraus – Apocalyptic Satirist*, Fig. 1 (p. 8).

[29] See *Bloomsbury / Freud: The Letters of James and Alix Strachey 1924–1925*, ed. Perry Meisel and Walter Kendrick (London 1986).

3

The Psychoanalytic Exodus
Romantic Antecedents, and the Loss to German Intellectual Life

Uwe Henrik Peters

The two major German-speaking countries, West Germany and Austria, are still facing a situation that is very difficult to describe historically. It is in some respects comparable to the psychological after-effects of the Holocaust on the German population, which caused a type of collective bad conscience and guilt feelings, but without a sense of mourning.[1] There is great admiration for the psychiatrists who emigrated from Germany, and particularly for the psychoanalysts who did so, but here too a lack of mourning for the loss and sometimes even a lack of awareness of it. I am at present writing a book about the German psychoanalysts who went into emigration between 1933 and 1938. This not always cheering task has led me to reflect not only on the loss to German intellectual life resulting from the exodus, but also on the deeper roots of psychoanalysis in German Romanticism.

The exodus

In 1933 about 2,000 psychiatrists of various orientations were living in Germany. By the beginning of the Second World War, about 600 had emigrated, settling in 80 different countries. Never before in cultural history had there been such an exodus. There are those in Germany who stress that at least two-thirds thus remained in the country and only one-third emigrated. This attitude, however, fails to recognize that the most active and productive of the people working in psychiatry left Germany and Austria; and that, of psychoanalysts, the vast majority emigrated. Very few analysts indeed remained, though August Aichhorn continued to live in Austria, and some analysts continued their work at the so-called Göring Institute in Berlin.[2] Others, among them Rudolf and Josephine Bilz, even became Nazis. But there were so few analysts remaining that the profession of psychoanalysis could not be revived after the war.

The reasons for the exodus of those working in psychiatry are not hard to find. It was not only the Nazis who viewed psychoanalysis as a Jewish science – Freud himself was well aware of the predominance of Jews within his circle.[3] Anti-Semitism was, of course, one of the main pillars of Nazi ideology. Furthermore, some of the psychoanalysts of the Twenties had had close contacts with the Communist and Social Democratic groups who were also targets of persecution by the Nazis. For instance, Wilhelm Reich and Marie Langer were psychoanalysts and Communists, while members of the Social Democratic underground organization 'Neu Beginnen' included Edith Jacobson and Thea (and Gerhard) Bry, both of whom now live in the United States.[4] Psychoanalysts like Richard Sterba (born 1898), who is still at work, joined their colleagues in emigrating although not themselves Jews, Communists or Social Democrats. Sterba, in fact, whose compilation of a dictionary of psychoanalysis was interrupted by emigration at the entry for 'delusions of grandeur [Größenwahn]', was the only non-Jew in the Vienna Psycho-Analytical Society in 1938.[5]

There is a not inconsiderable literature on how the worldwide dissemination of psychoanalysis, though not altogether the result of the mass emigration, was definitely speeded up by it.[6] And yet it is difficult to obtain a general survey. The breach in German cultural and intellectual life was so enormous that it is difficult adequately to convey its dimensions. Perhaps, however, as a mental exercise, one could try to transport the fruits that the world obtained through psychoanalysis and its offshoots after 1933 back to Germany. Imagine that the entire development of ego psychology (Anna Freud, Heinz Hartmann, Rudolf Löwenstein, Ernst Kris), which indeed was initially formulated just before the emigration, had taken place in that country.[7] Rudolf Löwenstein would have analysed Jacques Lacan in Berlin and not in Paris. Heinz Kohut and Otto Kernberg would have developed their theories of narcissism in Vienna and not in Chicago and New York. Margaret Mahler would have developed her individuation-separation theory in Berlin instead of New York.[8] Just imagine if Anna Freud had spent the second half of her life (1938–82) in Berlin, where some of the Freud family had moved, instead of London. Melanie Klein would not have gone to London to analyse Ernest Jones's German Jewish wife, Katherine, and his children. Friedrich ('Frederick' or 'Fritz') Perls would not have moved to South Africa through the intervention of Ernest Jones, nor founded a psychoanalytic institute and later developed his Gestalt therapy there.[9] Erik Erikson would have kept his stepfather's name, Homburger, or his mother's, Abrahamson, and stayed in Frankfurt. Erich Fromm would have remained in Heidelberg and with Frieda Fromm-Reichmann would have continued to hold psychoanalytic conferences there.[10] Obviously one could continue such reflections for some time, though appreciating full well that they cannot be admitted as evidence in the debate. But I would nevertheless like you, the reader, to imagine you are now in Vienna or Berlin – and speaking German instead of English. Perhaps you will be able then to empathize with the emotions of a German who loves his culture but finds it hard to accept part of its history.

Antecedents in German Romanticism

If one searches for parallels with Germany's particular historical situation, one may call to mind the Huguenots, who were expelled from France in the seventeenth century in great numbers. About 200,000 people were forced to leave their country and found refuge in Holland, England and, most of all, in Germany. At one time, Huguenots comprised 30 per cent of the population of Berlin. Germany gained immensely at that period from this influx from brilliant French intellectual life – the effects can still be felt today and have influenced Germany's cultural development deeply. For instance, some French Huguenots were involved in the German Romantic movement, as such names as Adalbert von Chamisso and Friedrich, Baron de la Motte Fouqué, both famous writers in their time, illustrate.[11] It was during the Romantic era, indeed, that most of the ideas that later formed the core of psychoanalytic theories were first conceived.

This fact becomes even more evident if, by contrast, one looks at mainstream German psychiatry at the time when psychoanalysis originated. In 1898, a year before Freud's *Interpretation of Dreams* was published, Kraepelin described the new clinical entity of 'dementia praecox'. In 1911 Eugen Bleuler changed the name to 'schizophrenia', a term still used all over the world. It is essential to note, however, that Kraepelin had combined his clinical description with a theory, based on the positivistic psychology of Wundt, which is still widely accepted by psychiatrists everywhere, and has been adopted in the current revision of the *Diagnostic and Statistical Manual* (*DSM* III).[12] This theory, which thus far has neither been proved conclusively nor disproved, refers to schizophrenia as an organic disease of the brain. This involves the discounting of the experiences of human life and interpersonal relationships, for example within the family, and also all the cultural aspects of life, as possible causes of mental disturbance; treating them first as relatively unimportant and eventually with total neglect. In fact, at the turn of the century, the situation of psychiatry was not very different in England, the United States or France from that in Germany. The treatment of mental and nervous patients was absolutely dominated by what we nowadays call 'biological psychiatry'.

Unlike other European countries, however, Germany can look back on an era of Romantic psychiatry which does not seem to have existed elsewhere in Europe, or in America, at the beginning of the nineteenth century or subsequently. This phase was, indeed, relatively short, but nevertheless it produced many concepts which are still important in the understanding of mental and nervous illnesses. The most far-reaching of these was that of the unconscious. The first books on it were written during the early nineteenth century,[13] and the idea put forward that the 'soul' formed an entity which stretched from the darkest depths of the unconscious up to the highest and lightest parts of the conscious. Dreams were regarded as belonging to the 'dark side' or 'shadow side [Nachtseite]' of man's nature and detailed attention was paid to them. In fact, 'night side' is the first term for the unconscious and includes dreams, delusions and so on. The fashionable philosopher Gotthilf Heinrich von Schubert (1780—1860), for example, published a very popular book, *Die Symbolik des Traumes* (Symbolism of Dreams), as early as 1814.

Johann Gottfried Langermann (1768–1832), the psychiatrist and asylum administrator who was for some years the private tutor of the Romantic poet Novalis (Baron Friedrich von Hardenberg, 1772–1801), had decided by 1797 against the concept of the brain as the only location and aetiological factor in mental disease, which of course is still the basic assumption of biological psychiatry. Nature and mind, Langermann argued, were completely different, and hence there was no reason to assume a necessary connection between physical and mental disease.[14] Whether or not it is possible for the mind to be disturbed without concomitant physical illness became a central issue of Romantic medicine. Even paranoia was viewed, not as implying a seriously diseased mind, but rather as a new and positively ingenious invention of that mind – a view Freud brought into serious discussion again a hundred years later. In a famous passage he echoes the Romantic view of the matter, invoking Goethe's phrase about the 'beautiful world' which can be rebuilt, after it has been destroyed: 'And the paranoiac builds it again, not more splendid, it is true, but at least so that he can once more live in it. He builds it up by the work of his delusions. *The delusional formation, which we take to be the pathological product, is in reality an attempt at recovery, a process of reconstruction*' (*SE* XII. 70–1).[15]

Madness is one of the topics by which the Romantic poets were fascinated. According to the notes Novalis left for the completion of his unfinished novel, *Heinrich von Ofterdingen* (1802–3), the hero was supposed to become the 'saviour of nature' through voluntary madness. The action of the anonymous work, *Die Nachtwachen des Bonaventura* (Nightwatches of Bonaventura, 1804), a typical product of the early Romantic period, takes place in an asylum and is primarily concerned with the topic of madness. The mad people in this book, in contrast to the sane, are the first to recognize the 'madness of the world'. This beautiful, though somewhat absurd, idea resurfaced much later in works of R.D. Laing such as *The Divided Self*.[16] It is well known that Laing's basic psychiatric ideas are originally Romantic, although also derived in part from psychoanalysis. Would anti-psychiatry have developed in Germany rather than Britain had the psychoanalytic exodus not taken place?

The Romantic doctors believed that the art of healing ('Heilkunst') in medical science, indeed every kind of healing, would of necessity affect the human soul because they believed the soul to be man's true centre, and that diseases only spread into the body and mind ('Geist') from it. If the soul resists disease, the body will not succumb. In fact, the idea that healing is an art, which only makes use of the results of science, is a romantic notion, though again strikingly modern.

In addition to the conventional medical treatment of the time, the Romantic doctors included social and psychological means in their armamentarium. Some of these were: induction of a somnambulistic state by 'magnetism', which we would now refer to as hypnotism; suggestion in the waking state or condition; utilizing the rapport between the doctor applying mesmerism and the patient, a long-lasting therapeutic relationship which establishes itself after a few mesmeric sessions. We now know it mainly under its Freudian terminology: transference / counter-transference. The Romantics also believed that human kindness, relaxation, making music, playing games, and generally enjoying oneself, gardening and doing manual work, and observing the beauties of nature (in this case the beautiful landscapes of the river Rhine) would not only benefit the patient but even cure him of mental anguish. All these measures were summed up under the term 'psychic cure' ('psychische Kur') which is in fact a combination of 'magnetic cure' and 'moral treatment'.[17] We find the term 'psychic cure' occurring again almost literally in Freud's 'psychoanalytic cure' ('psychoanalytische Kur'), which was how he termed his treatment originally. (There is a translation problem here, as the historical, that is to say Romantic, background of the phrase is totally lost in the English equivalent, 'psychoanalytic treatment'.)

In the second half of the nineteenth century Romantic medicine almost completely stagnated, and did not re-emerge until fifty years later in Freud's works. Only braidism or hypnotism, as mesmerism was called after 1843, kept up a marginal existence in European medical circles until Bernheim at Nancy and Charcot in Paris, from whom Freud learnt it, revived the practice. And it was hypnosis that we see, interestingly enough, forming the link with Freud's distinctive forms of therapy.

It should, at this point, be made clear that Freud was influenced not only by German Romantic psychiatry, but by other factors as well, among them the biological science of his time; the German classical tradition, above all Goethe; the Enlightenment ideal of tolerance as it was formulated and realized in his Jewish group, B'nai B'rith;[18] and also by the ideas of Darwin, and by Romantic theology (Schleiermacher). In acknowledging the cultural context in which psychoanalysis was embedded, we also become aware of the immense loss to German intellectual life which resulted from the psychoanalytic exodus. The humanistic ideas of Romantic psychiatry left the country along with Freud and his fellow psychoanalysts.

Historical dispersal and post-war reconstruction

The geographical situation should also be considered. Psychoanalysis developed in Vienna at a time when the city was the political and cultural centre of the Austro-Hungarian Empire, which in size, population and influence was comparable to other major European powers of the time such as England and France. This huge Austrian Empire was so completely destroyed by the First World War that not even all the German-speaking parts remained in the remodelled Austria. The population was reduced from about 65 million to 7 million. In other words, 90 per cent of the population of Austria-Hungary was distributed among the other successor states.

Germany, the other German-speaking empire, which had also before the war been comparable in size and influence to the European powers mentioned above, managed, by contrast with Austria, to keep most of its territory and population, with only minor losses. As Freud correctly pointed out, Berlin now replaced Vienna as the centre of power and culture for German speakers. The Austrian Adolf Hitler is an obvious example of someone adapting to this fact; otherwise his so-called National Socialist revolution would have been carried out in Vienna instead of Berlin.

Berlin also became the new centre of the psychoanalytic movement. Sigmund and Anna Freud spent a fair amount of time there well before the Nazis took over. The major reason for their visits was medical, in that Freud came for his oral prosthesis to be remodelled. But he also received many visitors while there, and even took to the air for his only flight in an aeroplane, to the island of Rügen. His medical treatment cannot have been the only reason why his sojourns in Berlin lasted so long. The same holds true for other members of his family – one of Freud's sons, for instance, owned a house in Berlin. Psychoanalysis was evidently drawn to the current German centre of power.

In 1930 the third psychoanalytic institute, after the ones in Vienna and Berlin, was founded in Frankfurt. As it was dissolved in 1933, it did not have time to become very active. After World War II, Frankfurt became the financial and economic centre of West Germany, being

situated geographically in the middle of this new country. The so-called
Frankfurt School (Frankfurter Schule) originated there and returned
there after the war, and it was in Frankfurt that Mitscherlich became
most influential. The University of Frankfurt was the only West
German university to offer an honorary doctorate to Anna Freud,
shortly before her death – typically enough, in psychology. Anna
Freud, who had always been sensitive to symbolic meanings, accepted
this honour without hesitation, although she had always until then
refused to visit West Germany and was now too frail to do so. The
three German psychoanalytic institutes in existence at the beginning of
the expulsion – in Berlin, Vienna and Frankfurt – also symbolize the
importance of psychoanalysis in Germany at that time, and their loss is
a sign of the immense depredations (among many others, of course)
which the Germans suffered because of Hitler.

The loss of psychoanalysis had another unfortunate effect, in that
almost all the non-psychoanalytical psychotherapists emigrated as well.
Shortly before, this branch of the psychiatric profession had wielded
increasing influence, as the six congresses of the 'General Medical
Society for Psychotherapy' (Allgemeine Ärztliche Gesellschaft für
Psychotherapie) showed quite clearly. Like their spiritual leader
Wladimir Gottlieb Eliasberg (born 1887), most of the non-analytical
psychotherapists were Jews and hence in danger of persecution.
Eliasberg emigrated, first to Austria, then to Czechoslovakia and later
to the United States, where he lived and worked until 1969. His last
book was on political propaganda.[19]

Although more non-analytical psychotherapists than analysts
remained in Germany – for example, Ernst Kretschmer and W.T.
Winkler, who studied Freud's works in the Marburg University
psychiatric department's library during bombing raids – their number
was too depleted to exert much influence. There was, indeed, even
some Nazi psychotherapy, but it is unimportant and will not be
considered here. Social Darwinism eventually infiltrated psychiatry and
hence the mentally ill joined the Jews as victims of the Holocaust.
About 100,000 mentally ill persons were killed by the Nazis.[20]

In addition to the losses in personnel, the literature of psychoanalysis
was comprehensively destroyed by the Nazis as well, and eliminated
from libraries. Nor was the post-1933 literature added to libraries'
holdings after the war. There are still quite a number of important
psychoanalytical works of which not a single copy can be found in West
Germany. It is, remarkably, often easier for a German historian of
psychoanalysis to visit the British Library in London than to try and
carry out research in, say, Cologne.

After the war the situation in Germany was peculiar indeed. Almost none of the psychoanalytic emigrants returned to their homeland[21] and those who had remained were too few to activate a vigorous new beginning. The Vienna Psycho-Analytical Society was refounded in 1946, but with only four full members, so that it no longer fulfilled the requirements for membership in the IPA (International Psycho-Analytical Association), and a ploy had to be used to circumvent the regulations. It is well known that the Nazi bureaucrats were meticulous record-keepers. They had dissolved the Psycho-Analytical Society and forced its members into emigration, but they had to carry out official procedures for the closure to become legally effective. When the warrant of closure arrived, however, the postman could find no one to whom to deliver it, so he had to go on without handing it over. This means that in actual fact the Psycho-Analytical Society continued in formal existence during the whole Nazi era.[22]

After the war, psychoanalysis in Germany for a long time faced a very difficult situation. Such fresh impetus as there was, is closely connected with the appearance of Alexander Mitscherlich. He had been deeply affected by his participation in the Nuremberg trials and wrote a book about the horrific experiments doctors carried out on concentration-camp inmates.[23] In Frankfurt he joined the re-established, Marxist-oriented Frankfurt School of philosophy and sociology. After the students' revolt of 1968 he became temporarily the spiritual leader of the German Left. Unlike the situation in America, in Germany psychoanalysis and psychosomatic medicine were seen for a long time as synonymous with a socialist outlook. As the climax of this development occurred at the same time as the general reforms which took place in universities and their medical faculties, it was possible to introduce psychosomatic medicine, and hence psychoanalysis, into the medical curriculum in German universities. Psychosomatic medicine, which was more or less identical with psychoanalysis, suddenly became an independent discipline within the framework of academic medicine, with its own professors, departments and hospitals. Surprisingly enough, the Federal Republic of Germany is the only country in the world today that has a Chair of Psychoanalysis at almost every one of its 25 medical schools.

Unfortunately, these favourable conditions have not so far led to any new creative impetus for psychoanalysis. Perhaps the future will look different; at present, however, there is little reason for optimism. To start with, the many chairs could not be distributed effectively because there was a lack of scientifically oriented psychoanalysis. Also, the first professors appointed found it hard to obtain medical staff with whom to work. The gap was filled by psychologists. Modern German psychiatry, therefore, shows a much stronger psychological element than the psychiatry of any other country. And yet the psychological debates – as long as they do not deal with history – have a special character that, using other analogies, might be summed up as 'late psychoanalysis'. I would not term it 'post-psychoanalysis'.

In other words, there are continuing, extremely abstract discussions on the subtleties of the various Oedipus, ego and narcissism theories. At the same time, the fact that many health-insurance companies are willing to underwrite the entire cost of even protracted psychoanalytic treatment – again an odd exception compared with many other countries – has led to unfortunate side-effects. Thus most conferences concentrate on 'technical problems' of treatment and charges.

In my opinion, this is yet another consequence of the loss Germany has had to suffer through the exodus of psychoanalysts. Freud somehow personally embodied the coherence of theory with practice, of science with humanity, and of complexity with discipline. At present psychoanalysis in Germany is something it surely should be least of all: namely, a very successful technical subdiscipline of both medicine and psychology. Psychoanalysis has become completely 'unromantic', in theory and practice, so its inheritance from the Romantics is also lost.

Notes

[1] A. and M. Mitscherlich, *Die Unfähigkeit zu trauern* (Munich and Zürich 1967/1973).

[2] August Aichhorn's only book, but well known, is *Verwahrloste Jugend* (Vienna 1925), trans. as *Wayward Youth* (New York 1935). Aichhorn was honoured after the war with a Festschrift on the occasion of his seventieth birthday, edited by one of his émigré analysands: *Searchlights on Delinquency*, ed. Kurt R. Eissler (New York 1949), which also contains a short biography. On the Göring Institute, see Geoffrey Cocks, *Psychotherapy in the Third Reich: The Göring Institute* (New York and Oxford 1985).

[3] See Dennis B. Klein, *Jewish Origins of the Psychoanalytic Movement* (New York 1981).

[4] See Myron Sharaf, *Fury on Earth: A Biography of Wilhelm Reich* (New York 1983); Russell Jacoby, *The Repression of Psychoanalysis: Otto Fenichel and the Political Freudians* (New York 1983); Richard Loewenthal, *Die Wiederstandsgruppe 'Neu Beginnen'*, Beiträge zum Thema Widerstand no. 20 (Berlin 1982); Gerhard Bry, 'Resistance; Recollections from the Nazi Years' (MS, Leo Baeck Institute, New York): an extract appears in *Jüdisches Leben in Deutschland. Selbstzeugnisse zur Sozialgeschichte 1918–1945*, ed. Monika Richarz (Stuttgart 1982), 281–91.

[5] Richard Sterba, *Handwörterbuch der Psychoanalyse* (Vienna 1936). See also Richard Francis Sterba, *Reminiscences of a Viennese Psychoanalyst* (Detroit 1982).

[6] See, e.g., Reuben Fine, *A History of Psychoanalysis* (New York 1979); *Histoire de la psychanalyse*, ed. Roland Jaccard, 2 vols. (Paris 1982); Ilse and Robert Barande, *Histoire de la psychanalyse en France* (Toulouse 1975); Mario Francioni, *Storia della psicoanalisi francese. Teorie e istituzioni freudiane* (Turin 1982); Paola Esposito, Stefano V. Rossi, Angelo Tamburini, *Origini e sviluppo della psicoanalisi in Italia (1907–1952)* (Bologna 1980); Eva Brabant, 'Histoire du mouvement psychanalytique hongrois' (*thèse*, Paris 1985).

[7] A. Freud, *Das Ich und die Abwehrmechanismen* (Vienna 1936), trans. as *The Ego and the Mechanisms of Defence* (London 1946); see also Uwe Henrik Peters, *Anna Freud, a Life Dedicated to Children* (London 1985). H. Hartmann, 'Ich-Psychologie und Anpas-

sungsproblem', *Internationale Psychoanalytische Zeitschrift*, xxiv (1939), 62–135, trans. as *Ego Psychology and the Problem of Adaptation* (New York 1948); E. Kris, *Selected Papers* (New Haven and London 1975); R. Löwenstein, *Practice and Precept in Psychoanalytic Training: Selected Papers* (New Haven and London 1982).

[8] See Sherry Turkle, *Psychoanalytic Politics: Freud's French Revolution* (New York 1978). H. Kohut, *The Analysis of the Self: A Systematic Approach to the Psychoanalytic Treatment of Narcissistic Personality Disorders* (New York 1971); O. Kernberg, *Borderline Conditions and Pathological Narcissism* (New York and London 1976). M. Mahler, *Selected Papers*, vol. I: *Infantile Psychosis and Early Contributions*; vol. II: *Separation-Individuation* (New York and London 1979).

[9] Phyllis Grosskurth, *Melanie Klein: Her World and Her Work* (London 1985). Fritz [Frederick S.] Perls, *The Gestalt Approach* and *Eye Witness to Therapy* (Palo Alto, Calif., 1973); see also Perls's autobiography, *In and Out the Garbage Pail* (1969; repr. New York and London 1972), and Martin Shepard, *Fritz, An Intimate Portrait of Fritz Perls and Gestalt Therapy* (New York 1975).

[10] Robert Coles, *Erik H. Erikson: The Growth of his Work* (Boston 1974). Rainer Funk, *Mut zum Menschen. Erich Fromms Denken und Werk, seine humanistische Religion und Ethik* (Stuttgart 1978).

[11] Adalbert von Chamisso was born Louis Charles Adelaide de Chamisso in Boncourt, France, in 1781. His novel *Peter Schlemihls wundersame Geschichte* (1814) describes the fantastic as if it were real. The man without his shadow represents, in the opinion of Chamisso, the man without 'fatherland', the émigré. Friedrich, Baron de la Motte Fouqué (1777–1843), derived the inspiration for his famous novella *Undine* (1811) from Paracelsus, and provided E.T.A. Hoffmann with the libretto for his opera *Undine*.

[12] *The Interpretation of Dreams* first appeared in 1899, though it bears the date 1900 on its title-page. Emil Kraepelin (1856–1926) first wrote extensively about dementia praecox in the 1899 edition, the 6th, of his textbook on psychiatry, but had given a presentation of it the year before. The *Diagnostic and Statistical Manual of Mental Disorders*, 3rd revision (*DSM* III), which appeared in 1980 and is widely used for diagnostic purposes in the USA and elsewhere, offers a new diagnostic system, based on the theories of biological psychiatry.

[13] E.g. Carl Gustav Carus, *Psyche. Zur Entwicklungsgeschichte der Seele* (Pforzheim 1846).

[14] These ideas can be found in Langermann's medical dissertation, *De methodo cognoscendi curandique animi morbos stabilienda* (Jena 1797).

[15] S. Freud, 'Psychoanalytische Bemerkungen über einen autobiographisch beschriebenen Fall von Paranoia (*Dementia paranoides*)', *GW* viii. 308, trans. as 'Psychoanalytic Notes on an Autobiographical Account of a Case of Paranoia (*Dementia paranoides*)', *SE* xii. 9–79.

[16] R.D. Laing, *The Divided Self: An Existential Study in Sanity and Madness* (London 1959).

[17] For more information on mesmerism, see Henry F. Ellenberger, *The Discovery of the Unconscious: The History and Evolution of Dynamic Psychiatry* (New York 1970); *Mesmerism: A Translation of the Original Scientific and Medical Writings of F.A. Mesmer*, trans. and comp. by George Bloch (Los Altos, Calif., 1980); Léon Chertok and Raymond de Saussure, *Naissance de la psychanalyse, de Mesmer à Freud* (Paris 1973), trans. as *The Therapeutic Revolution from Mesmer to Freud* (New York 1979). On 'psychic cure' see, e.g., Johann Christian Reil, *Rhapsodien über die Anwendung der psychischen Kurmethode auf Geisteszerrüttungen* (Halle 1803), and *Beiträge zur Beförderung einer Kurmethode auf psychischem Wege*, 2 vols. (Halle 1808).

[18] See U.H. Peters, 'Goethe und Freud', *Goethe-Jahrbuch, 1986* (Weimar 1986), 86–105; and Klein, *Jewish Origins of the Psychoanalytical Movement*.

[19] W.G. Eliasberg, 'Allgemeine ärztliche Gesellschaft für Psychotherapie 1926–1931.

History of the Six Congresses', *American Journal of Psychiatry*, cxii (1936), 738–40; *Politische Propaganda* (Neuwied, 1967).

[20] The first book on the holocaust of psychiatric patients was Gerhard Schmidt, *Selektion in der Heilanstalt 1933–1945* (Stuttgart 1965; 2nd edn., Frankfurt 1983). Other books followed: Friedrich Karl Kaul, *Nazimordaktion T4 – Die Psychiatrie im Strudel von T4* (East Berlin 1973; 2nd edn., under the title *Die Psychiatrie im Strudel der 'Euthanasie'*, Frankfurt 1979); Ernst Klee, *Die 'Vernichtung lebensunwerten Lebens'* (Frankfurt 1983). More recently, Robert Jay Lifton has published a vivid account of all Nazi medicine, *The Nazi Doctors: Medical Killing and the Psychology of Genocide* (New York 1986).

[21] There were a few exceptions. Otto Fleischmann returned to Vienna from Budapest and Robert Jockl from France.

[22] Wolfgang Huber, *Psychoanalyse in Österreich seit 1933* (Vienna / Salzburg: Ludwig Boltzmann Institut für Geschichte des Gesellschaftswissenschaften, 1977).

[23] *Das Diktat der Menschenverachtung. Eine Dokumentation von Alexander Mitscherlich und Fred Mielke. Der Nürnberger Ärzteprozeß und seine Quellen* (Heidelberg 1947).

4

Freud's Library and His Private Reading

Edward Timms

Freud was throughout his life an avid reader and built up a rich and diverse library. A substantial segment of that library is now on display at the Freud Museum in London. The books in the Museum form a handsome backdrop to the desk and the couch at which Freud's great work has done. But the aim of this paper is to suggest that they should not be regarded merely as a backdrop. On the contrary, they constitute a primary source of enquiry for anyone who seeks to understand the origins of psychoanalysis.

The range of Freud's library

The books in Freud's library at his home in the Berggasse were more diverse and numerous than the collection which survives in the London Freud Museum. The circumstances under which he brought part of his library to London are vividly recorded by Ernest Jones. After the Nazi occupation of Austria in March 1938, while awaiting the visa that would enable him and his family to leave for England, 'Freud went through his books, selected those he wished to take to London and disposed of the ones he no longer wanted'. There was a limit to what he could take out of the country, and when this had been reached there remained more than 1,000 volumes. These were handed to a Viennese bookseller for disposal. The bulk of them were purchased by the librarian of the New York State Psychiatric Institute, and before the end of 1939 that part of the collection had arrived in New York.[1]

The circumstances under which Freud was able to bring to London such a substantial part of his library, together with his furnishings and antiquities, are elucidated elsewhere in this volume. The essential point for the present argument is that the books now in London – about 2,500 volume in all – must be regarded as the heart of Freud's collection: the books which (like his works of art) were of particular value to him. One might have expected to find a unique collection of books dealing with psychoanalysis. What Freud in fact brought with him to London were only the remnants of his psychoanalytic library.

It was precisely books on psychoanalysis that made up the bulk of the collection of 1,000 volumes which he was willing to sell (and which went to New York). The heart of the collection which he brought to London was his non-scientific library: works of imaginative literature, on the fine arts, on history, archaeology and anthropology.

This surprising feature of the Freud Library in London has been remarked on in previous surveys. But it is now possible to make a more exact assessment of the range of Freud's cultural interests and literary erudition, on the basis of a computerized list of all the titles known to have been in his library at the Berggasse.[2] Novelists feature particularly prominently in his collection, from Balzac, Dostoevsky and Flaubert, Anatole France, Maupassant and Thomas Mann right through the alphabet to Stefan Zweig. Poetry (apart from Heine) was less well represented, though of course Freud had complete editions of Shake-speare and Goethe. Sets of Nietzsche and Burckhardt, Darwin and Frazer reflect his admiration for the great thinkers of the nineteenth century; and he was particularly proud of his 1911 edition of the *Encyclopaedia Britannica*.

In addition to this rich collection in the fields of literature and cultural history, Freud also brought a substantial selection of psycho-logical publications to London. After all, he was still a practising psychoanalyst. But it is to his literary and cultural library that I want first to draw attention. These books (as a recent survey puts it) 'reflect the tastes of a liberal, well-educated nineteenth-century gentleman with a firm background in the classics, both ancient and modern, rather than those of a doctor with certain specializations'.[3] More precisely, of a turn-of-the-century Viennese gentleman with that passion for cultural pursuits which was so characteristic of the assimilated Jewish community. There certainly seem to be few rare or exceptionally valuable books in Freud's collection. But one cannot fail to be impressed by the sheer breadth of his reading (just think of the kind of books read by medical students today). And the crux of the matter, of course, is not simply what Freud read, but what he *made* of his private reading.

'Private' reading?

The question hinges on what we really mean when we refer to 'private' reading. Ernest Jones emphasizes that Freud turned to literary authors primarily for relaxation and that this was essentially an 'external' interest. He was 'a great reader *despite* his preoccupations' as a scientist. And this view of Freud has been elaborated in a more recent study of Freud's private reading by Peter Brückner (1975). Brückner focuses on authors whom Freud read for relaxation and suggests that this reading had a compensatory function. The fantasy worlds created by great literature (we are told) consoled Freud for the renunciation of freedom and fulfilment imposed by society. Literature offered in its place at least the 'promise of happiness'. And Brückner argues that Freud was particularly attracted to authors in the tradition of the Enlightenment like Heine or Multatuli, whose work contained a socially progressive element.[4]

This view, although supported by interesting documentation, seems ultimately untenable. The attempt to situate Freud's 'recreational' reading in a separate compartment from his 'scientific' work just does not square with that feature which makes his achievement so distinctive: the way his psychoanalytical writings are shaped by literary allusions, which significantly contribute to the strategy of his scientific enquiries. Equally unsatisfactory is the converse approach to Freud's reading adopted by Frank Sulloway, one of the few scholars to have taken a close look at some of the books in Freud's library. In his influential study, *Freud – Biologist of the Mind* (1979), Sulloway analyses Freud's scientific reading without any reference to his literary and imaginative interests.[5] It seems more fruitful to avoid these kinds of compartmentalization. Freud's essential gift lay in his ability to synthesize ideas derived from both literary and scientific sources. Certainly his scientific discoveries cannot be fully understood without reference to their cultural matrix.

It deserves to be stressed that Freud was a reader of imaginative literature long before he had any scientific training. He read widely from early childhood, in French and English as well as German, and later acquired a knowledge of Greek, Latin, Italian and Spanish. According to Jones he began reading Shakespeare at the age of eight. 'Shakespeare', Jones continues, 'he read over and over again and was always ready with an apt quotation from his plays. He admired his superb power of expression and, even more, his extensive understanding of human nature.'[6] This hardly sounds like an 'external' interest. Indeed, one could argue that Shakespeare and Goethe shaped Freud's mind just as profoundly as Charcot and Meynert. What was it, after all, that stimulated Freud to study science in the first place? The famous fragment on 'Nature' attributed to Goethe, which he encounterd shortly before leaving school (*SE* v. 20, 8).

Freud's progressive outlook may (as Brückner suggests) have led him to identify with the values of the Enlightenment. But it was the literature of Romanticism that nourished his imagination. His admiration for E.T.A. Hoffmann is acknowledged in the most sophisticated of his literary essays, 'The Uncanny' (1919). And when we speak of his indebtedness to Shakespeare, we must remember that it was a very German – Romantic – Shakespeare that he was most familiar with: the translation by August Wilhelm Schlegel and Ludwig Tieck.[7] Part of the power of that translation is that in significant respects it is a mistranslation, enhancing the motifs of introspection and inwardness. It was Shakespeare who provided Freud with his earliest models of unconscious inhibition, as we see from a letter written to his friend Silberstein in 1872. He speaks there of his adolescent emotional inhibitions as 'my nonsensical "Hamlet-dom"'' – an appropriate image for his uncertainty as to whether he was more attracted by a girl or by her mother.[8] It was in drama and in imaginative fiction that Freud found his most suggestive models for the structuring of emotional experience. And it is not difficult to show that his sensitivity to literary symbolism made a profound contribution to his scientific investigations.[9]

Freud's syncretic imagination

To make this argument more specific, I want to focus on two books from Freud's library which contain clues to the working of his imagination. Any choice of two or three volumes – out of more than 2,000 – is bound to be arbitrary. But my choice is guided by the fact that a number of books in Freud's library are copiously marked or annotated, and thus reward special attention. Two books published in the late 1880s may be singled out for attention because of the glimpses they give of the way Freud's mind was working at a seminal period in his life. The first is perhaps unsurprising, because Freud refers to it several times in *The Interpretation of Dreams*: the 50-page pamphlet by W. Robert, *Der Traum als Naturnotwendigkeit erklärt* (Dreams Explained as a Natural Necessity) (1886). The second is more of a curiosity: an 1887 edition of *Macbeth* in French, published in Paris in a series of popular classics, with a detailed introduction by James Darmesteter.

The first problem is to discover approximately when Freud acquired these books; and then (a slightly different question) when he read and annotated them. In certain of his books Freud was thoughtful enough not only to inscribe his name but also the date of purchase: for example, the German translation of Darwin's *Descent of Man*, inscribed thus in 1875. But this is relatively rare. We can generally only establish an approximate chronology. The pamphlet by Robert was obviously read at some point in the dozen years between its publication and the completion of *The Interpretation of Dreams*.[10] With the edition of *Macbeth* the problem is more acute. Freud actually refers to Darmesteter's edition in his essay on 'Character-Types', published in 1916 (*SE* xiv. 322–4). So it is clear that he was reading – or rereading – this edition of *Macbeth* at that later date. Thus we cannot be sure whether his annotations date from 1915 or from the 1890s.

However, this *Macbeth* is such a cheap and ephemeral-looking edition that it seems more likely that Freud acquired it soon after its publication in 1887. I picture him, during his second visit to Paris in 1889, purchasing it at the railway station. What could be more rewarding, during the long return journey to Vienna, than to see what this French editor, Darmesteter, has to say in his extended introduction? Freud was of course already familiar with the play in German and perhaps also with the original English version.[11] What is striking about his marks in the margins of this edition is that they relate to the learned commentary, not to the text. They show that Freud *studied* great works of literature – he didn't just read them for relaxation. He studied *Macbeth* with the same kind of intense scholarly attention that he applied to the study of Sophocles and the Oedipus myth.[12]

Whatever the exact date of these marginalia, they serve to reinforce our awareness of Freud's fascination, from an early period and indeed throughout his life, with *Macbeth*. The play fascinated him not only because of its uncanny blend of premonition and hallucination. It also suggested complex psychological connections between good and evil, between conscious and unconscious motivation, which make Macbeth himself such a surprisingly sympathetic figure. It is this aspect of the play which is accentuated in Darmesteter's introduction, notably in a passage which Freud marked in the margin: 'Macbeth is not a calculating villain; there is in him no trace of Iago; he is a Hamlet with criminal tendencies'.[13]

My point is that the Freud of the 1880s and 1890s, his imagination nourished by Goethe, Shakespeare and Sophocles, was the *same* Freud who was systematically sifting through the psychological literature, particularly the theorizing about dreams. It is surely not too fanciful to picture him with *Macbeth* in one pocket of his overcoat, Robert's pamphlet *Dreams Explained* in the other. It is this ability to make connections between psychological theory and the literary imagination that we see at work in Freud's letters to Fliess, during the crucial period of his breakthrough to psychoanalysis. 'Shakespeare was right in juxtaposing fiction and madness', he writes in a note of May 1897 about hysterical fantasies. Even more striking is the celebrated letter of 15 October 1897:

A single idea of general value dawned on me. I have found, in my own case too, [the phenomenon of] being in love with my mother and jealous of my father, and I now consider it a universal event in early childhood.... If this is so, we can understand the gripping power of *Oedipus Rex*.... Everyone in the audience was once a budding Oedipus in fantasy and each recoils in horror from the dream fulfillment here transplanted into reality, with the full quantity of repression which separates his infantile state from his present one.

Fleetingly the thought passed through my head that the same thing might be at the bottom of *Hamlet* as well....[14]

In this evolving argument the literary examples are not some kind of embellishment, tacked on externally to the psychological theory. The new theory emerges from a mind predisposed to make connections between analytical psychology and imaginative literature.

To identify those 'fleeting' thoughts which underlie the early discoveries of psychoanalysis, it is worth taking a closer look at our second text from Freud's library, Robert's *Dreams Explained*. The excitement with which Freud read this ephemeral-looking pamphlet is indicated by the fact that on 17 of Robert's 51 pages there are emphatic underlinings or marginal marks. It is not difficult to understand why Freud was so enthusiastic. *Dreams Explained* is an *Interpretation of Dreams* in miniature, reviewing (as Freud was later to do) pre-existing theories of dreams and proposing a more sophisticated explanatory framework.

Essential features of Freud's theory are already anticipated in the pamphlet. Robert begins by arguing that there is nothing arbitrary about dreaming. It is subject, like every other aspect of natural behaviour, to the logic of cause and effect. Dreams are a form of natural excretion, physical in origin but perceived as a 'mental reaction phenomenon' ('geistige Reactionserscheinung', p. 9; marked by Freud in the margin). The stimuli for dreams are always things which have not been fully thought through, because our minds have been preoccupied with other matters. But such fleeting thoughts or impressions remain lodged in our minds, only to be reflected in our dreams (p. 10 and p. 11; both passages marked). Dreams are stimulated by sense impressions from the preceding day which have not been adequately assimilated; it is this which makes them difficult to explain (pp. 19–20; marked on p. 20).

At this point in his argument Robert introduces the key concept of 'dream-work' ('Traumarbeit', p. 21). This is significant because it must be one of the earliest occurrences of this word (perhaps it was Robert who coined it), but also because he defines and differentiates two functions of 'dream-work': to eliminate from the mental system impressions which cannot be properly assimilated; and to deepen the understanding of other impressions so that they are lastingly incorporated in the memory (p. 20; marked by Freud). Dreams thus form a 'safety valve' ('Sicherheitsventil', p. 26; marked). And the therapeutic function associated with sleep should really be attributed to dreams (p. 32; again marked).

Robert thus emphatically rejects the widely held view that dreams have a prophetic significance, suggesting instead that they merely give expression to impulses which have remained unconscious. Social factors may lead us to discount an instinctive antipathy felt on being introduced to a stranger; but this feeling will re-emerge in our dreams. Such dreams appear to have a prophetic or warning function. In fact they arise when an impression which has only been registered instinctively or 'unconsciously' ('unbewußt') 'has come to consciousness through dreamwork' ('durch Traumarbeit zum Bewußtsein gekommen ist', p. 34).

Although this very suggestive passage does not carry any marginal mark, it too may well have caught Freud's attention. And there can be no doubt that he was impressed by Robert's summing up of the inadequacies of previous dream interpretations, in a passage printed in emphatic type. The weakness of previous theories, says Robert, is that they have tried to discover the essential meaning of dreams *'within the dream itself'* ('im Traume selbst'), not by investigating *'its logical origin from within the waking consciousness'* ('seine logische Entstehung aus dem wachen Bewußtsein', p. 39). Freud marked this passage with two vertical lines in the margin. It does indeed anticipate his own strategy for the interpretation of dreams.

Freud acknowledges a certain indebtedness to Robert, particularly in his review of previous scientific literature in Chapter 1 of *The Interpretation of Dreams* (*SE* iv. 79–81). Returning towards the end of the book to Robert's theory, he concludes that 'we must accept his account of the *function* of dreams, though differing from him in his premises and in his view of the dream-process itself' (*SE* v. 579). But at other points he is at pains to distance himself from Robert's theory, particularly because Robert believes that dreams are simply stimulated by impressions from the previous day, ignoring those impressions 'which date back to earliest childhood' (*SE* iv. 177–8, 189). Freud refers in the course of *The Interpretation of Dreams* to at least 200 other theorists. His scattered references to Robert imply that *Dreams Explained* was merely one source among many – and not a particularly important one.

Freud's emphatic markings in the margins of Robert's pamphlet, however, put the matter in a new perspective. They suggest that Robert deserves more credit than he usually receives as one of the forerunners of the psychoanalytic theory of dreams. Since Freud's first recorded use of the word 'dream-work' follows closely on a reference to Robert, it seems likely that he was indebted to *Dreams Explained* for this key concept (*SE* iv. 178). Moreover there is evidence to suggest that his reading of Robert may have been the catalyst which in 1895, at the time when he was preparing *Studies on Hysteria* for the press, first stimulated him to attempt the interpretation of dreams. The primary factor which he emphasizes at this stage is an exact paraphrase of Robert's central argument. He attributes his dreams to 'the necessity of working out any ideas which I had only dwelt upon cursorily during the day – which had only been touched upon and not finally dealt with' (*SE* ii. 69–70, note).

What was it that enabled Freud to take the decisive step beyond Robert – to break through to a more comprehensive view of unconscious mental processes? The answer seems to lie with his syncretic imagination – his ability to synthesize an extraordinary range of divergent material: dream-work with self-analysis, the traumas of his patients with their repressed memories of childhood, recent emotional anxieties with early sexual experiences, processes of free association with a method of decoding symbols and verbal ambiguities which is essentially literary in character. All these elements converge to form in *The Interpretation of Dreams* a narrative which blends psychological observation with literary sensitivity. It is not fortuitous that the most celebrated passage in the book relates unconscious emotional development to the two most enigmatic characters in European tragedy – Oedipus and Hamlet (*SE* iv. 260–6).

Gradiva

The links between Freud's literary experience and his psychological insight can be elucidated even more clearly by taking a look at one further item in his library, his copy of Wilhelm Jensen's story *Gradiva*. This story is the subject of Freud's earliest systematic attempt to apply the theories of psychoanalysis to the interpretation of literature, *Delusions and Dreams in Jensen's 'Gradiva'* (1907). The parallels which Freud discerned between his own theory of dreams and Jensen's fictional use of dream motifs led him to formulate a fundamental question:

> When, from the year 1893 onwards, I plunged into investigations such as these of the origin of mental disturbances, it would certainly never have occurred to me to look for confirmation of my findings in imaginative writings. I was thus more than a little surprised to find that the author of *Gradiva*, which was published in 1903, had taken as the basis of its creation the very thing that I believed myself to have freshly discovered from the sources of my medical experience. How was it that the author arrived at the same knowledge as the doctor – or at least behaved as though he possessed the same knowledge?
>
> (*SE* ix. 54)

This is a conundrum which preoccupied Freud for many years. In his dialogue with other literary authors, notably his letters to Arthur Schnitzler, he was to raise the same question: 'I have often asked myself in astonishment how you came by this or that piece of secret knowledge which I had acquired by painstaking investigation' (letter of 8 May 1906).[15] The conundrum is more readily resolved if we recognize that Freud's discoveries did not derive exclusively from 'medical experience'. They derived from a mind which from an early stage, well before 1893, had been nourished by 'imaginative writings'.

Freud suggests that it was only considerably later that he became aware of the literary parallels. We must therefore assume that as a reader

6. Freud in his study in Vienna, with one of his favourite chow dogs.

7. Freud's desk in the Freud Museum, Maresfield Gardens, London.

he passed through a kind of 'latency period', during which the formative reading experiences of his childhood became obscured by his commitment to medical science. But the fact that they were no longer fully conscious does not diminish their significance. At the age of fourteen he was given a collection of the works of Ludwig Börne, in which he deeply immersed himself. Many years later he was astonished to discover that the method of free association, which he believed he had pioneered as a psychoanalyst, is in fact foreshadowed in one of those Börne essays, entitled 'The Art of Becoming an Original Writer in Three Days' (*SE* xviii. 264–5).

Freud's account of his reading of *Gradiva* is specially significant because it makes the convergence between literary and psychoanalytical methods fully explicit. Previously he had tended to rely on occasional interpolations or footnotes to suggest the parallels, as when in the case history of 'Dora' he acknowledges similar psychological insights in Schnitzler's *Paracelsus* (*SE* vii. 44, note). But in *Delusions and Dreams* he attaches the same degree of validity to the real-life example of 'Dora' as to the 'imaginary case' of Jensen's fictional hero (*SE* ix. 54). The private reading now is cited as testimony to the truth of the medical discoveries.

Gradiva is an unpretentious story about an archaeologist from north Germany, Norbert Hanold. During a visit to the ruins of Pompeii, he catches a glimpse of a young woman whose graceful stride reminds him uncannily of the figure depicted in a Roman bas-relief which he admired. His delusion is that he believes this young woman must be the reincarnation of a woman who was buried alive when Mount Vesuvius erupted and destroyed Pompeii nearly two thousand years earlier. Freud's commentary on this story in *Delusions and Dreams* is rightly regarded as one of his most subtle pieces of literary exegesis. His argument, which repays a close reading, is too complex to be re-capitulated here. But his own copy of Jensen's *Gradiva*, which has been rediscovered by the staff of the London Freud Museum, provides an additional source of insight, for it proves to be heavily annotated, not only with the kind of marginal lines and underlinings which we find in *Dreams Explained*, but also with many words unmistakably in Freud's hand.[16] Written with a blunt green crayon, often in abbreviated form, these cryptic comments provide vivid evidence of Freud's methods as a reader.

The features of the story which Freud's marginalia accentuate fall into several categories. Some of his notes are simply expressions of admiration ('schön', 'gut' or 'schlau'), or descriptive phrases which record a new development, such as a dream. But his most revealing comments accentuate features of the story which are certainly not apparent at a first reading. The word 'Wahn [delusion]' is repeatedly written in the margin, even though it scarcely occurs in Jensen's own vocabulary. Freud also shows himself to be sensitive to the network of symbolism in the story, particularly the archaeological imagery associated with its setting amid the ruins of Pompeii. The words 'Verschüttung' and 'verschüttet [buried beneath the rubble of time]' are identified by Freud on the penultimate page as the 'symbolic core' of the whole story ('symbolischer Kern', p. 150). For it turns out that the woman whom Norbert imagines to have been buried in the archaeological ruins is in fact a girl named Zoe Bertgang, who has re-emerged from the 'buried' memories of his own childhood. She walks with the same eye-catching stride which made the 'Gradiva' bas-relief so memorable for him.

Freud's marginal comments reveal his eye for ambiguities, particularly in those scenes which express Norbert's perplexity about the identity of the supposed 'Gradiva' (noted by Freud as 'doppelsinnig', p. 58, and 'zweideutig', p. 84). And he links this ambiguity to the blurring of the 'dividing line' between 'conscious' and 'unconscious' perception ('Scheidewand Bw/Ubw', p. 47). This elucidation of a concealed subtext becomes particularly significant at points where that subtext clearly transcends Jensen's authorial intention. Thus Norbert's preoccupation with the young woman's stride, her feet and her sandals, is left by Jensen in a haze of ambiguity. Freud identifies in these motifs a strong undercurrent of eroticism, making repeated marginal comments like 'erotischer Wunsch' (p. 70). He even hints at an element of foot fetishism ('erotisch[es] Fußinteresse', p. 88) which is very much at odds with the decorous mode of the narrative.

Jensen's story portrays a scholar absorbed in classical antiquity who through a series of mysterious encounters is reunited with a childhood sweetheart. The story has a conventionally romantic ending as the lovers, standing under a cloudless sky at the Hercules Gate in Pompeii, begin to plan their honeymoon. The final sentence of the story describes the scene, as Norbert stands aside to allow Zoe to walk ahead of him across the ancient stepping stones:

A serenely understanding smile flitted across his companion's mouth; enveloped in his dreamy gaze, Zoe Bertgang – Gradiva reborn – gathered up her dress a little in her left hand and stepped with her calm and agile stride across the stones through the brilliant sunshine to the other side of the road.

(p. 151)

For the ordinary reader this might seem like a harmonious happy ending. But Freud's reaction is recorded in one of his most vigorous marginal comments: 'Erotik! Aufnahme der Phantasie-Versöhnung [Eroticism! Acceptance of fantasy-reconciliation]' (see facsimile). In Norbert, as he follows Zoe's stride with his dreamy gaze, Freud

Uesuv breitete seine duftige Pinienkrone aus, und die ganze ausgegrabene Stadt erschien, statt mit Bimssteinen und Asche, von dem wohlthätigen Regensturz mit Perlen und Diamanten überschüttet. Mit den letzteren wetteiferte auch ein Glanz in den Augen der jungen Zoologentochter, doch ihre klugen Lippen entgegneten auf den kundgegebenen Reisezielwunsch ihres gewissermassen gleichfalls aus der Verschüttung wieder ausgegrabenen Kindheitsfreundes: „Darüber, denke ich, wollen wir uns heute nicht den Kopf zerbrechen; das ist eine Sache, die wohl besser von uns Beiden erst noch öfter in reiflichere Erwägung gezogen und künftigen Eingebungen überlassen wird. Ich fühle mich wenigstens zu solcher geographischen Entscheidung jetzt doch noch nicht völlig lebendig genug."

Das zeugte auch von einer der Sprecherin innewohnenden grossen Bescheidenheit hinsichtlich der Beurtheilung ihres Einsichtsvermögens in Dinge, über die sie bis heute noch nie nachgedacht hatte. Sie waren an das Herculesthor zurückgelangt, wo am Anfang der Strada Consolare alte Trittsteine die Strasse überkreuzten. Norbert Hanold hielt vor ihnen an und sagte mit einem eigenthüm-

lichen Klang der Stimme: „Bitte, geh' hier vorauf!" Ein heiter verständnissvoll lachender Zug umhuschte den Mund seiner Begleiterin, und mit der Linken das Kleid ein wenig raffend, schritt die Gradiva rediviva Zoë Bertgang, von ihm mit traumhaft dreinblickenden Augen umfasst, in ihrer ruhig-behenden Gangart durch den Sonnenglanz über die Trittsteine zur anderen Strassenseite hinüber.

9. Plaster cast of 'Gradiva' in Freud's study at Maresfield Gardens, London.

8 (left). Two pages from Freud's copy of Jensen's *Gradiva*, with Freud's marginal annotations.

identifies that undercurrent of eroticism which his own marginal notes
have traced through other equally innocuous-looking scenes. And
Freud's cryptic final phrase suggests that the 'reconciliation' is still
projected by Norbert on to the plane of 'fantasy'. The woman whose
graceful step he admires is still the idealized Gradiva, not the flesh-and-
blood Zoe Bertgang.

The glimpses which this annotated text offers of Freud's working
methods confirm my earlier redefinition of his private reading. He did
not simply read for relaxation. He was capable, when a book caught his
attention, of reading with a high degree of literary–critical sophistication. How patiently Freud must have read and reread *Gradiva* is shown
by his repeated use of the word 'Quelle' in the margins, identifying the
'origin' of some pattern of behaviour which is only revealed later (for
example, 'Zoe Quelle', p. 7, or 'Quelle später', p. 23). He deserves to
be recognized as one of the pioneers, not simply of modern psychology
but of the close reading of literary texts.

Freud's critical discrimination is also reflected in his numerous contributions to the debates about literary creativity at the Vienna Psycho-
Analytical Society during this same period.[17] It is hardly surprising that
his work was received so enthusiastically by leading writers of his day,
notably Thomas Mann. They recognized in his achievement an essentially literary component and acknowledged him as their ideal reader.
Arnold Zweig in particular emphasizes Freud's gifts as a literary critic.
'If only you would devote a few months to the writing of reviews of
novels', writes Zweig in a letter of November 1935, in response to
Freud's judicious analysis of his most recent book. 'In matters of
literary appreciation a whole school is indebted to you for its
existence.'[18]

To sum up my argument, I would like to take you in imagination back
to the Freud Museum in London. The display of Freud's books and
antiquities, desk and couch, carpets and pictures provides a visual
reminder of his greatest gift – his ability to synthesize disparate
elements into a coherent personal philosophy. At his home in the
Berggasse Freud's study, with his desk and books, was quite separate
from his consulting room with the famous couch. There were few
books in his consulting room, although there were many antiquities,
including – directly above the couch – a bas-relief of 'Gradiva'.[19] But
at the Freud Museum in London the furnishings have been rearranged.
The private study is no longer separate from the professional
consulting room. The layout of the Freud Museum thus epitomizes the
theme of my paper: the library and the couch are in the same room.

Notes

My thanks are due to David Newlands, first Curator of the London Freud Museum, and to his staff for kindly allowing me to examine books from Freud's library; and to Sigmund Freud Copyrights for permission to quote from Freud's handwritten annotations.

[1] Jones, II. 239; Ronald W. Clark, *Freud: The Man and the Cause* (London 1980), 510–11.

[2] Harry Trosman and Roger Dennis Simmons, 'The Freud Library', *Jn APA*, xxi (1973), no. 3, 646–87; Dorothea Hecken and Steve Neufeld, 'Reassembling Freud's London Library – A Report and Recommendations' (TS, Freud Museum, London, Apr 1986). *Die Bibliothek Sigmund Freuds nach den vorhandenen Verzeichnissen*, ed. Gerhard Fichtner, 2 vols. (Tübingen: Institut für Geschichte der Medizin, 1986).

[3] Hecken and Neufeld, 'Reassembling Freud's London Library', 4.

[4] Jones, I. 189 (emphasis added). Peter Brückner, *Sigmund Freuds Privatlektüre* (Cologne 1975), esp. 145–8.

[5] Frank J. Sulloway, *Freud – Biologist of the Mind: Beyond the Psychoanalytic Legend* (London 1979).

[6] Jones, I. 24.

[7] Freud refers to the Schlegel translation of Shakespeare in a letter of 14 July 1882 to Martha Bernays (*Letters*, 31). The edition of Shakespeare he owned, *Dramatische Werke*, trans. A.W. Schlegel and L. Tieck, 10 vols. (Berlin 1867), is in the London Freud Museum.

[8] Quoted in Clark, *Freud: The Man*, 24.

[9] See Edward Timms, 'Novelle and Case History: Freud in Pursuit of the Falcon', in *London German Studies II*, ed. J.P. Stern (London 1983), 115–34.

[10] Freud inscribed his name ('Dr Freud') on the cover, but unfortunately not the date when he read Robert's *Der Traum als Naturnotwendigkeit erklärt* (Hamburg 1886) (cf. *Die Bibliothek Sigmund Freuds*, ed. Fichtner, I. 287, which needs to be corrected on this point).

[11] Freud quotes from *Macbeth* in a letter to Wilhelm Knöpfmacher dated 6 Aug 1878 (*Letters*, 24).

[12] *Oedipus Rex* was the prescribed Greek text from which Freud had to translate a passage of 33 verses in his school-leaving examination in 1873 (see Clark, *Freud: The Man*, 30). The systematic way in which he studied literary interpretations of the Oedipus myth can be seen from one of the most heavily marked books in his library: Léopold Constans, *La Légende d'Oedipe étudiée dans l'antiquité, au moyen âge et dans les temps modernes* (Paris 1881).

[13] W. Shakespeare, *Macbeth*, ed. J. Darmesteter, 2nd edn. (Paris 1887), lxxix: 'Macbeth n'est point le scélérat qui calcule; rien en lui de Iago; c'est Hamlet dans le crime'. (Cf. *SE* xiv. 322, note, which misleadingly suggests that Freud read the first [1881] edition of this translation.)

[14] *The Complete Letters of Sigmund Freud to Wilhelm Fliess*, trans. and ed. J.M. Masson (Cambridge, Mass., 1985), 251, 272.

[15] *Letters*, 261.

[16] Wilhelm Jensen, *Gradiva – Ein pompeyanisches Phantasiestück* (Dresden and Leipzig 1903). I am grateful to Gerhard Fichtner (Tübingen) for confirming that the marginal notes are in Freud's hand; and to both Fichtner and Joseph Peter Strelka for helping to decipher illegible words.

[17] See *Minutes of the Vienna Psychoanalytic Society*, ed. Herman Nunberg and Ernst Federn, 4 vols. (New York 1962–75), esp. vols. I and II.

[18] Thomas Mann's essay, 'Freud und die Zukunft', is available in English translation in *Freud – A Collection of Critical Essays*, ed. Perry Meisel (Englewood Cliffs, N.J., 1981), 45–60. Zweig's letter is in *The Letters of Sigmund Freud and Arnold Zweig*, ed. Ernst L. Freud, trans. Prof. and Mrs W.D. Robson-Scott (London 1970), 112.

[19] For a photographic record of Freud's Vienna apartment, see *Berggasse 19: Sigmund Freud's Home and Offices, Vienna 1938*, photographed by Edmund Engelmann, with an introduction by Peter Gay (New York 1976).

5

Freud's Testament:
Moses and Monotheism

Ritchie Robertson

Moses and Monotheism was published, and indeed partially written, during Freud's exile in London, and was the last of his works to appear during his lifetime. Although he had begun it in 1934, and published the first two sections in *Imago* in 1937, he did not complete it until shortly after his arrival in Britain in June 1938. The German text was printed in Amsterdam by August, and published there early in 1939. The English translation by Katherine Jones, the wife of Ernest Jones, was published in Britain by the Hogarth Press on 25 May 1939 (not in March, as Jones states), and in the United States by Alfred A. Knopf on 19 June.[1]

The book has a close connection with the events of the 1930s that led to Freud's exile. The rise of Hitler and the ill-treatment of the German Jews impelled Freud to seek the causes of anti-Semitism in the distinctive character of the Jewish people, and to investigate their origins. As early as 1934 he told Arnold Zweig that he had found the formula: 'Moses created the Jews'. In the text, however, Freud acknowledges that his dealings with biblical tradition are autocratic and arbitrary, and that his structure has weak as well as strong points; while in his letters to Zweig he admits 'the weakness of my historical construction' and also seems uncertain about the genre of the work. He first refers to it as 'The Man Moses, a Historical Novel'. Later he admits that 'this historical novel won't stand up to my own criticism'.[2] 'I am no good at historical romances', he tells Max Eitingon. 'Let us leave them to Thomas Mann.'[3] His doubts are reflected in the repetitious and confusing form of the book. We seem to have a display of work in progress rather than a finished treatise.

The many shortcomings of *Moses and Monotheism* make it difficult to approach. Although its claims as a work of biblical scholarship can only too easily be demolished, the work remains intriguing and perplexing. In order to deal with it, I should like to treat *Moses and Monotheism* more as an imaginative than a scholarly work, one inspired by Goethe and

Thomas Mann as well as by biblical research. In it Freud allowed his imagination unusually free range, in order to explore the themes which he formulates as: 'what the real nature of a tradition resides in, and what its special power rests on, how impossible it is to dispute the personal influence upon world-history of individual great men' (*SE* XXIII. 52). But besides elucidating the explicit themes of the work, I want also to examine *Moses and Monotheism* as an implicit statement about the nature of Freud's identity as a Jew.

First of all, it may be helpful to recall, very briefly, the main theses of the book, without trying to reproduce Freud's intricate argument. Freud contends that Moses was an Egyptian, pointing out that Moses is part of an Egyptian name, meaning 'son', and arguing that the biblical story of Moses' being discovered among the bulrushes is essentially a 'family romance' distorted by Jewish chroniclers to conceal the fact that he was an Egyptian.

Freud then tries to explain the origins of Jewish monotheism. He points out its similarities to the monotheistic worship of the sun god Aten introduced by a Pharaoh of the Eighteenth Dynasty, Amenophis IV, who took the name Akhenaten. This monarch forbade any statue of Aten to be made, just as Moses' commandments later forbade the making of a graven image of God. Akhenaten's inscriptions emphasize the ethical values of truth and justice, which were later to be upheld by Moses' commandments and the prophets. Freud was not the first person to point out this resemblance and suggest a debt; his associate Karl Abraham had done so in 1912, in an article published in *Imago*, to which Freud, curiously enough, makes no reference.[4] And the connection is also made in one of the books he does quote, J.H. Breasted's *The Dawn of Conscience* (1934). Freud's own contribution is his account of the part played by Moses in bringing monotheism to the Hebrews.

Freud maintains that Akhenaten's adherents included a nobleman probably called Tuthmosis, a name later shortened to Moses. After Akhenaten's death and the restoration of polytheism by the priesthood, Moses preserved monotheism and satisfied his own ambition by imposing the doctrine on the Hebrews, whom he then led out of Egypt to the land of Canaan. Freud also adopts a theory put forward in 1922 by the biblical scholar Eduard Sellin, who interpreted some passages in Hosea as meaning that Moses was killed by his people just before entering the Promised Land.[5] In order to relieve their guilt, the Hebrews not only exalted Moses' memory, but went even further. As their conception of God developed, they formed him in the image of Moses. In affirming that their God had singled them out as his chosen people, they were really referring to the fact that Moses, the Egyptian prince, had condescended to choose them as the inheritors of monotheism.

Freud's next problem is to explain how the elevated doctrine that Moses had brought from Egypt managed to survive. For many generations it was submerged by the crude sacrificial cult of Yahweh, 'a coarse, narrow-minded local god, violent and bloodthirsty' (*SE* XXIII. 50), but resurfaced as the accepted religion of the Jews. It could not have survived merely in oral tradition, for that would not have given it the aura of unquestionable authority a religious doctrine needs. Freud's answer depends on the biological dictum that ontogeny recapitulates phylogeny – the development of the individual repeats that of the species. Transferring this principle from biology to psychology, he assumes that a nation has a collective mind in which great events affecting the nation as a whole are not forgotten but repressed. The process is analogous to the formation of a traumatic neurosis in the individual. The trauma is acquired in early childhood, is repressed during the latency period, and resurfaces after puberty as an obsessional neurosis, a compulsion to re-experience the original traumatic event. With the Israelites, the traumatic event was the killing of Moses. After a latency period in which they worshipped Yahweh, the memory of Moses and his doctrines resurfaced, so that the dead Moses was incomparably more powerful than the living one had been. These events are themselves made possible by the event which, in Freud's view, founded human society, the killing of the primal father by his sons who afterwards bore the burden of guilt.

There would be little point in attempting to defend this construction, and I have no intention of trying to rehabilitate *Moses and Monotheism* as a work of scholarship.[6] If, however, we begin to consider it as an imaginative work, we will recall that for many years past Freud's interest in Moses had amounted to an identification. This is clear from his paper on the *Moses* of Michelangelo, which concludes that the statue depicts Moses just after he has glimpsed the Israelites worshipping the golden calf. The paper was written shortly after the Psycho-Analytical Congress at Munich in 1913, at which it became clear that Jung was following Adler and Stekel into what Freud saw as apostasy.[7] In it Freud disputes the traditional view that Michelangelo depicts Moses dropping the tablets. Instead, in Freud's interpretation, Moses is clutching them to prevent them from falling to the ground. Thus he begins to rehabilitate Moses by challenging his biblical reputation of being impulsive and hot-tempered. Moses is now the man who keeps his head when all around him are losing theirs. He is a particular kind of great man: a guardian of the truth.

In *Moses and Monotheism* another component is added to this picture of Moses: the notion that he was killed by his followers. Freud gives credit for this idea to Eduard Sellin. But Sellin's suggestion rests on an extremely flimsy basis and has never been accepted by other biblical scholars. However, as Freud later points out, the murder of Moses was also suggested by Goethe. It is put forward as a semi-serious speculation in Goethe's ironic retelling of the story of Moses in 'Israel in der Wüste', which forms part of the 'Noten und Abhandlungen' appended to the *Westöstlicher Divan.*[8] We can safely assume that Freud had been familiar with this idea for many years and that it formed part of the original imaginative core around which *Moses and Monotheism* gradually took shape. But while Goethe supposes that Moses' followers killed him because they were tired of his ill-temper and incompetent leadership, Freud has Moses killed by people unable to endure the elevated doctrines he has taught them. He suffers, Freud says, the fate of all enlightened despots. Hence Moses is now the primal father killed by his sons, the figure whom Freud places at the origin of religion; and also the enlightened leader who offers his followers new truths which they are too blinkered to accept.

Next, why was Freud so anxious for Moses to have been an Egyptian? I want to ignore, as being too reductive, the common interpretation of *Moses and Monotheism* as a family romance in which Freud disavows his unassuming father and constructs a descent from a more imposing figure.[9] More promising – though still, I believe, mistaken – is the social interpretation offered by Marthe Robert. She argues that *Moses and Monotheism* expresses the emotional ambivalence arising from Freud's loyalty to his Jewish origins and his desire for success in the Gentile world. He severs himself from the Jews by declaring that he is no more a Jew than Moses was; and he severs himself from the Germans by identifying with Moses, who broke away from the Egyptians as Freud wished to break away from the Germans. This implies that *Moses and Monotheism* should be added to the long list of texts recently interpreted by Sander Gilman as articulating the 'self-hatred' which Freud himself described as 'an exquisitely Jewish phenomenon'.[10] And yet it is hard to believe that Freud ever wanted to repudiate his Jewish identity. In the preface to the Hebrew translation of *Totem and Taboo* he described himself as 'an author who is ignorant of the language of holy writ, who is completely estranged from the religion of his fathers – as well as from every other religion – and who cannot take a share in nationalist ideals, but who has yet never repudiated his people, who feels that he is in his essential nature a Jew and who has no desire to alter that nature' (*SE* xiii. xv). Nor does he adopt the frequent tactic of Jews who are uneasy about their social identity – that of acknowledging their own Jewishness but projecting their unease on to other Jewish groups, such as the Eastern Jews. Freud virtually never makes disparaging references to other Jews, in striking contrast to such contemporaries as the philosopher Fritz Mauthner or the novelist Jakob Wassermann.[11]

Perhaps the question 'Why did Freud want Moses not to have been a Jew?' is wrongly phrased. Instead, the question should be why Freud did not consider the obvious and plausible solution, that Moses was a Hebrew largely assimilated to Egyptian society, who recovered his loyalty to his people when he saw them being persecuted. Marthe Robert's explanation oversimplifies Freud's loyalties by blurring the distinction between assimilation and acculturation.[12] Freud seems to have accepted early in life that his unalterable Jewishness permitted only limited assimilation to Gentile society. He told an interviewer in the 1920s that since the rise of anti-Semitism in Germany and Austria he no longer described himself as a German but as a Jew.[13] But this did not diminish his loyalty to German and European culture. The literary allusions throughout his works show him to be, in Peter Gay's words, 'a cultivated German with an astonishing memory'.[14] He had practically no share in specifically Jewish culture, but felt himself to be no less a Jew for that.

In *Moses and Monotheism* Freud repeats his belief that the Jews are unassimilable, because of the minor but decisive racial and intellectual differences separating them from other nations. For Freud, therefore, a Jew could become acculturated to another society but not assimilated, for a Jew's identity was unalterable. This is why he represents Moses as an Egyptian. Moses could not be an assimilated Hebrew, because for Freud this was not a genuine possibility. Nor could he be an acculturated Hebrew, living in Egyptian society but not of it, for then his assumption of leadership over the Hebrews would have ceased to be a problem and would no longer have appealed to Freud's imagination. But Freud's identification with Moses does not necessarily imply, as Marthe Robert thinks, a fantasy in which Freud is no longer a Jew. Rather, it implies that Freud deliberately chooses to be a Jew. Instead of selecting one of the social identities offered to him, he creates a new identity for himself.

There is an obvious contradiction here. If a Jew cannot cease to be a Jew, how can someone else become a Jew? This contradiction did not originate with Freud, and cannot be explained away, for it is the contradiction at the heart of the concept of national identity. Recent history amply shows that, to a large extent at least, one's national identity is something one can choose. Millions of people have chosen to become Americans, or, more recently, to become Israelis. But if one's sense of national identity is to be strong and secure, one has to feel that one has not chosen it; it has to seem natural and unalterable, a birthright or a destiny. For this reason Ernest Gellner has recently written: 'Generally speaking, nationalist ideology suffers from pervasive false consciousness'. The contradiction within Freud's myth of Moses corresponds, therefore, to a contradiction within the very concept of national identity.[15]

I now come to the second question raised by *Moses and Monotheism.* Given that Freud's Moses creates the Jewish identity and imposes it on his followers, what is the content of that identity?

We have seen that Freud imagined Moses as the wise, restrained and responsible guardian of the truth, and that the truth preserved by Moses is the monotheism of Akhenaten. Now in studies of the origins of religion written in Freud's lifetime, Akhenaten held an honoured place, for his monotheism and his ethics were seen as anticipating those of Christianity, and hence the elements within Christianity which could be preserved in a secular and rationalist age. The account of Akhenaten by J.H. Breasted, on which Freud chiefly relied, is in this tradition. After describing Akhenaten's enlightened and universalist ideals, Breasted brushes aside the intervening millennia and identifies these ideals with 'the fundamental conclusions that form the basis of moral convictions, and continue to do so in civilised life'.[16]

Hence the monotheism of Akhenaten and Moses fits neatly into Freud's conception of intellectual development. Freud's basic model is of a gradual ascent towards a rationality which is best embodied in scientific enquiry. He acquired this model as a schoolboy, when his reading included Hume, Buckle and Lecky. In his anthropological writings he develops this into a sequence of 'three great pictures of the universe: animistic (or mythological), religious and scientific' (*SE* XIII. 77).[17] Freud's researches into irrational mental life led him increasingly to qualify this picture. *Totem and Taboo* shows how much in common civilized man has with the mental life of primitive peoples. The First World War shockingly confirmed the power of primitive feeling and elicited Freud's deeply pessimistic *Thoughts for the Times on War and Death* (1915). The militant rationalism of *The Future of an Illusion* (1927), however, shows that Freud had not discarded his belief in the eventual triumph of reason: 'The voice of the intellect is a soft one, but it does not rest till it has gained a hearing. Finally, after a countless succession of rebuffs, it succeeds. This is one of the few points on which one may be optimistic about the future of mankind.' (*SE* XXI. 53.)

If we ask how Judaism fits into this picture, the answer is a dialectical one. Freud regards Judaism as a traumatic neurosis, like other religions. But he considers it more advanced than other religions: ethically, because of its stress on truth and justice; and intellectually, because its prohibition of image-making trains its devotees in abstract thought. By comparison, Christianity represents a regression to a more emotional form of religion, in which the pleasure principle has more power. Judaism therefore offers a better starting-point from which to advance into the scientific age. This is why Jews are better equipped than Christians for the science known as psychoanalysis, and why Freud thought that Jung, as a Christian and a pastor's son, could only accept psychoanalysis after combating inner resistances from which Jews like himself were free.

Hence Freud constructs an intellectual progression from the monotheism of Akhenaten via that of Moses to the modern spirit of scientific rationality. This had, for Freud, an urgent contemporary relevance, because of the increasing influence of the Catholic Church in Austrian politics of the 1930s. Freud told Arnold Zweig that he delayed publishing the book because he feared the political influence of one Father Schmidt, an anthropologist, whose work Freud summed up as 'pious lies'. Wilhelm Schmidt (1868–1954) was a professor at Vienna University and an anthropologist of considerable eminence. His main work, *Der Ursprung der Gottesidee* (The Origin of the Conception of God), consists of 12 fat volumes containing over 10,000 pages. He had published in 1930 an anthropological manual in which he attacked Freud's *Totem and Taboo* for claiming that religion originated with totemism. Denying that totemism was a form of religion, Schmidt maintained that religion stemmed from a primeval monotheism still to be found among the most archaic peoples. Sir Edward Evans-Pritchard described Schmidt as 'a man of forceful personality as well as of great learning', but also called his arguments 'tendentious' and his use of sources 'dubious'.[18] His writing is aggressive, abusive and anti-Semitic. Schmidt was an influential figure whom Freud probably had reason to fear. By the time *Moses and Monotheism* was published, however, both Freud and the priest had fled from the Nazis into exile – the one in London, the other in Switzerland. But even in London, Freud met with clerical hostility. On 14 July 1939 the *Catholic Herald* printed a vitriolic review of *Moses and Monotheism* by Father Vincent McNabb, charging Freud with 'frank championship of atheism and incest', and shortly afterwards Father McNabb denounced Freud publicly from a platform in Hyde Park.[19]

A letter Freud wrote in 1938 from London to an English correspondent, who had feared that the book might harm relations between Jews and the Churches, shows how much *Moses and Monotheism* was intended to embody the intellectual ideals Freud associated with Jewishness. He denied that the book could be construed as an attack on Christianity, since its point of view was scientific:

Anyone considering the book from this point of view will have to admit that it is only Jewry and not Christianity which has reason to feel offended by its conclusions. For only a few incidental remarks, which say nothing that hasn't been said before, allude to Christianity. At most one can quote the old adage: 'Caught together, hanged together!'

Needless to say, I don't like offending my own people, either. But what can I do about it? I have spent my whole life standing up for what I have considered to be the scientific truth, even when it was uncomfortable and unpleasant for my fellow men. I cannot end up with an act of disavowal.[...] Well, we Jews have been reproached for growing cowardly in the course of the centuries. (Once upon a time we were a valiant nation.) In this transformation I had no share.[20]

In associating his Jewish identity with lofty ethical and intellectual ideals, Freud is maintaining the conception of the enlightened and rational Jew put forward in the eighteenth century by Mendelssohn and Lessing. In Freud's day this conception was under attack from many directions. From the beginning of the century onwards, Martin Buber had been insisting that the Jews were no less responsive than the Germans to the irrational imperatives of blood and soil. Else Lasker-Schüler had celebrated the 'wild Jews' of the Old Testament in her *Hebräische Balladen.* And Gershom Scholem had already begun recovering the traditions of Jewish mysticism in his studies of the Cabbalah.

Moses and Monotheism has a place in this development. Although it seems to uphold the image of the rational Jew, it also undermines Freud's rationalism by supporting his doubts about reason and implicitly denying his lingering belief in the perfectibility of man through reason. For he is arguing that ethical and intellectual doctrines are transmitted by irrational means. We no longer have the Enlightenment assumption that truth is discovered by a rational process of enquiry, consisting of examination of empirical evidence and open discussion in which the more reasonable side eventually wins. Instead, we learn that doctrines are transmitted by a 'great man' whose traits are those of the primal father. His authority imprints his teachings on his followers' minds. Only thus can his doctrines acquire the unquestionable certainty that they need in order to survive. Recalling Nietzsche's account of the imposition of memory by violence, in *The Genealogy of Morals,* one could perhaps say that *Moses and Monotheism* is Freud's most Nietzschean book; alternatively, that he is groping towards something like Weber's theory of charismatic leadership.

In describing how the leader's doctrines are rejected by his disloyal followers, the text contains an element of personal fantasy. Freud was well aware that the psychoanalytic movement itself was dismayingly fissile. He had already seen how liable psychoanalysis was to regress into a pseudo-religion, and had witnessed the defections of Adler, Stekel, Jung, Rank and Ferenczi. Yet the paradoxical implication concealed in *Moses and Monotheism* is that the disloyal followers are better guardians of the founder's doctrines than the loyal ones. The loyal followers will transmit his doctrines faithfully, but, lacking the stamp of irrational authority, the doctrines will eventually be forgotten. The disloyal followers will repress the doctrines, but eventually they will resurface, carrying a powerful emotional charge which will ensure their survival.

Moses and Monotheism, then, is a work full of unresolved contradictions. In it Freud affirms his Jewish identity, yet undermines that identity by revealing that it is an act of choice, not a natural birthright. And he affirms rationality while undermining rationality with his image of the charismatic leader. The ambivalence of its themes is reflected in the book's generic ambiguity, which leaves it poised uneasily between a scholarly treatise and a work of historical fiction.

Notes

[1] The dates are taken from a publisher's circular and from the *New York Times*, 21 May 1939, both in the Freud Museum. Contrast Jones, III. 258.

[2] *The Letters of Sigmund Freud and Arnold Zweig*, ed. Ernst L. Freud, trans. Prof. and Mrs W.D. Robson-Scott (London 1970), 91 (30 Sept 1934); 104 (14 Mar 1935); 91 (30 Sept 1934); 97 (6 Nov 1934).

[3] Quoted in Jones, III. 207.

[4] K. Abraham, 'Amenhotep IV. (Echnaton). Psychoanalytische Beiträge zum Verständnis seiner Persönlichkeit und des monotheistischen Aton-Kultes', *Imago*, I (1912), 334–60.

[5] E. Sellin, *Mose und seine Bedeutung für die israelitisch-jüdische Religionsgeschichte* (Leipzig 1922), esp. p. 43. The crucial passages are Hosea 5: 1, which Sellin (unlike most translators) interprets as referring to Shittim, the scene of idolatry and violence in Numbers 25, and Hosea 9: 7–14.

[6] The pertinent criticisms are succinctly made in the review by Salo W. Baron, *American Journal of Sociology*, XLV (1939), 471–7.

[7] Jones, II. 411; Martin S. Bergmann, 'Moses and the Evolution of Freud's Jewish Identity', *Israel Annals of Psychiatry and Related Disciplines*, XIV (Mar 1976), 3–26.

[8] J.W. von Goethe, *Werke*, ed. Erich Trunz, 14 vols. (Hamburg 1949–60), II. 207–25, esp. pp. 216–17.

[9] But cf. the detailed reading of *Moses and Monotheism* in the light of Freud's relations with his father in Marianne Krüll, *Freud and his Father* (London 1987), 194–208.

[10] M. Robert, *From Oedipus to Moses: Freud's Jewish Identity* (London 1977), esp. p. 167. Cf. Justin Miller, 'Interpretations of Freud's Jewishness, 1924–1974', *Journal of the History of the Behavioral Sciences*, XVII (1981), 357–74. Freud on self-hatred, Jones, III. 170. Cf. S.L. Gilman, *Jewish Self-Hatred: Anti-Semitism and the Hidden Language of the Jews* (Baltimore 1986).

[11] See Steven E. Aschheim, *Brothers and Strangers: The East European Jew in German and German Jewish Consciousness, 1800–1923* (Madison, Wis., 1982).

[12] See Marsha Rozenblit, *The Jews of Vienna, 1867–1914* (Albany, N.Y., 1983).

[13] G.S. Viereck, *Glimpses of the Great* (London 1930), 34. Cf. Dennis B. Klein, *Jewish Origins of the Psychoanalytic Movement* (New York 1981).

[14] P. Gay, *Freud, Jews and Other Germans* (New York 1978), 51.

[15] E. Gellner, *Nations and Nationalism* (Oxford 1983), 124. It is tempting to suppose that Freud perceived a resemblance between Moses and Theodor Herzl, but his references to Herzl are too scanty (perhaps suspiciously so) to permit certainty. See William J. McGrath, *Freud's Discovery of Psychoanalysis: The Politics of Hysteria* (Ithaca, N.Y., 1986), 313–15.

[16] J.H. Breasted, *The Dawn of Conscience* (New York 1934), 384; for sceptical comment on this appropriation of Akhenaten, see Cyril Aldred, *Akhenaten* (London 1968), 257.

[17] On Freud's debt to the evolutionary school of anthropologists, see Edwin R. Wallace IV, *Freud and Anthropology* (New York 1983).

[18] *Letters of Freud and Zweig*, 131 (17 June 1936). On Schmidt, see E.E. Evans-Pritchard, *Theories of Primitive Religion* (Oxford 1965), 104. For his attack on Freud and other writers on totemism (including Durkheim), see W. Schmidt, *The Origin and Growth of Religion* (London 1931; first published in German in 1930), 105–17. See also the obituary on him in *Mitteilungen der Anthropologischen Gesellschaft in Wien*, LXXXIII (1954), 87–96.

[19] See the cuttings from the *Catholic Herald* for 1939 in the Freud Museum.

[20] *Letters*, 448, 450 (31 Oct 1938).

6

The Fate of the Internationaler Psychoanalytischer Verlag

Murray G. Hall

Numerous accounts of the history and development of the Internationaler Psychoanalytischer Verlag (hereinafter 'Verlag') have been given by authoritative persons. None of these individuals, however, while narrating events at first hand, was in a position to witness personally or be fully informed about all the developments in the two decades in which the Verlag was active. More recent scholarship, based largely on these personal recollections – first and foremost those of Ernest Jones – has tended to misread, misinterpret, and even to present factual inaccuracies.[1] I would like here to clear up some of these misconceptions, by drawing on archival material consulted now for the first time, and to add a certain historical perspective hitherto lacking.[2]

The founding of the Verlag

In the course of its twenty-year history the Verlag was in many regards unique in the Austrian publishing landscape. The words 'mushroom atmosphere' have been used to describe the active scene in Austria following the proclamation of the First Republic in November 1918. What distinguished the Verlag from the dozens of newly established publishing houses in Austria was its longevity, as well as the fact that it was, in essence, a non-profit organization and that it offered a limited, specialized programme. Most of the firms which – some with almost no capital at all, others with a great deal of it – set out to repatriate Austrian literature, or at least to reap the benefits of relatively low domestic production and labour costs compared with neighbouring Germany, were gone again by the mid-1920s at the latest.[3] The Verlag itself at times only eked out an existence.

Another feature, at least for an historian, is the openness of the Verlag, which almost continually wrote its own history. Members of the International Psycho-Analytical Association and general readers were, as a rule, kept abreast of developments in and the fortunes of the

Verlag. While it was unique also in that it specialized in the publication and distribution of psychoanalytical writings, the Verlag could not, any more than the other houses, withstand the pressures of the book market and general economic developments. At the risk of oversimplification, we may say that its major difficulties up until 1933 were economic, while those after the watershed 1933 were political with economic overtones.

Before describing the events in the 1930s leading up to the demise of the Verlag in 1938, a word about its founding in 1919. As Freud related in the *Internationale Zeitschrift für ärztliche Psychoanalyse* in 1919, the financial backing for the Verlag came from a charitable fund in Budapest. The considerable sum of money was to be used to further the aims of the psychoanalytical movement.[4] For a number of reasons, the two journals published by the Association at the time had lost subscribers during the war, and it seemed inevitable that the publisher and bookseller Hugo Heller would decide to cease publication for lack of financial viability. The aim then was, by taking the journals out of the hands of a commercially oriented publisher, to secure regular publication and create a reliable system for distribution of both journals. Furthermore the Verlag planned to publish books and brochures on subjects from the field of medical and applied psychoanalysis. This laudable undertaking achieved its goal and published several hundred works which make up the corpus of psychoanalytical literature, despite the precarious financial situation at the end of the 1920s and in the 1930s.

The thick file once kept in Vienna by the Handelsgericht, a court regulating commercial enterprises, contains its share of dry, uninteresting material.[5] But it also contains a curious tale not told until now, namely the attempt by the Verlag to gain official legal recognition after having drawn up its statutes in mid-January 1919. Obtaining a place in the official trade register proved to be a problem in itself, but entirely within the parameters of Austrian bureaucracy. Indeed the process took about two and a half years.

The Chamber of Trade, Commerce and Industry, just one of the many authorities whose voice had to be heard in such cases, was totally against the use of the word 'international' in the company's name. In June 1921 the Chamber declared the use of the word to be 'unjustified'. The description could, it was argued, only be used for businesses which had considerable capital at their disposal and close ties with firms outside the boundaries of the former monarchy, or at least in cases where there were immediate prospects of such business connections.

This ruling prompted a five-page legal appeal on the part of the Verlag, one tantamount to a self-portrait at this early stage. It was pointed out that the operations were 'international' in the truest sense of the word, the name of the firm being taken from the International Psycho-Analytical Association, in existence since 1908, with branches in England, America, Holland, Switzerland, Germany, Hungary and Vienna. The name was based not on any fleeting trade relations, but on the 'internationality of science', something which had not suffered under the destructive influence of the war. As far as finances were concerned, the individual branches of the organization had foreign currency reserves far exceeding those which local companies could ever hope to amass. Besides, it was argued, the company at hand was primarily a non-profit organization serving the aims of science and in particular the needs of members of the Austrian branch, who could not afford to purchase books from abroad with the weak Austrian currency. Among the arguments in the lengthy appeal was a note of patriotism: the Verlag would be able to export and make known Austria's reputation and Austrian scholarship abroad. In late July 1921, the Chamber of Trade changed its mind and now found the word 'international' justified. The next day the Verlag was entered in the trade register. And during the following decade it did indeed gain an international reputation.

By 1931 the Verlag was by no means the only Austrian or German publishing company in financial trouble. Martin Freud took over the management of the Verlag in that year, and endeavoured to placate anxious creditors – with some success for the time being. The financial gap was bridged by obliging each member to subscribe the equivalent of $3 monthly. Later, individuals made private donations to keep the business going. As Ernest Jones relates, matters were so desperate in March 1933 that Freud conceived the idea of helping the firm by writing a new series of his *Introductory Lectures*.[6] Needless to say, the sale of his works had provided the financial backbone for its operation, but now the market was about to change.

Austrian writers, publishers and booksellers were traditionally over-dependent on the German book market and the Verlag was no exception. According to a survey made by the Austrian Booksellers Association in 1935, at the height of a German book-dumping campaign, domestic sales made up only 16.8 per cent of the turnover of the Verlag, as opposed to 26.5 per cent in Germany and 56.7 per cent elsewhere.[7] Here it is important to note that although Verlag publications bore the imprint 'Vienna–Leipzig', only the distributor, the wholesale agent for the firm, was located in Leipzig. Thus although more than 80 per cent of its output was sold via Leipzig, the books were not actually produced there. The imprint has led most scholars, including Jones, to draw completely false conclusions as to what part of the Verlag's operation was where.

Political pressures in the 1930s

The financial difficulties besetting the Verlag were compounded by political – one might even say 'racial' – ones following Hitler's rise to power in the spring of 1933. The desire to 'purify' the book market of purportedly destructive, non-German elements found its most stunning, although merely symbolic, manifestation in the book burnings of 10 May. Freud's works were fourth in the sequence to be thrown on the bonfire, while the herald of Nazi ideology solemnly proclaimed: 'Against the soul-destroying overvaluation of sexual life! For the nobility of the human soul! I consign to the flames the writings of Sigmund Freud'.[8]

The Nazi policy of burning and banning books has been depicted by historians in what tend to be simplistic terms. It is true that the publishing trade was abruptly divided into 'German-Aryan' firms on the one hand and 'undesirable' (usually Jewish) enterprises on the other. But in practice the policy towards undesirable firms or authors was by no means consistent. Nazi policy *vis-à-vis* the book trade was a mixture of chaos, cunning and contradiction. Thus despite the spectacular casting of Freud's books on to the bonfire, there appears to be no evidence that the publications of the Verlag were prevented after 1933 from being exported to Germany and sold through Leipzig. Prior to March 1936 they were certainly not banned on political grounds. A further incongruity can be noted in the fact that the Verlag, like other foreign-owned publishers (even those classified as 'Jewish'), was permitted still to advertise in the all-important *Börsenblatt*, the official publication of the book trade. Even at the end of December 1934 the Verlag was able to place a full-page ad in that journal for the *Almanach der Psychoanalyse* for 1935.[10] And until the Anschluss in 1938, Austrian publishers, especially those classified as 'Jewish', appear to have enjoyed certain privileges in Germany, since the Nazi government wanted to avoid the international complications that would have resulted from a ban.

The new state of affairs in Germany after 1933 did of course have adverse consequences for the Verlag. Publication of the journal *Psycho-analytische Bewegung* ceased in December 1933, and a 'special offer' enabled subscribers to purchase back issues. The reasons given for the suspension were that the overwhelming majority of subscribers were in Germany, and that the economic situation was worsening. The journal *Zeitschrift für psychoanalytische Pädagogik* suffered a similar fate, as here again most subscribers were in Germany. The reason given this time was somewhat more explicit: 'On account of the turnabout in the domestic political situation in Germany we have lost our entire readership'.

By January 1936 sales in Germany of books and journals published by the Verlag had been reduced to a quarter of their previous levels.[10] Martin Freud was optimistic that the market would not fall below that figure. But a short time later that market had to be written off altogether. An unpleasant surprise marked the turning-point in the Verlag's fortunes.[11] On 24 March 1936 Martin Freud was informed by his distributor, the wholesale bookseller Volckmar, in Leipzig that by order of the police chief there the Gestapo had been round and carted off 7,679 copies of the titles he listed. Martin Freud was later told that the entire stock of Verlag publications had been confiscated. The writings of Sigmund Freud featured particularly prominently in the list of works confiscated.

Rumours that the books were all to be destroyed, or indeed had already been destroyed, proved however to have no basis in fact. Martin Freud hastened to point out that the rumours were not spread from Vienna. The 'culprit' was Freud's other son, Ernst, in London, who told reporters his father's books had been confiscated or burned. This story, including news of a later intervention by Ernest Jones, was carried by the *News Chronicle* in London, with the headline: 'NAZIS BURN WORKS OF FREUD/LEIPZIG FACTORY LOOTED'. The story was picked up by the *Neues Wiener Journal* in Vienna, which appears to have been the only local paper to mention the Gestapo swoop.[12] The cloak-and-dagger operation remained completely unknown even to people in the German book trade, who went on ordering Verlag publications as if nothing had happened.

A possible explanation for the obvious deliberate harassment, coming three years after the book bonfires and several months before publication of the first official list of literature 'undesirable' in Nazi Germany, can be derived from a parallel case. Only days before the seizure of the Verlag stocks in Leipzig, the police chief had ordered the Gestapo to raid the same distributor, Volckmar, and to confiscate every book by Stefan Zweig on the premises, and all the other stock belonging to Zweig's publisher, Herbert Reichner of Vienna. Neither Reichner nor Martin Freud was officially informed of the police action. Nor were the reasons for it immediately apparent. There was no specific legislation in Germany banning either psychoanalysis as such or works on the subject, its teaching or practice. Psychoanalysis may well have been considered a 'Jewish' aberration, but it turns out that the Nazis had a different pretext for seizing the property of the Verlag—and an allegedly legal one at that. A decree of 28 February 1933, suspending numerous freedoms in the German constitution until further notice, had a first paragraph which read as follows: 'Printed works whose contents are liable to endanger public safety and order can be confiscated and withdrawn by police'.[13] The decree proved to be a blank cheque. Of course Freud's books no more endangered state security than did those of Stefan Zweig, but both authors became the victims of this general decree.

The day after receiving the news of the confiscation, Martin Freud sent a letter to the police chief in Leipzig requesting the release of the books, so that they could be transported back to Vienna. He waited three weeks for the terse reply: his application had been passed on to the ministry responsible and he would be informed in due course of the ministerial decision. Meanwhile, the Leipzig distributor and agent for the Verlag informed Martin Freud that he was severing business ties at the end of April. This was a potentially more disastrous blow than the various blacklistings.

Martin Freud had sent August Beranek to Leipzig and then to Berlin to plead his case before the Reichsschrifttumskammer, but Beranek returned to Vienna empty-handed after officials in Berlin intimated that if the Austrian government hadn't launched a diplomatic offensive in the meantime the books could have been released on the spot. Martin Freud got in touch immediately both with the Booksellers Association in Vienna and the Foreign Ministry, which intervened on his behalf through the Austrian Embassy in Berlin. Victimized publishing colleagues met to discuss the confiscations in Leipzig.

Martin Freud had a number of arguments in his favour. The Verlag – while branded as 'Jewish' and foreign-owned – was a member of a number of supra-national organizations, among them the Börsenverein für den Deutschen Buchhandel, whose non-German members were not subject to domestic German legislation and restrictions. Hence the apparently privileged position enjoyed by so-called 'Jewish' Austrian publishers in Germany itself, at least until the Anschluss. As Martin Freud pointed out in his correspondence with the Foreign Ministry and the Booksellers Association, part of the property seized belonged to foreigners and was thus a different class of 'booty'. This facilitated diplomatic interventions on the part of Britain, France and the United States.

Let me return briefly to Martin Freud's letter of 25 March 1936, addressed to the police chief in Leipzig. Both its condescending tone and subtle irony are worth quoting:

Our company has its base in Vienna, we are a strictly scientific publisher whose authors are for the most part of Aryan descent and foreign nationals (Americans, Britons, Dutch, French and Hungarians). We only distribute our books in Germany through our Leipzig commission agent on a relatively small scale and distribute them primarily to the Nordic countries and overseas, including Japan, South Africa and New Zealand. Of course we could have made these shipments directly from Austria, but we preferred to have our Leipzig agent, the F. Volckmar Company, take care of all distribution abroad on account of our confidence in German organizing talent, German precision and reliability, and German bookselling expertise.[14]

To cut a long story short, the problem was solved roughly four months later, during which period the Verlag was unable to sell its wares via Leipzig. Martin Freud was given permission to transport the confiscated property from Leipzig back to Vienna at his own expense. This information had been passed on through diplomatic channels several days in advance. In a letter of 14 July 1936 from the Austrian Embassy in Berlin to the External Affairs department of the Federal Chancellery in Vienna the envoy wrote:

As concerns the intervention undertaken in the above-mentioned matter, the German Foreign Office has informed the [Austrian] Embassy in Berlin that the President of the Reichsschrifttumskammer has ordered the release of the confiscated books belonging to the above-mentioned publishing house. In addition, the wholesale agent has been given permission to continue to sell the works in question abroad.

The claim that the Verlag was 'seized and liquidated by the Gestapo' in Leipzig in 1936, which one finds even in the work of recent historians, is thus very misleading. Even Jones's contention that the Verlag had to continue in Vienna as 'a gravely mutilated torso' is also not entirely correct. Nor does Jones say that the authorities did eventually release all the property.[15]

In a letter dated 17 July 1936, addressed to the legal counsel of the Booksellers Association in Vienna, Martin Freud revealed that the Germans were more generous than has hitherto been supposed. For as we have seen, he was allowed to leave part of the stock of books with Volckmar and to continue to sell books abroad from Leipzig. The same concession was made to Stefan Zweig's publisher. To what extent the release was a propaganda move on the part of the Germans, coming on the eve of the signing of the so-called 'July Agreement' between Hitler and the Austrian Chancellor, Kurt Schuschnigg, is difficult to say with certainty. The books of Stefan Zweig, seized just before Freud's, were later released, then confiscated once again, and then again released only days before the July Agreement was signed. There are numerous other examples of these German antics.

How was a German-language Jewish publisher to survive under such adverse circumstances? A further, rather unexpected answer is provided by newly discovered material which reveals that Martin Freud was seriously considering an alternative field of publication to keep the Verlag alive. A year after the seizure in Leipzig, in late March 1937, Martin Freud wrote again to the legal counsel of the Vienna Booksellers Association, to air an interesting proposition:

I have just gone over my company's balance sheet for the year just passed, 1936, and have come to the sad conclusion that I will not be in a position to continue operations on the previous basis or at all. Psychoanalysis has to all intents and purposes been banned from Germany. We only have the distribution rights for the German-language editions of most works of Prof. Freud, and it is apparent that because of the far too restricted markets brought about by the loss of Germany new psychoanalytical literature will no longer be able to be sold in sufficient quantities for it to be worthwhile for us or the authors.

Thus the Verlag had reached the end of the line financially a year before its politically enforced closure after the Anschluss.

Under the terms of its legal registration the Verlag was only permitted to publish works pertaining to psychoanalysis. In 1937 Martin Freud's only hope of staying in business was to expand the scope of his publishing and become active outside the confines of psychoanalysis. He came up with a modest plan to rescue the Verlag. What he had in mind was producing some five or at the most ten books a year with 'as neutral a content as possible' ('möglichst neutralen Inhalt'). That way, as he explained, he could meet overhead expenses not covered by the sales of the traditional fare. In order to ensure continuity, the company's name would have to be retained as publisher of the journals. On the other hand, he wrote, he would have to be able to publish the non-psychoanalytical works under a neutral name, 'because it would certainly appear ridiculous and dubious if a book on gardening or actuarial medicine came out under the banner of the Psychoanalytical Press'. Martin Freud emphasized that it was 'a question of survival' ('eine Existenzfrage') and hoped that the legal counsel would bring his influence to bear in broadening the field of operation of the Verlag. The firm was free from debt, but losses could be expected if the Verlag continued with works restricted to psychoanalysis. The only alternative, he concluded, was to liquidate the firm.[16] The counsel's reply is not on file, but it is clear that this scheme could not in any case have been implemented in the short time that remained before the Nazis marched into Austria.

Anton Sauerwald and the crisis of 1938

The consequences for psychoanalysis of the Nazi occupation of Austria have been described again and again from different points of view, notably by contemporaries of Freud like Ernest Jones, Richard F. Sterba, Max Schur and others. August Beranek's account, written in the 1960s, is in part factually inaccurate, while Wolfgang Huber's dissertation of 1977 is still the most reliable documentation we have.[17] Rather than review the contents of the various published recollections, I would like instead to present part of the hitherto unknown story of the man who, as Schur is one of the few to acknowledge, played an important role in Freud's fate, namely the chemist Anton Sauerwald.

Sauerwald was only thirty-five when, on 16 March 1938, he was put in charge of liquidating the Psycho-Analytical Association, the outpatients clinic or 'Ambulatorium', and the Verlag in the Berggasse. At this point he was one of the 20,000 to 30,000 appointed or self-appointed so-called 'wild' commissars who took charge of Jewish businesses in the city. Sauerwald was not officially appointed until late May 1938. The fact that the Verlag was not named among the 'Jewish firms still to be dealt with' in the list compiled by the new men calling the shots at the Booksellers Association, seems to suggest that its fate was a foregone conclusion, decided upon elsewhere. Indeed it was, for there could be no conceivable interest in allowing the business to continue.

Anton Sauerwald had studied science, medicine and law at the University of Vienna and graduated in 1929. In the early 1930s he went into business for himself, establishing a chemical laboratory in the 17th district. His special field was the making of explosive devices. Press reports after the war link him with the Nazi terrorist attacks in Vienna in 1933.[18] His lab was kept under police surveillance. Despite his youth, he was an authority in his own field.

Politically speaking, he seems to have been a typical Austrian, keeping all his options open. While wearing the membership pin of the Fatherland Front on one lapel, he had the swastika under the other. Sauerwald may well have been 'fervently antisemitic', as Jones infers – and his membership in the fraternity 'Germania' would support that argument. But when he began work at the Berggasse, he could not formally claim the status of 'illegal Nazi' – that is, of someone who had worked 'underground' for the Nazis prior to the Anschluss and who could thus expect special rewards from the new regime. It was only after March 1938 that he applied for membership in the Nazi party and was put on the waiting list. After the Anschluss the recruitment of party members was halted, and applicants frequently became so-called 'aspirants' ('Parteianwärter'). The actual awarding of official NSDAP membership often took place completely unbeknownst to the applicant, sometime during the war. Beranek, who himself appears to have been an 'illegal Nazi', even makes Sauerwald into an 'SA-Mann', a member of the Nazi Storm Troopers. In fact, Sauerwald was one of hundreds of thousands of Austrians who could claim, at least after the war, to have been 'sort of, but not really' Nazis.

Between 1939 and 1945 he served as a major in the Luftwaffe and was taken prisoner by the Americans. Upon his release he returned to Vienna on foot. The advice given in Austria in those days to anyone with real or imagined skeletons in his closet was 'Go west, young man'.

Sauerwald left for the Tyrol to join his wife, who had fled the city just before the dreaded Russians arrived. About this time a number of Viennese papers began to dredge up details from Sauerwald's sordid past. These largely erroneous reports appear to have been instigated by Freud's ill-informed nephew Harry, who was in Vienna as an officer in the US army. In a long article based on hearsay, half-truth and fantasy, Sauerwald was tried and convicted by the press in October 1945. The headline in the *Neues Österreich* read: 'SIGMUND FREUD'S BROWN MISERY. NAZI BOMBER DR SAUERWALD'. Among the salient passages were: 'Sauerwald plundered Sigmund Freud lock, stock and barrel' and 'the only possible verdict is: a beast without a soul'.[19] Sauerwald was placed on the wanted list, arrested in April 1947 and kept in custody for three and a half months.

He had to stand trial before a People's Court (Volksgericht) not once – as Schur suggests – but twice. On both occasions he was acquitted. The first trial found him not guilty of war crimes in connection with his role as commissar in charge of the Verlag, the Psycho-Analytical Association and the clinic. The second trial related to whether Sauerwald had actually been an 'illegal Nazi' prior to 1938. It turned out that he, like thousands of others after the Anschluss, had falsely claimed the coveted 'illegal' status in order to gain credit in the eyes of the new Nazi regime. The fact that his claims in 1938 proved to have been fraudulent was the basis for his acquittal in 1947. The People's Court found him not guilty of having been an illegal Nazi, and also acquitted him of the charge that he had committed fraud in his post-1945 registration documents by failing to mention his Nazi past.[20] Sauerwald was also involved at the time in another civil action to recover property rights of which he had been deprived.[21]

It is against this background that we must assess the impact of the events of 1938 on Freud and the Verlag. Anyone who studies existing accounts of what happened to Freud's personal effects, on the one hand, and the assets and property of the Verlag on the other, is bound to be thoroughly confused, so abundant are the contradictions and inconsistencies. I would like to clear up certain points and also to present Sauerwald's side of the story, based on his pre-trial testimony and his defence in court.

He built his defence on the one hand on his behaviour towards Freud and his family, and on his official actions as commissar on the other. By special order of the main office (Hauptamt) of the Nazi Security Service (Sicherheitsdienst or SD) in Berlin – which to my knowledge was seldom involved at this early a date in company closures – the Verlag was to be liquidated immediately, and further book sales strictly forbidden. The premises in the Berggasse, which had recently been renovated, were, according to a report from Sauerwald of mid-July

10. Freud's
house in the
Bergasse,
Vienna, after the
Anschluss, with
the Nazi flag
displayed.

1938, to be turned into a new 'Race Institute'. Eventually the premises
and furnishings were donated to the University of Vienna, which used
them for an Institute of Oriental Studies. The Psycho-Analytical Association's cash assets, totalling 20,000 to 30,000 Austrian Schillings,
were confiscated and transferred to a special account. The same was
true of the assets of the out-patients clinic, the Ambulatorium.

Speaking in his own defence, Sauerwald says he made every effort to
ensure that Freud and his family were not pestered by any Nazi
authorities. After the war, both Anna Freud and Marie Bonaparte were
willing and able to vouch for this, as will be seen from a letter of July
1947 from Anna Freud to Sauerwald's wife, among the court records,
on which I shall later draw. Sauerwald rightly points out that in his
'legal capacity' as commissar he was in no way obliged to assist Freud

and his family in personal matters. He goes on to describe the tremendous difficulties and obstacles he had to overcome in arranging the transport from Vienna of Freud's furniture, and especially his extensive library and the valuable collection of antiquities. The latter, he says, proved to be particularly difficult, for the authorities demanded 'Gutachten' approving their transport out of the country. Sauerwald says he intervened to make sure these special reports were in Freud's favour. The belongings could then be loaded on to three freight coaches and transported to London. The defendant also gives himself credit for obtaining permission for the two Austrian housemaids to leave with the family in June 1938. There has been speculation as to Sauerwald's motives for so obviously going beyond the call of duty. He himself said, after the war, that he acted of his own free will, completely unselfishly and out of respect for Freud.

In his biography of Freud Schur wrote that no one really knows why Sauerwald turned up in London in 1939. Sauerwald himself provides the answer. He says that after Freud emigrated, he travelled to London at Freud's request to discuss with him various business matters pertaining to the publishing company and its authors as well as bank dealings. During the visit Freud, who had not got to know Sauerwald personally, asked him to arrange for his doctor, Professor Pichler, to come to see him from Vienna, since Freud needed an examination and advice on further medical treatment. Sauerwald says he carried out this request, calling on Pichler personally to explain the situation. As Jones relates, Pichler did then journey to London for the sole purpose of examining his patient. Sauerwald's comment: 'Professor Freud was understandably pleased'. He then tells how he managed personally to enter Pichler's bills under 'moving expenses' and thus to spare Freud an extra payment.

What about the fate of the stocks of books belonging to the Verlag? Here again Sauerwald gives us detailed, authoritative information. Contrary to what one often reads, not everything was destroyed, despite the Gestapo order to that effect. A seemingly odd but clear distinction was made by the Nazis between works 'belonging to' ('zugehörig') – which apparently means 'written by' – Austrian nationals and those 'belonging to' foreigners. As a rule, every effort was made to avoid international complications. In fact, the settling of royalty and copyright claims outside the country proved to be an obstacle in carrying out the policy of ridding business life of Jews as quickly as possible. Some Jewish publishing firms in Austria continued to exist at least on paper until well into 1944.

The Internationaler Psychoanalytischer Verlag itself continued to exist after Sauerwald was called up for military service. Although he filed his final report in September 1940 – and it had taken that long to tie up loose ends with foreign debtors and creditors – it wasn't until the spring of 1941 that the company legally ceased to exist.

Sauerwald managed to save various quantities of books, including those 'belonging to' foreigners, using various means. He relates, for example, in his own self-defence that he expressly welcomed an offer by Marie Bonaparte to purchase and thus save the Verlag, and even tried to push the deal through with the help of the influential Nazi psychologist Professor Göring. The proposition was turned down, however, by the headquarters of the Security Service in Berlin and the Gestapo in Vienna, despite the prospect of foreign currency income. Sauerwald had worked out an arrangement with Marie Bonaparte (Princess George of Greece) by which the confiscated property would be saved by transferring it to the basement of the Greek Embassy in Vienna; but the plan fell through when that Embassy's 'extraterritorial' status was removed and it was reduced to a consulate. (Beranek, however, tells a different story. He claims *he* signed an agreement with Marie Bonaparte for the sale and says that the transfer of the books was foiled the very next day. A freight train carrying what he incorrectly calls 'the whole stock of books' ['das ganze Bücherlager'] never reached the paper mill in Styria it was heading for.)

Sauerwald also gives himself credit for having seen to it that, as he writes, 'almost all universities and institutes in Germany and Austria were given literature on psychoanalysis from the Verlag's stocks'. To this, according to Sauerwald, the Security Service gave its approval on condition the books were kept in storage and inaccessible. Some accounts speak of this as involving 45 crates of books, others of between 60 and 80 crates. Sauerwald then records his greatest achievement. He says that he personally struck a deal with the new Nazi director of the Austrian National Library, Paul Heigl, to have the library store a large number of crates, containing several copies of each book the Verlag had published. Most were said to be rare volumes. To prove his point, he presented the court with a list of the books which were then released after the war and returned to the Freud family via Amsterdam. 'I might add', he says, 'that these books will now provide the basis for the reconstruction of a new Psychoanalytical Press in Vienna'.

Another witness, Freud's lawyer Alfred Indira, testified that Sauerwald often took great risks by claiming to have the approval of the Security Service for some action when in fact he did not. In his first appearance before the People's Court, Sauerwald was able to refute the charges against him that he had used his position as commissar of the three organizations, including the Verlag, for personal gain.

The best summary of Sauerwald's role in this complex story is provided by the letter I have mentioned, written to his wife by Anna

Freud on 22 July 1947. It shows that Sauerwald deserves more credit than he has hitherto received for shielding the Freud family from the Nazi authorities and facilitating their move to London:

20 Maresfield Gardens
London, N.W.3.
22 July 1947.

Dear Mrs Sauerwald,

I am replying to your letter in lieu of my mother. I am the person who was always in direct contact with your husband in matters concerning my father.

My parents and I have in no way forgotten that we had every reason to be very grateful to your husband in a number of regards. We were in a very precarious situation at the time and there wasn't any doubt that your husband used his office as our appointed commissar in such a manner as to protect my father. In his dealings with him he always showed great respect and great consideration and did his utmost to prevent other functionaries of the regime from bothering him and as I well know he kept documents which could have endangered our lives hidden in his desk for quite some time. My brother and almost all our friends had already left Vienna by then and that meant there was no one to help me arrange my parents' and my own departure. He accompanied me at the time to various authorities in order to spare me inconvenience. I was especially grateful to him for the great effort he made in securing medical attendance on the journey. After all, my father was 82 at the time and seriously ill with cancer.

After we left the country Dr Sauerwald saw to it that we really had all our furniture and in particular the collection of antiquities which my father so loved sent on to us.

Last year we heard rumours that Dr Sauerwald had been arrested. I sent off at the time a letter in his favour to the authorities who I assumed were concerned with the case. Princess George of Greece, a friend of ours who was with us in Vienna in 1938 and who is equally grateful to Dr Sauerwald for protecting my father, did likewise. We were then told the rumour was unfounded.

I'm sure Princess George of Greece would be willing to repeat the statement she made in his favour now. If you would kindly tell me the name of the authority concerned, I will ask the Princess to send such a letter to them. Or to you, if you prefer.

It is my wish for you and your husband that the current problem will be resolved without any harm to him.

Yours,
ANNA FREUD[22]

Notes

[1] See esp. Hans-Martin Lohmann and Lutz Rosenkötter, 'Psychoanalyse in Hitler-deutschland. Wie war es wirklich?', in *Psychoanalyse und Nationalsozialismus. Beiträge zur Bearbeitung eines unbewältigten Traumas*, ed. Hans-Martin Lohmann (Frankfurt/Main

1984), 54–66; and Elis. Brainin and Isidor J. Kaminer, 'Psychoanalyse und National-sozialismus', ibid., 86–105.

[2] This archival material includes files in the Archiv, Österreichisches Buchgewer-behaus, Vienna; Vienna Booksellers Guild, Österr. Staatsarchiv: Allg. Verwaltungs-archiv and Haus-, Hof- und Staatsarchiv, Handelsgericht Wien.

[3] For further details see Murray G. Hall, *Österreichische Verlagsgeschichte 1918–1938*, 2 vols. (Vienna 1985).

[4] S. Freud, 'Internationaler Psychoanalytischer Verlag und Preiszuteilungen für psycho-analytische Arbeiten', *Int'l Z Psych*, v (1919), 137–8. And see ibid., vi (1920), 381 f.

[5] Handelsgericht Wien, Reg. C 55, 223. The file is kept in the Wiener Stadt- und Landesarchiv.

[6] E. Jones, *The Life and Work of Sigmund Freud*, 1 vol. edn., ed. and abridged Lionel Trilling and Steven Marcus (repr. London 1984), 613.

[7] Archiv, Österreichisches Buchgewerbehaus, Vienna. Verein 1935, file 423.2.

[8] 'Vierter Rufer: Gegen seelenzersetzende Überschätzung des Trieblebens! Für den Adel der menschlichen Seele! Ich übergebe dem Feuer die Schriften von Sigmund Freud.' Quoted in *'Das war ein Vorspiel nur...': Bücherverbrennung Deutschland 1933: Voraussetzungen und Folgen*, exhibition catalogue (Berlin: Akademie der Künste 1983), 212 f.

[9] *Börsenblatt*, vol. 101, no. 285 (7 Dec 1934), p. 5786.

[10] *Int'l Z Psych*, xxiii, no. 1 (1937), 189.

[11] The account which follows is based on correspondence between Martin Freud, the Booksellers Association in Vienna and the Ministry for External Affairs in Vienna, in the Archiv, Österreichisches Buchgewerbehaus, Vienna, Verein 1936, file 433, and Österr. Staatsarchiv, Haus-, Hof- und Staatsarchiv, N.P.A., Kt. 123 ('Beschlagnahme von Büchern des Internationalen Psychoanalytischen Verlages in Leipzig').

[12] *News Chronicle*, 7 Apr 1936, p. 13: '[...] Mr Ernst Freud said: "I was amazed to learn of the wholesale destruction of my father's works. I knew that his books were regarded with disfavour by the Nazi authorities but having regard to their interna-tional importance I never thought such action would be taken.[...]"'. The author would like to thank Dr Edward Timms for his assistance in obtaining a copy of this article. The Vienna report appeared in the *Neues Wiener Journal*, no. 15, 228 (10 Apr 1936), p. 6.

[13] 'Verordnung des Reichspräsidenten zum Schutze vom Volk und Staat', *Reichsgesetz-blatt*, Teil I, Nr. 17/1933. Ausgegeben zu Berlin, den 28. Februar 1933. For details of the Stefan Zweig affair, see Murray G. Hall, 'Literatur- und Verlagspolitik der dreißiger Jahre in Österreich. Am beispiel Stefan Zweigs und seines Wiener Verlegers Herbert Reichner', in *Stefan Zweig 1881/1981. Aufsätze und Dokumente*. Herausgegeben von der Dokumentationsstelle für neuere österreichische Literatur in Zusammenarbeit mit dem Salzburger Literaturarchiv (Vienna, Oct 1981), 113–36.

[14] Österreichisches Staatsarchiv, Abt. Haus-, Hof- und Staatsarchiv, N.P.A., Kt. 123, Zahl 40.488-13/36.

[15] Cf. Lohmann and Rosenkötter in *Psychoanalyse und Nationalsozialismus*: 'Am 28. März 1936 wurde der Internationale Psychoanalytische Verlag in Leipzig von der Gestapo beschlagnahmt und liquidiert'. Jones iii. 201, 236.

[16] Letter of 24 Mar 1937 in the archives of the Österreichisches Buchgewerbehaus, Vienna, File V 1937.

[17] R.F. Sterba, *Erinnerungen eines Wiener Psychoanalytikers* (Frankfurt/Main 1985; originally pub. in English as *Reminiscences of a Viennese Psychoanalyst*, Detroit 1982); M. Schur, *Sigmund Freud. Leben und Sterben* (Frankfurt/Main 1977); A. Beranek, 'Wie die Nazis den Internationalen Psychoanalytischen Verlag zerstörten', Pinkus Katalog 118 (Zürich, May 1969); W. Huber, 'Psychoanalyse in Österreich seit 1933' (D. Phil. diss., Salzburg 1977).

[18] *Neues Österreich*, no. 152 (18 Oct 1945), p. 3.

[19] Ibid.

[20] Landesgericht für Strafsachen Wien. Vg 8f Vr 2083/47 and Vg 1a Vr 2876/47. The author received special permission to consult the court records, which are not generally accessible. Complete details of the liquidation process carried out by Sauerwald can be found in the following files at the Allgemeines Verwaltungsarchiv in Vienna: Vermögensverkehrsstelle, Kommissare und Treuhänder 6717 and Handel 4874/VI.

[21] Sauerwald was forced to take legal action to obtain the release of his personal effects and library from his apartment in Vienna, which was given after the war to an 'anti-fascist'. See 'Der Vernichter der Freud-Bibliothek auf freiem Fuß', *Österreichische Volksstimme*, 20 Aug. 1947, p. 3.

[22] Because of the relative inaccessibility of Anna Freud's letter of 22 July 1947, the original German text is also put on record here:

Sehr geehrte Frau Sauerwald,

Ich beantworte an Stelle meiner Mutter Ihren Brief. Ich bin auch diejenige, die in den Angelegenheiten meines Vaters immer direkt mit Ihrem Mann zu tun hatte.

Meine Eltern und ich haben nie daran vergessen, daß wir Grund hatten, Ihrem Mann in verschiedener Beziehung sehr dankbar zu sein. Wir waren damals in sehr gefährdeter Lage und es war kein Zweifel darüber, daß Ihr Mann sein Amt als unser bestellter Kommissar benützt hat, um eine schützende Hand über meinen Vater zu halten. Er ist ihm selbst immer mit großem Respekt und großer Rücksicht begegnet, hat möglichst vermieden, andere Funktionäre des Regimes in seine Nähe kommen zu lassen und hat, wie ich weiß, längere Zeit Schriftstücke in seinem Schreibtisch verborgen gehalten, die uns hätten gefährlich werden können. Mein Bruder und fast alle unsere Freunde hatten damals Wien schon verlassen, so daß ich ohne Hilfe war, um die Ausreise meiner Eltern und meine eigene zu betreiben. Er hat mich damals zu verschiedenen Ämtern begleitet, um mir Unannehmlichkeiten zu ersparen. Besonders dankbar war ich dafür, daß er sich die größte Mühe gegeben hat, meinem Vater ärztliche Begleitung für die Reise zu sichern. Mein Vater war damals ja schon 82 Jahre alt und schwer krebskrank.

Dr. Sauerwald hat dann nach unserer Auswanderung dafür gesorgt, daß wir wirklich alle unsere Möbel und vor allem die Sammlung von Antiquitäten, die der liebste Besitz meines Vaters war, nachgeschickt bekommen haben.

Im vorigen Jahr ist einmal das Gerücht zu uns gedrungen, daß Dr. Sauerwald verhaftet ist. Ich habe damals einen Brief zu seinen Gunsten an die Behörde geschickt, die mir die zuständige schien. Das gleiche tat Frau Prinzessin Georg von Griechenland, eine Freundin unseres Hauses, die 1938 bei uns in Wien war und Dr. Sauerwald in gleicher Weise dafür dankbar, daß er meinen Vater beschützt hat. Wir bekamen aber damals die Antwort, daß das Gerücht auf einem Irrtum beruht haben muß.

Prinzessin Georg von Griechenland wäre sicher bereit, ihre Fürsprache von damals jetzt zu wiederholen. Wenn Sie mir die zuständige Behörde angeben wollen, so will ich die Prinzessin bitten, einen Brief dorthin zu richten. Oder an Sie, wenn Ihnen das besser erscheint.

Ich wünsche Ihnen und Ihrem Mann, daß die jetzige Sorge ohne schwere Schädigung für ihn vorübergeht.

Ihre

Anna Freud

The letter is in the court records in Vienna: Landesgericht für Strafsachen Wien, Vg 8f Vr 2876/47.

PART TWO

RECEPTION AND EXILE

7

The Jones-Freud Era, 1908-1939

R. Andrew Paskauskas

The accent in this paper is on Ernest Jones. This is justified in the context of a book entitled *Freud in Exile*, as it was Jones who in 1938, during the Nazi Anschluss of Austria, helped to rescue Freud and his daughter Anna from Vienna and arranged for their safe passage to London under diplomatic aegis. Besides, in the history of modern science and medicine Jones is regarded as the most important English-speaking exponent of psychoanalysis.

A British-trained neurologist, Jones fell under the spell of Freud's work, as well as Freud's personality, between 1908 and 1913, the period in which he lived and worked in Canada. He also played a crucial role in the reception of psychoanalysis in America, and in the psychoanalytic movement in Europe. When Jones returned to England at the end of 1913 he began a new phase in a career that would secure him a prominent place in the history of psychoanalysis. His three-volume *Life and Work of Sigmund Freud* (1953, 1955, 1957)[1] conclusively demonstrated his allegiance to Freud, and established his reputation as principal historian of the psychoanalytic movement.

What I have called the Jones–Freud era is situated temporally well before the appearance of Jones's biography of Freud, a work which contains the biases that ripened in an author who had played a major part in the history of the psychoanalytic movement. My analysis is based primarily on the unpublished letters between Freud and Jones for the period 1908–39. The correspondence consists of close to 700 letters (over 1,200 typescript pages): the letters from Jones to Freud are in English (about 900 pages); those from Freud to Jones are divided evenly between English and German (about 400 pages).[2]

Only fragments of this correspondence have been quoted in the literature on the history of psychoanalysis. In his biography of Freud, Jones refers to 170 of the letters in the appended notes, but quotes from only 35, leaving historians and readers at the mercy of his interpretation of certain passages. A mere 5 letters from Freud to Jones between 1925 and 1939 were published in Ernst Freud's edition of *Letters of Sigmund*

Freud 1873–1939 (1960), and only a few letters were employed by Max
Schur in his *Freud* (1972). There are 90 letters referred to or quoted by
Vincent Brome in his *Ernest Jones* (1983) and about 50 letters are
employed by Ronald W. Clark in his *Freud* (1980).[3] Neither Brome nor
Clark, however, provides a critical and scholarly perspective on the
historical issues. More recently, Riccardo Steiner has used a selection of
these documents effectively in his article of 1985 on the 'Controversial
Discussions'.[4] Phyllis Grosskurth's study of Melanie Klein (1986) is
marred by her sporadic, incomplete reading of the Freud / Jones correspondence.[5]

The letters between Freud and Jones shed new light on the nature
of the development of psychoanalysis. The correspondence contains
new historical evidence that reveals Jones's period of intellectual doubt
during his early years (1907–9); provides an intimate look at the
psychoanalytic method in operation – Jones's self-analysis (1909–14),
Freud's analysis of Jones's common-law wife, Loe Kann (1912–14), and
Sándor Ferenczi's analysis of Jones (1913); manifests Freud's style and
sensitivity as an analyst; establishes Jones's control over the translation
work undertaken during the 1920s; and demonstrates Freud's and
Jones's collaboration in grooming James Strachey as a translator well
before the appearance in the 1950s and 1960s of Strachey's Standard
Edition of Freud's *Complete Psychological Works* (24 vols., 1953–74).

The fundamental historical problem concerning the received view of
Freud and the development of psychoanalysis has been that Jones acted
both as a key figure in the development of psychoanalysis and as chief
historian of the movement. Jones's writing skills, his crisp logical
mind, and particularly his monopoly on unpublished documents have
combined in such a way that no other historian, writer or analyst to date
has been capable of outdoing him. Although certain attacks on the
fortress have been attempted, most researchers and writers in the end
have deferred to Jones.

Where his own life and work are concerned, Jones's authority as
historian of psychoanalysis has for the most part gone unchallenged.
But Jones's biases also surface in his historical and autobiographical
writings. His own accounts especially of his early period leave gaps that
can be filled by a careful reading of the Freud / Jones correspondence.

The Toronto period
With minor variations Jones's *Life and Work of Freud*, his *Free Associations* (1959), and the shorter historical pieces (1945, 1954, 1964) tell the
same story.[6] When Jones writes about the period between 1905 and
1913, for example, he gives the impression of having been a young but
confident psychoanalyst, making forays into the unexplored terrain of
Freud's psychology and related areas, and associating with the foremost

psychiatrists, neurologists and psychopathologists in England, Canada, the United States and continental Europe. Jones exaggerates his own role in the development of Canadian psychiatry and American psychopathology. He falsely claims that he was called to Toronto in the autumn of 1908 to take on the directorship of a new psychiatric hospital, which was to be modelled on Kraepelin's famous clinic in Munich, and – also falsely – that in 1910 he founded the American Psychopathological Association, an organization actually founded by Morton Prince.

Jones tends especially to exaggerate his role in the development of psychoanalysis. He situates himself historically as a practising psychoanalyst from 1905, and leads his readers to believe that he began his campaign for psychoanalysis as soon as he arrived in North America, a year before Freud's crucial appearance in America in September 1909. Thus, Jones claims that he converted James Jackson Putnam to psychoanalysis at the end of 1908, and that William James told him in 1909 that the 'future of psychology' belonged to his, Jones's, work.

What Jones leaves out of his historical and autobiographical accounts is significant. He sheds little light on the specific steps by which he became a psychoanalyst, merely remarking that he had begun to practise psychoanalysis in 1905, and had undergone a didactic analysis in 1913 with Ferenczi. Nor does he shed any light on the uncertainty he felt between 1907 and 1909 about entering Freud's circle of followers, or how this initial reluctance was reinforced by his closest companions, Loe Kann, his common-law wife, and Wilfred Trotter, his best friend. Finally, in his own discussions about his involvement with European psychoanalysts, Jones leaves out the crucial role he himself had played in Freud's break with Jung.

The Freud/Jones correspondence provides a more complete picture of Jones's relationship to the early history of psychoanalysis. For example, we can date Jones's first reading of Freud. This occurred in 1907, not prior to 1905 as Jones himself has suggested. Thus, Jones's role in the development of American psychoanalysis before Freud's appearance at Worcester, Massachusetts, in September of 1909, is relatively insignificant. Jones did not convert James Jackson Putnam to psychoanalysis in 1908. Freud did that in September 1909.

The letters reveal that the period between 1907 and 1909 was a crucial turning-point in Jones's intellectual and scientific development, that his first meeting with Freud at Salzburg in the spring of 1908 had a profound psychological impact on him, and that it was only after September 1909 that he declared to Freud that he would dedicate his life to psychoanalysis.

The correspondence sheds new light on the political and economic context of Jones's professional milieu in the medical arena of Ontario, and clearly indicates that Jones's claim that he was invited to Toronto to be director of a new Kraepelinian psychiatric clinic cannot be substantiated. Actually, Jones lost out on a possible career opportunity in Kraepelinian psychiatry when the Ontario government diverted funds from the psychiatric hospital project to the erection of a new prison. Jones's interest in forging a career in Canada strongly influenced him to continue his Kraepelinian research, at least until the end of 1910. The failure of the clinic project closed off that particular opportunity, and was the principal external factor shaping his career in Toronto, steering him towards the work of Freud.

Moreover, during this transitional period, Freud and Jung were not convinced of Jones's commitment to the psychoanalytic movement. Their correspondence of 1908 and 1909 reveals doubts about him. According to them, Jones was an 'enigma', 'incomprehensible', 'an intellectual liar', 'an opportunist', 'a fanatic' and 'a compromiser'.[7]

We cannot underestimate the profound personal impact that Freud had on the young Jones on the occasion of their second meeting at the Worcester gathering, when Freud and Jung had come to America to receive honorary doctorates at Clark University in September 1909. In his first letter to Freud, shortly after the conference, on 17 October 1909, Jones wrote: 'you have struck a powerful blow for the cause in America'. Then he declared to Freud:

the outcome of the story is that about six or eight months ago I determined not only to further the cause by all the means in my power, which I had always decided on, but also to further it by whatever means you personally decided on, and to follow your recommendations as exactly as possible.[8]

Indeed, after the Worcester meetings, Jones began to exude in America the missionary zeal on behalf of psychoanalysis for which he is now famous. Most significantly, he took an active role in the formation of the American Psychoanalytic Association (APA), which was founded in 1911 with Putnam as its first president and Jones as secretary. From Freud's point of view the establishment of the APA was a major breakthrough, and he later extolled Jones for conquering the Americans in less than two years.

During this North American – post-Worcester – period Jones also published more than 20 papers on all aspects of psychoanalysis, including his lengthy article on the 'nightmare' and the important essay on Shakespeare's *Hamlet*.[9] He delivered over a dozen papers on psychoanalysis at professional meetings held in various parts of the United States, including Baltimore, Detroit, Washington, Chicago and New York, and these were also published in leading American journals on medicine, neurology and psychiatry. Many were collected and published in his *Papers on Psycho-Analysis* (1913) and conclusively established his adherence to the psychoanalytic movement at a time when former adherents such as Alfred Adler and Carl Jung were attempting to undermine the fundamental tenets of psychoanalysis.

It was shortly after the Worcester gathering that Jones declared to Freud that he would dedicate his life to psychoanalysis. He was not a committed Freudian prior to September 1909, nor was he considered one by Freud. Freud's American visit was not only pivotal in the reception of psychoanalysis in the United States, it was a pivotal episode in Jones's conversion to psychoanalysis. The period between 1907 and 1909 was one of intellectual and scientific transition, in which Jones was preoccupied with Kraepelinian psychiatry and Bostonian psychopathology. His important psychoanalytic work and activity in general, and in America in particular, began after Freud's American visit, not before that date, as Jones himself has claimed in his historical writings. His work in helping to found the American Psychoanalytic Association in 1911 must be seen as his first major organizational activity on behalf of psychoanalysis in North America.

To address these issues, and to clarify the historical record, is not to attempt to denigrate Jones. As one psychoanalyst put it to me recently: 'The new view of Jones only enhances my pre-existing admiration for him, despite or even because of his opportunism, in picking psychoanalysis over Kraepelinian nosology or the psychotherapies of suggestion that were available at the time. . . . As a wily young fox [he] played his cards skillfully and came out on the side of the "psychology of the future" even in the process of helping to create it.'.[10]

The Freud/Jones correspondence also reveals the structure of Jones's psychoanalytic apprenticeship, including his self-analysis, Freud's analysis of Jones's common-law wife Loe, and Jones's analysis with Ferenczi. Space is lacking to go into the details here, except to mention that Loe Kann was analysed by Freud between 1912 and 1914. At a crucial point in the analysis, in early 1913, Jones insensitively committed an act of infidelity by engaging in sexual relations with one of Loe's female servants. As a result, Freud had to help Loe through an extremely difficult period in her emotional life, and his sensitivity and tact as a clinician are evident throughout this episode. Moreover, Freud's objectivity never waned. He did not reproach Jones for his behaviour, retaining his fondness for both Loe and Jones.

However, Loe decided to break off her intimate relationship with Jones, and this provided the impetus for a new era in Jones's professional and personal life. Jones's subsequent analysis with Ferenczi was sparked primarily by his remorse regarding his separation from Loe rather than as a 'didactic' analysis. The break with Loe was critical. But Jones was psychologically prepared for this. His self-analysis, coupled with Ferenczi's analysis, put him into a frame of mind that allowed him to enter a new phase in his personal and intellectual development. On 14 October 1913, he wrote to Freud: 'This year marks a turning-point in my career, and the change will be a *deep one*, both externally and internally.'

By the end of 1913, having resolved his personal relationship with Loe through his analysis with Ferenczi, and having successfully dealt with his personal problems, Jones had become a new man. These events signalled the completion of his psychoanalytic apprenticeship. The credibility he had achieved in Freud's eyes and among the closest Freudians by the end of the Toronto period in 1913 allowed him to take his place as a leading figure in Freud's inner circle of followers.

Jones's role in the development of psychoanalysis had a subtle component, one that cannot readily be grasped in his own historical writings. Consider this revealing passage in a letter of 19 June 1910 from Jones to Freud:

I feel it is a more sensible ideal to aim at developing one's own capacity in whatever direction that may lie than in merely trying to be 'original'. The originality-complex is not strong with me; my ambition is rather to know, to be 'behind the scenes', and 'in the know', rather than *to find out*. I realize that I have very little talent for originality; any talent I may have lies rather in the direction of being able to see perhaps quickly what others point out: no doubt that also has its use in the world. Therefore my work will be to try to work out in detail, and to find new demonstrations for the truth of, ideas that others have suggested. To me work is like a woman bearing a child; to men like you, I suppose it is more like the male fertilisation.

Such striking revelations are good material for the psycho-historian. However, I shall refrain from making psychoanalytic interpretations of Jones's relationship with Freud, a large chapter in itself, but will focus on this so-called 'behind-the-scenes' activity that forms a crucial part of Jones's orientation towards Freud and the politics of the psychoanalytic movement.

The Secret Committee

In the summer of 1912 Jones proposed to Freud that an unofficial council, or 'Secret Committee', be formed to watch over the development of psychoanalysis, to guard against possible defections, and to provide a source of comfort to Freud, relieving him of any worry about the future of psychoanalysis. On 7 August 1912 Jones outlined his ideas to Freud as follows:

My own thought is that the council should be quite unofficial and informal, therefore necessarily secret, and in the closest possible touch with you for the purposes both of criticism and instruction.... The idea of a united small body, designed, like the Paladins of Charlemagne, to guard the kingdom and policy of their master, was a product of my own romanticism....

11. The 'Committee', Berlin 1922: (*seated, left to right*) Freud, Sandor Ferenczi, Hanns Sachs: (*standing*) Otto Rank, Karl Abraham, Max Eitingon, Ernest Jones.

12. Freud and Ernest Jones in London, 1938, with (*far left*) Freud's eldest daughter, Mathilde (Mrs Robert Hollitscher), and his daughter-in-law, Lucie (Mrs Ernst Freud).

The membership of the Committee was established within a year of Jones's initial proposal. The first members of the group were Freud and Jones, Otto Rank of Vienna, Sándor Ferenczi of Budapest, Karl Abraham of Berlin and Hans Sachs of Vienna. In May 1913 Freud presented the members with a Greek intaglio that each of them later had mounted on a ring.

The role of secrecy within the political framework of the international psychoanalytical movement is historically significant. What was so extraordinary about Jones's proposal in 1912 was the fact that there was no mention of Carl Jung as a possible member of the Committee. Jung was president of the International Psycho-Analytical Association and editor of the *Jahrbuch für psychoanalytische und psychopathologische Forschungen*. And Jung and Freud had not yet severed their ties. Historically, the policy of excluding Jung from membership in the Secret Committee had tremendous repercussions on the crucial shift in power that occurred at the end of 1913 and early 1914 within the psychoanalytic movement. In the end, Jones displaced Jung in the power structure and took over his role as the most important Gentile among Freud's adherents. These events clearly signalled the end of Jones's apprenticeship and his entry into Freud's inner circle of followers.

When Jung resigned as editor of the *Jahrbuch* in 1913, Freud and Ferenczi wrote immediately to Jones as a member of the Secret Committee.[11] That gesture exhibits Jones's status within Freud's circle. His credibility was at its peak. As one of the Secret Committee, Jones was being consulted on what steps to take to deal with the Jung situation. He had entered the ranks of the initiated. His political abilities were put to the test, and he emerged as a master politician within the psychoanalytic movement.

Jones's ability to manoeuvre politically and be successful at it increased his credibility to such an extent that when Jung also resigned from the International Psycho-Analytical Association, in 1914, it was Jones who was seriously considered as the next official president. That in itself is historically significant, even though he had to wait until after World War I to assume the position.

Within three short years the tide had turned. At the beginning of his psychoanalytic apprenticeship, around 1910, Jones's status was relatively insignificant. Jung was considered Freud's closest adherent – the Crown Prince. By 1913, Jones had replaced Jung and entered on his career as the most important exponent of psychoanalysis in the English-speaking world. The clever way in which he was able to succeed Jung as Freud's heir-apparent can also be understood from the standpoint of his self-defined role as working 'behind the scenes'.

In 1913, after the early years of apprenticeship, Jones founded the London Psycho-Analytical Society, reconstituted after World War I as

13. Melanie Klein.

14. Ernest Jones in 1920.

15. James Strachey in Egypt, 1933.

the British Psycho-Analytical Society. He then founded and edited
(1920–39) the *International Journal of Psycho-Analysis*, and served as
president of the International Psycho-Analytical Association (1920–4,
and 1932–49). In the 1920s Jones founded the International Psycho-
Analytical Library, and the Institute of Psycho-Analysis, London,
where he gave younger European analysts such as Melanie Klein a
forum for their ideas. But these are facts we can glean readily from
Jones's *Life and Work of Freud* or his other historical writings.

As for Jones's 'behind-the-scenes' activities, again I turn to the
Secret Committee. That group resumed operations after World War I
and enlisted the independently wealthy Anton von Freund. After von
Freund's premature death, Max Eitingon joined the Committee. It is
significant that financial considerations influenced Eitingon's election
to the secret circle, and this ushered in a period of financing of psychoanalytic institutes and training programmes.

In 1920 a secret correspondence was also agreed upon, and the
Rundbriefe were circulated among the members between 1920 and 1925.
After the defection of Rank and the death of Abraham in 1925, the
correspondence continued between 1926 and 1936, and included the
letters of new members such as Anna Freud and the Dutch psychoanalyst J.H.W. van Ophuijsen. References to this particular group of
documents appear frequently throughout the Freud/Jones correspondence.

The activities of the secret group after World War I were of import
to the development of the psychoanalytic movement. The Committee
controlled membership in the International Association and the branch
societies, and managed the psychoanalytic journals and other publications. Moreover, under Jones's skilful control, major translation
projects were undertaken to put Freud's work into English, in an
attempt to correct the American translations which were deemed to be
poor renderings of Freud's writings. Most notably, this resulted in the
appearance by the mid-1920s of what we now know as Freud's *Collected
Papers*.[12]

Translation projects

The letters between Freud and Jones clearly exhibit Jones's participation in the major translation efforts of the 1920s. Jones again can be
observed in his typical role of operating from 'behind the scenes'.
Indeed, his involvement with the work of translation was more
extensive than has previously been suspected. On 10 April 1922, Jones
wrote to Freud: 'You know that it is essentially for you that we are all
working, which is why your inspiration and approval means so much to
us all. If I can produce a Collected Edition of your works in my lifetime
and leave the Journal on a soundly organised basis I shall feel that my

life has been worth living....' On 11 April 1924, while the final stage of the project to bring out the *Collected Papers* was under way, Jones wrote:

In the last few years I have personally revised every word of the translation of five of your books and have been only too glad of the opportunity. As you know it has long been my ambition to put out some of your work in a worthy form in English and I have even cherished the hope that in the future it might be possible to come to some arrangement whereby new translations could be published of the other books as well (*Traumdeutung*, etc.). ...

After the publication in 1923 of Freud's *Das Ich und das Es*, which we now know as *The Ego and the Id*, a dialogue ensued between Jones and Freud on the proper English translation of 'Ich' and 'Es'. On 29 September 1924, Jones wrote: 'You do not propose to invent another term (? Greek) for Es? It cannot be permanently used in psychology in that form, surely.' Some two years later, on 7 March 1926, Freud wrote: 'Sometimes I did have the feeling I should not have written *Das Ich und das Es*, for the Es cannot be rendered in English'. A few days later, on 11 March 1926, Jones replied: 'I did not understand your difficulty about "Das Ich u. das Es" in English. Are you not satisfied with "Id" = "Es". To me it is as good, but obviously neither word is a good technical term.'

Significantly, it was Jones who envisioned the idea of a 'standard' edition of Freud's writings, as early as 1920. On 27 January of that year, Jones wrote to Freud: 'I am anxious to publish your *Vorlesungen* (together with the *Fünf Vorlesungen*) as the first volume of our standard edition, and can find reliable translators. Have I your permission to start on this? ...' A month later, on 29 February 1920, Jones again referred to 'the projected Standard Edition of collected works, with just the *Vorlesungen* and *Fünf Vorlesungen* as the first volume'.[13]

The papers on problems of translation elsewhere in this book seriously question the adequacy of James Strachey's Standard Edition of Freud's psychological writings. But it is historically significant that Strachey was groomed, as translator, by both Freud and Jones in the early 1920s. Indeed, Jones had the task of translation in mind for Strachey when he first introduced him to Freud, in a letter of 7 May 1920. Jones wrote:

I write just today at the request of Mr James Strachey to ask if there is any hope of your taking him for analysis. He would prefer to start now rather than October if you have a vacancy. He is a man of 30, well educated and of a well-known literary family (I hope he may assist with translation of your works), I think a good fellow but weak and perhaps lacking in tenacity. He tells me he can spend £300 on fees, so doubts if he ought to pay two guineas a treatment if it were possible to pay less and go on for longer.[14]

By early 1921, Freud had enlisted Strachey into the ranks, as translator. In a letter of 7 February 1921, written in English, Freud reported to Jones that:

Strachey has finished the beaten child and will consult me on some points to-morrow. He is excellent but apt to fall into laziness if not admonished. He is ready to undertake another job which I proposed to him, to translate the 4 or 5 of my *Krankengeschichten* (Dora, Rattenmann, kl. Hans, Schreber and the Wolfmann (russian)), that would give a nice volume of our library, if you agree with the plan. It is true Brill pledged himself to do this work many years ago, but as he has not done it and is not likely to do it now I would have the nerve to discard him. In the circular I will say what my opinion of his case is.

Some years later, on 9 February 1924, Jones wrote: '[Strachey] is of course chiefly engrossed in his translation work, and makes no other contribution, e.g. to the work of the Society.'

Strachey continued to be involved in the major translation projects of the 1920s and 1930s, and would, typically, be Jones's and Freud's first choice. On 12 August 1924, Jones wrote: 'Strachey also, though terribly slow, has improved in his work so much that he now ranks as easily the best translator here or in America. . . .' On 2 June 1932, Jones reported that, of all the English translators, Strachey had proved to be 'most successful' and that 'all his work is very thorough and reliable and his judgement is remarkably balanced and of the greatest value'. Finally, when the issue of a new English translation of Freud's *Hemmung, Symptom und Angst* (1926) came up, Jones was hoping, as is clear in his letter to Freud of 27 June 1935, 'that we should be able to persuade Strachey to undertake this also. So by and by we shall recover the lost ground in providing a worthy translation of your work . . .'. Freud agreed. On 7 July 1935, he replied: 'Certainly, Strachey is the translator I would be most happy with'.

Thus Strachey underwent a kind of apprenticeship in the 1920s under the watchful eye of both Freud and Jones, who came to agree on Strachey's competence as a translator well before the appearance of the Standard Edition in 24 volumes that we know today.

The personal bond

Freud and Jones, however, did not always agree on all the issues to do with *die Sache*, the cause of psychoanalysis. To be sure, there were numerous disagreements between the two throughout the course of the Jones–Freud era. In the beginning they differed on the theory of anxiety, and, later, on telepathy, on Lamarckian theory, on the death instinct, on child analysis, on the theory of female sexuality, and on the question of lay analysis. Many of these issues come up frequently in the Freud/Jones correspondence. Any one of them could serve as a theme for a lengthy paper.

None the less, regardless of the disagreements, there was a deep bond of friendship between Jones and Freud, not always acknowledged by scholars and other commentators. Consider the evidence of Freud's affection in this passage taken from the Freud/Jones correspondence. On 20 November 1926 Freud wrote:

Dear Jones

Is it already really 20 years that you have been with the cause? The cause has really become wholly your own, because you succeeded in getting everything that was to be had from it: a society, a journal and an institute. What you have meant to it in return, we may leave to the historians to ascertain. That you can still become more is my firm expectation, once the many business matters which you still complain of now have been relieved by a smooth routine. Then you will find the leisure, on the basis of the experience you have gathered, to do more for co-workers and the new generation.

We may both be well satisfied with each other. I myself have the impression that you sometimes overestimate the importance of the dissensions [*die Unstimmigkeiten*] that existed even between us. It is indeed difficult to reach the point where people satisfy each other completely, one misses something in every person, and finds something to criticize. You yourself emphasized that certain differences also existed between Abraham and myself–, indeed the same applies to wife and children, but only those eulogizing the dead deny such traces of reality, the living may assert that such deviations from the ideal image do not spoil for them the enjoyment of reality.

You will be surprised to have the motive revealed that impedes my correspondence with you. It is a classic example of petty restrictions which our nature is subjected to. Namely, it is very difficult for me to write German in Latin script, as I am doing today. All sense of ease – with larger issues one says inspiration – leaves me immediately. But you have frequently let me know that you cannot read Gothic script, so that only two avenues of communication are left to me, both of which impinge on intimacy, either to dictate a typed letter to Anna or to use my awkward English.–...

Cordially
Your
FREUD

In many ways Freud reciprocated the affection that Jones showed in his own letters. And Jones's ultimate commitment to Freud stood fast. Of all Freud's colleagues Jones was in the end the most resolute supporter. Their personal and intellectual relationship was sustained from the first international psychoanalytical meeting in Salzburg in 1908 until Freud's death in 1939. Throughout this period, the intimacy between Jones and Freud was exceeded only a few times, perhaps, in Freud's relations with other adherents. Significantly, moreover, Jones's allegiance outlasted all the others. His last letter to Freud, who was by then living at 20 Maresfield Gardens, London, is particularly revealing. On 3 September 1939, Jones wrote:

Dear Professor,

This critical moment seems an appropriate one for me to express once more my personal devotion to you, my gratitude for all you have brought into my life and my intense sympathy for the suffering you are enduring. When England last fought Germany, twenty-five years ago, we were on opposite sides of the line, but even then we found a way to communicate our friendship to each other. Now we are near to each other and united in our military sympathies. No one can say if we shall see the end of this war, but in any case it has been a very interesting life and we have both made a contribution to human existence – even if in very different measure.

With my warmest and dearest regards

Yours always affectionately

ERNEST JONES

Jones's role in helping Freud, Anna Freud, and a host of other European analysts escape to London out of the clutches of the 'master thief H'[15] was clear evidence of his commitment to Freud and the science of psychoanalysis. This commitment, and the human and intellectual bonds that existed between Freud and Jones, form the historical basis for the events that led to Freud's arrival in London.

Notes

For permission to quote passages from the Freud / Jones correspondence, I would like especially to thank Mervyn Jones of London; Pearl King, Honorary Archivist of the British Psycho-Analytical Society, London; and Mark Paterson, Executive Director, Sigmund Freud Copyrights Ltd., Wivenhoe, Essex, England. I also thank the Social Sciences and Humanities Research Council of Canada for financial assistance which enabled me to undertake the research for this paper.

[1] E. Jones, *The Life and Work of Sigmund Freud*, 3 vols. (New York 1953–7), *Sigmund Freud: Life and Work*, 3 vols. (London 1953–7) and *The Life and Work of Sigmund Freud*, ed. and abridged Lionel Trilling and Stephen Marcus (London 1961).

[2] *The Freud / Jones Correspondence, 1908–1939* is to be published under the present author's editorship, by Harvard University Press, Cambridge, Mass.

[3] M. Schur, *Freud, Living and Dying* (London 1972); V. Brome, *Ernest Jones: Freud's Alter Ego* (New York and London 1983); R.W. Clark, *Freud: The Man and the Cause* (London and New York 1980).

[4] R. Steiner, 'Some Thoughts about Tradition and Change Arising from an Examination of the British Psychoanalytical Society's Controversial Discussions (1943–1944)', *Int'l Rev Psych*, XII (1985), 27–71.

[5] P. Grosskurth, *Melanie Klein: Her World and Her Work* (Toronto 1986).

[6] E. Jones: *Free Associations: Memories of a Psycho-Analyst* (London and New York 1959); 'Reminiscent Notes on the Early History of Psycho-Analysis in English-Speaking Countries', *Int'l Jn Psych*, XXVI (1945), 8–10; 'The Early History of Psycho-Analysis', *Journal of Mental Science*, C (1954), 198–210; and Richard I. Evans, *Conversations with Carl Jung and Reactions from Ernest Jones*, (Princeton, N.J., Toronto, London, New York 1964), 117–41.

[7] *The Freud / Jung Letters*, ed. William McGuire, trans. Ralph Manheim and R.F.C. Hull (Princeton, N.J., 1974), 145, 164, 165, 206, 208, 211, 212, 228.

[8] Unless otherwise noted, quotations from the Freud / Jones correspondence (1908–39) are from the collection located at Sigmund Freud Copyrights Ltd., Wivenhoe, Essex,

England. Where applicable, English translations of Freud's letters in German are by Frauke Voss and the author.

[9] E. Jones: 'On the Nightmare', *American Journal of Insanity*, LXVI (1910), 383–417; 'The Oedipus-Complex as an Explanation of Hamlet's Mystery: a Study in Motive', *American Jn of Psychology*, XXI (1910), 72–113.

[10] Personal communication to the author from Sanford Gifford, MD, Peter Bent Brigham Hospital, Boston, Mass., 22 Apr 1985.

[11] S. Ferenczi to E. Jones, 2 Nov 1913, Archives of the British Psycho-Analytical Society, London.

[12] S. Freud, *Collected Papers*, trans. under the supervision of Joan Riviere, 4 vols. (London 1924–5).

[13] These two letters of 1920 from Jones to Freud are contained in the Archives of the British Psycho-Analytical Society, London.

[14] Letter in the Archives, British Psycho-Analytical Society, London.

[15] Freud to E. Jones, 16 June 1934.

8

Early Divergences between the Psycho-Analytical Societies in London and Vienna

Pearl King

Freud's psychoanalytical writings were first reported on in Britain in 1893 by F.W.H. Myers, at a general meeting of the Society for Psychical Research, and the report was published in the proceedings of that Society. This was the first time that Freud's psychoanalytical ideas had been available in English.[1] It is interesting to note that it was while attending meetings of this body that both Joan Riviere and James Strachey came across psychoanalysis. A society concerned with exploring the unknown was a good stepping-stone to psychoanalysis. Freud himself eventually became an honorary member of it.

In 1898 Mitchell Clarke reviewed *Studies in Hysteria* by Breuer and Freud (1895) in *Brain*, a neurological journal, and in 1903 this review was seen by Wilfred Trotter, Ernest Jones's brother-in-law, who brought it to the attention of Jones. Both men were so intrigued with the ideas it contained that they decided to learn German in order to be able to read other papers by Freud in the original German.

Prior to this, Jones had qualified in medicine, with several gold medals, in 1900, and was working extremely hard building the foundations of what promised to be a very successful conventional career as a consultant physician and neurologist, when he first became interested in problems of psychopathology. Introduced to Freud's work, he began to put into practice some of Freud's ideas and used the new therapy on his first psychoanalytic patient from 1905 to 1906.[2]

In 1907 Jones met Jung in Amsterdam, and was invited to the Burghölzli Hospital where Jung worked. The following year, 1908, Jones took an active part in the first International Psycho-Analytical Congress held in Salzburg. He read a paper on 'Rationalisation in Everyday Life', introducing a new concept and giving a new meaning to the word.[3] It was here that he met Freud for the first time and thus began a personal and scientific association that was to last until Freud's death in 1939.

In London, Jones was finding the lot of the pioneer in psychoanalysis no less beset with trouble than Freud had done in Vienna. His difficulties were no doubt an important reason for his accepting in 1908 a post in Toronto, where he remained based until 1913. During this period he made numerous visits to Europe, which culminated in a period of personal analysis with Ferenczi. He was also extremely active in promoting the spread of psychoanalytic knowledge in Canada and the United States, where he helped to found the American Psychoanalytic Association in 1911. The first book on psychoanalysis to be published in English was the first edition of his *Papers on Psychoanalysis* (1912).

Returning to London in 1913, Jones found a few colleagues already interested in psychoanalysis. The most promising practitioner of analysis was David Eder, who had given the first account in England of analytic work, to an English professional audience. Very soon after Jones's return to London, he called together 15 colleagues at his house (only 4 of whom were actually engaged in the practice of analysis) and founded the London Psycho-Analytical Society on 30 October 1913, with himself as president and Eder as secretary. The 1914–18 War was a period of some scientific controversy amongst the.members of the recently formed London Society, concerning the role of infantile sexuality in the genesis of neurosis and the function of symbolism. These were the same differences that had developed between Freud and Jung before the war and had resulted in the latter's resignation from the International Psycho-Analytical Association.[4] The efforts of Jones to clarify the issues and restore unity in the group proved a failure and it was agreed in 1919 that the London Psycho-Analytical Society should be dissolved.

On 20 February 1919, the British Psycho-Analytical Society was formed and it was agreed that caution should be exercised in the selection of new members to ensure that they were genuinely interested in psychoanalysis. It became the seventh society to be affiliated to the International Psycho-Analytical Association.

The Society decided to start a library and to take steps to translate psychoanalytic writings into English. Joan Riviere, James and Alix Strachey worked with Jones on these tasks, and together they formed the Glossary Committee to work out how to translate Freud's concepts from German into English. In 1920 the *International Journal of Psycho-Analysis* was founded.

Meanwhile, steps were being taken to establish a setting within which the new British Society could function and develop. The Institute of Psycho-Analysis was set up in 1924, largely through the initiative and energy of John Rickman, to deal with financial and other matters concerning book publication, and especially to facilitate the publication of books in the International Psycho-Analytical Library

series with the Hogarth Press, who in 1924 thus became joint publishers
with the Institute.

In 1926, thanks to a very generous gift from Mr Prynce Hopkins, an
American benefactor, it proved possible to follow the example of the
Berlin Society and to establish a clinic for the benefit of 'needy patients'.
Premises were obtained at 96 Gloucester Place, and this house
continued as the headquarters of the British Psycho-Analytical Society,
the Institute of Psycho-Analysis and the London Clinic of Psycho-
Analysis until 1951, when the Institute moved to its present beautiful
building in New Cavendish Street, London.[5]

The selection and training of analysts

Let us consider for a moment what professional life was like for
psychoanalysts after the First World War. There was no organized
training, but it had been agreed in 1918 at the Budapest Congress that
all potential analysts should have some personal experience of psychoanalysis. Consequently, European and American analysts travelled to
Vienna, Berlin and Budapest to have some personal analysis for shorter
or longer periods.

During the 1920s several members of the British Society went to
Vienna for analysis with Freud; these included John Rickman, Joan
Riviere, James and Alix Strachey. Sylvia Payne, Barbara Low and Ella
Sharpe went to Berlin for analysis with Hans Sachs, while James and
Edward Glover, and later Alix Strachey, went to Abraham, who had
also been analysing Melanie Klein. In Budapest, Ferenczi had already
analysed Ernest Jones and Melanie Klein, and in the 1920s he also
analysed John Rickman and David Eder.

From this it will be apparent that the group of analysts who were at
the core of the emerging British Psycho-Analytical Society had had
personal experience of analysis in Vienna, Berlin and Budapest, and that
the approach to psychoanalysis current in those three Societies would
help to form the soil from which the British approach to psychoanalysis
developed.

In 1925, at the Bad Homburg Congress in Germany, the first conference of delegates from branch societies took place, to discuss the
whole problem of psychoanalytical training and the plan to form an
international training organization 'in order that there might be a
uniform system of psychoanalytical instruction in different countries'.

Max Eitingon's opening speech is an historical gem, and formulated
what are still the main principles underlying our current approach to
training, i.e. institutional responsibility for selection, training and qualification of candidates, supervised analyses of patients and theoretical
courses.[6] At the business meeting which followed, it was agreed that
each branch society should elect a training committee of not more than

7 members. Accordingly, in March 1926, the British Society elected its first training committee and they drew up draft suggestions for the selection and training of candidates for submission to the International Training Commission.[7]

By the first meeting of the International Training Commission, at Innsbruck in 1927, Eitingon could report that training in the three large Societies (Berlin, London and Vienna) was being caried out along similar lines, and that the special conditions of each country, whether they arose from cultural pressures or legal requirements, had not militated 'against the requirements arising out of the internal structures of our scientific theory and our practical work...'. He said that a training begun in London could be continued in Vienna and finished in Berlin, as the three centres were working in such a similar way.[8]

The question of the importance of medical qualifications for the practice of psychoanalysis was discussed at length both locally and at international meetings. Most of the European societies supported Freud's point of view on this question and were in favour of training lay as well as medically trained practitioners, in contrast to the point of view adopted by the American analysts, who would accept only medically trained candidates.

Divergences

However, while there was much similarity between the attitudes to the procedures and principles of training adopted by the two Societies, there were certain differences of emphasis or theoretical concern, in the sphere of psychoanalytical theory, which emanated originally from the particular interests of Ernest Jones from 1910 onwards. In his early contributions, he emphasized the importance of pre-genital and innate determinants over and above the influence of external or environmental stress, and their vital role in determining beliefs and perceptions of reality. Of particular importance was the role he ascribed to hate and aggression, and the influence of fear in relation to anxiety. Jones had not put these ideas forward as controversial issues, but as a consolidation of Freud's early formulations.[9]

By 1925 there were 54 members and associate members of the Society, and they came from a number of professional disciplines. Among the members were psychiatrists, specialists in neurology, general practitioners, teachers and university lecturers in psychology, English, logic and anthropology, university graduates, and those with no university degrees whom one could call 'gentleman (or gentlewoman) scholars'. As a group of professional colleagues they were probably not very different from the members of the Vienna Society.[10] There was one difference, however: while the majority of the members of the Vienna Society had had a Jewish background, at that period only two members of the British Society, Barbara Low and David Eder, were Jewish. The rest came from Scottish, English or Welsh Christian backgrounds, with a strong bias towards agnosticism and humanism.

These early psychoanalysts were fascinated and excited by the task of applying psychoanalytic ideas and understanding to the various problems and social issues with which they were concerned, either as citizens or in their professional capacity. The papers read at scientific meetings at this time covered a wide selection of topics applying Freud's ideas to child development, education, anthropology, child guidance, politics, history, literature and art, as well as to the treatment of neurotic and psychotic patients.

In addition to the task of translating the contributions of Freud and his continental colleagues, and applying them to their work with patients, the British members were developing their own psychoanalytic interests. These interests included the role of anxiety, hostility and aggression, the theory of symbolism, character problems, the origin and structure of the super-ego, problems of psychoanalytic technique, a psychoanalytic theory of psychoses, and the psychoanalysis of children.

The arrival of Melanie Klein

In 1925, encouraged by Alix Strachey, Melanie Klein wrote to ask if she could give some lectures on Child Analysis to interested members of the British Society, to whom Nina Searl and Sylvia Payne had read papers on the subject the previous year. These lectures took place in July 1925. In 1926, following the death of Abraham, Melanie Klein moved to London, and she was elected a member of the British Society in 1927. In view of their areas of common interest, it is not difficult to understand why the British Society was an appropriate one to give hospitality to her and her many ideas. Her arrival gave encouragement to analysts who were interested in exploring further the insights that could be gained from a study of the psychology and psychopathology of children and infants.

Up to the end of 1934 Melanie Klein had given 11 papers or short contributions before the British Society; these were received with interest and approval, if not always agreement. Members used her ideas if they were felt to be helpful, but failure to use them did not create animosity, nor was it taken as evidence of disloyalty to her, as it sometimes was in later years when she felt more under attack.

From 1929 onwards, the British Society increasingly flourished, after Ernest Jones had obtained a 'certificate of respectability' from the British Medical Association. Analysts were still excited by psychoanalysis and the discoveries that they were enabled to make with the help of Freud's work. Melanie Klein's contributions were looked on as further explorations of Freud's discoveries, rather than as new or alien ideas incompatible with psychoanalysis.

Jones himself, however, did not always agree with Freud, and his experience in the international movement had taught him that the unity and close identity of the theoretical conclusions, technique and practice of the early analysts was no longer possible, if psychoanalysis was to remain a science and not to degenerate into a theology. He felt that the alternative to this was essentially influenced by the British empirical tradition, which he shared with many of the indigenous early members of the Society, who had grown up in the intellectual climate that fostered 'gentleman scholars'.

He expressed this tradition in his opening remarks when chairing the symposium on 'The Relation of Psychoanalytic Theory to Psychoanalytic Technique' at the Salzburg Congress in 1924. 'In all these fundamental matters, therefore, both of theory and practice, my plea would be essentially for moderation and balance, rejecting nothing that experience has shown to be useful, while ever expectant of further increases in our knowledge and power.'[11]

In 1935 Melanie Klein published a paper on the psychogenesis of manic-depressive states, in which she extended her theories to cover various aspects of psychotic illness and claimed to show that the super-ego is developed at a very much earlier age than was formulated by Freud.[12] Edward Glover, himself a psychiatrist, was particularly resentful that a mere non-medical psychoanalyst was putting forward theories about the genesis of psychosis, which he claimed was the preserve of psychiatrists. Meanwhile, criticism of some of the Kleinian developments began to be expressed in London, notably by Barbara Low and Melitta Schmideberg (Melanie Klein's daughter), as well as by Edward Glover. Her critics particularly objected to her use of phantasy, her interpretation of Freud's concept of the death instinct, the early dating of the development of the super-ego, and the concept of internal objects, with its descriptive overtone and its tendency to reification rather than conceptualization.

The Exchange Lectures

In 1934 Ernest Jones was again elected president of the IPA, and he became concerned at the divergences that seemed to be growing up between London and Vienna on a number of topics, partly, though not entirely, influenced by the contributions of Melanie Klein in the British Society. Jones felt that these divergences arose in part from the growing lack of personal contact between the analysts in Vienna and in London, and the fact that 'nowadays far more psychoanalysis is learnt from the spoken word than through the written word'. He complained that as the habit of reading had declined, so 'the habit of writing had taken on a more narcissistic bent'. He then commented that 'the new work and ideas in London have not yet, in our opinion, been adequately considered in Vienna'.[13]

In order to deal with this problem of the divergence of points of view, Jones and Paul Federn, vice-president of the Vienna Society, arranged a series of 'exchange lectures' during 1935–6, in the hope that these differences might be mutually understood, if not resolved.

Jones himself gave the first paper, on 'Early Female Sexuality', and he described these divergences as follows: 'the early development of sexuality, especially in the female, the genesis of the super-ego and its relation to the Oedipus complex, the technique of child analysis and the concept of the death instinct'. He strongly disagreed with the phallo-centric view of female development and the underestimation of the role of the mother in the development of the child. He quoted Freud as saying: 'Everything connected with this first mother attachment has in analysis seemed to me so elusive, lost in a past so dim and shadowy, so hard to resuscitate that it seemed as if it had undergone some special inexorable repression'. Jones pointed out that there was a need for more work on the earliest years of a girl's attachment to her mother, and that this was what Melanie Klein and other British child analysts were exploring. He went on to say that 'differences of opinion in respect to the later stages of development are mainly, and perhaps altogether, due to different assumptions concerning the earlier stage'. In concluding this paper, Jones wrote: 'I think the Viennese would reproach us with estimating the early phantasy life too highly at the expense of external reality, and we should answer that there is no danger of any analysts neglecting external reality, whereas it is always possible for them to underestimate Freud's doctrine of the importance of psychical reality'.[14]

The first return paper was given by Robert Waelder, on 'Problems of Ego Psychology' (I have never been able to discover a copy). He not only gave it to a scientific meeting; a small group also met to discuss the differences with him in more detail. The next paper was given by Joan Riviere on 'The Genesis of Psychical Conflicts in Early Infancy'. In this paper she attempts to formulate the earliest psychical develop-mental processes in the child, the oral-sadistic impulses and their attendant anxieties, and the fundamental defence mechanisms against them employed by the ego, with reference to the defensive functions of projection and introjection. She hoped that a study of the factors operating in the first two years of life would throw light on 'ego-development and the genetic origin of the super-ego, together with the relation of these to infantile sexuality and libido developement'. The paper is interesting not only for the point of view that was presented, but also for its bibliography, which included work by a wide cross-section of members of the British Society who were in accord with various aspects of the approach that Joan Riviere was discussing. The return paper was again given by Robert Waelder, on 'The Problem of the Genesis of Psychical Conflicts in Early Infancy', in which he carefully discusses the points raised in Joan Riviere's paper.[15]

It is doubtful how much clarification or mutual understanding was achieved during these exchange lectures. Other more serious matters claimed the attention of psychoanalysts, which were a greater threat to psychoanalysis than such divergences. These were connected with the rise of Hitler and anti-Semitism in Germany, and the possible threat to Austria and therefore to the Vienna Society.

After the Anschluss

On the Continent the dark clouds of fascism and anti-Semitism were gaining ground. When the Nazi Party took over in Germany, Jones went to Berlin offering to help any Jewish psychoanalysts there and inviting them to London. Paula Heimann and Kate Friedlander were two of these who accepted.

In 1938 the Nazis occupied Vienna, and the life and liberty of Freud and his family and of his colleagues were in very serious danger. In this emergency, analysts in many parts of the world, but perhaps especially in England and America, immediately came to the rescue. Much of the responsibility was taken by Ernest Jones, supported by the British Society and the Home Office of the British government. Jones at once went to Vienna and, with the help of Princess Marie Bonaparte and the American Ambassador in Paris, he and John Rickman negotiated successfully with the Nazis for Freud, his family, and many colleagues to be allowed to leave Austria.

The British Society at this time welcomed and gave its membership to many members of the Vienna Society. Some of them subsequently went on to the United States, but a number settled permanently in England to the great enrichment of psychoanalysis in London. These latter included not only Sigmund Freud himself, but also his daughter Anna Freud and other leading members of the Vienna Society. Those who had been training analysts in Vienna were given the same status in the British Society.[16] But the acceptance of these Viennese colleagues also meant that differences between the Viennese and some British analysts had to be contained within the British Society, and the question would inevitably arise as to what kind of psychoanalytic theory and technique was to be taught to students.[17]

In October 1938 Melanie Klein read her paper 'Mourning and Its Relation to Manic Depressive States', in which she expanded her concept of the depressive position, the destruction of good internal objects when the child's hatred and sadism are active, and the process of reparation through the operation of love and the libido, which she linked with the process of mourning.[18] As Melanie Klein spelt out her contributions in greater detail, they began to be perceived by some as an alternative to the formulations of classical psychoanalysis. Furthermore, her theory of early development and the genesis of psychic functioning seemed to have consequences for the technique of analysis which some members did not feel were consistent with psychoanalysis as they knew it. Up to this time there had been widespread acceptance in the British Society of the view that Klein had made most important and valuable contributions to child analysis and that these had extensive implications in the wider field of general theory and technique. It became obvious, however, that this view was not shared by most of the Viennese colleagues. One result of this was the consolidation of the forces supporting Klein and the emergence of what later came to be known as the Kleinian Group, with the uncommitted members forming the main part of the British Society.[19]

With the outbreak of war, many psychoanalysts became involved in war work and others, particularly those who supported Klein, were evacuated from London, so that the original members of the British Society were often outnumbered at scientific meetings by their colleagues from European societies. As Melanie Klein and her colleagues did not return to London until late in 1941, the Wednesday scientific meetings must have felt like a fortnightly reunion of the ex-Viennese members of the Society, and this would have been an important supportive experience for them as they tried to cope with the pain of being refugees.

As my task was to consider early divergences between the Psycho-Analytical Societies in London and Vienna, I will leave the story at this point, for it now became the task of the British Society to try to assimilate the differences that I have been discussing.

However, I would emphasize that unless psychoanalysis is regarded as a closed system, incapable of extension, correction or development, its practitioners are bound to be confronted with new observations, which cannot always be satisfactorily accounted for with the help of existing psychoanalytic theories, and new hypotheses will be put forward to account for them.

This will always pose the question: How are they to be assessed and when should they be added to the general body of psychoanalytic knowledge and passed on to students? The problem facing us as psychoanalysts in this country has been: How can we nurture psychoanalysis, both as a theory and a therapeutic tool, and yet encourage its development without losing contact with the basic principles from which it has grown?.[20]

Marjorie Brierley has written: 'No science can remain alive if it ceases to grow and if the theory of psychoanalysis does not continue to develop, psychoanalysts will degenerate into a stereotyped cult'. In his description of psychoanalysis as an empirical science Freud gives us some guidelines. He wrote: 'It keeps close to the facts in its field of study, seeks to solve the immediate problems of observation, gropes its way forward by the help of experience, is always incomplete and always ready to correct or modify its theories'.[21]

Notes

[1] Ernest Jones, 'Reminiscent Notes on the Early History of Psycho-Analysis in English-Speaking Countries', *Int'l Jn Psych*, xxvi (1946).

[2] E. Jones: *Free Associations* (London 1959).

[3] E. Jones, 'Rationalisation in Everyday Life', in *Papers on Psycho-Analysis*, 3rd edn. (London 1923).

[4] W.H. Gillespie, 'Ernest Jones: The Bonny Fighter', *Int'l Jn Psych*, lx (1979), Part 3.

[5] P.H.M. King, 'The Development of Psychoanalysis in Britain', unpublished paper (1986) based on the first in a new series of Introductory Lectures entitled 'Psychoanalysis in Britain Today', given at Mansfield House.

[6] Report of IPA Business Meeting (1925), *Int'l Jn Psych*, vii (1926).

[7] P.H.M. King, 'The Education of a Psycho-Analyst: The British Experience', in *La Formation du psychanalyste* (IPA Monograph no. 3), ed. Serge Lebovici and Albert J. Solnit (Paris 1982).

[8] M. Eitingon, 'Report of the International Training Commission', *Int'l Jn Psych*, ix (1928).

[9] P.H.M. King, 'The Contributions of Ernest Jones to the British Psycho-Analytical Society', *Int'l Jn Psych*, lx (1979).

[10] H. Leupold-Lowenthal, 'The Minutes of the Vienna Psycho-Analytic Society', *Sigmund Freud House Bulletin*, iv, no. 2 (1980).

[11] E. Jones, Introduction to the Congress Symposium on 'The Relation of Psycho-Analytic Theory to Psycho-Analytic Technique', *Int'l Jn Psych*, vi (1925).

[12] M. Klein, 'A Contribution to the Psychogenesis of Manic-Depressive States', *Int'l Jn Psych*, xvi (1935).

[13] E. Jones, 'The Future of Psycho-Analysis', *Int'l Jn Psych*, xvii (1936).

[14] E. Jones, 'Early Female Sexuality', *Int'l Jn Psych*, xvi (1935), and in *Papers on Psycho-Analysis*, 4th and 5th edns. (London 1935).

[15] J. Riviere, 'The Genesis of Psychical Conflicts in Early Infancy', *Int'l Jn Psych*, xvii (1936); R. Waelder, 'The Problem of the Genesis of Psychical Conflicts in Early Infancy', *Int'l Jn Psych*, xviii (1937).

[16] A. Freud, 'Personal Memories of Ernest Jones', *Int'l Jn Psych*, lx (1979).

[17] P.H.M. King, 'Identity Crises: Splits and Compromise—Adaptive or Maladaptive', in *The Identity of a Psycho-Analyst* (IPA Monograph no. 2), ed. E.D. Joseph and D. Widlocher (New York 1978).

[18] M. Klein, 'Mourning and Its Relation to Manic-Depressive States', *Int'l Jn Psych*, xxi (1940).

[19] P.H.M. King, 'The Life and Work of Melanie Klein in the British Psycho-Analytical Society', *Int'l Jn Psych*, lxiv (1983), Part 3.

[20] P.H.M. King, 'Development of Psychoanalysis in Britain', unpub.

[21] M. Brierley, Introduction, *Trends in Psycho-Analysis* (London 1949); S. Freud, 'Two Encyclopaedia Articles'—(a) 'Psycho-Analysis' (1922: *SE* xviii).

9

Adrian Stokes

English Aesthetic Criticism under the Impact of Psychoanalysis

Stephen Bann

Adrian Stokes has a secure reputation as one of the most remarkable English writers on art of our century, and this reputation is underscored by the fact that he was perhaps the first critical writer of note in this country wholeheartedly and unreservedly to accept the relevance of psychoanalytic method to his work. The circumstances in which he developed his interest in psychoanalysis are already comparatively well known, thanks to the debt of friendship which Richard Wollheim has repaid in his essays and lectures on Stokes, and to the detailed work on the private papers by the young scholar Richard Read, which was condensed in the biographical appendix to the catalogue of the Stokes retrospective at the Serpentine Gallery (1982).[1] I do not propose to go over this ground again. But I should like just to sketch in the main features of Stokes's engagement with psychoanalysis, as a backdrop to my own brief investigation.

It seems clear that Stokes first discussed the theories of Freud with a friend at Rugby School, which he attended from 1916 to 1919. Over the next three years, which he spent as an undergraduate at Oxford reading Philosophy, Politics and Economics, he read translations of *The Interpretation of Dreams* and *The Psychopathology of Everyday Life* (these had of course been available in English since 1913 and 1914 respectively). But it was in the years 1929–30, after a period of intense depression, that he began to engage with Freud's ideas on a more serious level. About this time William Robson-Scott introduced him to Ernest Jones, and then to Melanie Klein, with whom in January 1930 he began seven years of analysis.

Even at this stage Stokes had begun to establish himself as a writer on art. Two early works of general cultural analysis, *The Thread of Ariadne* and *Sunrise in the West*, appeared in 1925 and 1926, and in 1929–30 he published a trio of essays on painters and sculptors of the Renaissance which were to herald the appearance of two grippingly original works. *The Quattro Cento: A Different Conception of the Italian Renaissance* (1932) and *Stones of Rimini* (1934). At roughly this period, Stokes's public commitment to the importance of psychoanalysis was demonstrated by his review of Klein's *The Psycho-Analysis of Children* in Eliot's *Criterion* (April 1933). But the overt references to Freud and Klein in his writings on art are delayed until the post-war period. It is as late as 1947, in a partly autobiographical work called *Inside Out* ('An Essay in the Psychology and Aesthetic Appeal of Space'), that he states unequivocally: 'From the heritage of Freud we may begin to understand the long and intricate history of our love and aggression, the springs of all our lives...'[2] In subsequent works, such as his *Michelangelo* (1955), the Kleinian basis of his aesthetic theory comes more and more to the fore, causing a rupture with his publisher, Fabers, and with influential art historians like Kenneth Clark. Stokes becomes more and more closely identified with psychoanalytic thinking, founding the Imago Group for discussion of topics of mutual interest in 1956, and conceiving one of his last major works, *Painting and the Inner World* (1963), as, in part, a dialogue with the psychoanalyst Donald Melzer.

I would not wish to challenge this overall account of Stokes's engagement with psychoanalysis. What I want to do, however, is to suggest another way of looking at the same story, which may have significant methodological implications for the study of the reception of Freud within this, or indeed any other, branch of English culture. For the version which I have just given is beyond doubt proleptic. It takes as its firm basis Stokes's unquestionable concern with applying Freudian and Kleinian concepts to the study of art and culture in the post-war period, and it detects in the earlier period, as early as Stokes's school days, signs of the interest that is eventually to mature. Yet Freud and Klein were demonstrably not the only points of reference in the young Stokes's world; perhaps their very significance to him was a function of other, more various cultural concerns.

It is obvious enough that from the mid-1920s, Stokes was intent on becoming a writer – and a rather specific sort of writer, who mingled elements of autobiography and art criticism in a heady blend of cultural and historical diagnosis. There had been writers like that in the past, and the clearest examples accessible to Stokes were the two Victorian sages and pioneers of aesthetic criticism, John Ruskin and Walter Pater. How are we to balance Stokes's reception of psychoanalysis against the vocation as an aesthetic critic that he appears to have conceived in the mid-1920s? This inevitably leads to a further, more testing issue. It is altogether too easy to represent Freud as an alien import to an English culture that had previously been hermetically sealed against infection. But Freud, as we know, read and valued Pater.[3] It is not too fanciful to imagine that the English aesthetic critics were in some sense working a furrow parallel to Freud's, and in this case Stokes would have found it only natural to step from one to the other.

This at any rate is my contention here. So my discussion of the impact of psychoanalysis will be confined wholly to the inter-war period, when Stokes's concern with the method was rarely made explicit in his writings, and it will attempt to keep in focus the central question: What does psychoanalysis offer to a critic who is also a writer, and a very special sort of writer?

The debt to Ruskin and Pater

The first point that I would make in trying to answer this question may seem to be a perverse one. I have recently had the opportunity to look, not only at the two published books of 1925–6, but also at some of the unpublished notebooks dating from Stokes's undergraduate days up to the period of the Second World War. What is very striking, especially for the period of the 1920s, is the absence in these sources of any manifest reference to Freud. *Sunrise in the West* (1926) places itself under the aegis of Cocteau's *Return to Order* (English translation published in the same year), and ranges remarkably widely over the areas of philosophy, culture, religion and the visual arts; it envisages the 'present position as one stage before the apotheosis of Western Civilization' and in so doing, picks a quarrel with Ruskin and declares a covert alliance with Pater. 'Nothing less than the pioneer waywardness of Ruskin, who subjugated his great sense of beauty *qua* beauty to serve in the harness of an inspired fanaticism, could induce a man as sensitive to art to deny the loveliness of the Loggia del Capitano which stands opposite the famous Basilica Palladiano in the piazza of Vicenza.' So writes the young Stokes, declaring his own attachment to the early Renaissance architecture which Ruskin vituperated. The alliance with Pater is apparent, I would suggest, in Stokes's evident choice of impassioned critical prose as his medium, since Pater, pre-eminently, had established critical prose, and 'aesthetic criticism', as the medium most appropriate for the representation of the bewildering complexity of the modern world. Stokes writes: 'History has been the search of poetry for her medium. It is prose.'[4] Nothing could express the essence of Pater more succinctly — one remembers that he chided the young Oscar Wilde with the remark: 'Why do you always write poetry.... Prose is so much more difficult'.[5]

The evidence of Stokes's notebooks seems to confirm these two leitmotivs: absence of Freud, inconvenient presence of Ruskin. It is worth noting that on occasions Stokes writes down lists of recently published or earlier books, presumably to introduce method into his reading. A list evidently compiled in 1928 ranges from novels like Huxley's *Point Counter Point* and Woolf's *Orlando*, to books on art like

Kenneth Clark's *Gothic Revival* and Sisley Huddleston's *Paris*, and works of history and cultural diagnosis like Mrs Nelson-Scott's *The Future of an Illusion* and *The Outline of Jewish History*.[6] For what it is worth, I find no mention of the translation of *The Ego and the Id*, published by the Woolfs in 1927.

It is scarcely very challenging to conclude that Stokes was dealing in the ideas that were current at the time, and finding his own voice within the echo chamber of early twentieth-century thought. His preoccupation with ecstasy, and with the contrasted values of hedonism and holiness, almost certainly relates to Pater's lengthy and exquisite oscillation between the beauty of religion and the religion of beauty, just as his references to St. Francis recall the honorary modernity conferred on the saint by publicists like Havelock Ellis. Stokes has certainly witnessed the Messianic streaking of D.H. Lawrence, but he is bold enough to claim, in opposition to Lawrence's cult of spontaneity, that 'Only the sophisticated can be truly free'.[7]

The presence of Freud in this crowded assembly is perhaps perceptible, but only when Stokes strikes the high points of his impassioned meditation. In an undergraduate essay from the notebooks, entitled 'A Plea for a New Method', we read the striking phrase: 'It is as if the individual was born on the stage in the middle of a play'.[8] From the notebook dated '1930 and before', we can take the following, unorthodox but fascinating passage:

What is desire? The brooding of the obsessed intelligence, the intelligence brooding upon smell and taste and shape. Desire does not come and go for consciousness. It leaps to the mind when eyes repudiate the clutch of sleep, or else, day light trickles upon dream, not some abstract dream, but on a still nearer vision of the near.

The object of desire is close, beneath a robe, behind a window. Oh that we did not see the distant! Then the close would not plague us. We should just take it if we could.[9]

I am taking it for granted that Stokes's affiliation to Freud, at this early stage, is not something declared by acknowledgements, quotations or adoption of Freudian terms, but by something quite different. One might say that Stokes is closest to Freud, and to the insights of psychoanalysis, when he is most obviously a writer – when he is most consciously using the resources of imaginative prose. And this obliges us to take into account a certain deep continuity in his long career. In 1926, in *Sunrise in the West*, he is already meditating profoundly on the work of Giorgione, whose Castelfranco altarpiece is chosen as the frontispiece to the book. In 1930, again, he confronts the mystery of Giorgione's work in an essay for the *Criterion*, and in 1945, finally, he returns to the *Tempesta*, doubling his commentary with a long section on fantasy whose Freudian basis is unmistakable. In a sense, Stokes's theme has not changed, and the specifically literary task of giving expression to it has not been made any easier by the adoption of the Freudian backdrop. In a sense, also, the passages in *Sunrise in the West* are not the beginning of the affair. Pater, in the 'School of Giorgione', and Ruskin, in 'The Two Boyhoods', had devoted some of their most eloquent and typical pages to the exposition of that painter's art.[10] We have the evidence of Stokes's 1925 diary for the fact that Ruskin was an omnipresent force for the young visitor to Venice. 'I think Ruskin must have been an eunuch although a great man,' he writes on 9 May 1925. 'He lashes me daily, hurls at me Stones of Venice.'[11] Well, the strength of that engagement is also visible, over a long term, in the character of the writing, and in the particular kind of biographical determination which Stokes gives to his aesthetic criticism.

Reviewing childhood

I want finally to demonstrate this point by making one or two detailed observations on the textual level, since this is ultimately the only way of validating what I have to say. Ruskin's essay 'The Two Boyhoods', which contrasts Giorgione's Venice with the London in which Turner and, by extension, Ruskin himself grew up, is a vivid, almost painful juxtaposition of a truly golden vista of late medieval Venice with the degraded aspect of the modern English city. Some commentators claim that Ruskin deliberately dated the Fall of Venice, from its medieval state of grace, to a year anticipating by exactly three centuries his own conception. However convincing this may be, the stark contrast of Utopia and Dystopia, of blissful boyhood and boyhood in the degraded modern environment, seems to be overdetermined by the circumstances of Ruskin's own life. There is no mediation, just as there was no possibility for Ruskin himself to draw upon the psychic resources accumulated in childhood to resolve the aggravated conflicts of adult life. In the case of Stokes, the entry into adult life also produces a psychological crisis, but it is a crisis resolved not only (I would suggest) through the analysis by Melanie Klein, but also through Stokes's capacity to re-configure his family romance through the terms and symbols of his writings.

In the notebook dating from Stokes's undergraduate days, there is an amusing little story called 'The Barrel Organ', which deals with a flight of fantasy during a boring lecture in a college hall. 'I am back again in my nursery amongst my toys', writes the narrator, and concludes with a speculation about the sound of the barrel-organ which originally distracted him:

For me the barrel-organ can paint the gentle world of childhood. Who knows? Perhaps 20 years hence, I will look back with seemingly disillusioned eyes on the golden times of today and think how sweet and happy they really were. Some melody will recall a host of memories – perhaps a barrel-organ will paint the petty struggles of this very day – the Lecturer goes droning on.[12]

Twenty years later, Stokes does indeed look back. His autobiographical essay, *Inside Out*, begins with the words: 'In the nursery, that is where to find the themes of human nature: the rest is "working-out", though it be also the real music'. Stokes has reaffirmed the importance of childhood, but he has turned on its head the nostalgic view represented by the juvenile essay. The point of *Inside Out* is to dramatize the opposition between the hostile, unresponsive landscape of Hyde Park – close by his childhood home in Bayswater – and the overwhelming experience of his introduction to Italy. In the process, certain details common to the two pieces of writing quite change their significance: the early essay refers warmly enough to 'those funny old beggars [in the Park] (Parkees, we used to call them)'. The later Stokes describes these beings as 'objects of apprehension', and even mentions having been once 'seized by a pack of parkees'. I am not concerned to dispute the superior truth of one of these two accounts, simply to say that the second – which is of course infinitely more sophisticated and interesting – obeys a structural imperative: the scene in Hyde Park must be dystopian so that the journey to Italy can be 'the approach to the counter-landscape, to the rested mother, to love and life'.[13] For Ruskin, there is no mediation between London and Italy. For Stokes, this mediation does take place. It takes place in the form of a journey which is mythologized and transmuted into a kind of second birth.

But I want to go further and be more specific than this. For me, the comparison between Ruskin and Freud brings out one remarkable feature. Ruskin, I suggest, experienced and expressed with an almost pathological intensity the symbolic richness of language which Freud was to analyse methodically in terms of the mechanisms of condensation, displacement and overdetermination. We find Ruskin protesting in a footnote to *The Queen of the Air* (1845): 'I am compelled, for clearness' sake, to mark only one meaning at a time. Athena's helmet is sometimes a mask – sometimes a sign of anger – sometimes of the highest light of aether: but I cannot speak of all this at once.' Here, and also in a neighbouring passage on the etymology of the word 'purple', which he describes as 'a liquid prism, and stream of opal', Ruskin both attests and bridles against the simultaneous presence of multiple meanings, which a mere linear elucidation can only disfigure and distort.[14] Now if Freud places the elucidation of multiple meaning on a new footing, endowing its processes with an overall architecture and design, we might expect those who have learned from him to be at the same time more self-conscious and more relaxed about the phenomenon. We might expect them to use it, not as an index of psychological stress, but as a sign of self-assurance. I will conclude by suggesting one particular instance where Stokes does this.

Writing on Giorgione

Back in that undergraduate notebook of 1922, where childhood is conventionally presented as a golden age, the experience of listening to the academic lecture is also conveyed in a conventional phrase: 'utter boredom'.[15] By 1930, Stokes is a more conscious stylist, and his use of the same adjective occurs within a succession of carefully selected phrases, all contributing to the evocation of Giorgione's effect of 'lassitude': 'Quiet observation had a supreme, a lyrical content. The only worthy discipline in such quiet commands utter relaxation, the discipline of precise images. Material will be warm colour, non-intense.'[16] Fourteen years later, in his book *Venice*, Stokes comes back once again to Giorgione, and this time it is with a specific picture, the *Tempesta*, in mind. Of the 'lack of tension' expressed there, Stokes has this to say:

Action of the landscape balances suspense of the figures, a balance to the effect of utter parity in their diversity, dependent as well, therefore, upon the reversed links; for instance, suspense from the flash of lightning (we await the thunder and the storm) and action by one of the figures in the very recent past. The woman has obviously bathed in the stream and is not yet altogether dry. She suckles the infant, an action of primal importance, for the mother as for the onlooker, inducing a sense of calm and self-sufficiency.[17]

These two passages are rather different in their emphasis. The first attempts to epitomize the general effect of Giorgione's painting, rather as Pater tried to do in his concept of the 'Giorgionesque'. The second addresses itself to a specific painting, no doubt the most celebrated of all Giorgione's works, and seeks to evoke its special qualities. The first, moreover, seems to try to envisage the effect of the Giorgionesque from the point of view of the artist, participating in his creative intention ('Material will be warm colour, non-intense'). The second, by contrast, provides an easy access to the world of the painting through the intermediacy of one of its participants: that standing male figure to the left, the 'onlooker' who acquires 'a sense of calm and self-sufficiency', is also the relay to ourselves as 'onlookers', according to strict Albertian practice.[18]

Much has been written about the *Tempesta*, both before and after Stokes took it as his subject: yet one of the really illuminating discussions, going far beyond the sterile dispute over iconography, has been the article by the French psychoanalytic critic, Marcelin Pleynet, which interprets the painting as an 'utérus-paysage'—a landscape as womb or matrix, both producing and produced by the suckling

16. *La Tempesta*, the painting by Giorgione in the Accademia di Belle Arti, Venice.

mother.[19] If we place the clever, yet unwieldy notion of the 'utérus-paysage' beside Stokes's more discreet insistence on 'utter relaxation', 'utter parity in diversity', we begin to get a sense of the different levels on which Stokes's shaping of language and experience may be proceeding.

The suggestion that the word 'utter' may be overdetermined in this context will perhaps appear very far-fetched at the outset. But let us retrace, by a slightly different track, the steps which Stokes took to find in Italy 'the counter-landscape...the rested mother'. Richard Wollheim tells us that one of the new concepts which Stokes learned from the Oxford philosophy of his day was the principle of 'identity-in-difference'.[20] It becomes clear, however, that Stokes interpreted this principle in a highly personal way; surely it is being evoked in the following striking passage from *Sunrise in the West* when he describes an evening at Como, beside the lake?

The scene is beautiful, complete in itself, transmuting all else into a bad dream, but – but what? It may be absurd but you cannot *entirely* forget that impossible journey from Milan.... You know only too well since you took your seat on the piazza that, so far from there being common denominators, you could not experience horror at enormity if you were not also capable of realizing the peace of the lake. One emotion needs a greater fire than this to be exalted at the expense of another.... Common denominators only *seemed* possible when contrast was less insistent and when, however different experiences might be, they could be related to one spirit.[21]

Certainly this passage appears to have a deep psychological importance. If we recall Stokes's other remark about being 'born on the stage in the middle of a play', it seems almost as if the 'seat on the piazza' were a place from which to experience that 'second birth' which Italy has made possible. Yet the image will not hold. The aggravation of the journey forces itself in upon the idyll of the lakeside view; indeed it comes to seem strictly necessary to it. At this early stage, we might say, the configuration of good objects is still being invaded by bad objects. But much has happened when, twenty years later, Stokes returns in autobiography to a piazza beside a Swiss/Italian lake, and in particular, his writing on Giorgione has progressed from the early book and article to the lengthy treatment of the *Tempesta* in *Venice*. He records, in one of the fragments from 'Living in Ticino 1947–50':

As I walk under the arcade of Locarno's main square, I see in a clear and liquid shade a café table with a light-blue cloth that touches a stone pier. I think I would be entirely safe there: leaning against the pillar I would be able to partake utterly of every thought: I would be immobile, provided for, as in the womb yet out-of-doors: existence within and existence without would be thinly divided: in the blue tablecloth I would clutch the sky.[22]

It is hard to miss the point that this is a description written by a person who is conversant with the terms of psychoanalysis. But the salient point which I am emphasizing is that it is written by an aesthetic critic who has used his own experience of psychoanalysis to re-configure the memories of his own life through the sustained act of writing. This has entailed not an impoverishment of linguistic experiment through submission to the law of technical terms, but a fuller recognition of the different registers on which language is capable of working – poetically, simultaneously. That use of the adverb 'utterly' is a small point of style, but against the instances already shown, and as a prelude to that description of being 'as in the womb, yet out-of-doors', it doubles its meaning with another layer of implication. It is an index (and certainly no more than an index) of the way in which Stokes's texts repay the closest investigation.

At the very end of *Venice* (the work which gains particular plangency from the fact that Stokes had to write it in separation from his beloved Italy, during the Second World War) there is a strong affirmation of his faith in the reparative properties of art. 'The external world is the sounding board of the emotions. That is self-evident: nevertheless, in contemplating the eternal poetry of Giorgione's *Tempesta*, it has seemed a discovery.' From the notebooks, it becomes apparent that Stokes initially wrote 'perennial poetry', and later changed it to 'eternal'.[23] Perhaps there is a reason why.

Notes

Extracts from the unpublished notebooks of Adrian Stokes are quoted by permission of Ann Stokes Angus. I am most grateful to her for giving this permission, and to Philip Stokes for making the material available to me.

[1] See in particular Richard Wollheim, 'Adrian Stokes: Critic, Painter, Poet', republished in 'Adrian Stokes 1902–1972', special supplement of *PN Review*, no. 15 (vol. VII, no. 1), 1980; also in the same number, Richard Read, 'Freudian Psychology and the Early Work of Adrian Stokes'; and *Adrian Stokes – A Retrospective*, catalogue of the exhibition held at the Serpentine Gallery, London, June–July 1982 (London: Arts Council of Great Britain, 1982).

[2] A. Stokes, *Critical Writings*, ed. Lawrence Gowing, 3 vols. (London 1978), II. 165.

[3] Ernest Jones records that when Freud was working on his Leonardo essay, Jones sent him the famous passage dealing with the Mona Lisa. Freud replied: 'Many thanks for the page from Pater; I knew it and had quoted some lines out of the fine passage' (Jones, II. 389).

[4] A. Stokes, *Sunrise in the West – A Modern Interpretation of Past and Present* (London 1926), x, 100, 111.

[5] Oscar Wilde, review of 'Mr Pater's *Appreciations*', *Speaker*, 22 Mar 1890, reprinted in *Critics of the 'Nineties*, ed. Derek Stanford (London 1970), 82.

[6] Notebook, entitled '1930 and before' on title-page, unpaginated. In all, about 25 contemporary titles are listed, together with roughly the same number of more varied sources which are more directly concerned with Stokes's studies of the early Renaissance.

[7] A. Stokes, *Sunrise in the West*, 135.

[8] Small notebook with marbled cover (man's profile with pipe on title-page). Stokes goes on to assert a 'position rather like Kant in our desires. Conscious of them and of things outside them but we cannot get outside them or judge them from the outside. We cannot conceive feeling or desire besides what we do, and we cannot help conforming to our desires.'

[9] Notebook, '1930 and before': the passage comes shortly after a 'Note from Burckhardt', in which Stokes discusses the 'idea of Fame', and a striking image of Sigismondo Malatesta 'Like a diver's helmet that pricks the water's surface as he rises from the deep, grows up and expands'. Richard Read has very aptly suggested that this image is a transformation of Pater's famous description of the Mona Lisa as a 'diver in deep seas' (*PN Review*, no. 15, 38).

[10] See W. Pater, 'The School of Giorgione', first published in 1877, and reprinted as part of *The Renaissance – Studies in Art and Poetry*, 3rd edn. (London 1888), and J. Ruskin, 'The Two Boyhoods', *Modern Painters*, vol. v (in *Works*, ed. E.T. Cook and A. Wedderburn, Library Edition [London 1903–12], vii). For a more detailed treatment of some of the connections among Ruskin, Pater and Stokes, see Stephen Bann: 'Writing on Giorgione', in *Literary Theory Today*, ed. M.A. Abbas and Tak-Wai Wong (Hong Kong 1981), and 'The Colour in the Text: Ruskin's Basket of Strawberries', in *The Ruskin Polygon – Essays on the Imagination of John Ruskin*, ed. John Dixon Hunt and Faith Holland (Manchester 1982). An excellent recent essay which stresses Stokes's kinship to Ruskin and Pater is David Carrier, 'The Presentness of Painting: Adrian Stokes as Aesthetician', in *Critical Inquiry*, no. 12 (Summer 1986).

[11] Grey linen-bound notebook ('A Diary' on title-page): entry for 9 May 1925.

[12] Small notebook with marbled cover, story entitled 'The Barrel Organ'.

[13] Stokes, *Critical Writings*, ii. 141, 144, 153.

[14] Ruskin, *Works*, xix. 307 n., 380.

[15] Small notebook with marbled cover.

[16] A. Stokes, 'Painting, Giorgione and Barbaro', *Criterion*, ix, no. 36 (April 1930), 491.

[17] Stokes, *Critical Writings*, ii. 129.

[18] See Leon Battista Alberti, *On Painting*, trans. John R. Spencer (New Haven, Conn., 1977), 78: 'whatever the painted persons do among themselves or with the beholder, all is pointed towards ornamenting or teaching the istoria'.

[19] See Marcelin Pleynet, 'Eloge de la peinture', in *Art Press*, no. 6 (Sept 1973): I have translated a substantial extract from this text in my essay in *Literary Theory Today*, 62–3. Pleynet suggests that 'we can also pass from the woman plus the child, whom she suckles while directing her look and her interest elsewhere, to the young man, whose look and attitude confirms the woman and denies the mother, and to the landscape as uterus – as productive base of the very possibility of the relationships which bind the ensemble together'.

[20] *PN Review*, no. 15, 31.

[21] Stokes, *Sunrise in the West*, 129.

[22] A. Stokes, *The Image in Form*, ed. Richard Wollheim (Harmondsworth 1972), 316.

[23] Notebook with green spine (title-page 'August 1938').

10

The Severance of Psychoanalysis from Its Cultural Matrix

Frederick Wyatt

Before addressing my subject, it may be helpful if I define my own place and my position in the field of psychoanalysis. I spent the years from 1938 to 1974 in the United States as a clinical psychologist and psychoanalyst, first as a belated apprentice with little scope and even less experience, struggling to get on with the business of living in a new country – and quite often having also to struggle to make a living. Then I tried to pursue an interrupted academic career, and at the same time to acquire the experience and the learning I sorely needed. For I did sense that those things alone can justify calling oneself a psychoanalyst. My own experience of America and the evolving fate of psychoanalysis there – its 'vicissitudes' – included, in the earlier years, being refused recognition as an analyst without medical dispensation: that is, I was considered a so-called lay analyst. These and other experiences ought to have protected me from too sanguine a view of the transformation of psychoanalysis in the States. Despite such experiences – or, maybe, just because of them – I still hope that I shall be able to present my observations with a reasonable degree of objectivity. At least I had the good fortune to meet a large number of analysts in exile and to get to know well some of the Viennese analysts who have made contributions to the history of psychoanalysis.

The limitations of my experience need to be clearly stated as well. They are those of location and job, and probably also of age, because I am younger by one analytic generation at least than nearly all the *émigré* analysts. I did practise psychotherapy and psychoanalysis almost all the time I was in America, but only on a part-time basis. In the main I was employed by a hospital or clinic, such as the one at the Harvard Medical School – or, more often, I was on the faculty of an academic institution. I wanted to have an academic career and gave a certain priority to it; that need not necessarily have been an obstacle to becoming an experienced analyst, but in some ways it was bound to present obstacles as well as opportunities, not only in the time it took, but also by way of the psychological fact of affiliation. As far as opportunities are concerned, a place in a university can provide impetus and stimulation in so many respects that some psychoanalysts at least should greatly profit from it.

I also clung to Academe because the status it provided gave me the backing for my clinical endeavours, which under existing conditions I needed. For the first twenty years of my stay in the States and for the reasons I have mentioned, I had only limited contact with psychoanalytic institutes, even though their major purpose should be to enable a communion of endeavour and help form an identity such as the practice of analysis demands. Thus for a long time academic institutions, like the University of Michigan, had to provide me with a sense of belonging, and they did a good job of it. These biographical data will, I hope, supply the frame of reference from which I shall approach my topic.

Effects of exile

What are the effects of emigration and exile?[1] It should not be difficult to list them, considering the world-wide abundance of experience of that predicament in our time. Let us start with general considerations, then apply them to the particular conditions of psychoanalysts and psychoanalysis. Anybody forced to move out of his country and into another one will have to worry, *first*, about his livelihood and that of his family, unless he has considerable means at his disposal, which is rarely the case. Much more often, he will have to work far below his competence and intellectual station. He may have to dig ditches or work in a scullery. Even if he should be lucky enough to make some use of his original competence, and be allowed to work in the field for which he has been trained, he will have to sustain many rebuffs and suffer discrimination. Some of these rebuffs will not be due to ill will, but to the difficulties of comprehension and the pitfalls of communication, which form the crux of the *émigré's* predicament. As a result, he will feel devalued and for a time, often without being clearly aware of it, may question his own worth. The consequence of all this, naturally, is an intense desire to get out of this marginal role, to accept the new situation as fully and as soon as possible, in order to become part of it.

Second, he will have to adapt as quickly as possible to the new country, its mores and its language. Language is the most obvious and often the most depressing barrier. If you don't understand what others are saying, you will feel isolated again and again. It will also make you insecure. Naturally, this will be especially hard for a person used to relying on being intelligent and well-spoken. If you can't express what you want to say, you will not count, and will feel dumb and boorish

Into the bargain. Barriers of language will reduce almost any person to helplessness and thus will unavoidably debase him in his own eyes. Deflated self-regard, again, leads to various forms of depression as much as to forced attempts at circumventing it, or of compensating for it in phantasy. A characteristic ploy is to turn disparagement back against the new environment, its values and ways, in a kind of smouldering discontent and anger barely restrained. With this goes the idealization of the former condition, now for ever lost through an inconceivable catastrophe. Other reactions are withdrawal and resignation, or an equally unrealistic elevation of the new country to the status of a Paradise Regained. At any rate, the alienation of speech leads to an alienation of self. Being an immigrant means a succession of blows to one's self-regard and, in a deeper sense, to one's fundamental identity. What I am is, after all, what I am worth, and if I cannot declare myself through speech and by what I can do, what then is left of me?

Third, the slow pace of adaptation to a new culture imposes more subtle trials. It is plainly difficult to understand a different way of life, especially when one is made to say and do things for which one has not been groomed. It takes a lot of trial and error to catch up on normal socialization. How long will it be until you can, as a matter of course, understand the cartoons in the *New Yorker* and the comic strips in the dailies? Any analyst coming from German-speaking Central Europe will remember the trials of doing therapy in the USA: how many cues he missed and how many innuendoes he didn't understand, referring as they did to stock figures of speech and convention, or the argot of special groups. I shall never forget the brash young man who confronted me disdainfully: 'What, doc, you don't know what "gay" means?' I couldn't tell him that the word had not occurred in any of the courses I had taken in English; nor did I tell him that I had fancied myself as speaking English quite fluently the day I set foot on his native ground.

Fourth, one has to settle with the past, a long and inevitably mournful task, to some extent akin to what Freud called the 'work [*Arbeit*] of mourning' (*SE* xiv. 244–5). The past may, in point of fact, have been as ambiguous as it had been for the analysts exiled from Austria and Germany. The Jewish members of this group had not been away long enough from the discrimination they had suffered in those countries for it to be dropped from memory. They could not afford to discard the anxious vigilance which had always dogged their steps. The political situation in Germany and Austria had been insecure for a long time.[2] In the case of psychoanalysis the powers of the state became increasingly hostile, and the economic situation continued to be labile, to say the least. The list of adversities could be extended. Nevertheless, the fact remained that the *émigré* analysts were as much tied to the conditions of their origin as we all are. It takes a long time to loosen these bonds, still longer to attach them to a new culture and country.

Adaptation to a new culture inevitably means giving up what, in essence, has been an integral part of the self. If conditions are friendly and the immigrant has reason to feel accepted by his new associates and by his environment he, in turn, will find his new environment fascinating and appealing, be it the sights of New York City, or the Golden Gate, or Puget Sound. He may find the ease and the informality of life enticing. Even so he will have to learn that, in order to adopt the new life and be adopted by it, he will have to abandon the old one, store away memories and with them the attachment to forms of gratification (including intellectual gratifications) to which he has been profoundly accustomed. The complex of cultural expectations – the books one reads, the reference to figures and forms of a common cultural tradition – will have to be dispensed with for the time being. All these, however, were parts of the self, meaning the self in a broader sense, *within a cultural matrix*.

Under the best of circumstances this will be a difficult and diminishing experience. In ordinary life, however, conditions are rarely optimal. If *we* are troubled, others will not bother to trouble with us. When we are beset by worries and setbacks, it will be difficult to give a show of ease and enthusiasm and thereby invite a reciprocal response. In short, the new culture is bound quite often to appear disappointing or unyielding or plain treacherous, as the many complaints about the unreliable friendliness of Americans have shown again and again. Timidity, restriction of language, the burden of multiple losses, all these make it difficult to accept the new and shut away the old. On the contrary, when things are difficult, it is tempting to hold on to the accustomed former culture or way of life, and set it against the new one which, as it is so complicated and seemingly murky and impenetrable, easily lends itself to being misunderstood and berated. Abraham Kardiner used to speak of the relatively large influx of German-speaking analysts as the 'Bei unsers' – he meant thereby to score off the people who always said disdainfully: 'Ja, bei uns war es anders' (freely translated: 'Well, where we come from, they did things differently').

Psychoanalysis in the United States

The complaint that psychoanalysis was 'corrupted' in the United States seems to me to derive from such experience, or more correctly, from the failure to understand the psychology of the *émigré*. Let us for the moment accept that psychoanalysis did indeed change there and that dominating traits of American culture – the terms used, of course, in the broad sense of contemporary anthropology – must have had their impact on it. I shall try to enumerate these. The expansion of psychoanalysis before the Second World War surely was determined by the insistent pragmatism of the pre- and also of the post-Depression years. It had to show its worth by demonstrating its effect. In other words, before it could be recognized as a universal instrument for understanding human conduct at large, applicable to an enormous variety of subjects besides and beyond the cure of souls, it would have to demonstrate that it was useful and could do something palpably practical about all kinds of bothersome symptoms. This demand did not yet touch on the principle, again of some relevance at present, that all psychoanalytic propositions do, after all, depend on being tested again and again under clinical conditions.

Psychoanalysis consequently came more strongly under the dominance of the medical profession, its aims and attitudes and, last but not least, its aspirations to maintain its economic status, its power and its prestige. We need to be reminded here that medicine in the States has for a long time held a special place. As sociologists have told us, the most desirable position in the community next to that of President of the United States has always been that of the medical doctor. That this circumstance had weighty consequences for psychoanalysis in the USA, there can be no doubt. It had much to do with moving psychoanalysis irresistibly into the orbit of medical thinking, of its social and its somatic–physiological orientation. It seems fair to say, then, that at least for some time the enormous intellectual scope of psychoanalysis was hemmed in, its potential for throwing light on the entire range of culture and conduct for a time curtailed. Having appointed itself the sole keeper of psychoanalysis, medicine was surely not an unequivocal blessing for its further development.

This situation changed quickly and noticeably with the influx of emigrant psychoanalysts from Germany and Austria, and a few years later also from France and England. It took some time for the immigrants to settle in, to learn the language, become familiar, explicitly and implicitly, with the mores of the country. But then they quickly advanced, and soon attained status in the psychoanalytic community. Think of Heinz Hartmann's position as director of research of the New York psychoanalytical group; or the enormous influence of the team consisting of Hartmann, Kris and Lowenstein; of Alexander in Chicago, of the Sterbas in Detroit, of Edith Buxbaum in Seattle, of Bernfeld in San Francisco; of Redl, Bettelheim, Erikson, Blos, Rapaport as psychoanalytical investigators and writers on topics which transcended the former, somewhat narrowly conceived ideas on theory and the psychoanalytic method.

The way in which these people and many others of similar importance helped to advance psychoanalysis in America will be a subject for historians of ideas (what in German is called, not inappropriately, 'Geistesgeschichte').[3] In general, one might say that their effect over the next thirty years was very strong. It would take a good-sized book to describe it in detail. The references for most papers published in psychoanalytic journals will show how extensive these contributions have been, and as far as I can see, the effect has almost universally been productive and beneficial.

To take one instance, American psychoanalysts for two or three decades came under the influence of psychoanalytic ego psychology, especially as taught and expanded upon in a series of articles by Hartmann, Kris and Lowenstein, and over a broader spectrum by all the psychoanalysts I mentioned before, and many others.[4] This by no means detracts from the stimulation coming from other endeavours, such as the Kleinian or object-relations theory. If the rise of ego psychology did indeed delay the reception of those other theories by analysts in the States – something of which I am not at all sure – one could argue that, a little later, it allowed more advanced and less parochial versions of those theories to have their impact. There were not as many heated and acrimonious debates in the States on those matters as, for instance, in England. I wonder if the effect of those schools, which by now is manifest, was not more constructive and truly stimulating just because it came a little later.

It might be of interest at this point if I tell you of a debate which is still going on among German psychoanalysts and others occupied with psychoanalysis in Germany. Three schools of thought gained influence there after the war, when it became possible to restore psychoanalysis and to train people to practise it, which for obvious reasons was very much needed. There was, *first*, the somewhat insecure and anxious orthodoxy of technique and theory of the surviving analysts and neophytes, which took its orientation from the state of psychoanalysis in the Thirties.

Second, another line emerged in the days of the student protest movement a little before 1968, and lasted for quite a few years thereafter. It was influenced by Wilhelm Reich, who had been resuscitated for just this event, though it was done with a kind of sardonic logic all of its own. It led to a revival of Reichian theories originating *not* among practising psychoanalysts and therapists but among students, joined in their thinking by some quarters of the intellectual Left. Paradoxically, Reich had left the ideas in question behind him long before, when he began to occupy himself exclusively with the study of the orgone. His political views during the last phase of his life, the time he spent in the USA, would have been so embarrassing for his new German admirers that they might have preferred to ignore them.[5]

In one, if not several, respects the Reichian revival converged with

the dominant ideological orientation of that time, the critical theory of
the Frankfurt School. Both encouraged a blending of psychoanalytic
with Marxist theories, which coalesced in what one might call the
chthonic view of psychoanalysis.[6] This version of psychoanalysis
focused, above all, on the instincts, conceived as struggling for freedom
in a perpetual battle against a tyrannical, hostile and demanding super-
ego, and made psychoanalysis into an altogether darkly romantic
'psychology of the unconscious'. Such it had been, indeed, in its early
phase, with the important difference that other trends towards future
developments were noticeably contained in it.

A more genuinely psychoanalytic impetus came, *third*, from object-
relations theory, popular in Germany for a worthy reason. British
analysts, including Balint, Klauber and many others, had taken an
especially strong supportive interest in the resurrection of psychoanalysis in Germany, and had devoted much time and effort to this
endeavour.

These three currents, different though they were in origin and intent,
converged with an entirely heterogeneous and highly ambiguous
political sentiment, or resentment, against the USA. This led to a
somewhat derisive judgement of American psychoanalysis. It was put
down as medicalized, restrictively service-oriented, and rather mindless
as far as the intellectual scope of psychoanalysis was concerned. To
appreciate these charges, it is important to understand that according
to this viewpoint the essential task of psychoanalysis is the critique of
society and civilization.[7] From this judgement derived a kind of pre-
judicial disdain of ego psychology, mainly, it appears, because it had
become the leading school of analytic thought in American psychoanalysis.

It would be fascinating to follow this argument and its rhetoric in
some detail. The debate I have outlined belongs in any case to the topic
of my paper, since it shows the inverse effect upon one of its countries
of origin of a direction psychoanalysis had taken in exile. Space being
limited, I should like only to point to a peculiar exercise in denial,
contained in the attack on ego psychology. The supposition is that it
excludes about half of Freud's work, from *The Ego and the Id* and
'Inhibitions, Symptoms and Anxiety' to 'Analysis Terminable and
Interminable'. This allegation overlooks the fact that ego psychology
did *not* originate with Hartmann, Kris and Lowenstein, or with
Erikson, much as they have contributed to it. It originated with Freud
and, of course, with Anna Freud. In addition, it would require a
considerable degree of self-induced myopia to overlook the contribution of American psychoanalysts, both native and immigrant, to the
theory and technique of psychoanalysis during the last thirty to forty
years.

A reciprocal interaction

I would suggest a different approach: the unfolding of psychoanalytic ego psychology and the seminal effect of European analysts should best be understood as *reciprocal*. It set goals and directions for the rapid expansion of psychoanalysis which, determined as it was by social and historical factors, might have taken place in any case. Albeit with some delay, a similar advance took place in most Western countries. In the States this expansion was to no small degree carried forward by *émigré* psychoanalysts. Through their work the more literary and humanist tradition of Freudian psychoanalysis also came to have some bearing on this development. However, those who were the leaders and pace-setters of the advance themselves changed with the changes they had brought about. They became more empirical, in the Anglo-Saxon sense which in its nuances still differs from the implications of the German term. They learned to limit speculation somewhat – which, to be sure, is a legitimate way for any science to approach a new topic. For in the wake of the early phase, which had encouraged what one might call the *mantic* attitude, the tolerance of luxuriant analytic phantasies had often become a little too great.

Analysts now learned to relate their hypotheses more closely to concrete clinical observations. They also, or at least some of them, became more used to establishing contact with other disciplines in the study of man, especially with psychology, sociology and anthropology. They were also made aware of the loopholes in analytic theory by a succession of critics, from Ernest Nagel and Karl Popper to Adolf Grünbaum;[8] and by and by they came to acknowledge the necessity of addressing themselves to this subject. In addition to the traditional preoccupation with culture, literature and the arts, with cultural antecedents and the past, psychoanalysts grew to be more interested in the immediate present – in the social environment and its disorders.

In his personable as well as highly personal autobiography, *Reminiscences of a Viennese Psychoanalyst* (1982), Richard Sterba writes:

When I met Robert Waelder the first time as *émigré* – he had settled in Philadelphia – he was very disturbed by the cultural differences between Vienna and his new place of activity. He said to me almost in despair: 'How can I teach here, where one cannot use a single classical quotation!' By *classical* he meant, of course, Latin and Greek. However, he must have adjusted very well to having to teach without what he at first missed so much, because he was soon widely known as a brilliant teacher of psychoanalysis.[9]

This quotation could well serve as a motto for my argument about the development of psychoanalysis in the American exile; in other words, for the effect of European psychoanalysts in America, of whom the largest number hailed from Vienna, as well as for their own transformation and that of psychoanalysis. While promoting important changes, year by year these psychoanalysts grew to become part of their new habitat, until it became a second home for them. With the changes they brought about, they also changed themselves. Putting it differently, while they were becoming productive agents of change in the new culture, its way of life subtly and inevitably affected and modified them too.

Sterba's book, without specifically aiming to describe this process, also shows that the transformation of psychoanalysts in Vienna had begun some time before the emigration. From being what one might call a closely knit band of dedicated disciples and explorers of a new intellectual continent, held together by their common purpose and their internal and outward relationship to Freud, they transformed themselves by and by into a School: both a practical school for the training of psychoanalysts and a school in the philosophical sense. Looked at from the point of view of social history and the history of ideas, this was bound to happen to psychoanalysis. In the States it happened according to the given social and cultural premises there, among them the dominant status of medicine and its power, or as people in Chicago like to say, its clout.

Freud's passing undoubtedly created a void to which organized psychoanalysis had to adapt. The rest was probably a natural and necessary development, applying as it does to all innovating and integrative movements. With the passage of time such movements become organized, codified, formalized. At the same time they continue to be subject to schisms. So too with psychoanalysis. There is surely no lack of comparable historical examples.

This is also true of the severance of psychoanalysis from the humanist tradition of Western and Central Europe, but especially that of Germany, from which psychoanalysis undoubtedly derives in many powerful though not necessarily obvious ways, as has been shown in several recent articles.[10] The unity of cultural achievement, the continuity of development vested in that ancient tradition, began to disappear in the American exile. The inability to quote from the classics of which Waelder complained may seem a small matter when compared with the enormous and frightfully destructive upheavals in which the world was then involved. But it does show in a nutshell, too, that it may signify a great deal more than making a show of one's learning. In a deeper sense, quoting from the classics is an appeal for, or a confirmation of, the continuity of an unbroken intellectual tradition.[11] In the States psychoanalysis lost this continuity, even though individual analysts held on to it and continued to contribute to it, as did Eissler in his study of Goethe, and Bettelheim in his analysis of fairy tales.[12]

What was lost was the unfolding of images and ideas from Sophocles through Shakespeare and Goethe to Freud – a continuity which for psychoanalysis had provided the support of a high cultural tradition to guide it and to confirm it. In Europe, psychoanalysis has still preserved some of that tradition, and old-timers like myself fervently wish and hope that it may hold on to it. How likely this is or how possible, future historians will have to assess. We may be wise to set our hopes, above all, on the range and power of the psychoanalytic purview itself – clinical, theoretical and applied – for no one of these can survive without the support of the others. The potential of psychoanalysis has not yet been fully realized. It seems to me that there should be an invigorating comfort in this fact.

Notes

[1] 'It is remarkable . . . that this theme has received little attention from the psychoanalysts, especially since they themselves have been involved in migration. . . .' This is the opening of an important paper by Leon and Rebeca Grinberg, 'A Psychoanalytic Study of Migration: Its Normal and Pathological Aspects', *Jn APA*, XXXII (1984), 13–38. These two analysts from Argentina, now resident in Madrid, have shared the predicament of many analysts in our time. The Grinbergs have also published (in Spanish) an extensive monograph on this subject, *Psicoanalisis de la migracion y del exilio* (Madrid 1984), which ought to be made accessible to readers in other languages.

[2] For some examples of this well-nigh universal experience, see Allan Janik and Stephen Toulmin, *Wittgenstein's Vienna* (New York 1973); H. Stuart Hughes, *The Sea Change: The Migration of Social Thought, 1930–1965* (New York 1975); Frederic V. Grunfeld, *Prophets Without Honor: A Background to Freud, Kafka, Einstein and Their World* (New York 1979); Peter Loewenberg, *Decoding the Past: The Psychohistorical Approach* (Berkeley, Calif., 1985). See also Peter G.J. Pulzer, *Political Anti-Semitism in Germany and Austria* (New York 1964).

[3] For an excellent survey of this migration as an event in intellectual and social history, see Hughes, *The Sea Change*.

[4] On the development of ego psychology in the United States, again see Hughes, *The Sea Change*.

[5] Those interested in what Reich did and thought at the time referred to should look into the correspondence between him and A.S. Neill of Summerhill School, *Record of a Friendship: The Correspondence between Wilhelm Reich and A.S. Neill, 1936–1957* (New York 1981).

[6] See Martin Jay, *The Dialectical Imagination: A History of the Frankfurt School and the Institute of Social Research, 1923–1950* (London 1973).

[7] H.-M. Lohmann: *Das Unbehagen in der Psychoanalyse* (Frankfurt a/Main 1982); *Die Psychoanalyse auf der Couch* (Frankfurt a/Main 1984).

[8] See, e.g., Ernest Nagel, 'Methodological Issues in Psychoanalytic Theory', in *Psychoanalysis and Scientific Method*, ed. Sidney Hook (New York 1959); Karl Popper, *Conjectures and Refutations: The Growth of Scientific Knowledge* (New York 1963); Adolf Grünbaum, *The Foundations of Psychoanalysis: A Philosophical Critique* (Berkeley, Calif., 1984).

[9] Richard F. Sterba, *Reminiscences of a Viennese Psychoanalyst* (Detroit 1982), 142.

[10] Didier Anzieu, 'The Place of German Language and Culture in Freud's Discovery of Psychoanalysis between 1895 and 1900', *Int'l Jn Psych*, LXVII (1986), 219–26; Ilse Grubrich-Simitis, 'Reflections on Sigmund Freud's Relationships to the German Language and to Some German-Speaking Authors on the Enlightenment', *Int'l Jn*

Psych, LXVII (1986), 287–94; A. Ernst Ticho, 'The Influence of the German-Language Culture on Freud's Thought', *Int'l Jn Psych*, LXVII (1986), 227–34; Madeleine and Henri Vermorel, 'Was Freud a Romantic?', *Int'l Rev Psych*, XIII (1986), 15–38; Janine Chasseguet-Smirgel, 'Das Paradoxon der Freud'schen Methode', *Zeitschrift für Psychoanalytische Theorie und Praxis*, I (1986), 131–51.

[11] Frederick Wyatt, 'Literatur in der Psychoanalyse', in *Freiburger literaturpsychologische Gespräche*, vol. v (Würzburg 1986).

[12] Kurt R. Eissler, *Goethe: A Psychoanalytic Study* (Detroit 1963); Bruno Bettelheim, *The Uses of Enchantment: The Meaning and Importance of Fairy Tales* (New York 1976).

11

Psychoanalysis – The Fate of a Science in Exile

Ernst Federn

In the long history of exiled scholars and scientists, psychoanalysts have had to face very special problems. For much of that history, though exile meant loss of home and friends, it did not mean loss of language. That was either Latin or mathematics or both. Exile in previous periods seldom also meant loss of social status, since academic achievements, like diplomas, prizes or published works, were recognized everywhere. Psychoanalysis could not share in these advantages. Its exiles must be placed among those of literary and political personalities. This social feature deserves attention. Indeed, I consider it as crucial for a true understanding of my topic.

Freud's exile was an exception. England received him not as an exiled refugee, but rather as a homecoming hero. Symbolically this was expressed by the fact that the officers of the Royal Society, which made him a member, came to his home to bestow this honour on the old and sick Freud. I was also told that the borough of Hampstead where Freud was to settle arranged that German-speaking policemen be specially selected for duty there to accommodate the expected visitors. Nevertheless Freud considered himself to be an exile. A copy of his book on Moses was sent to Paul Federn as a 'greeting among exiles', as Freud put it in his dedication. ('Herrn Dr. Paul Federn als Gruß unter Exilierten, Verf. London 1939').

While the members of the Royal Society accepted Freud as their equal, the equivalent institution, the Akademie der Wissenschaften in Vienna, never considered Freud a scientist so far as psychoanalysis was concerned. His achievements in neurology were, of course, not important enough to earn him membership. Psychoanalysis is still today, in the eyes of many philosophers of science, no science at all. Within the realm of German culture, to which he unquestionably belongs, Freud was perhaps considered a great writer, at most a great scholar. The only honour he ever received from this cultural community was the Goethe Prize of the city of Frankfurt. That these, the Royal Society and the Goethe Prize, were the only two honours Freud ever received (if we overlook his having been made an honorary citizen of Vienna), symbolically underscores my main thesis: the exile of psychoanalysis was so exceptional and had such special consequences because in its culture of origin it was not a 'science' in the English sense of the word.

'Science' and 'Wissenschaft'

We must deal here with a linguistic problem of philosophy that is expressed in the different meanings of the words 'Wissenschaft' and 'science'. Historically it can be traced back at least to the differences between the philosophies of Kant and Hume. Though the valid point can be made that in his philosophy Freud followed Hobbes rather than Hume or Kant, this in my opinion refers to Hobbes's psychology rather than his epistemology. Philosophically Freud was more likely influenced by Kant, Hegel, Schopenhauer and Brentano, to name only the most important figures. It is not easy to determine exactly which of these had a decisive influence, since Freud himself denied the value of philosophy altogether. He considered himself a scientist in the sense of the school of Helmholtz. This concept of scientific method, valid in the nineteenth century, had its origin with Auguste Comte and the Enlightenment. A hundred years later it is no longer valid in its original meaning.

In German culture we have accepted the distinction between 'Naturwissenschaften' (sciences), and 'Geisteswissenschaften' (humanities or 'human sciences'). The practitioners of the one are called in English 'scientists', of the other 'scholars'. Freud did not know this distinction and used the term 'Wissenschaft' for both, in fact very different, fields of knowledge. This rather confusing picture was made more intricate through the development of the Austrian school of positivism, the Vienna Circle around Moritz Schlick. Its proponents, notably Otto Neurath, Carnap and others, tried to create a 'universal science' ('Einheitswissenschaft'). Freud took part in this discussion through some of his students and disciples, chiefly Heinz Hartmann, Ernst Kris and Robert Waelder. These three were the 'philosophers' in the Vienna Psycho-Analytical Society: of them Waelder alone was a trained physicist; Hartmann was a medical doctor with an inherited interest in the social sciences, and Kris an art historian. These three men were later, as exiles in the USA, to carry on the discussion of psychoanalytic epistemology in a country where only a few exceptional men knew what they were talking about.

Nevertheless, for the fate of psychoanalysis the question of whether psychoanalysis is a science was to become crucial because it merged with the other question to which Freud made an undeniable contribution: whether psychoanalysis is part of medicine or of psychology. Later efforts began to classify it as a social science, and finally as a hermeneutic science belonging to philosophy. Freud for his part always maintained that it was a new science, not subsumed by any other existing branches, though partaking of their ethics and attitudes. We have to keep in mind that 'Wissenschaft' in Freud's sense was opposed to 'Glaube' (conviction). The opposing attitudes are: 'I believe because I cannot know' and 'I know because I am able to prove'. Important in this context are also the different associations of 'Wissenschaft' and 'science'. The German word implies 'creating knowledge', the English 'knowledge already gained'. The German emphasizes the process, the English the result. The German language is essentially psychologically oriented, the English pragmatic. Before I advance my argument any further, may I give an example from another field: Marx and Engels also believed they had erected a 'scientific' theory which proved that socialism must eventually be established according to the innate 'laws' of society. The alternative would be the destruction of those laws, which meant barbarism. We know today, after Einstein, Planck and Heisenberg, that such 'laws' do not exist even in nature. In this sense psychoanalysis unwittingly created the paradigm for modern natural science, not vice versa.

I can now present to you adequately the true tragedy that befell psychoanalysis in exile. Not only did that exile mean loss of home, but also loss of language and loss of its philosophical bearings. This loss was all the harder to bear as language and philosophy also meant economic and social status. In the USA the exiled psychoanalyst was not even recognized as a professional man unless he was awarded an academic degree in the new country. Paul Federn failed the examinations three times, before a legal solution was found which permitted medical doctors with a degree from the time before 1914 to practise medicine. Non-medical analysts like Theodor Reik had to struggle to find a niche within the laws of the country, mostly in the fields of counselling and social work. The pressures of economic necessity, the dismal prospect of never returning to one's home – few psychoanalysts were politically-minded enough to be able to envisage Hitler's defeat – forced the average exiled psychoanalyst to adjust as quickly as possible to the philosophy of the country of exile.

We know that Freud himself doubted whether the people of the United States would ever understand his work.[1] He considered them too superficial and too pragmatic. We do not know whether Freud included England in this prejudice. Historically, England was much more often a friend of Austria than an enemy, while the USA for a hundred years after independence considered Austria as her chief antagonist. Freud, as typical a Viennese as they come, was always a friend and admirer of England, albeit of the England that created Oliver Cromwell. Indeed, the exile of psychoanalysis in England took very different forms from that in the USA.

Distortions in America

In the USA under the influence of Hartmann and Kris the Americanization of psychoanalysis became decisive. Hartmann's concept of the ego dominated psychoanalytic theory for about twenty years. Although Hartmann was not opposed to non-medical analysis and Kris was not a medical doctor, what became the psychoanalytical establishment accepted the American point of view that psychoanalysis is part of psychiatry. This decision was a tragic one: as Freud predicted, his psychoanalysis at least was drastically distorted in the USA. Of course ideas cannot die. But what happened was that Freudian psychoanalysis in the original sense is hardly practised, taught or developed any longer in the USA. Its literature produced in the USA is only vaguely recognizable as having anything in common with what Freud had in mind. This development was foreseen by many Freudian psychoanalysts. The mere fact that the term 'orthodox psychoanalysis' originated in the USA is symbolic. We know that Freud was opposed all his life to two developments: the creation of an orthodoxy, a church, and the subordination of psychoanalysis to the medical profession. Both became true of psychoanalysis in the USA. Therefore in my eyes Freudian psychoanalysis has ceased to exist there. This does not mean that many individual followers of Freud do not continue to practise in the States and to struggle for recognition.

An example from the recent literature may illustrate what I have just said. In 1984 Morris N. Eagle, a psychologist trained in the USA who became chairman of the Department of Psychology at York University in Ontario, Canada, published a book under the title *Recent Developments in Psychoanalysis. A Critical Evaluation*, with a picture of Freud on the cover. This book was hailed by Robert R. Holt as 'the best survey of the current status of psychoanalytic theory that I have seen' and by Robert S. Wallerstein as 'a truly formidable achievement'. Let me present only one quotation: 'Although psychoanalysis is a treatment, Freud nevertheless believed that its place in history would be secured because of its contribution to an understanding of the structure of the mind'.[2] Freud is here turned upside-down and 'corrected' by Eagle, who represents a majority of American psychoanalysts. What Freud had said was that *because* psychoanalysis is a tool for understanding man's psyche it can also be used for treating its ailments.

I cannot enter into a detailed discussion of Eagle's book. Although it is admirably written and contains some excellent criticism of many post-Freudian theories, it is not about psychoanalysis. This is fully understandable, because Eagle is a follower of pragmatic philosophy in the sense of Peirce's formulation: 'every truth has practical consequences and these are the tests of its truth'. Eagle and American psychoanalysts cannot understand Freud because for them the concept of the unconscious mind is a hypothesis to be tested by therapy, whereas for Freud – to use a distinction made by Robert Waelder – the unconscious is a discovery which does not need repeated verification.[3] Similarly the existence of the American continent does not need to be proved again by every newcomer to its shores. I believe that this contradiction is insurmountable. Those who still hold the opinion that the unconscious mind is only a hypothesis are in the same category as people who cannot believe in evolution.

Developments in England

I shall turn now to the very different situation in England and again start with a quotation. It is from the introduction to the book *Freud and Society* by Yiannis Gabriel: 'Freud is one of the very few thinkers who have definitely and irreversibly changed the way we think about the world and about ourselves.' In America, however, Gabriel identifies a different development: 'The adoption of psychoanalysis by American culture like that of other immigrants was accomplished only after considerable dues had been paid. Many of Freud's key ideas were distorted beyond recognition.'[4] Why this striking difference in the fate of exiled psychoanalysis in these two countries which, as the expression goes, are separated by the same language?

I believe the most important factor was two women: Anna Freud and Melanie Klein. Curiously, both were non-medical analysts. But they would not have made their impact on England if it had not been for the many English medical analysts who remained true Freudians. Also the meticulous scholarship of Strachey's Standard Edition helped to ensure that exile in England did not have the same disastrous effect on psychoanalysis as in the USA. In England psychoanalysis could take another course and develop its own school which, though it differs from that of Freud, has not abandoned the discovery of the unconscious. In England, also, the psychoanalytic societies have not excluded non-medical analysts from membership – nor have they developed such a rigid orthodoxy of thought and training.[5]

In this context I must pay tribute to Anna Freud and speak of her role. She adopted England as her new home and worked for the country's children, as is well known. I have characterized Anna Freud in other papers as the great preserver of Freud's work, rather than as an innovator, her creation of child analysis notwithstanding. Perhaps that was the price she had to pay for being an exile: to limit her work to preserving Freudian psychoanalysis and preventing its 'distortion beyond recognition'. The exiled Anna Freud needed a very long time, perhaps too long for the good of continental psychoanalysis, to overcome the trauma of having been driven from her home. Finally she did make peace with her city of birth. When, at the unveiling of the first monument to Freud in Vienna, Harald Leupold-Löwenthal greeted her as guest of honour, Anna Freud contradicted him forcefully: 'I am not a guest here, I was born here and I was here even before my father wrote *The Interpretation of Dreams*'.

As to the second woman I have mentioned, Melanie Klein, she was never an exile. Brought to England by the most distinguished English psychoanalyst, Ernest Jones, and under no duress, she may have been freer to make her contribution – which, whether one agrees with it or not, has certainly widened the horizon of psychoanalytic observation and theory. Nothing comparable in quality had happened in the USA prior to the arrival of the European analysts.

Why was it that exile in the USA so distorted psychoanalysis, while in England it made it grow? To answer this question I must return to my first statement, that psychoanalysis was not only exiled from home, but from language and philosophy as well. I am convinced that neither the exile of Descartes to Sweden, disastrous as that was for him, nor that of Einstein, Fermi, Szilard and the other great scientists and scholars, had any negative influence on their work. Rather it enhanced it. Even an economist like Schumpeter did not suffer with respect to his work; where could one study capitalism better than in the USA? None of these exiled scientists and scholars had to struggle with the losses which befell psychoanalysts: (1) social status; (2) the tool of their work: the spoken language; and (3) the soil of their existence: their continental philosophy.

A further proof is the difference between the fate of those psychoanalysts who emigrated voluntarily to the USA and those who had to flee there. It was easier for the first group, and their efforts to ward off the influence of American culture were for a while even successful. It looked as if the contributions of Herman Nunberg, Helene Deutsch, Erik Erikson and others who came more or less voluntarily to the States, might be readily accepted by American psychoanalysts and even take root. But the essentially pragmatic approach, so foreign to the psychoanalytic method, proved in the long run to be stronger and more persistent. The exiled analysts unfortunately did not try to continue and reinforce the work of these who had come before, but on the contrary adapted quickly to the American scientism. After thirty years who still reads those real Freudian analysts?

Is this development final and is psychoanalysis as it was created by Freud dead in the United States? One could come to that conclusion after the publicity and kudos accorded to people like Masson and

Sulloway. Pragmatists will believe that it is the fate of all scientific discoveries to be overthrown by new paradigms. I am not a pragmatist and I am convinced that the USA will eventually see a new acceptance of Freud. If his work can now be translated into Chinese, why should it be impossible for it to take root again in the USA?

Notes

[1] See Bruno Bettelheim, *Freud and Man's Soul* (London 1985), 18–19 (quoting from Freud's introduction to an article in the *Medical Review of Reviews*, xxxvi [1930]).

[2] Morris N. Eagle, *Recent Developments in Psychoanalysis. A Critical Evaluation* (New York 1984), 154.

[3] See Robert Waelder, *Basic Theory of Psychoanalysis* (New York 1960).

[4] Yiannis Gabriel, *Freud and Society* (London 1983), 1.

[5] See Edward Glover, 'Psychoanalysis in England', in *Psychoanalytic Pioneers*, ed. F. Alexander, S. Eisenstein and M. Grotjahn (New York 1966).

12

Wilhelm Stekel: A Refugee Analyst and His English Reception

Martin Stanton

A life recalled

Wilhelm Stekel was found dead in his hotel room in London on Wednesday, 25 June 1940. A glass stood empty on the bedside table, and beside it lay a neat stack of letters. His clothes were hung neatly in the wardrobe. A few books, notes, and the daily newspaper were arranged on the table. The hotel staff had discovered him, and informed the police. A post-mortem was requested, and the coroner duly revealed that the old man had poisoned himself. He added that the suicide had resulted from an unbalanced state of mind. This shocked the hotel staff, and indeed all those who had come into contact with Stekel during his last days. Depressed he was – who was not at that time, with nightly bombings and most of Europe invaded by the German armies? He had been deathly pale – but then he was seriously ill, and had been for some time. But all the same, to quote one of the hotel guests, 'He was a kindly gentleman, full of that Central European charm'.

It is tempting to see this scene as the summary of Stekel's life: a deranged mind, a man that could not cope any more, an alien. One could recreate his last hours. He took a bath, then clipped his fine beard and moustache, for, on his own admission, he was extremely vain. One could also picture his last thoughts, following, maybe, the famous cinematic sequence of flashbacks displaying the sum of his life. He would surely have recalled his childhood in Bukovina, then part of the Austrian Empire, but after 1918 part of Romania, and now part of the Soviet Union. He would walk again through the small whitewashed house in Boyan, where he was born on 18 March 1868, remember the sour taste of poverty which invaded his early youth. (Some 5,000 to 6,000 Jews died of starvation in Bukovina annually.) He might then reconstruct the family circle: his father, who was illiterate, and had to leave home and travel far and wide to earn money to send to the family; his mother, who came from a good professional middle-class Jewish background, and encouraged her young son's educational aspirations, if not instilled them in him; his sister, who became a governess, and his brother who became an office clerk.

His memories might stray to Czernowitz, the capital of Bukovina, where he attended the *Gymnasium*, and he might even rehearse the four languages spoken there, Romanian, Polish, Ukrainian and German. Stekel always claimed proudly that his first language was Ukrainian, and that he learned it from his wet-nurse Marysia. He also claimed, half humorously, that he inbibed her fiery temper through her milk, or 'the warm primal liquid', as he called it. Into this scene would surely rush a pack of dogs, if only because he loved them all his life from childhood on. The fiercer the dog, the more he loved it. Indeed, an old Viennese lady told me that she remembered very clearly how the Stekel dogs used to terrorize the Gonzagagasse. When questioned about it, Stekel would reply angrily, 'Quark!', one of his favourite words, which means both 'nonsense' and cream cheese, one of Marysia's specialities.

From here, he might have travelled on in his fantasies to Vienna, and relived some key episodes in his life as a medical student. Inevitably, there would be music, for he played both the violin and viola in a Viennese orchestra, composed a set of highly successful children's songs, and remained a passionate devotee of chamber music. Even near the end of his life, in 1939, during a convalescence in Tonbridge in Kent, his great joy was to be able to play the piano, a battered but well-tuned Bechstein. From Vienna, he might also have recalled his work with Richard von Krafft-Ebing, author of *Psychopathia Sexualis*, and coiner of the terms 'sadism' and 'masochism'. Stekel no doubt had a great deal of personal experience to relate directly to these terms, first and foremost through an unhappy marriage to his first wife, Malvina. He regarded her name as synonymous with malevolence, and indeed he suffered from persistent and chronic problems of impotence throughout his relationship with her. These led him to consult Freud for some eight sessions in 1902. Freud taught him that mother-fixation was the major cause. Despite their two children, Stekel grew further apart from his wife, and divorced her just after the First World War, to marry soon after Hilde, an attractive member of his circle. She had been a pupil of his, and helped him henceforth with his clinical work.

At this point in the phantasmagoric sequence we have imaginatively attributed to Stekel, the name Freud would certainly have evoked some powerful associations. First, probably, would figure the intermediaries, the colleagues employed to transfer messages to Freud: the gaunt, death-obsessed Herbert Silberer, whom Stekel felt had been rejected by Freud, and who was precipitated by subsequent emotions into suicide;[1] and Fritz Wittels, sharer of cards, Trabuko cigars and black coffee at Berggasse 19, misogynist, and creator, in large part, of the conflict with Karl Kraus. Wittels had joined Stekel's group of 'active' analysts briefly in 1923, and had written a biography of Freud, *Sigmund Freud: der Mann, die Lehre, die Schule* (1924), which vindicated Stekel's account of his difficulties with the IPA; but he soon changed his mind, and in 1925, supported by Freud, successfully reapplied to join the Vienna Psycho-Analytical Society.

Stekel had himself written to Freud, a letter dated 12 January 1924, asking for a similar reconciliation, and Freud replied the following day, as was his manner, claiming that 'on a certain occasion' Stekel had deceived him 'in the most heinous manner', adding after this, in brackets, *'Zentralblatt'*.[2] The 'heinous' occasion was in fact the disagreement engendered by Stekel's refusal to accept Viktor Tausk as the *Zentralblatt*'s book-review editor. Stekel had felt irretrievably insulted by Tausk, who said Stekel could neither spell nor write grammatically. Freud apologized to Stekel for Tausk's insults, but was more concerned about a business deal that Stekel had conducted with the *Zentralblatt*'s publisher, Bergmann, in Wiesbaden, without Freud's knowledge or consent. According to an internal memo by Paul Federn, dated 31 January 1929, Stekel wrote to Federn and Wittels to ask Freud's pardon. But he also wrote to Freud on a number of other occasions, the last time from London in 1939, where they both happened to find themselves as refugees. Freud did not reply. By all accounts, Freud's view remained that he expressed in the 1924 letter: 'I admit that you have remained loyal to psychoanalysis and have been of use to it; you have also done it great harm'.[3]

In classical melodrama, I suppose, Stekel would also have assessed his achievements in his final hours. Perhaps first the work of his circle in Vienna, especially Emil Gutheil, who later edited his papers, and continued his work in America; then, Anton Missriegler, co-editor of the *Fortschritte der Sexualwissenschaft und Psychoanalyse*, and author of the revolutionary *Lebensbeichte eines Kriminellen* (1933), who, sadly, later renounced Stekel and 'Jewish psychology', in conformity with the aims of the suitably Aryanized 'German General Medical Society for Psychotherapy' (Deutsche Allgemeine Ärztliche Gesellschaft für Psychotherapie) – whose international and Swiss section president at the time, incidentally, was none other than Carl Gustav Jung.[4] Stekel's group also incorporated a large international section, many of whom, in fact, were forced through anti-Semitism to become international: Ernst Bien, Ernst Rosenblum, Fritz Wengraf, Walter Schindler in Berlin (later to become a prominent figure in London).[5] This group, under Stekel's leadership, formed two institutions: the Viennese Institute for Active Psychoanalysis (Institut für Aktive Psychoanalyse in Wien), and the Vienna Active Psychoanalytical Ambulatorium (Aktivanalytisches Privatambulatorium in Wien). A major difference between the groups and the Vienna Psycho-Analytical Society and

Ambulatorium was that Stekel was fiercely opposed to lay analysis. A psychiatric qualification was a pre-condition of membership to all Stekelian groups. The Institute, and Stekel personally, trained scores of psychiatrists in psychoanalytic technique, and offered free psychoanalytic treatment through the services of the Ambulatorium. Stekel also gave regular lectures on psychoanalysis to the American Medical Association in Vienna.

In addition, he gained considerable notoriety in Vienna as a journalist. This activity was frequently derided by other analysts. Ernest Jones, for example, dismissed Stekel as 'a born journalist in a pejorative sense... indeed he earned part of his living by writing regular feuilletons [or gossip columns] for the local press'.[6] In fact, he wrote for quite respectable papers, the *Neues Wiener Tagblatt*, the *Frankfurter Zeitung*, the *Prager Tagblatt* and the *Vossische Zeitung*. More significantly, he also contributed to experimental Expressionist journals like *Daimon*, which was edited by Jacob Moreno Levy, the founder of psychodrama; *Die Gefährten*, whose contributors included Alfred Adler and Martin Buber; and *Das Ziel*, for which Stekel wrote a famous article on free love entitled 'Sexual Enlightenment'.[7] Stekel actually committed some pretty radical views to print in this period. For example, he attacked the use of ECT and the abuse of narcotic drugs in mental hospitals; he was also an ardent pacifist, and renowned for his proposals to introduce psychoanalytic methods in prisons, borstals and schools.[8]

Stekel's creative output also included numerous books during the inter-war period. He revised his celebrated book on 'Dreams' (for he too wrote one), completed the 10 volumes of a series on 'Disorders of the Instincts and Emotions', wrote what is probably his most useful book, *The Technique of Analytical Psychotherapy*, and, in England, his 'last will and testament', as he called it, his *Autobiography*. Since 1950 most of these writings have been out of print,[9] and they have often been damned by faint praise. For example, to quote Ernest Jones again: 'For a few years he retained a remarkable capacity for divining the unconscious counterpart of conscious mental processes, and he made... a real contribution to our knowledge of symbols'. 'Divining' is the key word here, for in Jones's view, Stekel never went beyond guesswork. Similar comments are to be found in Lou Andreas-Salomé's *Freud Journal*: 'Stekel is a good fellow', she wrote, 'not essentially bad, but on the other hand without the intellectual qualities to be able to penetrate deeply'. We know from her biographers that 'penetrate' ('durchdringen') was a word laden with personal and contradictory connotations for her.[10]

Stekel is also often given brief credit for coining a few useful terms, notably 'anxiety hysteria' in his 1908 book on neurotic anxiety states, and 'thanatos', which he launched in the 1909 *Jahrbuch der Psychoanalyse*. He is also often cited as a pioneer of short-term analysis. Unfortunately, such credit is usually qualified by dismissive comments on Stekelian 'bombastic phraseology', and 'passion for the latest jargon'.[11] It is certainly true that Stekel frequently changed his terminology, much to the annoyance of his contemporaries. Notable in this was his switch to the terms 'parology' and 'parapathy' in 1908, just when the majority of analysts were accepting 'psychosis' and 'neurosis' as the definitive terms. It is also clear that Stekel had a partiality for contradictions, and frequently excelled himself in displays of theoretical crudity.

Even so, such observations fail to appreciate the strength of Stekel's work, that is, the priority and meticulous attention he gave to clinical material, over and above any theoretical concern that may have been prevalent at the time. This is illustrated by the extensive inclusion of case histories in his work, even at the expense of the coherence of his argument. Stekel made a point of including exceptions to his own rules. Most important, probably, in hindsight, was his brief but detailed account of his analysis of Otto Gross in 1914. Gross, the charismatic, anarchist, promiscuous, cocaine-riddled, Expressionist, early psychoanalyst, had previously been analysed by Jung, who had expeditiously classified him as psychotic. Stekel did much to discredit this diagnosis, and indeed cast considerable doubt on the accuracy and integrity of Jung's psychiatric studies at this time.[12]

A further illustration of his peculiar combination of strengths and weaknesses can be seen in the huge dream archive he constructed in Vienna, by sending a set questionnaire to artists great and small. The questions were rather slanted, like 'Do you have repetitive dreams? Do you daydream? Do you commit crimes in dreams? Do you have reasonable, sober [*nüchtern*] dreams, or fantastic ones?' and 'Do you use dreams for your artistic work?', but the answers must be considered a gold mine for anyone working on artistic production in Vienna at the time, as the respondents included theatre directors like Burckhardt, poets like George, and writers like Werfel, as well as many now forgotten talents.[13]

Motives for suicide

Behind this imaginative rewind of Stekel's life, however arbitrary or partial it may appear, lie a number of inescapable narrative assumptions, all of which imply a basic ethical question: In what way are we constructing this suicide as some kind of ideal event, attributed, as we have seen, to a legally declared deranged mind, disorientated in the process of remembering? Furthermore, how, if at all, does this act relate to his past, to his theories, or to an attempt to expound his motives? What evidence is there? First of all, there is his *Autobiography*, which he asked his wife to publish, and which he refers to as his 'last will and testament'. Remarkable as this book is, especially its last chapter entitled 'A Refugee from the Nazis', it contains a number of inaccuracies and omits important detail. It clearly is not meant to provide an apologia for suicide; indeed, much of it is taken from journal entries. There is not, for example, an obvious sense of chronology.

Moreover, Stekel makes scant reference to his responsibilities, in particular his patients, which is extremely unusual, as we have already noted the great importance he gave to case-history material. We know, though, that he left letters for each of his patients, supposedly containing some explanation of his decision to commit suicide. These, of course, will remain private for some time to come. He also left a letter to the British people, thanking them for their hospitality, and praising their fortitude; and a letter to his wife, who had been recuperating in hospital after a serious operation. He had been extremely concerned that she should be secure financially, and indeed in simple practical ways. He mentioned to her, for example, that she could still use his library subscription. So we might conclude from this that, however deranged he may have been declared to be legally, the act and its consequences seem to have been premeditated in some detail.

The reason I mention this, and raise these related questions, is that historians of psychoanalysis have tended to take the opposite line, and to group Stekel with other suicides among pioneer psychoanalysts, such as Johann Honegger in 1911, Karl Schrötter in 1912, Viktor Tausk in 1919, Otto Gross in 1920, Herbert Silberer in 1923, to mention only a few. Paul Roazen, for example, in his book *Freud and His Followers* (1976), has commented that 'It remains troubling that these early analysts should so frequently have killed themselves or otherwise come to bad ends. . . . A number of lives seemed to have been sacrificed for the sake of the triumph of Freud's work'.[14] This approach seems to me to rest on a whole host of misguided assumptions: first, the outright moral condemnation of suicide, leading, in extreme cases, to the reduction of all possible motives for suicide to 'mental derangement'; second, the assumption that the suicides of all these analysts related directly to Freud, and partook of some classic Oedipal tragedy, in which real or phantasized rejection by the Master had dire consequences; then all those assumptions about the dangers of psychoanalysis – its 'contagion', and the supposed fragility of analysts in the face of their own and their analysands' unconscious; and finally, and perhaps most importantly, a wild overestimation of the role of theory in priming, informing, or even comprehending these suicides.

These assumptions have not only contributed to the malicious gossip which has enshrouded and obstructed research on the work of the early analysts, but also shifted attention from the complex problems of relating the theoretical and practical work of these individuals to the imposition of crude ahistorical theories that are set up supposedly to explain personal disputes. General theories about psychoanalysts' suicides, in particular, have proved extremely damaging; and Kurt Eissler's book *Talent and Genius* (1971) set an impeccable precedent in exposing their distortions. Let us take, for example, one detail that has been used to justify the grouping together of early psychoanalysts' suicides. It has been claimed that the discussions on the subject of suicide held by the Vienna Psycho-Analytical Society, on the Wednesdays 20 and 27 April 1910, actually clarified or even helped precipitate the acts later committed by participants. It is true that substantial contributions to the debate were made not only by Tausk and Stekel, but also by Paul Federn (another analyst who was to end his own life). But if you read these contributions carefully, either in the *Minutes*, vol. II, or in the separate publication *Über den Selbstmord* (1910), you will find very divergent views expressed.[15] Federn's view that 'suicide is a normal reaction to negative experiences in life', raising still prevalent issues like euthanasia, Tausk's distinctions based on Schopenhauer's philosophy, and Stekel's reaction to both their views through the 'talion thesis', that is, that 'no one kills himself who has not wanted to kill someone else', all actually contributed to a general attempt to distinguish categories of suicide. Far from being some turgid, intense personal wrangle, foreboding imminent separation of their paths, the debate actually centred on an exposition by Ernst Oppenheim (an Adlerian) of a book by Dr A. Baer on the rapid increase in child suicides.

My specific purpose here is to suggest that Stekel's suicide was neither the 'summary' of his life and views, nor an act that forms a part of a homogeneous set. Stekel's suicide had nothing to do with Freud, or the 'future' of psychoanalysis, and offers no lurid detail. He did not tie a rope around his neck and put an army pistol to his right temple, like Tausk; nor did he hang himself on a set of window bars, leaving a torch shining on his face so his wife would see him when she came home, as Herbert Silberer did; nor was he found dead in the street, ravaged by drugs, starvation and debauchery, like Otto Gross. Quite simply, Stekel's suicide was neither that spectacular not that unusual in the context in which he found himself. He was a seventy-two-year-old Jewish exile, gravely ill from a diabetic condition which had left him largely immobile, and subject to comas; he had no valid passport, merely temporary papers issued by the American Embassy in Zürich, which entitled him to entry into the United States as a tourist only. He wished to travel to California, but was becoming much too ill. His permit to stay in Great Britain was subject to regular review and renewal, and his wife, although also gravely ill, had already been 'deported' with other female 'unfriendly aliens' to the Isle of Man. He committed suicide the day after France had signed an armistice. *The Times* of that day (and it was the paper on his hotel room table) included reports on mass round-ups and shootings of Jews in Paris, where his son Eric, a musician, was living. For a week, the press had discussed German plans for the invasion of Britain, down to such details as black lists and the English phrase book distributed to German troops. Stekel had long considered the possibility of suicide in such circumstances: 'should things become worse', he wrote in his *Autobiography*, 'I had resolved to commit suicide rather than be placed in a concentration camp'.[16]

The refugee's dilemma

When I say that suicide was not 'unusual' in this context, I am referring not to psychoanalysts as such, but to refugees in general, especially the Jewish refugees from Nazism. It is often pointed out that the only pioneer psychoanalyst to die at the hands of the Nazis was Isidor Sadger; and that surely more would have suffered the same fate had Freud not stayed in Vienna for as long as he did to offer the protection of his world renown. True though this may be, it understates the enormity of the refugee problem and the pain and suffering experienced by the estimated 802,000 people who managed to escape the Nazis before borders were closed in 1939. In this respect, psychoanalysts were no different from anyone else. Although accurate statistics are hard to obtain, given the restrictions still in force on German archives from this period, it has been estimated that up to one-fifth of European refugees committed suicide (around 160,000), either in the process of fleeing, or afterwards, through the inability to assimilate to their new country.[17] Clearly, one should be cautious in categorizing suicide as 'deviant' in this context, or in viewing it, as Stekel did in 1910, as 'one of the terminal forms of neurosis'. It seems value-laden, to put it mildly, to dismiss someone as 'unbalanced' because he determines to take his own life rather than face the gas chambers. In any case, the fact that many committed suicide should not preclude study of the difficulty and suffering endured by those refugees who survived. In this sense, I think it is important, in discussing the English reception of Stekel, to look at the structure of the reception of refugees in general.

There is thus a further and final dimension to my imaginary account of Stekel's life-rewind: he was not alone in having to abandon all his belongings and leave the Westbahnhof in Vienna on the 9 p.m. train for Zürich on 11 March 1938, the day Hitler marched into Vienna. Like those of everyone else, his options for travel were extremely restricted.[18] After 1933, the major powers 'regulated' their quota systems to 'control' their intake of European refugees; the United States, for example, admitted 51,153 Europeans in 1931, but only 7,634 in 1933. They committed themselves officially to admitting 26,000 in 1938, but financial guarantees and administrative difficulties caused long delays.

Britain followed a similar policy, imposed severe restrictions on the kinds of employment refugees were allowed to pursue; doctors of physics and chemistry, for example, were supposed to take up domestic service. Special restrictions were imposed on artists, who had to apply to the Home Office for permission to perform in public. A general law, in force in France and Britain, for example, limited to 10 per cent the proportion of refugee artists from any one country allowed to perform in a particular field (a special exception was made in the case of balalaika orchestras, where they allowed the Russians a quota of 15 per cent, for fear that the orchestras might otherwise disappear). The Jewish Agency was asked to provide financial guarantees to cover the maintenance of each Jewish refugee who had found employment and was granted permission to stay in Britain. Needless to say, this placed an incredible burden on the British Jewish community, which was already under considerable emotional and financial pressure. Stekel commented grimly in his journal: 'My experiences as a refugee are in a measure depressing. People fear you are hard up and that you are going to ask for financial aid. Their behaviour changes after the first reserve has worn off, and it changes still more after they learn you do not need money. I could relate some stories along these lines, but I prefer to hurry on. . . .'[19]

Finally, the passports of Austrian and German Jews were first stamped with 'Israel' in them, then declared invalid. Furthermore, there were no international agreements forthcoming to protect the rights of refugees. The Nansen International Office for Refugees, established in August 1930 under the auspices of the League of Nations, provided only for Russians, Armenians, Assyrians, Assyro-Chaldeans, Turks and refugees from the Saar. It made no provision for refugees from fascist regimes. In fact, a convention to deal with the problems of Italian, German or Spanish refugees was set up only on 10 February 1938, and proved hopeless to administer in the face of the enormous numbers queuing outside the respective embassies to obtain the necessary papers. Stekel noted in Switzerland:

I went to the American Consul who advised me to get an immigration visa, but he added that he did not have the power to issue one. It would be necessary to go to the Chief Consul at Zürich. At the American Consulate at Zürich there was such a queue of refugees that half the day passed before I could enter. I sent the Consul my visiting card and the letter of introduction from the consul at Bern, and in five minutes I was ushered in to see him. But the information I received was depressing. The place where I was born was now Rumanian territory, therefore I had to be treated as a Rumanian, and might have to wait seven or eight years for my quota number. It would be necessary for me to visit

America as a tourist. Through the connections of my friend, Mumenthaler, I was able to procure a certificate of identification as quickly as possible. As an exceptional case, I was given a return visa, which made my credentials as valid and valuable as a passport. Thanks to the invitation of the Tavistock Clinic in London to deliver six lectures on my active method of psychoanalysis, I received my English visa by wire before I touched English soil. I wished to avoid the possibility of being refused at the frontier....[20]

The picture I have given so far of Stekel's English reception has been pretty grim: a suicide, following from illness, the pain and suffering of being a refugee, and apocalyptic Weltschmerz. Fortunately, there is some lightness too. In his letter to the British public, and in his *Autobiography*, he describes what he had appreciated in Britain; such as manners, the kindness of a few people, and the English countryside. There were also a few things that he did not appreciate, such as the apparent absence of 'comfort stations' in London. 'Comfort station' was an expression he had picked up in New York, denoting a public toilet, and he complains bitterly in his *Autobiography* of the discomfort he had to suffer from a prostate condition in this kind of environment. He attributed British lack of concern about such practical necessities to 'the horrors of the Protestant ethic'.

Stekel managed as a refugee to continue work he had started in Vienna. First, his work for Jewish refugees: like the novelist Stefan Zweig, he gave lectures the proceeds of which went to the refugee fund. Stekel and Zweig met in Brazil in 1936 after both giving lectures in a 'Jewish Culture' series; and incidentally, interesting parallels can be drawn between the narrative form of Stekel's *Autobiography* and Zweig's classic *The World of Yesterday*, particularly their concluding chapters. Secondly, Stekel continued his study of dictatorship; probably the most celebrated exposition of his views was contained in John Gunther's best-seller *Inside Europe* (1936), and in Gunther's interview with him published in *Look* Magazine of 7 May 1940.

Thirdly, and most important to him, maybe, was the opportunity to visit A. S. Neill's Summerhill School at Leiston, Suffolk. Stekel, like Wilhelm Reich, was a long-standing admirer of Neill's anti-authoritarian educative methods, and had in fact trained some of Summerhill's teachers. After Stekel's suicide, Neill wrote to Reich: 'I had a soft spot in my heart for him, for behind his childish egoism there was something very warm about him'. About Neill, Stekel wrote: 'the future of the world depends upon teachers like these, for the world must be rebuilt by a new generation such as this. Though I do not share Mr Neill's political views, he and I are good friends, and I wish there were many more idealists such as he'.[21] This comment, made in the last months of his life, can hardly be said to indicate a pathologically depressed or deranged mind.

17. Wilhelm Stekel, towards the end of his career.

In summary, my conclusions are few and simple: I suggest we regard Stekel's suicide as a logical reaction to extremely adverse circumstances, motivated by chronic illness and the pressures of exile. It was not motivated by his psychoanalytic theories, in fact it contradicted them, and it should not be taken as a reflection on the value of his work. Nor did it reflect on his ability to adapt to Britain, and its culture; on the contrary, he wished to stress how happy he had been, and how relatively easy he had found it to continue his work. Personality defects he certainly had, but then who has not? And the mix of good and bad comment on him suggests he was neurotically human, not megalomaniac or pathologically deceitful. It is to be hoped that at some point, critics and researchers will cease to plow the furrow of very old conflicts involving Freud and the Vienna Psycho-Analytical Society, and will see that even so-called 'deviants' like Stekel contributed widely and generously to psychoanalysis, and to mental health as a whole.

Notes

[1] Wilhelm Stekel, 'In memoriam Herbert Silberer', *Fortschritte der Sexualwissenschaft und Psychoanalyse*, I (1924), 408 ff.

[2] S. Freud, letter to W. Stekel dated 13 Jan 1924, *Letters*, 352.

[3] Ibid., 353.

[4] Cf. Aniela Jaffé, 'C. G. Jung and National Socialism', in her *From the Life and Work of C. G. Jung* (London 1972), 78 ff.; V. W. Odajnyk, 'The German Case', in his *Jung and Politics* (New York 1976), 86 ff.; W. Huber, *Beiträge zur Geschichte der Psychoanalyse in Österreich*, and *Psychoanalyse in Österreich seit 1933* (Vienna 1977/8).

[5] Dr Walter Schindler (1900–86) remained a Stekelian, and practised active analysis throughout his professional life. In London, after 1945, he became a consultant psychotherapist at St. Bartholomew's Hospital, and gave regular lectures on subjects ranging from the aetiology of sexual deviations to the psychoanalysis of the creative arts. He was a founder and major contributor to *Group Psychology*, a journal based in Germany but with a world-wide distribution. In 1980, he published *Wilhelm Stekel, Aktive Psychoanalyse – eklektisch gesehen* (Bern). Cf. Schindler's obituary in the *Proceedings of the Royal College of Psychiatry*, Feb 1987.

[6] E. Jones, II. 152.

[7] W. Stekel, 'Sexuelle Aufklärung', *Das Ziel* (ed. A. J. Schranzhofer), no. 2 (May 1913).

[8] Cf. *The Autobiography of Wilhelm Stekel*, ed. Emil A. Gutheil *et al.* (New York 1950), 50 ff.; and W. Stekel, *Unser Seelenleben im Kriege* (Berlin 1916).

[9] In 1945, Samuel Lowy, MD, a Czech refugee and a prominent figure in the Department of Psychological Medecine at St. Bartholomew's Hospital, London, inaugurated an important re-edition of Stekel's work in English. Crucial in this were *The Technique of Analytical Psychotherapy* (1950), and *Conditions of Nervous Anxiety and their Treatment* (1949), both with introductions by Lowy.

[10] E. Jones, *Free Associations: Memories of a Psychoanalyst* (London 1959), 219; *The Freud Journal of Lou Andreas-Salomé* (New York 1960), 35.

[11] Cf. D. Rapaport, *Organization and Pathology of Thought* (New York 1951), on Stekel's 'polyphony of thought'.

[12] Stekel's case history of Gross is contained (under the pseudonym 'M.K.') in vol. VIII of *Störungen des Trieb- und Affektlebens* (1927), ch. 12, 'Die Tragödie eines Analytikers'. This was published in English under the title *Sadism and Masochism* (London 1935). Cf. Emmanuel Hurwitz, *Otto Gross, Paradies-Sucher zwischen Freud und Jung* (Zürich 1979); Kurt Kreiler, *Von geschlechtlicher Not zur sozialen Katastrophe* (Frankfurt 1980); and Josef Dvorak, 'Opiumträume in Bad Ischl: Wilhelm Stekel analysierte Otto Gross', *Forum*, Sept 1985, p. 45 ff. For Jung's view of Gross, see *The Freud/Jung Letters*, ed. William McGuire (London 1974), 156.

[13] Archiv der Stadt Wien, File ref. IN 153, 613.

[14] Paul Roazen, *Freud and his Followers* (repr. Harmondsworth 1979), 430.

[15] *Minutes of the Vienna Psychoanalytic Society*, ed. Herman Nunberg and Ernst Federn, 4 vols. (New York 1962–74); *Über den Selbstmord insbesondere den Schülerselbstmord* (Diskussion der Wiener Psycho-analytischen Vereinigung, no. 1, 1910).

[16] W. Stekel, *Autobiography*, 270.

[17] Joseph B. Schectman, *The Refugee in the World – Displacement and Integration* (New York 1963).

[18] Cf. the moving and now classic account of Sir John Hope Simpson, *Refugees: Preliminary Report of a Survey* (London: RIIA, 1938).

[19] W. Stekel, *Autobiography*, 277.

[20] Ibid., 275.

[21] *Record of a Friendship: The Correspondence between Wilhelm Reich and A. S. Neill, 1936–1957* (London 1982), 40; W. Stekel, *Autobiography*, 281–2.

PART THREE

PROBLEMS OF TRANSLATION

13

The Question of Revising the Standard Edition

Malcolm Pines

The Strachey 'Standard Edition' of Freud's works, 23 volumes of which were published between 1955 and 1967, was then, and still is, a great scientific and literary achievement. The replacement of earlier diverse translations which often misrepresented and distorted Freud's writings, which were in conflict with one another and confused the reader, by a uniform edition for which the work of translation was shared among a small, highly skilled, knowledgeable team of psychoanalysts who devoted a massive amount of attention to issues of terminology and to the clarification of concepts, was greeted with almost universal praise, admiration and gratitude. It was a great psychoanalytic publication, a considerable financial risk.

Generations of psychoanalysts have been raised on Strachey. They have learned from Strachey's great editorial skill in tracing the historical development of Freud's concepts, classifying the constant revisions Freud made in the light of further analytical experience and increased theoretical sophistication or the demands of criticism of his ideas; and they have appreciated the magisterial quality of the language and the cool clarity of style of a writer nourished on the European tradition of classical translation. Few at the time questioned whether Strachey's translation represented as authentic a version of Freud's ideas as possible. The authority of Anna Freud reinforced this almost universal acceptance.

What then has happened, especially in the last decade, that the Strachey version has begun seriously to be questioned and challenged? Several factors have to be taken into account. It is inevitable that the achievements of one generation will be challenged by the next. This is healthy, and demonstrates the liveliness and evolution of psychoanalytic thought. Nowadays, non-German-speaking analysts are learning German so as to be able to read Freud in the original and form their own impressions of his ideas. They appreciate Freud's mastery of German style, the subtleties and achievements of which have recently been presented to us by the Canadian analyst and literary scholar, Patrick Mahony.[1] Others, on the basis of a close examination of Strachey's work, have argued that his Freud is not the authentic Freud, that Strachey subtly and powerfully amended Freud's ideas so that eventually they presented a far greater uniformity than Freud himself had intended. It has been seriously argued, for instance, that what we accept as the structural theory is more Strachey's invention than Freud's.[2] If so, the consequences are far-reaching indeed, as generations of analysts have been brought up to regard the structural theory as a great achievement of Freud's model-building, the foundation of much later theoretical superstructure. Opposition to the structural model, arguments that it was mechanistic and over-schematic, too far removed from the facts of human development and from clinical experience, have led to radical revisions such as Fairbairn's emphasis on the primacy of object relations and to Kohut's on the primary significance of self-experience. But if Freud never ceased to describe the experience of the self, did not completely substitute the conceptually abstract ego for the experience-close self, do self psychologists and object-relations theorists need to diverge so radically from Freud? Do we need Kohut's two paradigms of guilty man and tragic man?[3]

The rallying cry of 'Back to Freud' was first heard from Lacan in France, where there still is no uniform complete edition of Freud, though one is now in preparation. Only in France have Freud's own words been so closely scrutinized, so carefully translated; nowhere else has so much theoretical sophistication been applied to 'The Language of Psychoanalysis'.[4] One of Freud's papers, 'Negation' (1925), has been translated into French in 27 different versions. Recently, too, a completely new Spanish translation has been produced and greeted with much praise. Moreover, Freud's writings are now widely studied in universities by non-analysts from many disciplines, who recognize the great significance of psychoanalysis for twentieth-century culture.

In 1989 the copyright in Freud's writings expires. The way will then be open for new translations to be made. Will Strachey be challenged by new translators, new editors? This is almost certain to be the case. Does Strachey need to be revised, either conservatively or radically? Does Freud need to be retranslated *ab initio*, or can we continue to base our English version on the work of the small team of translators who devoted a major part of their professional lives to this great labour? Can any small group of analysts ever again constitute an assembly of skills and talent such as made this work possible?

I have outlined elsewhere some questions, the answers to which would involve the cooperation of Germanists, translators, philosophers and historians of science as well as psychoanalysts.[5] The work is immense, important and provocative and will challenge many cherished assumptions.

It may be useful to recall the social context of Freud's childhood and youth and how this may have influenced him in the development of psychoanalysis. Freud was a child of the 1860s, enlightened, liberal years in Austria, when full political emancipation was granted to the Jews. In his school and university days he was drawn to pan-Germanic nationalism and was a member of the Vienna Reading Circle which eagerly studied Schopenhauer and Nietzsche. He was deeply imbued with classical German literature and philosophy and originally wanted to enter politics through the law. He was converted to the study of science and philosophy through his reading of Goethe, was spellbound by the personality and teachings of Franz Brentano during his studies at the University of Vienna. Later Freud largely suppressed information about these early studies and enthusiasms, as did his biographer, Ernest Jones, and the influences have only recently been revealed.[6]

The scientific model that Freud embraced and avowed was that of the school of Helmholtz, which repudiated vitalism. Much of Freud's work can be seen to be influenced by these mechanistic models, but the question has repeatedly been raised whether other influences, less recognizable, are not also important and powerful in a fuller appraisal of his standpoint. German medical and scientific thought in the mid- to late nineteenth century had repudiated its predecessor, the influential school of Romantic science and medicine. Recently the Vermorels have pointed to the many traces of Romantic thought in Freud's work, and a fuller biographical study would amplify this suppressed aspect of his personality.[7]

Freud's psychoanalysis is a study of conflict between the instincts and the ego and super-ego, between the instinctual forces themselves. His own life exemplifies the conflicts between the scientist and the poet, the classicist and the romantic. He lived out these conflicts in his love of Greek, Roman and Egyptian civilizations. The conflict is also reflected in his neurotic travel symptoms, which for many years prevented him from reaching Rome and which he himself analysed as his identification with Hannibal, the Semitic hero who opposed the Rome that in Freud's mind represented oppressive Catholicism.

How do these biographical and contextual matters relate to the Strachey translations? Strachey avowed that his aim was to represent the thought of Freud as a man of science of the nineteenth century, writing for other men of science of that same era. How adequate, we may now ask, is this both as aim and as goal? Some of the answers to this question are explored in the papers that follow.

Freud's writings attract readers far beyond Strachey's definition. His influence is as wide as that of any other thinker of the nineteenth or twentieth century, and it is clearly his style, his prose, his personality that attract and intrigue philosophers, artists, historians and lay persons far beyond the intended field of scientists and psychologists. The thoughts of such a man will repeatedly be scrutinized. For most Anglo-Saxons, and for many other cultures, the access to Freud is through Strachey. To study Freud is to study Strachey, the medium through whom his message is transmitted.

I myself accept that many of the recent reappraisals of Strachey's work are valid and that substantial revisions are needed. Our progressive understanding of Freud's personality and his ideas should be reflected in the translation. The translation itself is now being studied as a living document of the development of psychoanalysis in the English-speaking world during the decades 1920–50, with the complex historical, political and scientific dimensions that that development entailed, as well as of the significant personalities involved in the translation.

In time, the defenders of the sacrosanctity of the Strachey translation will, I believe, come to see the value of this renewed study. It will surely revitalize psychoanalysis itself as well as contributing greatly to the history and philosophy of science.

Notes

[1] P. Mahony, *Freud as a Writer* (New York 1982).

[2] D. Ornston, 'Strachey's Influence: A Preliminary Report', *Int'l Jn Psych*, LXIII (1982), 409.

[3] H. Kohut, *The Restoration of the Self* (New York 1977).

[4] J. Laplanche and J.-B. Pontalis, *The Language of Psycho-Analysis*, trans. D. Nicholson-Smith (London 1973).

[5] M. Pines, Guest Editorial, *Int'l Rev Psych*, XII (1985).

[6] W.J. McGrath, *Freud's Discovery of Psychoanalysis: The Politics of Hysteria* (Ithaca, N.Y., 1986).

[7] M. and M. Vermorel, 'Was Freud a Romantic?', *Int'l Rev Psych*, XIII (1986), no. 1, 15.

14

'Die Weltmachtstellung des Britischen Reichs'[1]

Notes on the Term 'Standard' in the First Translations of Freud

Riccardo Steiner

The purpose of this paper is to give a brief outline of the original adoption of the term 'standard', in so far as it had a bearing on the 'Standard Edition' of the works of Sigmund Freud. It would perhaps be useful to begin by putting the question in its historical perspective, since I am convinced that to deal with even such an apparently marginal issue as the introduction and use of the term 'standard' can help us to understand the specific form which the translation of Freud's work took in this country. Such a historical perspective (although, for reasons of space, it must be very condensed here)[2] would help explain not only the importance of that particular translation at the time of its first appearance but also its enduring immobility or, if you prefer, its static perseverance ever since.

In the specific case of the Standard Edition of the works of Freud, and the use of the term as laid down in Strachey's General Preface of 1964, one needs first of all to clear up some of the misunderstandings that form an immediate obstacle. Otherwise one is liable to make gross errors of historical judgement and to overlook some important cultural and (for want of a better word) institutional implications; and many ideological implications will be lost to view. For 'ideology' I am inclined, with some reservations, to follow the definition offered by Althusser in his pamphlet *Philosophie et philosophie spontanée des savants* (1967). The fact is that, however one views these implications – ideological, cultural, institutional, etc. – they have resulted in a situation in which this particular translation has come to assume the aspect of a special phenomenon in itself, and it is almost the only example of its kind in the contemporary history of textual translation.

Although the translation of Freud's work was signed by James Strachey, his wife Alix, Anna Freud and the rest of his collaborators,

this translation was actually an enterprise that owed many of its fundamental aspects to earlier days. To trace the origins of the enterprise and
above all the recurrence and virtual permanence of certain terms, in
particular certain technical terminology that Strachey chose to use in
the translation, we shall have to go back as far as the years Ernest Jones
spent in the USA and Canada, and the period of his collaboration with
Brill and Putnam at the beginning of the century.

A certain variety of historical methodology, held in particular esteem
in Britain, insists with some justification on the need to provide
rigorous proof and documentation of any assertion, in order to avoid
facile speculation or hazardous formulations. Far be it from one such
as myself to call into question the value of such a robustly empirical
approach. Nevertheless, though it may not be immediately possible to
provide a full range of 'rigorous proof' to support my analysis, I hope
to be able to get at some of the conscious and unconscious intentions
of those involved in the enterprise of 'standardizing' Freud's language
in English. By examining the pragmatic intentions of those who
worked at a more or less unconscious level on the 'standardizing'
process, we can gain an insight into the specific quality of the cultural
venture which began originally with the translation of some of Freud's
fundamental concepts. All these key concepts are to be found in the first
papers written by Brill, Jones and Putnam in America during the first
decade of this century. While these initial attempts were being made to
translate some of the basic Freudian terms, Brill produced in 1909 a
translation of a selection of Freud's papers from the *Studien über
Hysterie*, and this was soon followed by a translation of the *Drei Abhandlungen zur Sexualtheorie* and *Die Traumdeutung*.

   Taken together, these translations, although not openly declared to
be massively and officially concerned with the standardization of
Freud's technical language, none the less present many of the fundamental characteristics of the later enterprise. This is what I meant in
referring to the more or less unconscious intentions of the first
translators of Freud. I am thinking especially of the tacit decision on the
part of all those directly concerned to select and employ a specific
terminology, such as 'the ego' for 'das Ich', 'the unconscious' for 'das
Unbewußte', 'displacement' for 'Verschiebung', 'condensation' for
'Verdichtung', 'resistance' for 'Abwehr', 'repression' for 'Verdrängung', 'dream work' for 'Traumarbeit', 'primary and secondary
process' for 'primäre und sekundäre Prozeß', 'libido' for 'Libido',
'presentation / idea / representation'   for   'Vorstellung',   'instinct /
impulse' for 'Trieb', 'mind / soul' for 'Seele', and so on. The use of this
terminology was soon to be followed by the adoption of other technical
terms, such as 'homosexual', 'heterosexual', 'oral', 'anal', 'fixation',

'perversion', 'sado-masochism', 'narcissism', etc., all of which constantly recur in the early papers of Brill, Jones and Putnam. Such terms quickly came to constitute a primary core that is found repeatedly from this time on.[3]

From the letters exchanged between Jones and Freud and between Freud and Putnam,[4] it is clear that Freud had already entered into a tacit understanding with Jones and Brill. This understanding owed its origins to their famous meeting in Vienna in 1908, which probably provided the basis of an embryonic agreement on the characteristics required for a translation of Freud's language, especially his so-called technical vocabulary. From Jones's account of that meeting we can gather, for example, that Freud himself suggested the term 'repression' to translate the German 'Verdrängung'. Gilman and Anzieu are certainly right in stressing that Freud's use of a Latin, and especially, ancient Greek vocabulary, and his great interest in ancient Greek culture, had very precise historical and cultural causes which cannot be simply identified with those of Jones, Brill and Putnam.[5] Yet, as we shall see presently, Jones continued in his tentative efforts to make psychoanalysis penetrate the well-stocked arsenals of the Anglo-American psychiatric and psychological establishment, using the phalanxes and legions of Greek and Latin terminology, and it seems that Freud did not present any open opposition to his efforts. After all, despite their differences, Freud's cultural background of studies in neurophysiology and psychiatry had much in common with that of Jones. In fact he supported Jones's efforts and accepted Jones's strategy of attempting a piecemeal penetration of and influence on the type of language current in medical, psychiatric and psychological circles. This strategy was based essentially on an adaptation of psychoanalysis and its language.[6] At the same time it is true that Freud would occasionally allow himself some 'poetic licence', for example in his acceptance of the word 'soul' to translate 'Seele' in some instances.

In the main, then, the technical terminology was proposed early and with Freud's assent. One needs to give only a perfunctory glance at H.W. Chase's translation of Freud's Clark lectures to see that Chase was relying on a terminology already in circulation, recently coined by Brill and Jones. Freud himself supervised the translation of these lectures and in so doing must have accepted the particular terminology employed. What resulted, though not yet a thoroughgoing 'standardization' of technical terminology, was a 'uniformity' of terms that tended towards the 'monosemic'.[7] This vocabulary could be presented to the educated Anglo-American public of doctors and psychologists whom Jones had in mind, without risk of disturbing or outraging them.

Obviously if we wish to understand the significance of this

operation, we must consider not only Jones's personal cultural background and ideas but also the general cultural climate of Britain and America at that time. In the preface to his *Papers on Psycho-analysis* of 1912, Jones explicitly refers to the natural sciences, for example physiology and biology, and to the fact that psychoanalysis had for the first time 'reduced' the 'psychical' to the 'physical' and thus shed its links with philosophical and moral tendencies associated with such thinkers as Nietzsche and Bergson. The only philosopher with whom Jones was prepared to compare Freud was Karl Pearson. Jones referred to Freud as the 'Darwin of the mind', and his comparison between Freud and Pearson clearly indicates that he saw Freud in the light of Pearson's writings on an 'economy of thought' and the sophisticated positivism of such a text as *The Grammar of Science*.[8] But above all, the overt link to natural science must be understood in the context of the discussions on sexuality conducted by the institutions and in the internal publications of the medical and psychiatric professions, and of the effect of censorship on public access to discourse about sexuality.

A long and almost esoteric tradition had kept the general public in blissful ignorance by barring it from direct access to publications dealing with the arguments on sexuality. This centuries-old tradition was typical of the medical profession both in Britain and on the Continent. One should beware of exaggerating these factors; there was always a divorce between official scientific discourse and what the medical profession practised or said in private. Nevertheless, when Brill published the first English translation of *The Interpretation of Dreams* in 1913, the edition carried an official warning that 'the sales of this book are limited to members of the Medical, Scholastic, Legal and Clerical professions'.[9] While I am not in complete agreement with the theories put forward by Michel Foucault in his *History of Sexuality* (vol. I, 1978), one cannot ignore the relevance of certain linguistic details of psycho-analytic discourse, such as the excessive use of Latin and Greek, to modes of power and control at that time.

In addition to these factors, there was the enormous 'prescriptive power' of such a standardized language, with its potential of establishing a network of institutions directly concerned in the teaching and transmission of psychoanalysis. The adoption of a standardized language came to assume great importance. It immediately legitimized the profession, so to speak, giving it a 'status' and equipping psycho-analysts with a professional language of their own with which to confront the medical profession in general. Psychoanalysts thus acquired a linguistic instrument at the same time as gaining a separate identity in professional terms.

Jones and Brill spoke of a literal translation of Freud. Whatever precisely they may have meant by that, we can see that from the outset they considered themselves the only true translators of Freud, authorized by him no less than if he had directly bestowed on them his linguistic blessing. Having received the eucharist directly from his hand, they felt themselves empowered in turn to depute others to carry on the translation, while they established precise laws of procedure.

From this time on, Jones insisted that whoever wished to translate Freud had to have prior knowledge of psychoanalysis and first-hand experience of psychoanalysis in practice. This led in turn to all the problems of what the French psychoanalyst Granoff calls 'filiation':[10] from whom, for example, was one to learn psychoanalysis in order to translate? A whole series of very complex problems arises here, to which we must add the rivalry, both conscious and unconscious, between Jones and Brill themselves over who was to have the final say in the standardization of Freud's language. When Jones returned to Britain in 1913, his overriding aim was to take personal control of the translation project in order to create a cultural and administrative setting which would enable him to limit or even eliminate the participation of Brill, and to assume overall control of the dissemination of Freud's thought in Britain.[11]

Between 1913 and 1923 Jones not only continued his work of translation, introducing new terminology such as 'omnipotence of thoughts', 'pain' (for 'Unlust'), 'ego ideal', 'parapraxis' and probably 'anaclitic', but also produced a number of full terminological glossaries. With the publication in 1913 of the first number of *Die Internationale Zeitschrift für Ärztliche Psychoanalyse*, these glossaries came to be referred to as the 'Codex' of the most important psychoanalytical terms. Jones had editorial responsibility for the English-language section of this 'Codex'. He also appended a glossary of psychoanalytical terms to the second edition of his own *Papers on Psycho-Analysis*, published in 1918, and added an updated version of the same glossary to the third edition, in 1923.

If one follows in detail the growth of interest in psychoanalysis in Britain during that period – for example the foundation of the London Psycho-Analytical Society in 1913, and of the British Psycho-Analytical Society in 1919, the various conferences held and their published proceedings and the open controversies raging in the columns of the national press – one quickly perceives that a sort of informal 'standard-ization' was indeed taking place. This happened on the basis of the experience acquired in America and through the free circulation of a specific terminology which, with continual usage and repetition over time, was passed on to others, until eventually it acquired the potency of a norm. Essentially this 'standardization' had its roots in a Latin and ancient Greek vocabulary, as the pre-existing terminology of psychiatry and academic psychology had had.

It was not till the end of the First World War, however, with the explosion of interest in psychoanalysis, that Jones was able to bring his plans to fruition. He published the first English-language edition of the *International Journal of Psycho-Analysis* in 1920; he started a project to establish an 'International Library'; and he initiated the discussions that were eventually to induce Freud to cede to him the British publication rights for all the works not already translated by Brill and others. It is in a letter to Freud dated 29 February 1920, and another to Rank dated 26 February 1920, that we find Jones's initial definition of his plan to produce a 'Standard Edition' of the writings of the 'Herr Professor'. Whether his definition was appropriate and one can actually consider his plan as *leading to the present Standard Edition* is another matter.

In order to understand fully the complexity of Jones's plan, we must refer to his editorial in the first number of the *International Journal of Psycho-Analysis*. In that brief piece Jones outlines and justifies his project of standardization. Typically, he refers explicitly to the examples of the 'physical' and 'chemical' sciences, insists on the at least provisional necessity of what he calls a 'strongly supported central organ, systematically and comprehensively *codifying* all that is published on the given subjects' (my emphasis), which would have the function of avoiding misinterpretations of Freudian psychoanalysis through, for instance, 'dilution of the meanings of its new ideas until they may be regarded as harmless'. He goes on to make explicit reference to the way opposition to psychoanalysis had developed in America

under all sorts of specious guises and by the aid of various seductive catchwords . . . A notable, and perhaps unique feature of this . . . defence against Psycho-analysis is that it conceals its negative antagonistic nature by pretending to develop a more positive attitude towards Psycho-analysis; it makes use of its technical terms, *Libido*, 'repression', etc., but in such a way as to rob them of their intrinsic meaning.[12]

Jones and his immediate collaborators felt that they alone were authorized to establish translation guide-lines for the English-language edition. They considered themselves uniquely capable of transmitting Freud's thought in English. (In this regard it is by no means surprising that, in 1922, Jones compared himself and his collaborators to the Church of England.)[13] Even in the *Statuten der Internationalen Psycho-analytischen Vereinigung*, one finds no such explicit reference to the links between psychoanalysis and the natural sciences. In its pages, the general tendency was to speak of 'Psychoanalyse als reine Psychologie [psychoanalysis as pure psychology]', and only then to link it to 'Medizin [medicine]' and the 'Geisteswissenschaften [humanities]'.[14] Freud himself tried more than once to connect psychoanalysis to the natural sciences, knowing (as of course did Jones) that their discourse was itself figurative: "The shortcomings of our description would probably disappear if for the psychological terms we could substitute physiological or chemical ones. These too only constitute a metaphorical language, but one familiar to us for a much longer time and perhaps also *simpler* [my emphasis]'.[15]

Jones's project during these years took on specific characteristics directly related to the cultural peculiarities of Britain and, above all, to his own medical training in neurophysiology and psychiatry. This is particularly evident in the brief comments, also published in the first number of the *International Journal of Psycho-analysis*, in which Jones outlines some of the peculiarities of the English character, linking them directly to the specific peculiarities of the English language and Anglo-Saxon culture in general. English, he maintains, is primarily a vernacular insular language which, unlike Latin or Greek, does not allow much emotive distance when dealing with discussions on sexual matters. He refers openly to the problem of eliminating all references that might prove too dangerously connotative, and he also discusses the group personality and group culture, both professional and social, of the contemporary British medical profession as though it were a meta-historical phenomenon and as such immune to change.[16]

The origins of his approach and its ideological implications are surely too obvious to warrant any further commentary. When, a few years later, in 1924, Jones went on to publish the official glossary of terms for translating Freud, compiled with the help of a committee which included Freud himself, Joan Riviere and James and Alix Strachey, he made explicit reference to the importance of using the ancient Greek and Latin patrimony of the English language. In this way a sort of *lingua franca* was brought into being. Although Freud did not explicitly agree, he did not disagree. He supported the Glossary, informing Jones in a letter of 15 February 1922 that his daughter Anna and John Rickman (while he was still in Vienna) were using it.

These were the years when the English language was beginning to assume international dominance in the scientific, cultural and economic fields, often at the expense of French and German. One of the most interesting aspects of the Glossary is its three-way division of terms, an attempt to translate the so-called technical terms of Freud's language based on a sort of *lectio difficilior*. This division reflects Jones's personal preference for terms with ancient Greek and Latin roots. Firstly there are those terms already uniformly 'standardised' – this is the actual word used by Jones (p. 1); then come those terms which would require further discussion and experimental use before they could be 'standardised'; and finally there were terms which would not require any discussion because they were not technical. The Glossary was revised more than once in the following years, to accommodate terms added later by Freud's translators. But from what we have observed of the large number of terms already officially standardized in the first Glossary of 1924, it comes as little surprise to find that about 90 per cent of the items in that list had been coined by Brill and Jones as early as 1908–10, and they remained unchanged in later editions of the Glossary.[17]

In addition, it is essential to note the huge increase in authority and prestige which the adoption of the standardized Glossary as the only authorized source for Freud translation brought to the British Psycho-Analytical Society. We must not forget that the administrative problems of such an institution were closely linked to its financial endeavours to stay afloat, and these depended on its establishing a definitive dominance in the field of psychoanalysis.

Thus it is clear that, from those earlier times to the present day, there has been a gradual process of 'standardization' which can be traced back to the choices and uses of terms arrived at in 1908–9. James Strachey (whether completely willingly or not) participated actively in the production of the first Glossary, allowing the introduction of the famous term 'cathexis' studied by Darius Ornston, and many other technical and non-technical terms.[18] Strachey's participation is evident from his personal copy of the Glossary, which contains handwritten notes in the margins. These marginalia suggest numerous additions to the existing terminology, all of them enhancing the already significant ancient Greek and Latin flavour of the translation.[19] As Bettelheim, Ornston and others have argued, Strachey completed retrospectively the 'standardization' of Freud's literary style.

One could write an entire chapter on the way Freud supported Strachey from the start, opposing the ambivalent attitude of Jones, based as it was on feelings of rivalry and jealousy that both Stracheys, whom he had sent to Vienna, had had the chance to be analysed by Freud himself. Jones showed the same attitude of rivalry towards Joan Riviere and to some extent towards John Rickman, and it was always connected with the question of who was to have final and personal control over the Freud translation.[20] The support Freud gave to Strachey is clearly and officially expressed in the *Rundbrief* dated 'Wien 11 November 1920' and signed by Freud and Rank: 'In Strachey aus Cambridge, der sich jetzt in Wien aufhält, haben wir einen sehr guten und tüchtigen Übersetzer gefunden; er soll jetzt eine Arbeit vom Professor übernehmen, wahrscheinlich: Ein Kind wird geschlagen. [Strachey, from Cambridge, who is staying in Vienna at the moment, is proving to be a very good and thorough translator; he is about to take on a translation from the Professor, probably "A Child is Being

Beaten"].' And Freud, as well as Anna Freud after him, continued to support Strachey until the end of his life.[21] But we must not ignore the fact that when Alix and James Strachey commenced their work of translation in the '20s, they took as model the work already begun by Brill and, above all, by Jones. The latter was based on a rendering of the technical terminology of Freud, sometimes arbitrarily chosen by Jones and very often tending towards the production of a monosemic language. This fact, that Strachey was actively involved in translating the technical language of Freud following the rules of standardization established by Jones, *significantly influenced his later translation and standardization of Freud's style.*

All this carries a further set of ideological implications. We have seen that it was necessary to adapt psychoanalysis to the particular cultural environment in which Freud's work was being translated; but there also arose a sort of 'élitist' tendency which ran the risk of sometimes distorting Freud's thinking by making it too 'technical', sacrificing the complexity of the connotative as well as the denotative aspects of his language, even rendering it occasionally too prescriptive, too aristocratically distant. Let us not forget the associations that the term 'standard' has in English, especially in written English.[22] Freud's literary style, by contrast, was markedly determined by variable factors, such as the subject he was dealing with, the particular public he was addressing, the situation in which he was writing.[23]

With all these reservations in mind, a line of continuity is evident, even at the institutional level. For instance, the composition of the Publications Committee of the British Psycho-Analytic Society remained almost unchanged for over thirty years, and this helped to ensure a continuity of cultural and ideological viewpoint which partially explains some aspects of the English translation and the ways psychoanalysis developed in Britain. This is notwithstanding the curious fact that the term 'standard' itself seems to have disappeared for many years, reappearing officially only in the '50s, in a document in which Strachey announces to the British Society his intention of publishing a 'Standard Edition' of the works of Freud.

The continuity is also demonstrated by a curious episode which occurred during the intervening years. It concerns Jones's attempts to have Freud's complete works published immediately after Freud's death. He wrote to various analysts who had emigrated to America and to prominent cultural figures in Britain, requesting their collaboration or assistance in his efforts. Two things are striking here: his insistence on the term 'uniform translation', and his conviction that only he himself, Strachey, and those of the generation of pioneers who had initiated the original work of translation under Jones's guidance were truly authorized to translate and give a standard 'uniformity' to the work of Freud in English, because they alone had received the direct blessing of the Master.

As Jones states in a letter to Strachey of 28 September 1939, discussing his proposal to produce a complete edition of Freud in English: 'If it is done after our time it can never be done so well'. As I have tried to show, in the '50s Strachey was simply redoubling his efforts to follow a plan which had been almost completely formulated many years previously. He had, of course, his own idiosyncrasies of personal choice and preference, and these are very different from those of Jones, owing to their dissimilar cultural backgrounds and personalities – one has only to think of Strachey's well-known relationship with the Bloomsbury group. But in the main he was reworking translations already done by others, especially Riviere. He openly acknowledged this in a letter to Jones of 14 December 1957: 'The Metapsychological Papers plus die Traumdeutung were the main things of Freud that called for *retranslating* and editing' (my emphasis).

In effect, therefore, Strachey was trying to resolve a series of problems of translation set at the beginning of the '20s, if not before, by the Glossary Committee headed by Jones. Documents show some of Freud's views on questions of translation. On 14 July 1921 he wrote to Jones, referring to Strachey's translation of *Massenpsychologie und Ich-Analyse*: 'I could only go through the first half of the translation. I found it absolutely correct, free of all misunderstandings and I hope the rest will prove the same. I am no judge of the style, it seemed to me plain and easy. *Your claims for elegance may be stronger than mine* [my emphasis].' Freud was happy with Riviere's work too, calling it 'good, uniform work', in a letter to Jones of 17 May 1922. Furthermore, James and Alix Strachey discussed translation problems with Sigmund and Anna Freud later on, at the time they were translating the *Krankengeschichten*, in 1924–5.[24]

All these factors should help us to understand the historical context and the reasons why certain decisions were taken in the '20s. Were those decisions, taken in those years and under those particular conditions and ideological pressures, responsible for the imposition of a sort of Anglo-American Newspeak on psychoanalysis? Though I am personally of the view that such influences can be exaggerated, I cannot help being persuaded by Rank's accusation, in 1921, that Jones was furthering 'die Weltmachtstellung des Britischen Reichs [the position of the British Empire as a world power]'.[25]

To understand the historical importance of the decisions taken in the '20s, we should perhaps also take account of other considerations, which play a part in any field of study but have a particular significance tor psychoanalysis. I refer to the phenomenon of the 'viscosity' of institutions, their power to guarantee their own perpetuation. One of the chief ways they achieve this is by means of a simplified language which creates a code of communication among members, binding them together according to certain determined and hierarchical principles, and thus providing them with a sense of security at both a conscious and an unconscious level. This sense of security ensures that they will identify almost by reflex with the linguistic code. Thus they in turn pass on or teach this code to others, and the institution exercises a 'hegemonic', dominant role over its adherents.

Also significant is the fact that authorized expressions and technical terms require a passage of time before they can become 'standard' in the written language. Indeed it is this slow process which guarantees their later permanence and resistance to change. In time they form the cultural and communicative bricks with which the institution that created them builds itself into an edifice. The process is analogous to what Thomas Kuhn refers to as the 'necessary degree of dogmatism' that enables mature scientific thought to take place.[26]

All these factors contribute to our understanding of the 'enduring immobility' or 'static perseverance' of some aspects of the translations produced initially by Brill, Jones and his group, and taken up later by Strachey. And we must not ignore the particular unconscious charisma exercised by the transmission of psychoanalysis via the analytic treatment itself, and the special way psychoanalysis was and is taught, which have given Freud's language a unique power even in translation.

It is of course impossible to analyse here in detail the complex political and financial interests concerned in the struggle for control of psychoanalysis, both at a local level and at the level of the International Psycho-Analytical Association which, from the 1940s, was largely composed of the psychoanalysts who had fled from Nazi persecution to America and England. The 'Anglo–American alliance' meant that the International Psycho-Analytical Association itself came to stand as the principal guarantor of the translation and standardization of Freud's language. One has to remember that English is still the official and dominant language of the Association today.

As far as the particular mode of transmission of psychoanalysis is concerned, I have already noted the important role played by Freud himself in authorizing this transmission and its direct influence on Brill, Jones, the Stracheys, Riviere, Rickman, Anna Freud and others. Knowing well the unconscious emotive force involved in such privileged relationships of authorization, it is easy to see why, even to this day, it is difficult to measure the part played by this influence. In no other case do the problems of transmission play such a critical part, except perhaps that of the Bible or certain works by Karl Marx. Anyone concerned directly with the process of translation is aware that even the most perfect of renderings has a very limited life-span – twenty or thirty years at most.

It is clear, now that the first generation of pioneers in the field of psychoanalytical studies has disappeared, that we are witnessing a transformation and transferral of the early identifications and rivalries. We run the risk of establishing new 'standards', in our effort to correct the old terminology, re-examine the criteria of choices in the translation, and so on. There is no doubt that an enormous task lies ahead. We must first of all establish an accurate German text of Freud's work, studying as far as possible the cultural and linguistic basis of his style and his sources, and collect *all his writings* into a proper German edition, before we can think of beginning a new translation.[27] An enterprise of this kind – preparing a new 'real' Standard Edition of Freud, whether in German, English or any other language – always involves a risk of dogmatism, especially if the institutions that sponsor and guarantee the enterprise are inflexible, not prepared to open themselves to change, unwilling to accept the value of a plurality of suggestions and interpretations based on a plurality of experience. The most serious risk is that we might come to believe that, with the aid of modern technology, we can arrive at the 'true' Freud.

Apart from the problems of establishing the original text, deciding whether it is indeed possible to get at the 'true' Freud in German, or whether here too one is forever doing no more than simply 'interpreting' him – after all, the Austro-Germanic language used by Freud is not the German of today – we cannot ignore the fact that, as Borges has so eloquently demonstrated, a translation can never be more than an approximation. I refer here not so much to Borges' famous fictitious translator of *Don Quixote* as to his very beautiful tale of the professor of geography who, in his efforts to produce an accurate map of a little-known region, comes to the conclusion that the only perfect map would be one as large as the region itself – though even this would not completely satisfy him.[28]

Rather than get bogged down, therefore, in trying to establish new standard criteria for rendering the 'true' Freud, we should perhaps more profitably try to establish the best criteria for understanding and translating a Freud who speaks directly to us in our times, with the specific set of problems that belong to our age. Such questions (and hopefully such answers) belong to a historical moment that is quite different, culturally and socially, or even simply psychoanalytically, from that of Jones and Strachey. Whenever linguistic problems are debated, sometimes heatedly, what is at stake is never simply a linguistic problem *per se*, but the new historical and social reality which speaks out at these moments because it, precisely, is involved in a process of change. In sum, I would argue that only a 'dead' text, or one from Holy Scripture, permits of one and only one translation.

While it may be true that psychoanalysis is concerned with the atemporality of the unconscious, as a discipline it is by no means atemporal. Even its language is bound by the necessity of change, and this applies to the language of its original texts as well, if they are to survive and remain relevant to changed times – if, in other words, these texts are to provide new answers to the questions of new generations. The 'true' original text, far from producing final answers for all time, survives specifically on the basis of its capacity to elicit new questions through its constant reinterpretation. And this will always be the case, as long as we are prepared to accept that our new questions and our new answers, even those related directly to the new translation of the work of Freud, are already dated at the moment they are committed to paper; that is, in our here-and-now as well.

Notes

I would like to thank Sigmund Freud Copyrights Ltd. and Miss Pearl King, Honorary Archivist of the British Psycho-Analytical Society, for their permission to quote from unpublished correspondence between Freud and Ernest Jones, and from other documents. Reference to all letters not otherwise attributed is to letters held in these archives. I would also like to thank Dr Naomi Segal for her generous editorial help with this article.

[1] The title phrase is from an unpublished letter from Otto Rank to Ernest Jones, dated 2 Feb 1921, Archives of the British Psycho-Analytical Society.

[2] Those interested in further details may like to consult R. Steiner, 'An International World-Wide Trademark of Genuineness . . .?', *Int'l Rev Psych*, xiv (1987), no. 1. This is the first of a series of three articles on this subject to appear in the *Review*.

[3] Also such terms as 'interpretation of dreams' and 'free association'; see B. Bettelheim, *Freud and Man's Soul* (London 1983), 67–71.

[4] For reference to the Freud/Putnam correspondence see *James Jackson Putnam and Psychoanalysis*, ed. N.J. Hale (Cambridge, Mass., 1971). As for the Freud/Jones correspondence, which is as yet unpublished, I quote from copies of the letters held in the Archives of the British Psycho-Analytical Society and in the Sigmund Freud Archives at Colchester.

[5] I refer to an unpublished paper by S. Gilman circulated to the Publications Committee of the British Psycho-Analytical Society in autumn 1984, and to the excellent paper by D. Anzieu, 'The Place of Germanic Language and Culture in Freud's Discovery of Psychoanalysis Between 1895 and 1900', *Int'l Jn Psych*, lxvii (1986), no. 2.

[6] See Freud's letters to Jones (those written in English) and also the commendation Freud made of H.W. Chase's translation of his lectures, when he participated, along with Jung, Ferenczi and others, in the Clark University conferences in the USA in 1909.

[7] See Steiner, *Int'l Rev Psych*, xiv (1987), no. 1.

[8] E. Jones, Preface to *Papers on Psycho-analysis* (London 1913), 27. Jones recommended Pearson's *The Grammar of Science* (4th edn., London 1911) to Freud, who appreciated the book very much; see letter of Freud to Jones dated Vienna, 2 Feb 1912. In Freud's personal library in London, there is a copy of *The Grammar of Science* with copious underlinings in red pencil, which seems often to have been referred to by Freud. In

my opinion, he had recourse to this work at the time he wrote his *Metapsychological Papers* (Steiner, article in preparation, see n. 2).

[9] S. Freud, *The Interpretation of Dreams*, trans. A.A. Brill (London 1913), inserted sheet.

[10] W. Granoff, *Filiations: l'avenir du complexe d'Œdipe* (Paris 1975).

[11] I refer here to the second in my series of articles, 'An International World-wide Trademark of Genuineness . . .?', in preparation, to be published in 1988.

[12] Editorial by E. Jones, *Int'l Jn Psych*, I (1920), 3–4.

[13] E. Jones, letter to the Archbishop of Canterbury, 12 July 1922.

[14] For the German text of the *Statuten*, see *Int'l Z Psych*, v (1919), 143.

[15] S. Freud, *Beyond the Pleasure Principle* (London 1922), 22. It must not be forgotten that the official translator of this book was C.J.M. Hubback; but Jones began a translation of his own, and strictly supervised Hubback's translation. This was the period when Jones was preparing the official *Glossary for the Use of Translators of Psycho-Analytical Works* (London [1924]). Freud's remarks are therefore of great significance for understanding the editorial Jones wrote for the Glossary, where he again refers directly to the language of the natural sciences and its characteristics.

[16] E. Jones, 'A Linguistic Factor in English Characterology', *Int'l Jn Psych*, I (1920), 256–61. See also Darius Ornston, 'Strachey's Influence', *Int'l Jn Psych*, LXIII (1982), 409–26, and R. Steiner, forthcoming article (see n. 2).

[17] For instance: 'ego', 'unconscious', 'repression', 'preconscious', 'condensation', 'displacement', 'instinct', 'representation', 'dramatization', 'primary and secondary process', etc.

[18] There is evidence of Strachey's more personal reaction against Jones in the correspondence between him and his wife of the years 1924–5; see *Bloomsbury / Freud: The Letters of James and Alix Strachey 1924–1925*, ed. P. Meisel and W. Kendrick (London 1985); D. Ornston, 'The Invention of "Cathexis" and Strachey's Strategy', *Int'l Rev Psych*, XII (1985), no. 4.

[19] This copy of the Glossary, from an edition published in the 1930s, is held in the Archives of the British Psycho-Analytical Society. In the margins are more than 130 new terms or corrections added in the hand of James Strachey. It is quite possible that these were used by Alix Strachey in her *New German–English Psycho-Analytical Vocabulary* (London 1943).

[20] I refer here to an unpublished paper of mine, read at the special meeting on Strachey's translation organized by the British Psycho-Analytical Society in January 1984. Using the correspondence between Jones and Freud, I gave evidence of the way Jones tried to control the translation of Freud's papers and books. This is also confirmed by several remarks in Jones's letters to Rank. Jones was obsessed by the translation of Freud's works, and he thought he had the right to have the final say on it, especially on the technical vocabulary. For instance, in a letter to Rank dated 2 Feb 1921, after attacking Riviere, Jones states: 'I am so anxious that all [Freud's] work should be as well translated as combined brains can do . . .'. Or see a letter from Jones to Rank of 10 Apr 1922: 'I shall doubtless have to revise the Professor's writings as well as Mrs Riviere, even if she has the time for it; I don't think she would take the sole responsibility for it'. A very similar statement occurs in a letter to Freud of the same date, 10 Apr 1922, where Jones writes: 'with regard to the revision of translations, I should like to make an exception with your own work and also do not think Mrs Riviere would care to undertake the sole responsibility of this, though she might do an intermediate revision. . . . *If I can produce a Collected Edition of your works in my lifetime and leave the Journal on a soundly organised basis, I shall feel that my life has been worth living though I hope to do more for Psa. even than that* [my emphasis].'

[21] See for instance a letter from Freud to Jones dated 7 July 1935: '*J. Strachey ist mir gewiß der erwünschteste Übersetzer* [my emphasis] [Strachey is certainly the translator I would be most happy with]'.

[22] See R. Quirk, *The Use of English*, 2nd edn. (London 1968); R. Williams, *The Long Revolution* (London 1961); G. Orwell, *Collected Essays, Journalism and Letters*, 5th edn., vol. III: 1943–5 (London 1984).

[23] D. Ornston, *Int'l Jn Psych*, LXIII; B. Bettelheim, *Freud and Man's Soul*; Patrick Mahony, 'Further Considerations on Freud as a Writer', unpub. paper, 1984.

[24] In the Archives of the British Psycho-Analytical Society there is a series of letters from Anna and Sigmund Freud to James and Alix Strachey, and vice versa, dated in the early 1920s – the period when the Stracheys were translating the case histories. There is no doubt, at least from these documents, that Freud, helped by his daughter Anna, was closely following the translation done by Strachey. He also answered specific questions in a series of unpublished notes on the 'Dora' case, etc. I hope to publish these documents in the near future.

[25] To be fair, one needs to put Rank's remark in its context; Jones was complaining about misprints for which the Verlag in Vienna was responsible in their publication of papers on psychoanalysis in English. At that time both the *International Journal of Psycho-Analysis* and the International Library were published under the aegis of the Verlag in Austria.

[26] R. Steiner, 'Some Thoughts on Tradition and Change in Psychoanalysis', *Int'l Rev Psych*, XII (1985), no. 2; T. Kuhn, *The Structure of the Scientific Revolutions* (Chicago 1970).

[27] R. Steiner, unpub. letter to the Chairman of the Publications Committee of the British Psycho-Analytical Society, April 1983, on the problems relating to a new translation of Freud's work in English.

[28] This paradigm can actually be found earlier, in Lewis Carroll's *Sylvie and Bruno Concluded*, first published 1893; see *The Complete Works of Lewis Carroll* (London 1939), 556–7. I am indebted for this reference to Naomi Segal.

15

How Standard is the 'Standard Edition'?

Darius Gray Ornston, Jr.

When James Strachey's better-known brother set out to describe the Victorian era, he complained that he had too much material. Lytton Strachey pondered how a writer could be brief but fair – and still honour his own freedom of spirit. He described what he called a subtle strategy, that is '[I] will row out over that great ocean of material, and lower down into it, here and there, a little bucket, which will bring up to the light of day some characteristic specimen... to be examined with a careful curiosity.... It [will be] my purpose to illustrate rather than explain'.[1] On the second page of his *Eminent Victorians* Lytton Strachey went on to describe certain drawbacks to Standard Editions, in his case, Standard Biographies.

'To illustrate rather than explain'
Two years after Lytton had published his 'Victorian visions', James Strachey consulted Dr Ernest Jones. He was thirty-three years old, recently married and very much at a loss for what to do with himself. Although he asked to be referred to Dr Sigmund Freud for psycho-analytic treatment, instead he was shipped off to Vienna as one of Freud's pupils and translators. Strachey must have pulled a steady oar, because he gradually came to play a major role in bringing Freud's psychology across. Beyond that, we still know very little about the making of the 'Standard Edition'.[2]

Although we have ample evidence that Freud approved of Strachey as one of his English translators, we must now consider a very different question. Why was an edition of Freud's psychoanalytic works, published in a language foreign to him long after he died, given such absolute credibility and overweening authority?

One paradoxical reason may be that there are major differences between what Freud wrote and what James Strachey made of it – or, more precisely, between the way Freud wrote and the 'Standard Edition' which James Strachey put together for his own reader. *Freud's own imaginative pictures of unconscious life are much more variegated than*

Strachey's. Freud remained master of his metaphors by choosing somewhat irreconcilable imagery from many different fields including, of course, nineteenth-century biology.[3] Where Freud steadily shifts his descriptions of what goes on unconsciously and portrays his own conceptions with many different comparisons, *Strachey simplifies.*

We must remember that Freud had all kinds of advantages over Strachey. For one thing, Freud was not writing a 'Standard Edition'. He was reworking various ways of imagining what goes on unconsciously, that is, steadfastly sketching whatever he could see of his own ways of trying to make sense of the unconscious – at one time or another. Strachey was following a predetermined programme, probably a Grand Design in the mind of Ernest Jones.[4]

Freud also had the advantage of writing in plain and ambiguous German, that is, in a scientific tradition which expects a real scientist to describe an unsettled conception indefinitely. In this kind of describing psychology, conceptual inconsistency and flexibility ('Geschmeidig-keit') are necessary virtues and a gifted writer is empowered to say several different things at the same time. This kind of science will give grave difficulty to a person who has accepted the catechism of Ernest Jones.[5]

Furthermore, I believe Freud assumes a reader who is ready to get involved, who can enjoy several irreconcilable senses and read between the lines. Freud seems to trust his reader and therefore, he often relies on the engaging language of everyday experience.[6]

Strachey recognized that his own wording sounded weak when compared to Freud's. For example, Freud chose a descriptive term for the way we all recall and sort apart our own experience in order to 'feel our way into' another person's psychic life ('uns einzufühlen'). Writing to his wife in English and also at certain places in his formal translation, Strachey chose to use a literal translation of this descriptive German word 'Einfühlung', although Jones would insist that 'empathy' was the 'recognised official psychological word for it'. Some day, when their correspondence is opened to independent scholars, we may learn why Strachey neither remarked on nor explained his diverse translations of the same German terms, and why the Stracheys relied on Ernest Jones for advice about what Freud meant to say.[7]

Strachey said he had *very* English writing in mind;[8] and we also know he was addressing naïve souls who took it for granted that language is made up simply of words. One who appreciates Freud will always be able to enjoy another view: language also makes sense as patterns of sound and word plays on catch-phrases. Strachey wryly told Jones about a group of Americans who 'seemed to think that if they could be told the "right" translation the meaning would automatically be conveyed to them'.[9]

For reasons which must have made sense at the time, then, Strachey broke up some of Freud's descriptive conceptions and also condensed some of his lively imagery into fewer terms. In the table on p. 206 are two examples of the way Strachey congealed some of Freud's descriptive language into more consistent and simpler imagery such as 'structure' and 'discharge'. Later I will describe Strachey's use of the term 'subject'. As any editor will do, Strachey emphasized what he took for fundamental and quietly played down or cut out what he saw as inessential.

Why is the 'Standard Edition' so important to psychoanalysis?
I don't think anyone has really studied this question, but we can run through a few obvious reasons. The first is that psychoanalysis had caught on rapidly in the United States. Because the English-speaking peoples are dreadful about languages, some good translations were essential.

Strachey's translations became important because they were good, but that doesn't answer our question, because there were so many good English translations between the wars. A systematic comparison could be made of Brill and Baines and Riviere and Putnam and the many other good translations which still have certain advantages over Strachey's. To say that Strachey was given more to do than the others, or that his Edition contains much more than the others, does not settle this matter because we have been asked to begin to think about *why* this happened.

Freud was never satisfied. He took such pains to paraphrase, to find yet another informative comparison. And he said quite explicitly that this was his scientific strategy, that we can only describe with the help of comparisons and that we have to keep on changing our descriptions of our own conceptions because none of them will do for very long.[10]

What would *Freud* have made of a single and standardized English translation of his many radiantly shifting sketches, so scrupulously variegated? No one knows. Jones and Anna Freud agreed with Strachey, seeing Freud as 'completely unbusinesslike' if not careless in the handling of his copyrights and translations. Perhaps. *Another view is that Freud favoured diverse wording as essential to his descriptive science.*[11]

Some have suggested that Freud would have approved of Strachey's version. I can see no reason why not, because, well into the 1930s, Freud continued to approve and encourage many other translators of his works, including the very unfashionable A.A. Brill.[12] Why then would Freud have wanted to discourage Strachey's attempts? And we know from R.A. Paskauskas that Freud went along with Jones and preferred Strachey for certain assignments.

However, we have no evidence that Freud preferred Strachey's 'scientific language', let alone that he would have approved of the

MASSENPSYCHOLOGIE

UND

ICH-ANALYSE

VON

PROF. SIGM. FREUD

INTERNATIONALER
PSYCHOANALYTISCHER VERLAG G. M. B. H.
LEIPZIG WIEN ZÜRICH
1921

18. Title-page of the original 1921 edition of *Massenpsychologie und Ich-Analyse*, with the Verlag's vignette of Oedipus and the Sphinx.

Standard Edition. Whatever understanding Freud may have had of Jones's intentions, his opinion of Strachey's final production will never be known because he died long before these books were published. And even if he had put his imprimatur on the very English 'Standard Edition', that would not help a person who is trying to make an independent judgement about the ways in which Strachey changed what Freud wrote.

Uwe Peters speculates about how differently Freud's inheritance might have developed in an Austro-German culture. If Strachey had not contrived a taut craft for Freud's subtle prose, would Freud have disappeared among the Romantic writers of an earlier age?[13] Or was the metapsychological jargon consolidated in the years immediately after Freud died more like a stabilizing sea anchor – which only became a drag when it was time to move?

Must any 'Standard Edition' suppress alternatives? Is that what we have Standards for? Or could a critical edition discuss some other ways of putting things? Well, of course, some day there will be several critical editions, although, for reasons I will come to later, none of us will live to see them.

If, then, Strachey's team felt they must settle any unsettling questions, this would also explain why Strachey tells us so little about the many choices he had to make. He writes as if his own reading of each term and passage were the only one. I believe this tells us something about the bumptiously metapsychological fashion of Strachey's time. If I were to name only one way in which Strachey's edition is indeed 'an amateur production', as Strachey said in his General Preface (1966), it would be his systematic exclusion of alternatives.

I don't see how we can understand Strachey's necessarily selective use of assorted advisers, nor his reasoning, until we have clearer sets of perspectives on psychoanalysis after Freud died. What role did Alix Strachey play? Was Anna Freud still learning English when the binding decisions were made? Why did Joan Riviere withdraw, and what is in those huge bundles of her correspondence with Freud locked up in the Library of Congress until after the next millennium? What difference did it make that Jones was more of a foreigner than most of us, that is, an expatriate Welshman by way of Canada who had learned some German late in life? Did anyone keep notes on the meetings of Jones's very English 'Glossary Committee'? And so, on and on.[14]

Why was Strachey's version so eagerly mistaken for scripture? Perhaps we should ask why the other King James edition still holds up. The King James is often wrong, but precious few scholars seem to care about that because it *sounds* right.

To say that among psychoanalysts a canonical tradition took the place of scientific scholarship just re-words this embarrassing question: How could any paper or book, based on a standardized *translation*, have passed for serious scholarship? And then, how could any single translation – done by a man who said he seldom looked at Freud's original manuscripts, and who also said that often there was no reliable original[15] – ever have been mistaken for 'the Standard' and then so eagerly accepted by so many sensible people, some of whom surely knew better?

Bigotry must have something to do with such blind acquiescence. For one thing, there is that sad German diffidence towards the English language. And German deference is only worsened by those native English-speakers who still mistake a certain dialect of southern England for 'the standard'. Suddenly we have stumbled into a huge socio-linguistic question and perhaps an emotional quagmire. I don't think the rise and fall of the British Empire, nor colonial attitudes, are enough to explain why even to this day, in some circles, English is accorded a strange supremacy – and not just English, but the mannerisms and dialect peculiar to a once self-certain social caste.

And then, those two horrible wars did not help – not at all. The ruins of war, resentment, shame and alienation confuse at least another whole generation. In this symposium we have begun to learn about the awkward predicaments of some badly torn, grateful and vulnerable German-speaking analysts who did get out in time.

Strachey tells us that 500 American subscribers underwrote his edition in advance, 'an act of pure and indeed unreasonable faith'.[16] I think we can also understand the predicament of people who have invested heavily, are unable to judge and yet convinced they have no decent alternative.

Many people whose mother tongue was German, and who had been reading Freud in German, noticed differences and sent in suggestions, but we don't even know where their letters are – let alone have access to them. Furthermore, many alternative translations of single words or whole passages have already been salted into the psychoanalytic literature, but these are seldom indexed and impossible to find. Why have we paid so little attention to Freud's own descriptive terms and so eagerly adopted the 'international vocabulary' promoted by Ernest Jones?

We do know that some analysts saw alternative readings as unscientific and that Jones was one of them. Jones laid out a programme based on his own, now ingenuous, assumption that a 'classical nomenclature' would be free of any personal associations. Although he went right on to complain that German scientists, and only German scientists, refused to comply with the 'classical nomenclature' which he, Jones, saw as the essence of science, Jones did *not* remark that Freud continued to picture his ideas in plain German. Freud never gave up the common metaphors and technical expressions of his own time (or somewhat earlier), and usually he stepped around Jones's selections. Freud simply avoided most of Jones's 'international vocabulary'.[17]

Despite Jones's brave new hope for a technical terminology free of feelings, human beings crave simple certainty and they are loyal to a fault. Synthetic Latin words connote a factual consistency which has eluded psychoanalysis.[18] And yet, for all of the elemental reasons, some analysts are still quite passionately attached to what they feel must be the proper way of wording things. Their terms are not neutral now, if they ever were. If you doubt me, at your next psychoanalytic meeting stand up and try to discuss any alternative translation of Freud's *Das Ich und das Es*.

One of the differences between German and English is that, for a long, long time, the English language has been thoroughly latinized and frenchified, while Jones's observation about German scientists' preference for their descriptive mother-tongue is still valid. Jones's 'nomenclature' sounds stranger in German, and deep differences prevail. We now know that the Stracheys and John Rickman vigorously opposed Jones's choices for *The Ego and the Id*, and we know that Jones turned the tide; but we do not know how or why.[19]

In fact, we know from their published letters that the Stracheys disagreed with many of Jones's choices, and we have some clues to their predicament. Strachey did tell us about a few of his own assumptions, and an informed reader who can grasp the essence of historical method, who can perform a sympathetic act of creative imagination, may begin to understand.[20]

Although most of the research materials are still closed to independent scholars, I think the Stracheys' letters show that they did as they were told. James Strachey stood discreetly by his crew. At times against his better judgement, he used his own musical ear to clean up Freud's subtly compelling sounds and demonically throbbing intensities, almost all of the natural rhythms and intimate effects which might offend his own proper English reader.[21]

Why is Freud more immediate than Strachey? In one of his many enlightening studies, Mahony has pointed out that Strachey shunted most of Freud's lively dreams and engaging anecdotes from the present tense into the past. For example:

Eine große Halle – viele Gäste, die wir empfangen. – Unter ihnen Irma, die ich sofort beiseite nehme, um gleichsam ihren Brief zu beantworten, ihr Vorwürfe zu machen, daß sie die 'Lösung' noch nicht akzeptiert. Ich sage ihr:... [A large hall – we are receiving many guests – *Irma* is among them. Right away I take her aside in order to answer her letter and scold her because she doesn't accept my 'solution'. I say to her:...] (*GW* II–III. 111).

THE STANDARD EDITION
OF THE COMPLETE PSYCHOLOGICAL WORKS OF

SIGMUND FREUD

Translated from the German under the General Editorship of

JAMES STRACHEY

In Collaboration with

ANNA FREUD

Assisted by

ALIX STRACHEY and ALAN TYSON

VOLUME XVIII

(1920–1922)

Beyond the Pleasure Principle

Group Psychology

and

Other Works

LONDON

THE HOGARTH PRESS

AND THE INSTITUTE OF PSYCHO-ANALYSIS

19. Title-page of volume XVIII of the Standard Edition; note that *Massen-psychologie* (cf. p. 199) has been mistranslated as *Group Psychology*.

Even though one does shift tenses more often in German than in English, Strachey's silent penchant for the simple past is just one of many ways in which he sounds remote when compared to Freud.[22]

In the Golden Age of Metapsychology, when an analyst might see himself a flawless mirror, whose 'functions' were neutralized and 'conflict-free', and whose true regressions were 'in the service of the ego', it was natural for Strachey to suppose that he had little interest in theory and to believe he could set his own convictions aside.[23]

As he did with so many metaphors that were traditional in German scientific writing, Strachey saw 'psychic energy' as Freud's 'discovery'. He said this notion was essential and called psychic energy the *most* fundamental of Freud's concepts. However, Freud had never said anything like that, and in fact had not even used the loosely personified imagery of 'Besetzung' in that very early paper where Strachey dug up his own definition of 'cathexis'.[24]

Strachey also said Freud came to put more value on what he, Strachey, called 'structure' than on function – although Freud never said that either. Freud did often tinker with what he regarded as no more than a second topology, but Strachey crystallized Freud's various versions of this ancient idea into 'the structural theory'. Similarly, Rapaport and Gill could not find definitions of 'structure' and 'metapsychology' in Freud's works until they put together their own.[25]

These are Strachey's opinions and they are not Freud's. Strachey didn't know that 'Energie' and 'Struktur' had been common in Romantic medicine, and were still common in nineteenth-century German psycho-biologies. Therefore, he read them as original to Freud.[26]

Furthermore, as Hirschmüller, and also Ritchie Robertson, have reminded us, Freud is unreliable when not misleading about his own sources. For example, Romantic medical writers had used the same terms he chose for very similar topical schemes, and it is quite likely Freud knew about this.[27]

Strachey had left medical school after three weeks and he had no scientific training. In his reluctantly post-Victorian England, a scientist was a logical positivist and there was only one scientific method. I doubt whether Strachey was ready to think about science in any other way. It followed that there was only one correct reading of Freud – as a logical positivist.[28]

John Bowlby says 'spontaneity and intuition' are 'proceedings far removed from science'. Among many of the English and Americans this traditional conceit runs deep. Another view of this ancient tension was traditional in Freud's time. For example, the pre-eminent surgeon scientist at the University of Vienna during Freud's student years put it:

Der Proceß des Forschens und des Gestaltens des Erforschten ist ein psych-
ologischer Vorgang, ohne dessen Entwicklung weder Wissenschaft noch
Kunst produciert wird. Es gehört zu den trivialen Thorheiten unserer Zeit, in
Wissenschaft und Kunst eine Art von Gegensatz sehen zu wollen. Die Fantasie
ist die Mutter beider.
[The process of research and the shaping of this exploration is an ongoing
psychological activity. Without its development neither science nor art can be
produced. One of the trivial foolishnesses of our time is wanting to see an
opposition between science and art. Phantasy is the mother of both.][29]

I think Strachey and Jones also were burdened with 'The Whig
Interpretation of History'[30] – their assumption that real science must
develop in orderly stages and relentlessly for the better. While Freud
would seize and use any old comparison which might inform,
Strachey's tale is a logical progression with occasional lapses.
Therefore, Strachey had to tidy up.

Freud's Romantic irony

I believe that in order to feel Freud's attitude towards his own animated
theories one must sense his irony, his steady Romantic irony. By that
I mean, Freud subtly mocks his own grand schemes and often
undercuts his own exaggerated claims. Typically, he tells us he has
never ('niemals') abused the power of suggestion in order to talk a
patient into anything, and on the following page we find him bullying
the young wife of a colleague into having sex with her husband.[31]

Freud's irony has not been studied yet but by resolutely *personifying*
his many mechanisms, authorities, territories, apparatuses and what-
have-you; by *resisting definitions* and *relying on poetic word play and
ambiguity*; and by *tirelessly shaping a fresh context* when he does find a use
for the imagery of an earlier century – Freud engages, delights and
persuades precisely because he never seems taken in by any one perspective for very long.

For example, by putting the same rough conception in as many
different ways as he can find, Freud forestalls an eager reader who is
looking for THE WORD. Freud cajoles or seduces one into trying this,
while wondering about that, and always reckoning from one's own
experience and recall. Freud's very *variety keeps one from making too much
out of any one way of putting an idea*. Strachey's Freud is easier to read
because he seldom sounds sceptical, let alone ironical, about such
ponderous matters as metapsychology.

Take another example: Strachey read Freud as an objective scientist
who was studying a subject. Naturally, it follows that, as he translated
Freud's short paper on constructions, Strachey had to use the word
'subject' quite often, although Freud had not found a place for the
German word 'Subjekt' anywhere in this paper. Strachey has Freud's

'betreffende Punkt' or 'relevant point' as a 'subject'. Freud's 'Thema' or theme, Freud's 'Analysierte' or analysand, and Freud's 'Kranke' or patient all boil down to Strachey's 'subject', as does the 'Inhalt' or content of Freud's construction. Strachey also inserts the word 'subject' gratuitously: Freud's 'aktive Äußerungen des Analysierten [active expressions of the analysand]' are 'behaviour of the subject of the analysis' in Strachey's English version. Strachey was writing a different kind of science.[32]

Freud			Strachey
der Aufbau	die Gliederung	die Ordnung	
der Bau	das Gebäude	die Struktur	
der Überbau	das Gebilde	der Träger	structure
die Bildung	das Gefüge		
abfliessen	ableiten	entladen	
abführen	abstossen	entlasten	discharge
ablaufen	abströmen	verlaufen	
der Analysierte (analysed person, analysand)			
das Individuum (individual)			
der Kranke (patient)			
der Punkt (point)			subject
der Inhalt (content)			
das Thema (theme)			
von denen (of which)			

In Freud's portrayals the analyst is a person working with another 'person' to bring the past alive in order to try to understand. Freud developed 'a radically new definition of the doctor and patient relationship'.[33] Because he saw their psychological processes as the same, Freud chose to use the same words to describe them. Strachey did not see this. Therefore, and silently, Strachey separates Freud's choice of the same words to describe the psychology of both analyst and patient. He does this all the time.[34] Once again we are talking about the much more meaningful matter of tone and style, rather than trivial quarrels about which technical terms to use.

In sum, Strachey's translation was good, and when we learn more about the problems he faced and the spirit of his time, we may be able to understand his choices. However, for now, Strachey clumps Freud's variegated conceptual descriptions into fewer terms, and he systematically separates some of what Freud chose to describe as the same – for example, the psychological processes of patient and analyst.

What can be changed and what will happen?

No one knows, because the basic research on Freud's scientific sources and style has barely begun. Most research material is, as I have said, still closed off from open investigation and alternative readings. New translations are forbidden by copyright, and the holders of those archives and copyrights have yet to come forward, announce and explain their policies. Naturally it has been very difficult to engage competent scholars.

However gradually some archives may be opening up. And in a year or so the English copyright will expire. Some day alternative readings will not only be permitted but encouraged, openly debated and even published. If context meant more than terminology in Freud's psychology, then distribution and scientific discussion of experimental translations would be one essential step towards a critical edition.

In time, Freud's role in the history of his discipline will come into perspective. We will be able to see more of his sources, his assumptions, his stylistic devices and his errors. Some day such critical work will no longer be seen as an attack on Freud or on the institutions set up to take his place. Strachey's own historical niche should come clear and stay secure. However, at this early stage of scholarly study any salty phrase about what Freud really meant, or about what Strachey was up to, must be washed down with a lot of caution.[35]

Scriptural use of either Freud or Strachey will one day seem a sad, all too human, symptom of our time. People who go on about Freud's 'definition', as if there were one and only one definition of anything at all in Freud's works, will be mistrusted. At least I hope so. And in my idyll the history of psychoanalysis will belong to science; and no one will ever plumb the depths, let alone come up with the final word.

Notes

The research for this paper was supported in part by the Fund for Psychoanalytic Research of the American Psychoanalytic Association. I am grateful to Patrick Mahony and Burness E. Moore, as well as to the editors of this volume, for generous readings and several suggestions.

[1] L. Strachey, *Eminent Victorians* (London 1918).

[2] J. Strachey: *Remarks on the 50th Anniversary of the British Psycho-Analytical Society*, 30 Oct 1963 (Mansfield House, London), 22–4; General Preface, *SE* I. D.G. Ornston: 'Strachey's Influence', *Int'l Jn Psych*, LXIII (1982), 409–26; 'Freud's Conception is Different from Strachey's, *Jn APA*, XXXIII (1985), 379–412; 'The Invention of "Cathexis" and Strachey's Strategy', *Int'l Rev Psych*, XII (1985), 391–9. R.A. Paskauskas, this volume, Chapter 7.

[3] W. Schönau, *Sigmund Freuds Prosa* (Stuttgart 1968).

[4] J. Strachey: *Remarks*, 1963; General Preface, *SE* I; J. and A. Strachey, *Bloomsbury/ Freud*, ed. P. Meisel and W. Kendrick (New York 1985); R. Andrew Paskauskas, personal communication; Ornston, *Int'l Rev Psych*, XII.

[5] Ornston, *Int'l Rev Psych*, XII.

[6] S. Bernfeld, 'Freud's Earliest Theories and the School of Helmholtz', *Psychoanalytic Quarterly*, XIII (1944), 341–62; Schönau, *Sigmund Freuds Prosa*; U. Pörksen, 'Zur Terminologie der Psychoanalyse', *Deutsche Sprache*, III (1973), 7–36; P. Mahony: *Freud as a Writer* [1982], 2nd edn. rev. (New Haven, Conn., 1987); *Cries of the Wolfman* (New York 1984); *Freud and the Rat Man* (New Haven, Conn., 1986).

[7] J. Strachey: *Remarks*, 1963; General Preface, *SE* I; J. and A. Strachey, *Bloomsbury/ Freud*, 170f., 177; Ornston, *Int'l Rev Psych*, XII.

[8] J. Strachey, General Preface, *SE* I. xix.

[9] Letter cited in Ornston, *Int'l Rev Psych*, XII, 394. Mahony's books (see n. 6) are the best available on Freud's rhythms and evocative puns.

[10] S. Freud, *Die Frage der Laienanalyse* (1926), *GW* XIV. 222, via B. Bettelheim, *Freud and Man's Soul* (New York 1983); Ornston, *Int'l Rev Psych*, XII.

[11] Jones, III. 50, 132; J. Strachey, General Preface, *SE* I. xxi; A. Freud, Preface, *SE* XXIV. vii; cf. Ornston: *Int'l Jn Psych*, LXIII; *Jn APA*, XXXIII; *Int'l Rev Psych*, XII.

[12] E.A. Ticho, 'The Influence of the German-Language Culture on Freud's Thought', *Int'l Jn Psych*, LXVII (1986), 227–34; I. Grubrich-Simitis, 'Reflections on Sigmund Freud's Relationship to the German Language and to Some German-Speaking Authors of the Enlightenment', *Int'l Jn Psych*, LXVII (1986), 287–94; S. Freud, *Die Traumdeutung* (1900), *GW* II–III, 104, footnote added in 1930.

[13] K. Eissler, 'Creativity and Adolescence', *Psych Study of Child*, XXXIII (1978), 461–517.

[14] E. Jones, *Free Associations* (London and New York 1959); J. Strachey: obituary for Joan Riviere, *Int'l Jn Psych*, XLIV (1963), 228–30; General Preface, *SE* I; Ornston, *Int'l Rev Psych*, XII.

[15] J. Strachey, General Preface, *SE* I.

[16] Ibid., *SE* I. xx.

[17] E. Jones [*et al.*], *Glossary for the Use of Translators of Psycho-Analytical Works* [1924] (*Int'l Jn Psych* suppl no. 1); Ornston, *Int'l Rev Psych*, XII.

[18] C. Rycroft, *A Critical Dictionary of Psychoanalysis* [1968] (Totowa, N.J., 1973); S.A. Leavy, 'Psychoanalytic Interpretation', *Psych Study of Child*, XXVIII (1973), 305–30.

[19] Jones, *Glossary*; J. and A. Strachey, *Bloomsbury | Freud*.

[20] H. Butterfield, *The Whig Interpretation of History* [1931] (repr. New York 1965).

[21] J. and A. Strachey, *Bloomsbury | Freud*.

[22] Freud, *Die Traumdeutung*: my translation; compare Strachey's ('A large hall – numerous guests, whom we were receiving. – Among them was Irma. I at once took her on one side, as though to answer her letter and to reproach her for not having accepted my "solution" yet. I said to her:...', *SE* IV. 107). P. Mahony, 'Towards a Formalist Approach to Dreams', *Int'l Rev Psych*, IV (1977), 83–99.

[23] J. Strachey, *Remarks*, 1963; *Int'l Jn Psych*, XLIV; General Preface, *SE* I; J. and A. Strachey, *Bloomsbury | Freud*.

[24] J. Strachey; Editor's Introduction (1953), *SE* IV. xvi; 'The Emergence of Freud's Fundamental Hypotheses' (1962), *SE* III. 62f.; Ornston, *Int'l Rev Psych*, XII.

[25] D. Rapaport and M.M. Gill, 'The Points of View and Assumptions of Metapsychology', in *Collected Papers of David Rapaport*, ed. M.M. Gill (New York 1959): Ornston, *Jn APA*, XXXIII.

[26] J. Strachey, *Remarks*, 1963.

[27] A. Hirschmüller, 'Sublimierung', *Forum der Psychoanalyse*, I (1985), 250–64; R. Robertson in ch. 5 of this volume; H. Ellenberger, *The Discovery of the Unconscious* (New York 1970); Ornston, in preparation.

[28] D.W. Winnicott, obituary for James Strachey, *Int'l Jn Psych*, L (1969), 129–31; J. Strachey, *Remarks*, 1963; Ornston: *Jn APA*, XXXIII; *Int'l Rev Psych*, XII.

[29] T. Billroth, *Briefe von Theodor Billroth*, ed. G. Fischer, 2nd edn. (Hanover 1896), letter no. 147 to Prof. Wm. Lübke, 27 July 1875, p. 192.

[30] Butterfield, *Whig Interpretation of History*.

[31] S. Freud, 'Konstruktionen in der Analyse' (1937), GW XVI. 49ff.

[32] Ibid., GW XVI. 45 (SE XXIII. 259).

[33] I. Grubrich-Simitis, 'Sigmund Freuds Lebensgeschichte und die Anfänge der Psycho-analyse', *Neue Rundschau*, LXXXII (1971), no. 1, 313.

[34] Ornston, *Int'l Jn Psych*, LXIII.

[35] Mahony: *Freud as a Writer*; 'The Discourse of Sigmund Freud', unpub. MS. Ornston, review of Bettelheim, *Freud and Man's Soul*, *Jn APA*, XXXIII (1985), Book Supplement, 189–200.

16

Reservations about the Standard Edition

Alex Holder

I would like to begin by expressing a sense of disappointment and concern: some three years ago a working party was set up by the Publications Committee of the British Psycho-Analytical Society to investigate the claims that Strachey's 'Standard Edition' of Freud's works, however magnificent, had many flaws and ought to be revised or even replaced. Well over two years ago this working party recommended a radical revision of Strachey, so radical indeed as to be tantamount to a new translation. It based its recommendations on the view that Strachey's translation presented a perspective on Freud which was very peculiar to Strachey, to his era, and to his own cultural, scientific and philosophical background and beliefs; furthermore that the Strachey translation and its presentation lacked the rigour by which works of scholarship in other disciplines are judged.

This radical suggestion understandably generated a great deal of anxiety, which had many sources, perhaps the most serious being the threat of losing something which we had taken for granted, had grown up with, and which we had all assumed to be the authentic voice of the Master. Now that I have lived and worked in Germany for more than three years and have immersed myself in the original Freud again – with all the criticisms levelled against Strachey's translation at the back of my mind – I have become even more alive to how different Freud sounds when one hears him speaking in his own voice.

Another possible source of anxiety is the awareness of the enormity of the task of retranslation and the absence of any guarantee that the revised version will be an improvement on Strachey.

All this led the working party to suggest various possible compromises, such as the publication of a supplement, in which problematical issues would be examined in depth, factual errors corrected, etc., and which would serve as a gloss to the 24 volumes of Strachey.

Since then there has been silence; to my knowledge there have been no moves in the direction of implementing plans even for a compromise solution, let alone the more radical proposal.

What could this mean?

- Do we need more *evidence* to convince us of the inadequacies of Strachey's translation? or is there still a widespread belief that Strachey is good enough?
- Do we need more *time* to allow us to get used to the idea of losing something that has been central to our psychoanalytic education and to which we feel such a close relationship?
- Or are we awaiting another Strachey, an individual of similar gifts who has the time and energy for so forbidding a task, even when undertaken in collaboration with others?
- Or was the whole wave of criticism perhaps only a storm in a teacup?
- Or is it felt that it is, quite simply, impossible to translate Freud into English satisfactorily – or at any rate to improve on Strachey – just as the Germans despairingly feel in attempting to translate Winnicott into German?

I have recently had occasion to read a paper by a colleague on 'Analysis Terminable and Interminable', in which he also touches on the difficulty of translating Freud into English, citing the very title, 'Die endliche und die unendliche Analyse', as a demonstration of these difficulties. 'Endlich' as an adjective (used thus by Freud in his title) means that something, in this particular instance an analysis, can be brought to an end, that it is 'finite'. The opposite would be 'infinite', 'unending'. A more literal translation of the German original would thus be 'The Finite and Infinite Analysis'. The author of the paper takes the view that Strachey's choice of the words 'terminable' and 'interminable' evokes connotations of precise time limitations, real objects, etc., and rather derives from the terminology of the natural sciences. He therefore endorses one of the main criticisms levelled against Strachey, namely that the latter's language places Freud in the realm of the natural sciences ('Naturwissenschaften') and thereby distances him from the 'Geisteswissenschaften' where he truly belongs.[1]

That said, I wish to make it clear that I in no way underestimate the importance of Strachey and the tremendous influence he has had on the development and spread of psychoanalysis in the English-speaking world. (It is a fact that psychoanalytic contributions from that language area over the past few decades have been more numerous than from any other.) I think that just because Strachey's achievement is so magnificent in many respects, just because his annotations, commentaries, cross-references etc., have been so helpful and useful in guiding us through the jungle of Freud's revisions, additions, modifications of points of view, enigmatic and apparently contradictory formulations – just because of all this we have never seriously questioned the authenticity of the actual translation, or asked ourselves how close to the original it really is and how faithfully it reflects the spirit and meaning of that original. Faced with the notion – indeed, the claim – that it is not Freud but Strachey's idiosyncratic *version* of Freud that we have been reading, we want to turn a blind eye to that notion because of its implications.

As an analogy, it is rather like having come to know and admire a well-known work of art, and then to have experts discover that later additions by others have been superimposed on the original canvas, which they proceed to remove in order to reveal the original. The restoration may prove quite a shock. Or, to take another example even closer to my own experience: having grown up listening to the music of Bach, Handel, and other composers of that era performed by full orchestras on modern instruments, some years ago I first heard the same music played on the authentic instruments and by the small ensemble of players for which it was originally written. What a difference, and one which took some getting used to!

Over the last three years I have become more and more convinced that Strachey took considerable liberties in his translation; as I have read more of Freud in the original, I have gained a quite new apprehension of him, a sense of immediacy, of being addressed in a very personal way, in a style both beautiful and literary which is far removed from the language of scientific discourse. That style elicits a totally different response from the one I had when I read Freud in Strachey's translation during my psychoanalytic training in London. In this respect I agree with Bettelheim that Strachey makes Freud sound much more formal, technical and abstract than he is. In particular, Strachey's introduction of terms derived from Latin and Greek adds a dimension which is almost totally absent from the original.

I will give just one example to illustrate this point. It concerns Freud's term 'Besetzung' which Strachey chose to render as 'cathexis'. This is a foreign term with which the ordinary English reader has no associations whatsoever. It is certainly not a word in daily use. This is very different from the German 'Besetzung', an extremely common, everyday word, with clear and strong military connotations but also with associations to the word 'besitzen', to possess. 'Besetzung' literally means 'occupation', as for instance the occupation of a strategically important position, a town or a country. As a term used by Freud in postulating the movement of hypothetical psychic forces, it immediately brings to mind, in the German original, one of Freud's favourite metaphors of advancing and retreating troops or armies. This was the term he used, for instance, in his discussions of libidinal development and progression, or when he tried to elucidate processes of regression and fixation. Such links, which a German reader makes automatically – consciously or unconsciously – between these metaphors and the notion of 'Besetzung' are absent in Strachey's translation. However, this example at the same time highlights the pitfalls and difficulties in any attempt to translate Freud literally, for the word 'occupation' also has the quite separate meaning of 'job' or 'profession', which is not present in the German 'Besetzung'. It will be one of the many obstacles confronting future translators of Freud.

When I first examined Strachey's translation for the purpose of evaluating its fidelity to the original, I embarked on a little experiment which yielded some interesting results. I picked, almost at random, Freud's paper 'Die Verdrängung' ('Repression')[2] and started to translate it as literally as possible, while trying at the same time to produce a readable English text. I then compared my version with Strachey's and examined the differences in actual translation, not taking into account differences in style and rhythm which, of course, present the translator with a further huge problem – one that Patrick Mahony, for instance, has addressed.[3]

In the first sentence alone of the paper on 'Repression' I found five instances of varying translations of crucial words or phrases.[4] The first concerns the word 'Schicksal'. Incomprehensibly, Strachey discards the obvious English equivalent, which is 'fate' (as we meet it indeed in the compound 'fate neurosis [Schicksalsneurose]'), and chooses instead the much more abstract term 'vicissitudes'. 'Fate' has many more connotations, just as the German 'Schicksal' has.

Let me mention briefly at least two of the other variants in order to convey something of the problems to be faced in a retranslation of Freud. Where Freud uses 'unwirksam' (literally 'ineffective'), Strachey chooses 'inoperative', a term with mechanical, scientific connotations which are totally absent from the German original. Freud's compound 'Triebregung' in the opening sentence takes us right to the heart of a long-standing debate as to the most adequate way of translating 'Trieb'. Since Freud himself made a clear differentiation between 'Trieb' and 'Instinkt', Strachey's choice of 'instinct' for 'Trieb' is strange and misleading. But even if we agree that it won't do, it still leaves us with the problem of finding a better alternative. Equally, we can raise questions about Strachey's choice of 'impulse' to convey the sense of '-regung' of the original. To me the word 'impulse' conveys something much more powerful and peremptory than does the German 'Regung' which literally means 'a stirring'. Furthermore, there are immediate associative links in German from 'Regung' to 'Aufregung [excitement]', 'Erregung [stimulation]', etc.

I think we have to accept that no translation will be able to replicate such associative links and all the connotations that are triggered in the mind of a German-speaking reader (and even more so a German-born reader) when he studies the real Freud.

Freud himself was the first to place psychoanalysis alongside education and government as one of the three impossible professions. Sometimes I begin to wonder whether a totally satisfactory rendering of Freud in English, or any other language for that matter, is not an equally impossible task.

Nevertheless I am left with the conviction that Strachey can be improved upon and that for the sake of present and future generations of English-speaking psychoanalysts (and students of the human mind) the transmission of the true heritage which Freud has bequeathed is a task which ought to be undertaken, or at least attempted, as soon as possible.

Notes

[1] Helmut Junker, 'On Reading Freud: Comments on "Analysis Terminable and Interminable"', unpub. paper.

[2] S. Freud, 'Die Verdrängung', *GW* x (1915), 247; *SE* xiv. 141.

[3] P. Mahony, *Freud as a Writer* (New York 1982).

[4] Freud's German sentence reads: 'Es kann das Schicksal einer Triebregung werden, daß sie auf Widerstände stößt, welche sie unwirksam machen wollen' (*GW* x. 248). Strachey's translation is: 'One of the vicissitudes an instinctual impulse may undergo is to meet with resistances which seek to make it inoperative' (*SE* xiv. 146).

17

On the Difficulties of Retranslating Freud into English

Reading Experiences of a German Analyst*

Helmut Junker

Having had the opportunity to teach psychoanalysis at an English-speaking institute for about a year, I became aware of serious discrepancies between the German of Freud and the Strachey translation. To my great surprise the Standard Edition was in some respects easier to understand than the German original. It even seemed theoretically more *correct* than the original. How can these paradoxes be explained?

When Strachey's text is read page by page, not compared sentence by sentence with the German original but for its own style, it sounds like an original. This seems to be a consequence of the fact that any translation of a text is already and necessarily an interpretation. I got the impression that the Standard Edition is a fully elaborated and reliable work within the confines of Strachey's intention. Strachey is to be admired for achieving what he promised in his introduction to the translation: 'The imaginary model which I have always kept before me is of the writings of some English man of science of wide education born in the middle of the nineteenth century' (*SE* i, xix). This apostrophized Englishman, however, is different from a Viennese Jew, with his socio-economic, political and cultural background. It may be that a shift has taken place, during the last sixty years, from the idea of explaining Freud to empathizing with Freud. Yet Strachey's conception has to be accepted as a whole and unique *œuvre* and – beyond noting its mistakes – cannot be ameliorated without interfering with it deeply. And retranslation faces the immense problem of 'a conception of Freud' which has to be worked out by the translator before translating a single word.

The Freudian text raises some idiosyncratic obstacles: the innocent translator assumes that there is *one* (and only one) given meaning, and

* The editors are grateful for permission to reprint this paper, which first appeared in the *International Review of Psycho-Analysis*, xiv (July 1987), 317–20.

his task is to render this meaning within the categories of 'correct' and 'incorrect'. His work done, he is criticized with reference to the adage: *traduttore–traditore*. For the naïve procedure of translating remarkably reduces the full meaning of a Freudian text, and leads to slightly puzzling and restricted results. In the German original of a given passage the words are sometimes obscure, or have different meanings according to their context; Strachey, however, decided to give them one clear meaning. This makes his version at once easier to read and seemingly more correct. For better or worse: Freud's language has an 'openness' which is not fearful of ambivalence or rhetorical ingredients, sometimes using a negative when the word lexically is affirmative, is not even scared by contradictions. Thus Freud permits to some extent different translations, all of which would have some claim to being correct.

Furthermore, Freud's multi-methodological approach opens the way to variant readings and interpretations that may stress, or neglect, certain medical, philosophical, sociological or literary elements in his language. Some proof for the last statement can be found in the various biographies of Freud, each of them having a different basic idea from which the author conceptualized his work. You may think of Schur or Jones, Clark or Sulloway, Bernfeld or Roazen. Each has also a different scientific approach to the *œuvre* itself. Although these authors contradict each other in the very essentials, they all nevertheless belong in and contribute to the interpretation of Freud. Before translation can start, philological investigation seems necessary to gain a broader knowledge and understanding of the Freudian literary style within the German written language.

The uniqueness and completeness of Strachey's Freud brings me to the conclusion that his work has created a version of Freud, not a translation. To give this some proof: If Strachey were retranslated into German by a translator who did not know the original, the result would again be surprising. It would sound peculiar, seeming to be similar, but very different from the original. Most striking is the often latinized and abstract language. In present-day German publications on psycho-analytic subjects you find such language employed intentionally. It is considered modern. As Germans re-imported analytic knowledge from the English-speaking world after the Second World War, this abstracted and latinized language was perceived and labelled as 'scientific'. It differs greatly from the language Freud wrote.

These observations may be seriously limited by my understanding of English. Not being bilingual, I understand the words lexically and probably miss the connotations that are available to the English reader. Reading Freud in German, I am alert to connotations which go beyond the strict lexical meaning and allow further associations to develop, whereas reading him in English I reduce meaning to a basic understanding only. Such a question could be tested philologically, i.e. with English-speaking students allowed to associate about Strachey's text, and the results compared with those of German-speaking students who use the corresponding original text of Freud. I do not know, moreover, whether latinization and abstraction belong irrevocably to the English language, lead to its praised clarity, and simultaneously limit it to a form of philosophical positivism. Possibly the limitation arising from the search for a definitive meaning is not perceived as a loss, and is balanced by other means within the English language.

To raise another point: Even going back to Freud, in German-language discussions among analysts in Germany, one finds considerable and substantial differences in understanding. This is due not only to the already-mentioned differences in methodological approach, but to the understanding of the language itself. Elderly people 'read' (and understand) the special Austro-German usages of words, for they have a living picture of the society of Vienna around 1900 and its language. This does not mean that Freud writes an Austrian variety of German. But someone who visualizes the Viennese scene and has internalized it in his own idiosyncratic structure will add a meaning to words which is correct – though not strictly and identically as understood by someone of a different age and cultural background.

Analysts of a younger generation – among whom I count myself – can only attain the sensitivity just described by *rereading* Freud in an effort to amplify the meaning, to 'get everything out of it'. Young analysts, however, students reading Freud for the first time, unable to read historically, will understand the text differently. They read Strachey's footnotes, translated and printed in the Freud *Studienausgabe* along with the German text, and unknowingly get slightly confused.

This again is not a question of incorrect or correct, but underlines the crucial importance of developing a conceptualization: Which of the different Freuds should be translated? What is the 'state of mind' ('Geistesverfassung') of the new translator who after eighty years of history, which means after eighty years of interpretation, approaches this work? The words may be identical, but the process of interpretation has added meaning or suppressed it. Who reads Freud correctly? If Freud were to be translated by a group of analysts, could they be neutral and unanimous in their views? The French analysts are aware of this problem, never having achieved a complete French Standard Edition.

For every translator is a first reader. He or she becomes a competent one by rereading. This rereading opens up a process of communication between the text and the rereader, and such a process has bearing on the latter's professional capacity. The meaning is no longer that of the first reading, understood and frozen forever. Instead an additional meaning appears and will take possession of the translator. Addition, however, requires a logical hierarchy; a new process starts to impose itself on this broadened knowledge. This implies secondarily a counter-process to select and to justify the selection. Can this be done by the mere translation of words?

My firm belief is that history cannot be discounted and no one can annihilate the time between. A translator of today cannot be one of the year 1900 or 1905, trying to translate out of time. It is impossible for his knowledge to consist of the knowledge and the 'Zeitgeist' of that time. In my opinion this is one of the most difficult problems in the task of retranslating Freud. Who, then, is the translator we are looking for?

Strachey was in the enviable position of being able to declare himself *the* translator, openly demonstrating his conception of the 'true' Freud. Deficient as that conception may be (and is) in various aspects, the new translator or translators − and most probably it will be not a single person but a group − must arrive at a conception of their own. It is for these reasons that a French Standard Edition has never come into existence. Besides, I can only admire the group of French analysts who by translating and retranslating Freud arrived at some 25 different versions of the brief work 'Die Verneinung [Negation]'. Similar studies might help the group of future translators to understand their own conceptualization and to strengthen it by such tests.

I fear that any particular translation will be appreciated only by a particular group who presume it to possess the scientific truth, and will be blamed by all others. I frankly believe it will be impossible for any one translation to satisfy the different groups of analysts who read Freud within their different frames of reference. And this may also be a problem for the same reader at different times. If an analyst reads a Freudian text, say every five years, when did he read it correctly? Were these his 'findings' of 1960, 1965, 1970, 1980, 1985? Who can decide which was the right interpretation? What about the misreadings of the early years which slowly became petrified, the decay of living words into stereotypes? Analytic knowledge is organic in its development; it can be compared to a tree: each of the tree's annual rings is different, because of different life-climates and life-circumstances, both private and professional. It is difficult to say of ourselves what within the tree gives it its static strength, which wood is dry or rotting, and where the juice comes from that flows up to the branches. You may also say: Words are living creatures, they need a special biosphere to survive, and often they die.

To summarize: It is very difficult to find a common conception of Freud's *œuvre* which would be acceptable to the different groups of analysts. It would be narrow-minded to favour one group over others. For this reason I doubt whether the problem can be solved by *one* translation, and it seems to me to be scientifically more fruitful to comment than to translate. In practice, this would be to adopt a classical means of interpreting a work in a foreign language. The page would be divided into three columns: on the left the original text, in the middle the chosen translation, and on the right (where it would occupy the greatest space on the page) a commentary which would allow for and take into consideration the different possible readings. By this method the reader could prepare himself by reading the commentary, and the already experienced reader find within that commentary a means of amplifying his knowledge and a stimulus to read the original.

PART FOUR

PERSPECTIVES FOR THE FUTURE

18

Psychoanalysis as a Social Institution

An Anthropological Perspective

Ernest Gellner

The invitation to contribute to this symposium was no doubt prompted by the publication of my book, *The Psychoanalytic Movement*. If I myself begin by mentioning this book, it is not because I want to plug it, but simply because you don't often get a misprint on the *title-page*, let alone a Freudian misprint. This makes it something of a collector's piece. The book I wrote was meant to have the subtitle 'The Cunning of Unreason'– 'Die List der Unvernunft', an allusion of course to the famous Hegelian phrase. The printer changed it to 'The *Coming* of Unreason'.[1] I would like to think that Sigmund is chuckling in his grave. By the time it was noticed it would have cost the publishers too much to change it, and they left it as it was.

The other introductory remark I have to make is that I hope I'm not here under false pretences: the symposium programme said that I was going to talk about anthropology. This sounds as if I were going to talk about the implications of psychoanalysis *for* anthropology; which is an interesting subject about which people have indeed written much. But what I am in fact going to do is the other way round. I am going to perform a kind of intellectual experiment ('Gedankenexperiment'): if one were to look at psychoanalysis as a social institution, which of course it is, in the way that a social anthropologist does, which of its features would one fix on?

A social anthropologist is a kind of sociologist, but one whose style of thought and approach is influenced by the involvement of social anthropology with simpler societies. Once upon a time the subject was in effect actually defined as the study of such societies. It is no longer so, and there is no longer any simple definition of it, in fact no neat definition is available at all. All the same, this orientation has obviously had an impact. Its consequence is a tendency of social anthropologists to be functionalists, at least in the loose sense of being very much on the look-out for the interlocking of institutions. When this is turned into a doctrine, into the view that society is a kind of self-winding watch, a system of mutually supportive self-preserving institutions, it is of course simply false, or at best a half-truth. But as background orientation, guiding your method, indicating what you are trying to find, it is not at all bad, because it makes you look for certain things.

When one looks at simple societies one does very frequently find a kind of pleasing integration, pleasing at least to the outsider, in whom it is liable to strike a spark of envy, and lead him to some kind of romantic populism. He sees, with envy, a society which is an interlocking whole. Rank, background belief, salvation and fears, all are linked, and techniques for avoiding what is most feared, and for obtaining what is most desired, are welded to a system of personal relationships. Endeavour, identity, and personal links, all form a single fairly coherent system. The beliefs confirm and highlight the individual's status, the statuses are all organized into a system which in turn is reinforced by the ritual, and ranking confirms the faith. And then ritual feeds back again into the system, it incarnates and reinforces beliefs, and elements in the whole link into each other. This is satisfying and gratifying to people in our condition, where this kind of mutual support is most conspicuously lacking.

The general features of our society – if one may briefly sum them up – result in the lack of a well-established social structure. One simply does not know where one is. The price of equality, egalitarianism and mobility is that one has to start from scratch and *work* for one's relationships. Such rituals as survive are, on the whole, disconnected from daily life, and they are largely make-believe, folklore knowingly consumed as such. Seriously held background belief doesn't reinforce one's life experiences; on the contrary, this society depends on a growing science and technology. And the price of growth is instability, technicality, unintelligibility, and a high degree of specialization, which separates the background beliefs which are serious, truly serious, from the beliefs in terms of which one lives one's daily life. And so one has had to invent for the first time a special word for the ordinary world, 'die Lebenswelt', as something distinguished from the serious world of scientific enquiry. As the French philosopher Bachelard said, the world in which one thinks and the world in which one lives are no longer the same.

These then are the features which characterize the society we live in: and the achievement, the real historic achievement, it seems to me, of psychoanalysis is that it has managed to correct all this, and to some extent invert and restore the previous situation, and to do so in an altogether contemporary, in no way archaicizing style. Of the various belief systems that have emerged in the modern world, psychoanalysis is by far the most successful. I think it has only one rival, and that one is successful in a quite different way: the rival is of course Marxism, and Marxism has been successful in the sense of having in effect become one of the world's official religions.

But Marxism is conspicuously unsuccessful as a system of solace, support and orientation for individuals in crisis. This is one of the marked features of life in the Soviet Union. That country has the great difficulty of creating convincing rites of passage and rituals for daily life: when it is done in a Marxist idiom, they turn out to be very flat and uninspiring. Marxism is very poor in that respect. It does or did constitute a kind of rousing Messianism of our *collective* salvation, but it offers no individual salvation, nor indeed any support in individual crises. Psychoanalysis by contrast does this superbly well. What I did in my book was to sketch out a kind of answer to the question of *how* it manages to do it; I tried to offer the kind of theory which, ideally, should be well supported by a good piece of ethnographic research. It is not actually my fault that the research has not been carried out, but I do not apologize for putting forward the hypothesis of what the answers would look like if it *were* done, in the hope that it may indeed come to be done.

All I have time for here is to indicate the way the answer runs. First of all, at the level of doctrine, psychoanalysis has succeeded in squaring the circle: on the one hand, it is unambiguously and firmly naturalistic. Unlike the comforting belief systems inherited from the past, it does not invoke any kind of transcendence, which would be offensive to the secular modern spirit. It does not involve one in a kind of belief which for many people would be archaic and unacceptable. At the same time, however, it fully satisfies the requirement of separation of the sacred and dangerous, on the one hand, from the humdrum and ordinary on the other. It does so by postulating a realm which possesses all the qualities of transcendence, without actually being literally transcendant. The realm is hidden, it is powerful, it is menacing and dangerous; it is both separate and distinct, it is *where the action is*, it is in the region where our salvation and damnation are determined. The Unconscious has all these traits, and on top of that, there is every indication that it actually exists. It is entirely compatible with our other background beliefs.

Take the famous progression Copernicus, Darwin, Freud, the successive steps of making man part of nature. The Unconscious really makes sense if Darwin is right, as obviously he is. If we are continuous with nature, you would indeed expect to find something like the great powerful drives within us, forces which are continuous with our biological nature. Here we are in an area where other modern theories of man, whilst trying to do justice to the naturalistic background vision, have conspicuously failed. They tend to fail on one of two scores: either by failing to do justice to the quite obvious power of our instinctual drives, or on the other hand by failing to do justice to the extraordinary semantic complexity of the inner and outer worlds we live in. This complexity manifests itself in terribly intricate structures, partly shared, partly private. All the assumptions, for instance, contained in the pervasive economists' model, of a *homo economicus* in pursuit of sharply specific aims, simply fail to do justice to the brutality, deviousness, tortuous obscurity of our inner life, to all the things which we know from experience to mask our real driving forces.

On the other hand, some kind of crude biologizing of our inner selves *also* fails to do justice to the semantic complexity of our passions and of their objects and discriminations. One really important thing about the Freudian Unconscious is that it does justice simultaneously to both these features, and that it constitutes a kind of naming, and a proper recognition, of the region where the two meet. And when dark drives encounter complex meanings, this capacity to bring the two into relation with each other perhaps constitutes the major factor in explaining how Freudian language and terminology and style have come to prevail. It does justice to what we know about our inner lives, to the power of dark drives *and* to semantic complexity. This was one of the most important factors, the factor on which my book focuses. This is why psychoanalysis has conquered the language and thought of the Western world.

Now the integration of background belief with our life situation which it effects is, once again, most remarkable. One striking feature of modern man is that, although on the one hand he has been firmly placed inside nature, in another sense he has been firmly taken outside it. Nature is no longer a menace. In fact it barely exists. One is only interested in the weather because it affects one's holidays, one's weekend, one's hobbies; otherwise it makes virtually no difference. The life-style, economic and social activities of modern industrial societies are barely affected by whether the modern industrial city happens to be located in a tropical rain forest or in some northern tundra. We all expect to live out our appointed span, and sudden and premature death is something that happens to other people. If it happens to anyone close to us it constitutes a major scandal. We are no longer frightened of nature, and it really makes no difference to us. I am only speaking about the prosperous part of the world, of course. Nature, which was part of what was feared, in an age when the vagaries of the weather or climate could make the difference between hunger and having enough to eat, has gone. Nature has ceased to be a significant part of our environment.

Our environment is now made up virtually exclusively of other people and of meanings. What we call 'work' is really the manipulation of meanings and of other people. At any rate that is what the middle class and upwards consider as work. There is still a part of the population which is in contact with nature, but it is shrinking. Even its members tend to press buttons on machines rather than actually shovelling bits of mud from one place to another, which is what work used to be. Now if you consider jointly the fact that our environment is *other people*, but at the same time our society is very loosely structured, that human relationships are not prescribed and imposed, certain crucial consequences follow. It is not only that our spouses are not prescribed for us in the way they sometimes are in simpler societies; our friends aren't prescribed either, nor our workmates. One has to work for the latter relationships, so to speak to make them. Personal relationships are not prescribed, but are very much at risk.

Add to this the fact that, almost by definition, the overwhelming majority of us are mediocre. That is what 'mediocre' means. Hence our success or failure, in this loosely structured environment consisting of *other people*, depends for its quality on how we 'get on with them', on how our persistent relationships function. It doesn't really depend on our performance in some purely technical sense. There may be some people so brilliant that they can afford to have horrible relationships, and some others so hopeless that nothing will really help them. But these are small minorities. For most of us, our fate, contentment, status, dignity, self-satisfaction, in a loosely structured world made up of other people and nothing else, depend on our personal relationships which, at the same time, are neither guaranteed nor organized. In other words, human relationships constitute the area of maximum risk and justified apprehension.

Psychoanalysis is a doctrine which offers or implies the promise of salvation in precisely this area of maximum fear. In this respect it very closely resembles our previous belief systems, which generally concentrated on what was then the area of maximum danger. Human relationships have now acquired this quality, which once used to haunt *nature*. Human relations seem lawless and law-bound at the same time. One has the strong feeling that events within this realm are not random: the same kinds of things happen to everyone over and over again. At the same time, if you try to formulate the laws governing this realm, the generalizations invariably turn out to be either vacuous or false.

One feels there must be some mechanism controlling this area, and yet it seems to be beyond our grasp or power to control. Chomsky, who is I suppose the foremost living theorist of human *competence*, did once formulate the suggestion that our basic mental equipment may be not only such that we learn complex grammar with astonishing ease, but also that we are incapable of understanding human behaviour. I am not defending the theory, but it is interesting that somebody as high-powered as he should have suggested it.

Many of us must feel this way: we are helpless and scared and at the mercy of unintelligible forces which pervade the very realm which governs us. In psychoanalysis we find at long last a theory which claims to give access to and control of that realm. Here, once again, there are similarities between traditional belief systems, and a kind of formal parallelism between them and psychoanalysis. It displays a dovetailing of ontology and epistemology: the basic model showing how the world really works, and the theory of knowledge concerning how the crucial realm is to be reached, strongly support each other.

Basically Freudianism claims there is but one access to this crucial realm, namely free association interpreted in a Freudian way. Moreover this penetration of reality is not available to everyone: there is an interesting and suggestive ambiguity about whether self-analysis is possible or not. It *has* to be possible, because otherwise the whole thing could never have got started. On the other hand, it must not be encouraged too much, because if it were too easy, it would erode the monopoly of access. It would destroy the aura, linked to a sense of guilt, which marks the boundaries between that realm and the ordinary sufferers, which gives them hope, but also keeps them in check and in awe. The neat dovetailing of the theory concerning how the crucial realm works with the doctrine concerning how it can be approached, *and* the linking of the path of discovery to the promise of salvation, or at least alleviation, is one of the most fascinating aspects of Freud.

There is the nature of the relevant ritual. The central characteristic of modern man, at least the point most celebrated by sociological analysts, is a kind of compulsive rationality. This is the Weberian theme of the orderliness, the Cartesian separation of all issues, the requirement of orderly procedure which is both tedious and stressful. Now in most societies, the sacred has always been marked off by a kind of deliberate inversion. The Freudian elevation of free association into the channel of discovery also constitutes this kind of saturnalian inversion. For us, an ordinary saturnalia, in which we put on funny clothes, and get high, is only a kind of artificial make-believe playtime. It doesn't *really* turn us on, or link us to deep, fatal reality. But when we are systematically free-associating, that really is an inversion of our deepest and most compulsive and obligatory habits. Normally, our honour resides in our orderliness. Its abandonment really does signal an exceptional condition, by the inversion of the normal order of things.

And take again that one-to-one relationship, which admittedly is mitigated in group therapy. This too is highly appropriate for an individualist age, if you accept, as by and large I do, the Durkheimian thesis about the intimate link of the sacred to the social.[2] What do you do in a very individualist age such as ours, where all the intermediate groupings which lie between intimate relationships, on the one hand, and the national state, on the other, are pretty feeble? I am at present teaching – at Cambridge – in a university where the ritual re-enactment of collegiate commensality is prominent; but everybody knows that it's largely theatre, that it's not for real. It is a kind of consumer association for enacting a return to an earlier age. As such it is very enjoyable, but it has no ultimate emotional reality or force. By contrast, individual relationships do have it. So that the ultimate reduction of the therapeutic or soteriological relationship to a one-to-one relation is entirely congruent with the requirements and spirit of the age. Rituals confirm the social order and mirror it. They bring heightened emotion, illumination and salvation, whilst re-enacting crucial relations in a symbolic and ritual form. In a deeply individualist age, the soteriological ritual is appropriately contained in face-to-face single relationship.

In ritual, in method, in substantive doctrine, in the linking of salvation to a definite person, in the selection of the type of suffering to be alleviated, in the technique deployed for its alleviation – in all these respects psychoanalysis seems ideally fitted to the conditions of the age. This was my answer to the question which my book had set itself: how was this astonishing conquest of our thought and language accomplished, in a period well under half a century, and unaided by special resources? It was an extraordinary conquest, by a terminology and a doctrine, of the speech and thought of the entire Western world, and of many regions outside it.

Finally, I would stress one phenomenon that badly needs to be studied. In as far as our world desperately requires pastoral services, they are in general modelled on the psychoanalytic paradigm. The amount of anguish dispersed in this amorphous society is very large. The provision of a kind of secular priesthood in the form of counsellors is something which was spread with a fabulous speed. It has remained largely undocumented. The basic style, posture, ethos, ethic of this new pastoral clerisy is largely borrowed from the psychoanalytic tradition. This is something which deserves very thorough investigation.

Notes

[1] E. Gellner, *The Psychoanalytic Movement, or The Coming of Unreason* (repr. London 1985). For the concept of 'the cunning of reason' see G.W.F. Hegel, *The Philosophy of History*, trans. J. Sibree (New York 1956), 32–3.

[2] E. Durkheim, *The Elementary Forms of Religious Life*, trans. J.W. Swain (London 1915).

19

Changing Theories of Childhood since Freud*

John Bowlby

Psychoanalysis has always been a developmental discipline, and almost every analyst believes that a knowledge of how personality develops during infancy and childhood is a necessary part of his or her therapeutic equipment. Yet there has been no agreement about it, and, since Freud's first attempts to sketch a theory, many alternatives have been proposed. Even so, none has been widely accepted and the area remains intensely controversial.

Perhaps the most widely adopted shift from Freud's early formulations has been to focus attention on a child's early relationships with his parents, particularly his mother, and to de-emphasize or discard drive theory. To describe and theorize about these and other emotionally loaded relationships a variety of terms have been introduced: 'significant other', 'dependency', 'overdependency', 'symbiosis' and 'object relations', among others. This shift was already foreshadowed in Freud's later writings[1] and has had many proponents. They include, in this country, the object-relations theorists Melanie Klein, Balint, Fairbairn and Winnicott, and in the United States the neo-Freudians Sullivan, Horney, Frankel-Brunswick and Fromm; among those most recently influential has been Margaret Mahler. Nevertheless, although all the resulting schemas have in common a focus on early mother-child relationships, there are great differences among them. One is the age at which it is believed certain key developments occur; another is the weight given to the influence that a mother's way of treating her infant and child is thought to have on his subsequent development – a weight that varies from the trivial to the substantial. Although all rely extensively on the traditional psychoanalytic method of reconstructing development retrospectively from what is observed or inferred during treatment sessions, both Winnicott's and Mahler's ideas are distinctive

* The editors are grateful for permission to reprint parts of this paper which appeared under the title 'Developmental Psychiatry Comes of Age' in the *American Journal of Psychiatry*, CXLV, January 1988, pp. 1–10.

by having been deeply influenced by direct observation of normally developing infants and young children with their mothers. It is no coincidence that my own ideas are closest to theirs.

During my training in the British Psycho-Analytical Society during the 1930s the focus of my interest was always on relationships. This leaning was greatly reinforced by my having a Kleinian analyst (Joan Riviere) and Melanie Klein as a supervisor. Simultaneously I was working at the London Child Guidance Clinic, where I learned a great deal about the effects on children of the way their parents treat them, and how parental treatment that is pathogenic for a child is commonly a consequence of the parent's own unhappy childhood. I was also struck by the ill-effects that seemed to follow major disruptions in relationships. Since it appeared that these adverse influences were of immense importance, but were little recognized and even disputed by my psychoanalytic colleagues, I decided to study them. The development of my work and ideas is chronicled elsewhere;[2] here I will proceed at once to describe the picture of child development that has been emerging from systematic observation during recent years and that I now share with a rapidly increasing number of developmental psychologists and clinicians. The label used to describe our conceptual framework is 'attachment theory'.[3]

Attachment theory

Attachment theory is a version of object-relations theory, from which it grew, and sets out to explain the same clinical phenomena. It has exploited a number of new ideas, not available in Freud's time, that have seemed to fit the data, and which have come principally from the related disciplines of cognitive psychology and control theory, and from ethology with its strong neo-Darwinian underpinning. In its initial formulation, observation of how young children respond when placed in a strange place with strange people, and the effects such experiences have on the child's subsequent relations with his parents, was especially influential. Whilst giving systematic attention to the influences of family events on a child's socio-emotional development, attachment theory, like all versions of psychoanalytic theory, seeks to understand these influences in terms of their effect on the child's instinctive urges, feelings and thoughts – his internal world. Distinctive features of the approach are that it adheres to usual scientific procedures and seeks evidence from whatever sources seem to promote understanding.

Before going further let me assure you that in speaking of scientific method I am not referring to psychoanalytic *therapy*. To be useful, psychotherapy entails a personal relationship between therapist and patient, resting on spontaneity and intuition – proceedings far removed from science. But it also requires an understanding of personality development and psychopathology, and it is in furthering that understanding that I believe scientific method to be indispensable.[4] Without it, we have no criteria for resolving differences.

The starting-point of attachment theory is the hypothesis that emotional bonds between one human being and another are primary and have a distinctive biological function of their own. Thus the propensity to form strong emotional bonds with particular individuals is seen as a basic component of human nature, already present in germinal form in the neonate and continuing through adult life into old age. During infancy and childhood bonds are with parents (or parent substitutes) who are looked to for protection, comfort and support. During healthy adolescence and adult life these bonds persist, but are complemented by new bonds, commonly of a heterosexual nature. Although food and sex sometimes play important roles in such relationships, the relationship exists in its own right and has an important survival function of its own, namely protection. Thus, within the attachment framework, bonds are seen as neither subordinate to nor derivative from food and sex, as traditional theories have proposed. Nor is the urgent desire for comfort and support in adversity regarded as childish, as most earlier theories have implied. Instead, the capacity to form bonds with other individuals, sometimes in the care-seeking role and sometimes in the care-giving one, is regarded as a principal feature of effective personality functioning and mental health.

As a rule care-seeking is shown by a weaker and less experienced individual towards someone regarded as stronger and/or wiser. A child, or older person, in the care-seeking role keeps within range of the care-giver, the degree of closeness or of ready accessibility depending on circumstances: hence the concept of attachment behaviour.

Another basic component of human nature is the urge to explore the environment, to play and to take part in varied activities with peers. This behaviour is, of course, antithetic to attachment behaviour. When an individual (of any age) is feeling secure, he is likely to explore away from his attachment figure. When alarmed, anxious, tired or unwell, he feels an urge towards proximity. Thus we see the typical pattern of interaction between child and parent known as exploration from a secure base. Provided the parent is known to be accessible and will be responsive when called upon, a healthy child feels secure enough to explore. At first these explorations are limited both in time and space. Around the middle of the third year, however, a secure child becomes confident enough to increase time and distance away – first to half-days and later to whole days. As he grows into adolescence, his excursions are extended to weeks or months, but a secure home base remains indispensable none the less for optimal functioning and mental health.

During the early months of life an infant shows many of the component responses of what will later become attachment behaviour, but the organized pattern does not develop until the second half of the first year. From birth onwards he shows a germinal capacity to engage in social interaction and pleasure in doing so.[5] Within weeks, moreover, he is able to distinguish between his mother-figure and others by means of her smell and by hearing her voice, and also by the way she holds him. Visual discrimination is not reliable until the second quarter. Initially crying is the only means available to him for signalling his need for care, and contentment the only means for signalling that he has been satisfied. During the second month, however, his social smile acts strongly to encourage his mother in her ministrations.

The development of attachment behaviour as an organized system, having as its goal the keeping of proximity to, or of accessibility to, a discriminated mother-figure, requires that the child should have developed the cognitive capacity to keep his mother in mind when she is not present: this capacity develops during the second six months of life. Thus, from nine months onwards the great majority of infants respond to being left with a strange person by protest and crying, and also by prolonged fretting and rejection of the stranger. These observations demonstrate that during these months an infant's representational model of his mother is becoming readily available to him for purposes of comparison during her absence and for recognition after her return.

A major feature of attachment theory is the hypothesis that attachment behaviour is organized by means of a control system within the central nervous system, analogous to the physiological control systems that maintain physiological measures such as blood pressure or body temperature, within set limits. Thus the theory proposes that, in a way analogous to physiological homeostasis, the attachment-control system maintains a person's relation to his attachment figure between certain limits of distance and accessibility. As such, it can be regarded as an example of what can usefully be termed environmental homeostasis. Among situations that activate care-seeking is anything that frightens a child or signals that he is tired or unwell. Among situations that terminate care-seeking and release him for other activities are comfort and reassurance. Since control systems are themselves sources of activity, traditional theories of motivation which invoke a build-up of psychic energy or drive are rendered obsolete.

In all personal relationships emotional expression plays a leading part, and in none does it play so large a part as in the intimate exchanges of mother and child. Throughout the first year and much of the second they have no other means of communication, and even after language has developed, emotional expression continues to be of enormous importance. As a result of sensitive research, there is now a much

clearer picture of the role of emotion during development than there
was earlier.

By four months an infant is capable of expressing at least the
following five differentiated emotions: interest, enjoyment, sadness,
fear and anger. Although such expressions are usually brief, they tend
to be repeated and involve not only facial expression but characteristic
movement of the whole body. Moreover, each is elicited only in the
presence of (and sometimes only in the absence of) specific persons.[6] A
sensitive mother is soon adept at recognizing these different emotions
and also in identifying the situations in which they occur.

Infants, too, are adept at discriminating an adult's facial expressions.
In fact, experiment has shown that even a neonate can discriminate
between a smiling face, a surprised one and a sad one by responding in
a distinctive way to each.[7] We are a far cry from the idea of infantile
narcissism.

In a review of his findings a leading researcher in this field has
concluded that 'emotional states should be defined within personal
interaction rather than as supposed moods of an isolated individual',[8]
a conclusion that is highly consistent with attachment theory.

This leads to consideration of the third major component of human
nature relevant to this exposition, namely care-giving, which is the
prime role of parents and complementary to attachment behaviour.
When looked at in terms of evolution theory the occurrence of altruistic
care of the young is readily understood, since it serves to promote the
survival of offspring (and often of other relatives as well) and thereby
the individual's own genes. Nevertheless, this form of explanation
constitutes a radical shift from most psychological theorizing, including
Freud's, which has mistakenly assumed that individuals are by nature
essentially selfish and that they consider the interests of others only
when constrained to do so by social pressures and sanctions. Nothing,
I believe, that stems from an ethological perspective has more far-reaching implications for understanding human nature than this reappraisal
of altruism.

Returning now to the attachment control system within the child, it
is evident that for it to operate efficiently, it requires to have at its
disposal as much information as possible about the self and the
attachment figure, not only in regard to their respective locations and
capabilities but in regard also to how each is likely to respond to the
other as environmental and other conditions change. Observations lead
us to conclude that towards the end of the first year of life a child is
acquiring a considerable knowledge of his immediate world; and that
during subsequent years this knowledge is best regarded as becoming
organized in the form of internal working models, including models of
the self and the mother. The function of these models is to simulate

happenings in the real world, thereby enabling the individual to plan his behaviour with all the advantages of insight and foresight. The more adequate and accurate the simulation, of course, the better adapted is the behaviour based on it likely to be. Although our knowledge of the rate at which these models develop during the earliest years is still scanty, there is good evidence that by the fifth birthday most children are using a sophisticated working model of mother or mother-substitute which includes knowledge of her interests, moods and intentions, all of which he can then take into account.[9] With a complementary model of himself, he is already engaging in a complex intersubjective relationship with his mother who, of course, has her own working models both of her child and of herself. Because these models are in constant use, day in and day out, their influence on thought, feeling and behaviour becomes routine and largely outside of awareness.

Since as clinicians we know that long before a child reaches five the patterns of interaction between him and his mother are vastly diverse, ranging from smooth-running and happy to being filled with friction and distress of every kind and degree, and that they are also apt to persist, the more we know about how they originate the better. It is here that recent research by developmental psychologists has made such huge strides.

Patterns of attachment and their determinants

Three principal patterns of attachment present during the early years are now reliably identified, together with the family conditions that promote them. One of these patterns is consistent with the child developing healthily and two are predictive of disturbed development. Which pattern an individual develops during these years is seen to be profoundly influenced by the way his parents (or other parent-type figures) treat him. This conclusion, which is as important as it has been controversial, is unpopular in some circles and, in consequence, is constantly challenged. Yet the evidence for it is now weighty and derives from a number of research studies of socio-emotional development during the first five years. This research tradition was first set by Ainsworth during the 1960s, and has since been exploited and expanded, notably in the USA by Main, Sroufe and Waters, and in Germany by Grossmann.[10]

The pattern of attachment consistent with healthy development is that of *secure* attachment, in which the individual is confident that his parent (or parent-figure) will be available, responsive and helpful should he encounter adverse or frightening situations. With this assurance, he feels bold in his explorations of the world and also competent in dealing with it. This pattern is found to be promoted by a parent, in the early years especially by the mother, being readily available, sensitive to her child's signals and lovingly responsive when he seeks protection and/or comfort and/or assistance.

A second pattern is that of *anxious resistant* attachment in which the individual is uncertain whether his parent will be available or responsive or helpful when called upon. Because of this uncertainty he is always prone to separation anxiety, tends to be clinging, and is anxious about exploring the world. This pattern is promoted by a parent being available and helpful on some occasions but not on others, and by separations and, later, especially by threats of abandonment used as a means of control.

A third pattern is that of *anxious avoidant* attachment in which the individual has no confidence that, when he seeks care, he will be responded to helpfully but, on the contrary, expects to be rebuffed. Such an individual attempts to live his life without the love and support of others. This pattern is the result of the individual's mother constantly rebuffing him when he approaches her for comfort or protection. The most extreme cases result from repeated rejection and ill-treatment, or prolonged institutionalization. Clinical evidence suggests that, if it persists, this pattern leads to a variety of personality disorders from compulsively self-sufficient individuals to persistently delinquent ones.

There is much evidence that, at least in families where care-giving arrangements continue stable, the pattern of attachment between child and mother, once established, tends to persist. For example, in two different samples (Californian and German) the patterns of attachment to mother at twelve months were found, with but few exceptions, still to be present at six years.[11] Furthermore studies in progress in Minneapolis[12] have shown that the pattern of attachment characteristic of the pair, as assessed when the child is aged twelve months, is highly predictive also of behaviour outside the home in a nursery group three and a half years later. Thus children who showed a secure pattern with the mother at twelve months are likely to be described by their nursery teachers as cheerful and cooperative, popular with other children, resilient and resourceful. Those who showed an anxious avoidant pattern are likely to be described later as emotionally insulated, hostile or anti-social and as unduly seeking of attention. Those who showed an anxious resistant pattern are also likely to be described as unduly seeking of attention and as tense, impulsive and easily frustrated or else as passive and helpless.

Ample confirmation of the teacher's descriptions comes from independent observers and laboratory assessments of the same children.[13] Similarly, an experimental study done in Germany shows that at three years of age children earlier assessed as securely attached respond to potential failure with increased effort, whereas the insecurely attached do the opposite.[14] In other words, the securely attached children are responding with confidence and hope that they can succeed whilst the insecure are already showing signs of helplessness and defeatism.

In a number of these studies detailed observations have been made of the way the children's mothers treated them. Great variability is seen, with high correlations between a mother's style of interaction and the child's pattern of attachment to her. For example, in one such study, made when the children were two and a half years old, mothers were observed whilst their children were attempting a task that they could not manage without a little help. A mother of a secure toddler enabled her child to focus on the task, respected his attempts to complete it on his own, and responded with the required help when called upon: communication between them was harmonious. Mothers of insecure infants were less sensitive to the toddlers' state of mind, either not giving support and help when appealed to or else intruding when the child was striving to solve the problem himself.[15]

In discussing these and similar findings, Bretherton emphasizes the easy flow of communication between a mother and her child in the secure partnerships and concludes that this easy communication is only possible when a mother is intuitively alive to the crucial part she plays in providing her child with a secure base, variously encouraging autonomy, providing necessary help or giving comfort according to her child's state of mind.[16]

Mothers of insecure infants deviate from this sensitive pattern of mothering in a great variety of ways. One, common amongst mothers of avoidant infants, is to scoff at her child's bids for comfort and support.[17] Another, well-known to clinicians and the effects of which are now being observed by developmentalists,[18] is a mother who fails to respect her child's desire for autonomy and discourages exploration. This is usually a mother who, not having had a secure home base during her own childhood, is consciously or unconsciously seeking to invert the relationship by making her child her own attachment-figure. In the past this has too often been labelled 'overindulgence' or 'spoiling', which has led to appalling confusion about what is best for a child.

It is not difficult to understand why patterns of attachment, once developed, tend to persist. One reason is that the way a parent treats a child, whether for better or for worse, tends to be self-perpetuating. Thus a secure child is a happier and more rewarding child to care for, and also is less demanding than an anxious one. An anxious ambivalent child is apt to be whiny and clinging; whilst an anxious avoidant child keeps his distance, is bad-tempered and prone to bully other children. In each of these cases the child's behaviour is likely to elicit an unfavourable response from the parent, so that vicious circles develop.

Although for the reasons given patterns, once formed, are likely to persist, this is by no means necessarily so. Evidence shows that during the first two or three years a pattern of attachment is a property of the relationship: for example the pattern of child to mother may differ from that to the father, and also that if the parent treats the child differently the pattern will change accordingly. These changes are amongst much evidence reviewed by Sroufe that stability of pattern, when it occurs, cannot be attributed to the child's inborn temperament as has often been claimed.[19] On the contrary, the evidence points unmistakeably to the conclusion that a host of personal characteristics traditionally termed temperamental and often ascribed to heredity are environmentally induced. True, neonates differ from each other in many many ways. Yet the evidence is crystal-clear from repeated studies that infants described as difficult during their early days are enabled by sensitive mothering to become happy easy toddlers. Contrariwise, placid newborns can be turned into anxious, moody, demanding or awkward toddlers by insensitive or rejecting mothering. Not only did Ainsworth demonstrate this in her original study, but it has been found again and again in subsequent ones. Those who attribute so much to inborn temperament will have to think again.

Thus, during the earliest years features of personality crucial to psychoanalysis remain relatively open to change because they are still responsive to the environment. As a child grows older, however, clinical evidence shows that both the pattern of attachment and the personality features that go with it become increasingly a property of the child himself and also increasingly resistant to change. This means that he tends to impose it, or some derivative of it, upon new relationships, as with his teacher in the Minneapolis study. Similarly, experience shows that he tends also to impose it or some derivative of it on to a foster mother or a therapist.

The tendencies to impose earlier patterns on to new relationships, and in some measure to persist in doing so despite absence of fit, are, of course, the phenomena that gave birth to psychoanalysis. They are also the phenomena of transference that during recent decades have led an increasing number of analysts to embrace the object-relations version of psychoanalytic theory and, in my own case, to advance the attachment version with its postulate of internal working models of self and attachment-figure in interaction. Thus far, therefore, the picture presented can be looked upon as a much modified and updated variant of traditional psychoanalytic thinking in which great emphasis is placed on the particular pattern into which each personality comes to be organized during the early years, with its own distinctive working models or, to use the traditional term, internal world, and on the strong influence thereafter that each individual's internal world has in shaping his or her life.

Notes

[1] S. Freud: 'Female Sexuality', in *Collected Papers* (London 1931), *SE* xxi. 223; *An Outline of Psycho-Analysis* (London 1940), *SE* xxiii.

[2] J. Bowlby, 'Attachment and Loss: Retrospect and Prospect', *American Jn of Orthopsychiatry*, lii (1982), 664–78.

[3] J. Bowlby, *Attachment and Loss*, vol. I: *Attachment* [1st edn. 1969] (London 1982).

[4] J. Bowlby, 'Psychoanalysis as Art and Science', *Int'l Rev Psych*, vi (1979), 3–14.

[5] D.N. Stern, *The Interpersonal World of the Infant* (New York 1985).

[6] J.J. Gaensbauer, 'The Differentiation of Discrete Affect', *Psych Study of Child*, xxxvii (1982), 29–66.

[7] E.V. Demos, 'Affect in Early Infancy: Physiology or Psychology', *Psychoanalytic Enquiry*, i (1982), 533–74.

[8] C. Trevarthen, 'Instincts for Human Understanding and for Cultural Co-operation: Their Development in Infancy', in *Human Ethology*, ed. M. von Cranach *et al.* (Cambridge 1979), 530–71, 581–94.

[9] P. Light, *The Development of Social Sensitivity: A Study of Social Aspects of Role-Taking in Young Children* (Cambridge 1979).

[10] M.D.S. Ainsworth *et al.*, *Patterns of Attachment: A Psychological Study of the Strange Situation* (Hillsdale, N.J., 1978); M.D.S. Ainsworth, (i) 'Patterns of Infant-Mother Attachment: Antecedents and Effects on Development' and (ii) 'Attachments Across the Life Span', *Bulletin of the New York Academy of Medicine*, lxi (1985), 771–91, 792–812; M. Main and D.R. Weston, 'The Quality of the Toddler's Relationship to Mother and to Father: Related to Conflict Behaviour and the Readiness to Establish New Relationships', *Child Development*, lii (1981), 932–40; M. Main and J. Stadtman, 'Infant Response to Rejection of Physical Contact by the Mother: Aggression, Avoidance and Conflict', *Jn of the American Academy of Child Psychiatry*, xx (1981), 292–307; M. Main, N. Kaplan and J. Cassidy, 'Security in Infancy, Childhood and Adulthood: A Move to the Level of Representation', in *Growing Points in Attachment: Theory and Research*, ed. I. Bretherton and E. Waters (Monograph of the Society for Research in Child Development, serial no. 209) (Chicago 1985); L.A. Sroufe: 'Infant-Caregiver Attachment and Patterns of Adaptation in Preschool: The Roots of Maladaptation and Competence', in *Minnesota Symposium in Child Psychology*, vol. xvi, ed. M. Perlmutter (Minneapolis 1983); 'Attachment Classification from the Perspective of Infant-Caregiver Relationships and Infant Temperament', *Child Development*, lvi (1985), 1–14; E. Waters, B.E. Vaughn and B.R. Egeland, 'Individual Differences in Infant-Mother Attachment Relationships at Age One: Antecedents in Neonatal Behaviour in an Urban, Economically Disadvantaged Sample', *Child Development*, li (1980), 208–16; E. Waters and K.E. Deane, 'Defining and Assessing Individual Differences in Attachment Relationships: Q-Methodology and the Organization of Behaviour in Infancy and Early Childhood', in *Growing Points in Attachment Theory and Research*, ed. I. Bretherton and E. Waters (Chicago 1985); K.E. and K. Grossmann and A. Schwan, 'Capturing the Wider View of Attachment: A Reanalysis of Ainsworth's Strange Situation', in *Measuring Emotions in Infants and Children*, vol. II, ed. C.E. Izard and P.B. Read (Cambridge 1986).

[11] Main, Kaplan and Cassidy in *Growing Points in Attachment*; M.G. Wartner, 'Attachment in Infancy and at Age Six, and Children's Self-Concept: A Follow-up of a German Longitudinal Study' (doctoral diss., Univ. of Virginia 1986).

[12] Sroufe in *Minnesota Symposium*, vol. xvi.

[13] Ibid.; P. LaFrenier and L.A. Sroufe, 'Profiles of Peer Competence in the Pre-School:

With Relations Between Measures, Influence of Social Ecology and Relation to the Attachment History', *Developmental Psychology*, xxi (1985), 59–69.

[14] P. Lütkenhaus, K.E. and K. Grossmann, 'Infant-Mother Attachment at Twelve Months and Style of Interaction with a Stranger at the Age of Three Years', *Child Development*, lvi (1985), 1538–42.

[15] L. Matas, R.A. Arend and L.A. Sroufe, 'Continuity of Adaptation in the Second Year: The Relationship between Quality of Attachment and Later Competence', *Child Development*, xlix (1978), 547–56.

[16] I. Bretherton, 'New Perspectives on Attachment Relations: Security, Communication and Internal Working Models', in *Handbook of Infant Development*, ed. J. Osofsky, 2nd edn. (1987).

[17] Main, Kaplan and Cassidy in *Growing Points in Attachment*.

[18] L.A. Sroufe *et al.*, 'Generational Boundary Dissolution between Mothers and Their Preschool Children: A Relationship Systems Approach', *Child Development*, lvi (1985), 317–25; M. Main and J. Solomon, 'Discovery of an Insecure Disorganized/ Disoriented Attachment Pattern', in *Affective Development in Infancy*, ed. T.B. Brazelton and M. Yogman (Norwood, N.J., 1986).

[19] Sroufe, *Child Development*, lvi.

20

Freud and the Question of Women

Naomi Segal

In his conviction that no utterance is innocent, Freud offers us the means to deconstruct him. In this brief introduction to his relation to feminism, I shall try to focus on some linguistic tangles in Freud's text that have got lost – or rather, tidied away – in translation.

My first instance comes from that classical text for feminist readers of Freud, the New Introductory Lecture on 'Femininity' (*SE* xxii. 112–35). These 'lectures' were written for publication, not for delivery. They appeared in 1932. In the fifth, 'Femininity', Freud begins (as he did often enough) by dwelling on the limits and problems of his authority to speak. It seems slightly as if he is aware that the whole thing – lecture, lecture hall, dais, audience and even theory – is somehow spurious and unreal. So he pauses obsessively on the relation of speaker to audience that must be conjured up before anything can follow.

First he goes over the arguments of the preceding four lectures, concerned that perhaps 'these lectures are without a *raison d'être*'. Then he modestly introduces the present subject:

Today's lecture, too, should have no place in an introduction; but it may serve to give you an example of a detailed piece of analytic work, and I can say two things to recommend it. It brings forward nothing but observed facts, almost without any speculative additions, and it deals with a subject which has a claim on your interest second almost to no other. Throughout history people [*Menschen*] have knocked their heads against the riddle of the nature of femininity . . .

Nor will *you* have escaped worrying over this problem – those of you who are men; to those of you who are women this will not apply – you are yourselves the problem. (*SE* xxii. 113)

This lecture has been fully criticized by both Luce Irigaray in *Speculum de l'autre femme* (1974) and Sarah Kofman in *L'Enigme de la femme* (1980, 1983), but neither makes anything in particular of the pronoun in the last phrase of this passage, which bears a more careful examination. For the English 'you are yourselves the problem', the German original is 'sie sind selbst dieses Rätsel' (*GW* xv. 120).[1] Now if the lectures *had* been delivered, the phrase would have been interestingly ambiguous: the women in the audience could never have known for sure whether they were being spoken to or spoken about, since 'sie', when it is not seen in writing, can suggest either 'you' or 'they'. But this is a written, not a spoken text, and Strachey's embarrassed misreading covers up for the startling fact that the phrase is actually in the third person. The passage should read: 'to those of you who are women this will not apply – they are themselves the problem'. In other words, Freud is unable to continue the mode of direct address, even though it is logically necessary, when he imagines himself speaking to the female members of his fictitious audience.

One of feminism's key arguments is that, in public (that is, mostly, in published) discourse, women are the object, not the subject, of language. This is notwithstanding the myth of women's incessant chatter; it is now well established that in mixed contexts, women speak less of the time than men. The myth of women's excessive speech is a compensatory one designed both to cover up a blatant injustice and also to account for an obscure fear in men that women's speech may somehow threaten theirs. What surely no one could disagree with is that in public women tend to be spoken of. Not only do they do little of the speaking (there are exceptions, of course!) but they are also rarely seriously addressed. Freud's evasion of the second person is a typical if unconscious political ploy.

The advent of psychoanalysis was a crucial turning-point. It substituted for the passive theatrical performance of Charcot's hysterics in the Salpêtrière the private and painstaking listening of Freud's method. As Stephen Heath puts it: 'Charcot sees, Freud hears'.[2] For the hysteric to speak and be listened to is something that had perhaps not happened since the witch trials. And when she had spoken she would, after all, not be burned but be offered the curative prospect of exchanging her torment for everyday unhappiness – quite an improvement. But there is a drawback. She could not entirely expect to be heard. If for example she claimed her father had raped her, she would gently but firmly be shown that this had not actually happened in reality but was a piece of infantile fantasy. Or if she had a passion for another woman's 'adorable white body' (*SE* viii. 96), as 'Dora' did, she would be taught that her true desire was for the woman's husband or, more deeply, for the woman's lover, her own father.[3]

I have chosen these instances because the two failures to hear – or, to be more exact, the two distortions by interpretation – are key examples of what women may not say to Freud. Paternal rape and female homosexuality tend to disappear from the psychoanalytical argument, the first all at once in the abandonment of what is euphemistically called 'the seduction theory' (at this point, as Nancy Chodorow remarks, fathers become the 'victims of childhood fantasy') and the second by a complicated reasoning in which, as Irigaray demonstrates, each woman is deemed to be playing the part of a man.[4] Enough has been said and written recently about the question of fathers and daughters. I shall come back to the latter case – the question of women's mutual desire – later on in my argument.

The second linguistic example I want to look at – and another which loses its most problematic aspects with translation into English – is Freud's famous last word on the subject of women, uttered in a letter to Marie Bonaparte: 'what do women want? [was will das Weib?]'. Here again a member of the female sex is addressed in the third person. And in addition, she finds herself translated into the neuter.

None of us is qualified to speak, or to answer, for our whole group. (When Jupiter jovially informs Juno that women get more pleasure out of sexual intercourse than men, all Ovid's narrator tells us is that 'she held the opposite view'.[5] They resort to Tiresias to arbitrate. Can you guess whom he agrees with?) Neither Marie Bonaparte nor I can answer Freud's question; all the more since its very phrasing makes us the dark continent that has no mind or voice. German has three very common nouns for women ('Mädchen', 'Fräulein', 'Weib') that are neuter in gender. 'Der Mensch' means a human being, but *das* Mensch' means an unruly or whorish girl. I am, then, not only not a 'you' but not even a 'she'; I am an 'it'.

Yet Freud took his place within women's discourse. It was Bertha Pappenheim (under Breuer's pseudonym, 'Anna O.') who invented and named the 'talking cure'. Women's speech fed and formed early psycho-analysis, female analysts were welcomed into the developing movement, and yet its theories centre on men's development and on an Oedipal triangle that makes every one of us (ideally) Jocasta. Penis envy, female masochism, all the woman's share is secondary, prob-lematic, shadowed by a presumption of lack; her gentler nature (so called) makes her less aggressive, her active aims can only be for passive goals; her whole history is of a progressive relinquishment and re-trenchment which, when perfectly and cruelly achieved, offers no dividends in the creativity of sublimation, and is seen impossibly as both more complicated and 'simpler' than the development of a man. The 'advance in intellectuality' that brought monotheism out of polytheism was, the later Freud argues, an abandonment of the use of sense-perception by which we see who our mother is in favour of the kind of thought process by which we deduce who our father is.[6] This sounds right enough, except when we remember that Freud is the theorist who bases the whole course of male and female psychosexual development on the moment when the child 'catches sight of' the

female genital and automatically prefers the *visible* penis over the clitoris
and vagina which provide the eye with 'nothing to see'. As Lacan
ruthlessly perceives (ruthlessly because he is supremely uninterested in
the political base of this difference), everything male is assigned a plus,
everything female is a minus.[7]

The case against Freud has been put by many feminist writers already
– some of them, let's not forget, directly in Freud's own time. Many of
the same arguments are reappearing in contemporary French critiques
of Freud. The early debate concentrated on the most exasperating and
dangerous doctrines of penis envy and feminine masochism. Essentially, feminists used the advances in anthropology and the evidence of
direct experience to argue that these diagnoses were biased by the
politics of patriarchal domination; they were, in other words, explicable
and changeable. In many ways, as I began by saying, Freud's method
has provided techniques that are useful to feminism. The talking cure,
for instance, was adapted to become a different kind of release through
the early and still continuing method of 'consciousness-raising': women
discuss common problems and experiences together and thus cure the
most grievous disease – isolation. Or again, 'where id was, there ego
shall be' (*SE* xxii. 80), 'wo Es war, soll Ich werden': feminist studies
of history, anthropology, law, literature and so on seek out the women
or the women's voice hidden behind the masculine surface of these
fields and bring to light what has been repressed. But in other ways,
Freud's theories, and the way they have been used, have consolidated
the oppression of women rather than alleviated it.

Feminism and psychoanalysis and feminism

I want to begin by reviewing the major arguments that were put
forward by feminists against Freud's theories, especially in the late
1960s and early 1970s; then I shall try to show how feminism has more
recently returned to him, making use of him either because of or in spite
of his overt arguments. I shall end by coming back to a question of
language, looking in particular at the arguments of several readers of
the 'Dora' case history – for here, in linguistic and other symptoms,
Freud has been discovered at his most irritable and cornered, caught
properly in a second-person dialogue that does not work out his way.

In 1927, Ernest Jones pointed out the bias in Freud's 'phallo-centric
view'. Karen Horney wrote articles in the '20s and '30s demonstrating
the social basis of penis envy and proposing in males a parallel envy of
motherhood and a terror of the female genital that expresses a sense of
inadequacy *vis-à-vis* the mother, not the father. Anthropological work
such as Margaret Mead's *Sex and Temperament in Three Primitive Societies*
(1935) helped to expose cultural variations on the patriarchal theme of
male aggression and female submission. The first key text of modern

feminism that looks at Freud is Simone de Beauvoir's *Le deuxième Sexe* (1949), in which a fairly good knowledge of Freud's theories supports a confident rejection of many of his arguments. Beauvoir accepts that boys are proud of their genital but disputes that this need make girls ashamed of theirs. She stresses the 'total situation' (p. 74) that causes women's complexes and disadvantages. Above all, she quarrels with psychoanalysis's '[systematic rejection] of the idea of *choice*' (p. 76), its insistence on sexuality as 'an irreducible datum' (p. 77) and its anti-existentialist tendency to look backward deterministically rather than forward at the forming of 'projects'. In her view, woman is caught not between masculine and feminine identifications but between 'the role of *object, Other* which is offered her, and the assertion of her liberty' (p. 83).[8]

It was in the late '60s that the contemporary phase of feminism really began. Mary Ellmann's *Thinking about Women* (1968) is a witty critique of the use of 'sexual analogy' in criticism and other writing. In a sense, such a critique could only have been written in a post-Freudian era: Freud's own suspicion of language and awareness of sexual imagery provide guide-lines for the deconstruction of critical discourse that Ellmann undertakes. But she derides Freud's revelations of sexually analogical thinking as 'codifying and pervading our modern sense of reiteration – of habits, rather than surprises, of the mind' (p. 8). She restores the surprise by showing where patriarchy biases the imagery. Here, for example, is her comment on bisexuality:

Most comments upon bisexuality have not . . . disturbed Freud's view of the matter. So far as women are perceived also to be bisexual, they are disliked. The evidence in women of what is considered any masculine propensity is felt to be unpleasant, prompted by envy (Freud again) or excessive ambition. On one level of diction such women are called *pushy* or *driving*, on another *phallic*. And of course this last term is, in these contexts, always reproachful: men may congratulate themselves upon the productivity of their own mental wombs, but they are displeased to come upon women with mental penises.   (p. 21)

'At his best, Freud persuaded softly – he was too brilliant to assert' (p. 154), Ellmann adds more than a hundred pages later. Her own attacks are equally soft and deadly: if women's pubic hair is an effort of nature to hide the embarrassing lack of a penis, for instance, what on earth explains men's? And, like many of this generation of feminists, she concentrates special attention on the private symptomatology of Freud's patronizing letters to Martha Bernays at the time of their engagement.[9]

One of the least dated documents of '60s feminist writing is Kate Millett's powerful doctoral thesis, *Sexual Politics* (1969, 1970). It ranges from prehistory through the recent history of women's rights and wrongs, and ends with a section of literary criticism, seeking out the political biases of texts by D.H. Lawrence, Henry Miller, Norman Mailer, and one good guy, Jean Genet. The analysis of Freud's influence appears in a section headed 'The Counter-revolution 1930–60'; like Betty Friedan in *The Feminine Mystique*, published some six years earlier, Millett sees the post-Freudian legacy as both the symptom and the cause of the rush to send women back to domesticity after the reforms achieved by the first phase of nineteenth-century feminism. Her reading of Freud begins from the assumption that 'we must ask ourselves not only what conclusions he drew from the evidence at hand but also upon what assumptions he drew them' (p. 179). Her objections to penis envy are based on a common-sense empiricism which argues, like Beauvoir's, that it seems strange to judge girls' as well as boys' reactions to the genitals upon the normative model of the male body. Millett reasonably questions Freud's belief that girls as well as boys 'discover' the female genital; and adds, 'it is especially curious to imagine that half the race should attribute their clear and obvious social-status inferiority to the crudest biological reasons when so many more promising social factors are involved' (p. 183). Juliet Mitchell's critique of 1974 rightly shows that this argument, like many others put by feminists in the '60s, lacks all interest in and sympathy with the idea of the unconscious. That this objection is only partly effective, I shall try later to show.

Millett's common-sense quarrels with the arguments of psychoanalysis are legitimate ones. 'It is interesting', she notes, 'that Freud should imagine the young female's fears center about castration rather than rape – a phenomenon which girls are in fact, and with reason, in dread of, since it happens to them and castration does not' (p. 184). Though she is wrong in saying that Freud focuses girls' *fears* on castration – he believes they gradually accept it as a pre-given fact – she is right in highlighting an extraordinary omission and marking what it tells us of the coercive nature of psychoanalytic theories on women. Similarly, she observes that 'Freudian logic has succeeded in converting childbirth, an impressive female accomplishment, and the only function its rationale permits her, into nothing more than a hunt for a male organ. It somehow becomes the male prerogative even to give birth, as babies are but surrogate penises' (p. 185). What Irigaray calls the 'homosexuality' of the structure that sees women as channels for the reproduction of men, or (which is little different) the means of exchange among men, is as sharply revealed by Millett's critique as it is by Irigaray's exposure of the male effigies involved (in Freud's mind) in the lesbian embrace.

Where Juliet Mitchell argues that Freud must be read as descriptive, Millett insists his theory is prescriptive. As 'pure *description*', she says (p. 194), his writings point out the most significant differences in the sexual arrangement of patriarchy; but the effects of his revelations are conservative at best, counter-revolutionary at worst: everyday unhappiness instead of burning may be merely a slower form of torture.[10] There are many who would argue today that psychoanalytic treatment at the hands of a non-feminist analyst can do a woman more harm than good.

Three books appeared in 1970, popularizing the feminist argument in England: by far the best known is Germaine Greer's *The Female Eunuch*; the others are Eva Figes's *Patriarchal Attitudes* and Shulamith Firestone's *The Dialectic of Sex*. The first two have little time for Freud and his ways. Greer co-opts his 'fact' of the castration of women as her key metaphor, commenting: 'the characteristics that are praised and rewarded [in women] are those of the castrate – timidity, plumpness, languor, delicacy and preciosity' (p. 21). She regards the influence of what she calls 'the psychological sell' as a last resort to bind the mind of the woman who has managed to come through infancy and adolescence without adapting to 'her feminine conditioning' (p. 21). Psychoanalysis, in Greer's view, is a form of 'paternal guidance . . . an extraordinary confidence trick' (p. 107); and she points out that Freud's 'argument is a tautology which cannot proceed beyond its own terms, so that it is neither demonstrable nor refutable' (p. 108). She too places Freud in his historical moment and argues that 'facts are [taken as] irrelevant in what is basically a value system' (p. 114).[11]

Eva Figes discusses Freud's theories immediately after an analysis of the figure of Lilith in the writings of the rabbis. She regards Freud as another 'Jewish patriarch' (p. 28) defending a similarly 'entrenched position', and quotes from the letters to Martha Bernays to illustrate Freud's 'willingness to accept the contemporary roles of male and female as right and inevitable' (p. 29). She sees the correctness of Freud's descriptions but shows that they are effectively prescriptions too: 'as Freud said, woman *is* hostile to the demands of civilization – when the civilization is totally masculine, the only one that Freud recognized' (p. 49); or, 'Freud . . . demanded not that woman should give up her will, but her masculinity, which in effect demanded the same thing. And by saying that she had to renounce her masculinity at puberty, he was in fact admitting that her attributes as a human being were fundamentally similar to those of the male' (p. 127). She too sees psychoanalysis as a 'subtle psychological taboo' (p. 135) which freezes 'the would-be emancipated woman . . . in her tracks' and stops her 'from going further', and cannot forgive Freud, with all his insights, for being 'unable to see beyond the immediate social situation' (p. 136) to any possibility of change.[12]

Shulamith Firestone switches tack somewhat. To her, psychoanalysis is 'the misguided feminism'; in a nice mixture of metaphors, she judges it 'our modern Church' (p. 46) in which, we may as well admit, 'the emperor had no clothes on'. The research of Masters and Johnson, for

example, has proved that the idea of the vaginal orgasm is physiologic-
ally a myth. But she argues that '*Freudianism and feminism are made of the
same stuff*' (p. 49). By the 'rediscovery' of sexuality, Freud focuses on the
repression (social and psychological) that is intrinsic to the way we
experience our bodies. She links the two theories together in the
argument that 'Freud was merely the diagnostician for what feminism
purports to cure'. His failure, in Firestone's view, is that he tried to 'put
into practice a basic contradiction – the resolution of a problem within
the environment that created it' (p. 50). The Oedipus complex needs to
be understood '*in terms of power*' (p. 51), especially in the reaction of the
child to its realization that its mother 'is half-way between authority and
helplessness' (p. 53). Both mother and child are trapped in the Oedipal
family; the child only grows up by leaving the mother's prison behind,
actually by conspiring in her entrapment (if a male) or by finally
reproducing it if a female. Children of both sexes, joining the ranks of
their mother's oppressors, feel guilty and thus aggressive towards her
(this argument is fully and beautifully developed by Dorothy Dinnerstein in her 1976 book *The Mermaid and the Minotaur*). Firestone ends by
showing how '*Freudianism subsumed the place of feminism as the lesser of two
evils*' (p. 64). In America in the '40s, she repeats, it was used powerfully
to send young women back to the hearth and the home.[13]

The debate was restated in 1974 by the publication of Juliet
Mitchell's *Psychoanalysis and Feminism*. In this highly influential book,
Mitchell goes back over Freud's theories on women in considerable
detail, then demolishes the post-Freudians Reich and Laing, whose
ideas find greater favour with many feminists; she goes on to attack the
reasoning of the critiques of Freud that I have just outlined; and ends
with an apologia for Freudianism that (in parts explicitly, in parts
implicitly) owes a great deal to Lacan. Her position is outlined on the
first page:

> the argument of this book is that a rejection of psychoanalysis and of Freud's
> works is fatal for feminism. However it may have been used, psychoanalysis
> is not a recommendation *for* a patriarchal society, but an analysis *of* one. If we
> are interested in understanding and challenging the oppression of women, we
> cannot afford to neglect it.   (p. xv)

Mitchell criticizes the feminist critics of Freud for their neglect of the
two fundamental innovations of psychoanalysis: the 'discovery' of the
unconscious and infantile sexuality. She points out that the vocabulary
of the first area is too new, the second too confusingly familiar, to be
easily appreciated. The mainly empiricist objections of feminist thought
avoid these difficulties and just leave aside what is too awkward to
digest. Mitchell argues (as such influential object-relations feminists as
Nancy Chodorow have since) that only an acceptance of unconscious

processes can explain the perpetuation and, especially, the internalization of women's oppression. We cannot learn what to do about it unless
we acquaint ourselves with the unspoken ways in which it is acquired.
Sharing the attitude of the French women's group 'Psychanalyse et
politique' (since renamed 'Politique et psychanalyse'), she 'denounces
radical feminism's rejection of psychoanalysis, but this does not imply
. . . an acceptance of the present patriarchal practice of psychoanalysis,
nor of the many patriarchal judgements found within Freud's own
work' (pp. xxi–ii).

But there are serious problems in Mitchell's exposition of Freud's
thought. She argues that 'Freud found the unconscious because
nothing else would explain what he observed' (p. 6), but this hypothetical finding immediately hardens into 'objective knowledge'.
Everything that follows assumes that Freud's 'findings' are unimpeach-
able, not so much because they are proved as because – and this, of
course, cuts both ways – they cannot be disproved. Of the Oedipus
complex, for example, Mitchell argues that it 'is the *repressed* ideas that
appertain to the family drama of any primary constellation of figures
within which the child must find its place. It is not the *actual* family
situation or the conscious desire it evokes' (p. 63). Fine – but what if
it were not the repressed ideas that appertain to the family drama; what
if they are something different? Could we ever know?

The empirical is never wholly abandoned by psychoanalysis. Even
Lacan is happy to quote the actual behaviour of babies in front of
mirrors when it suits his argument. Mitchell sides with Freud against
Melanie Klein in rejecting the idea of the super-ego as a 'combined
parent-figure' because, as she puts it, 'it *is* the father and not the two
parents [in patriarchal culture] who plays this particular role' (p. 72).
Here by an italicized 'is' she is inserting us back into the world of
experience, for in this context it is useful to her to note who wields
power in the 'real world'. Conversely, the terms of reality, fact,
evidence are co-opted by Freud and his apologists so that they speak of
the disavowal of the *fact* or '*evidence*' of female castration (Mitchell,
p. 85), a mixture of registers if ever there was one. The completeness of
the female body is surely the most deeply disavowed fact of all psychoanalytic theory.

Mitchell argues that in the unconscious psychical reality (which she
never really defines) the penis is universally dominant. How much can
be claimed for psychical as opposed to social reality is a question
examined by Teresa Brennan in the next paper. But it is immediately
obvious that Mitchell fails to question the teleology of Freud's analysis
of women's development. Because most women do make the changes
of genital zone, love object and so on upon which patriarchal sexuality
depends, she accepts wholly Freud's argument that they must. The

'must' of (assumed) evidence turns in a trice into the 'have to' of prescription. How can it not? Women do have to do these things. But this does not tell us why, nor is the argument perhaps able to stand far enough away to tell us how. There are other theories, taking in the existence of unconscious reasoning, which could account for it. Freud's argument, effectively simply telling us that women do make these changes, is scarcely more than a tautology.

'The Freud the feminists have inherited is often a long way off-centre', Mitchell argues (p. 301); 'neither Freud's contribution on femininity nor the science of psychoanalysis are anywhere near unflawed or complete – but a return to these would seem to be the way forward' (p. 302).[14] Since her restatement of the debate, the writings of Freud and Lacan, as well as those of the object-relations analysts, have been incorporated, digested, reread by feminists. To a great extent, the argument has now moved over to France and is channelled through Lacan, although such French thinkers as Irigaray, Kofman and Hélène Cixous have taken direct issue with Freud's writings. Jane Gallop, in her *Feminism and Psychoanalysis: the Daughter's Seduction* (1982), stops only briefly to quarrel with Mitchell's book (whose title her own up-ends) before moving on to what she sees as the father–daughter conflict between Irigaray and Lacan. I want to return to a more specifically linguistic arena, using a recently published collection *In Dora's Case* (1985), to pick up some points and problems from this set of readings of Freud's 'Dora' case history.

'What Dora Knew'

For a literary critic, this volume is particularly exciting: in chapter after chapter, the twelve essayists (not all of them feminists) find something new and stimulating to say about the same text. 'Hysteria', Charles Bernheimer observes, is 'the illness of the other, typically of the feminine other . . . hysteria, psychoanalysis, and feminism . . . traverse each other in a complex relation of contestation, implication and solidarity' (p. 1). These contemporary rereadings of the 'Dora' text seek to return to Freud's thought by deconstructing this (as he called it) 'fragmentary' text.[15]

I want to consider two connected motifs in these analyses of the 'Dora' text: first, Freud's obsession with finding out 'what Dora knew'; and second, a lapse of reasoning and of language connected to the question of oral sex.

The failure of the case is, as Freud and later Lacan and others stress, all to do with transference and counter-transference. Now it seems that, while counter-transference may be understood simply as a mirror-image of transference – in Suzanne Gearheart's words, 'the distortion or bias imposed on [Freud's] psychoanalytic theory and practice by [his historical and social] limitations and [his] desires' (p. 105) – it can also mean a rational co-optation of unconscious responses which can then be made use of in the practice of analysis. Thus the analyst, though s/he has unconscious responses, can make these conscious ('wo Es war, soll Ich werden') in the form of knowledge. In Winnicott's comparison between the mother and the analyst, the key unrelinquished distinction between them is that mothers are supposed to act by pure feeling, while the analyst 'needs to be aware'.[16] In the 'Dora' case, we find Freud jealously guarding his privileged position as what Lacan calls 'le sujet supposé savoir' ('the subject presumed to know');[17] for this reason, he pursues the question of the authorization and source of Dora's sexual knowledge, for his knowing must at all costs subsume hers.

In her article in *In Dora's Case*, Toril Moi points to the avowed fragmentariness of Freud's text as a symptom of his obsession with the sources of Dora's knowledge as 'female, oral, and scattered. Freud, on the contrary, presents his knowledge as something that creates a unitary whole' (pp. 195–6). She goes on:

> knowledge and theory must [to Freud] be conceptualized as whole, rounded, finished – just like the penis . . . Freud's masculine psyche perceives Dora as more fundamentally threatening than he can consciously express. Instead, his fear of epistemological castration manifests itself in various disguises: in his obsessive desire to discover the sources of Dora's knowledge, and in his oddly intense discussion of the fragmentary status of the *Dora* text.   (pp. 196–7)

A similar point is made in Neil Hertz's essay: he sees the counter-transference as an identification between Freud and Dora, in which 'a first point of resemblance [is that] neither Dora nor Freud tells all' (p. 226). Both of them keep secret the satisfactions they get from their mutual speech: 'Dora refuses to "know" that when she coughs she is picturing to herself a scene of oral gratification; and Freud has every reason to deny that his own conversations with girls like Dora are titillating' (p. 229). In using the term 'gynaecological' of his procedures and 'gynaecophilic' of Dora's homoerotic tendencies, 'it is as if Freud had a strong interest in clearly marking off the separation of the two realms, in keeping *logos* uncontaminated by *philia* – that is, in defusing the erotic content of acts of knowledge' (p. 230). Hertz focuses particularly on the danger figured for Freud in 'the possibility of oral sexual intercourse between [Dora and Frau K.], the scenario – sensual and discursive at once – that Luce Irigaray was subsequently to call "quand nos lèvres se parlent" ' (p. 235): 'when our lips speak together', 'lèvres' meaning both lips and labia. Hertz concludes:

> I don't think this is a sign that Freud was squeamish about lesbian love but rather that he was anxious to preserve certain clarities in his thinking about the transfer of knowledge. It required a vigilant effort, it would seem, to draw

the line between the operations in the hysteric, which produce the text of her illness, and those in the analyst, which seek to interpret and dissolve that text . . .   (p. 236)

This, I think, is the crux of the problem, and I return here to the failure of Freud and psychoanalysis either to address or properly to hear the woman's speech. In his anxiety to be the sole subject of legitimate knowledge, he makes her voice into text – *his* text – and, in dividing her from her knowledge, he also divides her from the other woman (Frau K. or her mother, in Dora's case) with whom she shares knowledge and to whom, *in his absence*, she speaks. His refusal to address her comes originally from the threat he perceives in the grouping of women. If women are kept as an object of discourse (not least, of smutty jokes) between men, then they are separated from each other and disallowed both desire and knowledge.

The other problem highlighted in this volume by such critics as Lacan, Moi, Hertz and Gallop, is Freud's strange misreading of 'oral sexual intercourse' in its more conventional sense. He takes it that the oral sex Dora believes her impotent father to have had with Frau K. is fellatio, when logically it must have been cunnilingus. As Lacan puts it: 'cunnilingus is the artifice most commonly adopted by "men of means" whose powers begin to abandon them' (p. 98). Moi suggests that Freud's illogicality 'reveals his own unconscious wish for gratification' (p. 191). Hertz quotes Freud's observation that ' "[Dora] must be thinking of precisely those parts of the body which in her case were in a state of irritation – the throat and oral cavity" ' (p. 228). But none of them appears to see that this would imply that Dora was thinking of cunnilingus not simply between Frau K. and her father but between Frau K. and herself.

Jane Gallop brings the discussion back to language. She notes how, precisely when he is concerned to show how free of euphemistic coyness he is, Freud drops embarrassedly into French: ' "j'appelle un chat un chat" ' (p. 209). But 'chat' or 'chatte', as she points out, is slang for the female genital. 'So in this gynaecological context, where he founds his innocence upon the direct use of technical terms, he takes a French detour and calls a pussy a pussy' (p. 209). This is an apt observation, and fits well with the other critics' diagnosis of Freud's unwillingness to imagine oral sex as directed towards the woman's pleasure; but one thing is missing. There is not one 'pussy' here, but two. Freud is avoiding the unpalatable thought, not just of Dora's knowledge and desire for Frau K., but also of Frau K.'s for Dora. It is the two women together, knowing, speaking or making love, who are repressed from the text and the theory.

There is no time to look here at the many alternative readings of female development being offered by contemporary feminist research into the relations of mothers and daughters. But we might glance at one more symptomatic phrase. When Freud writes 'wo Es war, soll Ich werden', he opens himself up to a further rereading. If, as I suggested earlier, feminism borrows this principle of uncovering and bringing to light the repressed, it is reversing and exposing the phrase as Freud uttered it. Abandoning the dry latinisms of Strachey's mistranslation, we can read it as 'where it was, there I shall be'. 'I' is Freud, of course; 'it' is the neutered woman whose linguistic space he both displaces and appropriates. But this is the moment for the 'it' to be taken back again by a feminist reading which translates it as 'she', or 'I', or even 'we'.

Notes

Throughout this article, references to a cited text appear in brackets after quotations. A passage without a page reference is taken from the last-cited page.

[1] Strachey's translation of 'Rätsel' as 'problem' is of course a major distortion, suggesting an element of blame that is entirely absent from the somewhat disingenuous German term – more accurately to be translated 'riddle'.

[2] S. Heath, 'Difference', *Screen*, xix (1978), no. 3, p. 58.

[3] In the discussion that followed my reading of this paper, one male psychoanalyst assured me that such crude reactions are no longer typical; another male analyst disagreed with him. My argument is, of course, directed against Freud not against his followers, but my impressions are based on the reports of women analysts and women patients as well as on my own analysis of Freud's texts.

[4] N. Chodorow, *The Reproduction of Mothering* (Berkeley, Calif., Los Angeles and London 1978), 160; L. Irigaray, *Speculum de l'autre femme* (Paris 1974), 120–3.

[5] Ovid, *Metamorphoses*, Bk. i, trans. F.J. Miller (London 1916), 147.

[6] This argument appears in two places: in a footnote to the 'Rat man' case history (probably added in 1923), *SE* x. 233; and in *Moses and Monotheism*, *SE* xxiii. 113–14.

[7] J. Lacan, *Le Séminaire XX: Encore*, ed. J.-A. Miller (Paris 1975), 68.

[8] S. de Beauvoir, *Le deuxième Sexe* (Paris 1949; trans. as *The Second Sex*, London 1953), quoted from the Penguin edn., trans. by H.M. Parshley (Harmondsworth 1972).

[9] M. Ellmann, *Thinking About Women* (New York and London 1968), quoted from the Virago edn. (London 1979).

[10] K. Millett, *Sexual Politics* (New York 1969, London 1970), quoted from the Virago edn. (London 1977).

[11] G. Greer, *The Female Eunuch* (London 1970), quoted from the Granada edn. (St. Albans 1981).

[12] E. Figes, *Patriarchal Attitudes* (London 1970), quoted from the Virago edn. (London 1978).

[13] S. Firestone, *The Dialectic of Sex* (London 1970), quoted from the Women's Press edn. (London 1979).

[14] J. Mitchell, *Psychoanalysis and Feminism* (London 1974), quoted from the Penguin edn. (Harmondsworth 1975).

[15] *In Dora's Case: Freud, Hysteria, Feminism*, ed. C. Bernheimer and C. Kahane (London 1985). Further quotations are all from this edn.

[16] D.W. Winnicott, 'The Theory of the Parent–Infant Relationship', *Int'l Jn Psych*, xli (1960), 585–95; the quotation, p. 593.

[17] See *Le Séminaire XI: Les quatre Concepts fondamentaux de la psychanalyse*, ed. J.-A. Miller (Paris 1973), 209–20. This phrase is usually mistranslated as 'the subject supposed to know'.

21

Controversial Discussions and Feminist Debate

Teresa Brennan

Psychoanalytic feminist debates have encountered the same problem that dominated much of the 'Controversial Discussions', the series of scientific meetings of the British Psycho-Analytical Society held in 1943–4, prompted by the theoretical and practical differences between Anna Freud and another child analyst, Melanie Klein. The problem is and was psychical reality. Over forty years ago, it was an unresolved issue in the Discussions. It is now an issue in recent writing on psychoanalysis and feminism. Yet it is appropriate and useful to begin with this other occasion when psychical reality was discussed.

This is not to say that either side in the Controversial Discussions was right or even clear about psychical reality, simply that their different understandings of the concept help define its meaning, and situate its bearing for feminism. In the remainder of this introduction, I will indicate what the concept of psychical reality meant in psychoanalytic theory before the Controversial Discussions began; its meaning for psychoanalysis in general was synonymous with its meaning for Freud. It is because the concept became an issue in the Controversial Discussions that they contribute to defining the concept, and to our understanding of the problem psychical reality poses for feminism.

Feminism is about change. It tries to change the situation of women and men in social reality, but can it change it in psychical reality? And how far is social reality affected by psychical reality? Answers depend on what psychical reality involves. The concept came into its own when Freud abandoned his first explanation of an hysterical symptom. He had attributed it to childhood seduction. He afterwards discovered that it was due not to an actual seduction, but to a phantasy of it.[1] The main idea here is that the repressed phantasy, living on in psychical reality, had the same effects as a real event. Freud still believed of course that real events are traumatic. What was going on was the shift in emphasis to unconscious phantasy; a shift that introduced psychical reality as a concept and, as Laplanche and Pontalis among others point out, founded psychoanalysis.[2] To pre-empt any misunderstanding over what this paper is about, I should say now that it is not concerned with the 'real event' of seduction.[3] Incestuous seduction and incestuous rapes certainly occur, may be increasing, and girl children are their main traumatized victims. This is a vital, paramount feminist concern, but it is not the aspect of psychical reality that concerns me now.

Psychical reality came to have a broad and fundamental importance in Freud's writing. Laplanche and Pontalis, who have given it more thought than most, say that when Freud speaks of it 'he means everything in the psyche that takes on the force of reality for the subject'. 'Frequently [he] means nothing more than the reality of our thoughts, of our personal world, a reality at least as valid as that of the material world and, in the case of neurotic phenomena, decisive.' But '[i]n its strictest sense, "psychical reality" denotes the unconscious wish and the phantasy associated with it'.[4]

On the face of it, there is nothing in these definitions that rules out change. If there were, there would be no point to psychoanalysis as a therapeutic practice. Yet if we consider psychical reality in the context of an ongoing feminist debate on psychoanalysis, problems are evident. I will give a summary account of the feminist debate, before attempting to define psychical reality further. Then, defining it further, I will show that psychical reality has two meanings in feminist debates, as it does in the Controversial Discussions. One 'psychical reality' is obviously modifiable. The other at first seems intractable.

The feminist debate

Feminism's debate on psychoanalysis involves four positions. Naomi Segal has discussed three of them. I will briefly recapitulate, before introducing the fourth. The first position is an outright feminist repudiation of Freud's psychoanalysis on the grounds that it is a phallocentric, biological explanation of patriarchy's origins. The view that patriarchy is based on biology is a primary feminist target: an abiding feminist claim is that oppressive reality owes its origin to social and historical contingencies. Other positions on psychoanalysis and feminism are more complicated, as they value psychoanalysis but either write out or re-situate Freudian phallo-centrism. One such position is that of the French psychoanalyst, Luce Irigaray.[5] She criticizes Freud's assumption that women are psychically disadvantaged by the lack of a penis, but her criticism does not grow out of the feminist critique of biological determinism. Irigaray is influenced by, while reacting against, Jacques Lacan's interpretation of Freud, an interpretation which is central to most of the feminist writing concerned with psychical reality. Like Lacan, Irigaray thinks of the psychical effects of the penis in symbolic terms. Perhaps because her work is not situated in the expressly socio-historical, anti-biologistic Anglo-American context, English-speaking critics often mistake Irigaray for a biological determinist. As Margaret Whitford argues, they overlook Irigaray's own context.[6]

However it is in the Anglo-American socio-historical context that the problems with psychical reality emerge. They emerge especially in relation to two attempts at appropriating psychoanalysis for feminism, which (along with other studies such as Dinnerstein, 1976) exemplify a third position on the subject. One is Juliet Mitchell's (1974), the other Nancy Chodorow's (1978).[7] Using Freud and Lacan, Mitchell suggests that psychoanalysis might extend the Marxist theory of ideology because it theorizes a socio-historical product. Chodorow argues that psychoanalysis can be used to extend socialization accounts of how gender difference is internalized, but her argument relocates the origins of men's domination of women in socio-historical facts rather than the psychical centrality of the penis.

The fourth position in the debate comes about when Jane Gallop in 1982 argues that Mitchell in *Psychoanalysis and Feminism* tried to read Lacan's theories on the non-contingent or transhistorical nature of desire as theories about something which could be made historically contingent.[8] In the same year, Mitchell makes a similar claim. She goes on to say that psychoanalysis is not a socialization theory, nor an extension of the theory of ideology.[9] On the basis of Lacan's theory, Mitchell argues that to reread psychoanalysis without Freud's (or Lacan's) phallo-centrism is to forget 'psychical reality'; and thereby to 'reduce' psychoanalysis to a 'sociology'. She says that psychoanalysis is not a theory of how socially created sexual relations are internalized. It is about the construction, rather than the internalization, of sexual difference.

Mitchell's arguments are popular in Britain; Nancy Chodorow's are frequently criticized.[10] Given that feminism rejected psychoanalysis because it was 'biologically based', one would expect a favourable feminist reception for Chodorow's sanitized psychoanalysis, which claims psychoanalysis for feminism by getting rid of its messy instincts, which criticizes Freud's biological and other non-contingent assumptions, which situates the perpetuation of inequality between men and women in the fact that women have the primary responsibility for early infant care, and which argues that inequality will subside when men and women share that responsibility. But while Chodorow's and similar arguments had a favourable feminist reception in the States, they have been criticized in Britain on the grounds that they 'sociologize' psychoanalysis.

That some feminists should criticize others for 'sociologizing' is surprising, as the criticism has less to do with the immediate demands of a feminist politics than with defending or defining a particular understanding of psychoanalysis. By the immediate demands of a feminist politics I mean the need to know how an oppressive social reality can be changed. In saying that Chodorow 'sociologizes' psychoanalysis, these critics seem to say that psychoanalytic explanations of sexual difference cannot be reduced to socio-historical facts, including the fact that women have the main responsibility for infants. By saying that psychical reality cannot be reduced to sociology, they imply that psychical reality involves more than contingencies. The question is what?

Now it is possible to define 'psychical reality' without giving up the idea that psychical reality is basically an internalized version of social reality. For instance, when Chodorow argues that gender difference is the product of internalized social relations, she none the less refers to a kind of psychical reality. She stresses that internalization involves more than a direct correspondence between social and psychical life, and discusses how psychical life has its own specific mechanisms:

Internalization does not mean direct transmission of what is objectively in the child's social world into . . . unconscious experience. Social experiences take on varied psychological meanings depending on the child's feelings of ease, helplessness, dependence. . . . Internalization involves distortions, defenses, and transformations [and it] is mediated by fantasy and by conflict.[11]

Yet this is just about as much space as Chodorow gives psychical reality. It is important that she recognizes psychically specific mechanisms (her critics have not allowed that she does so, with the exception of Adams).[12] But it also matters that Chodorow sees psychical reality as no more than a set of mechanisms for refracting social reality, where social reality paints the picture, but the view of it is distorted. Mitchell and other feminists with similar views clearly have something more complex in mind when they link psychical reality to phallocentrism and to the construction (not the internalization) of sexual difference. I will return to this more complex view in my discussion of Lacan. More immediately, I note that while in the feminist context the nature of psychical reality is a new concern, it is not new for psychoanalysis. Psychoanalysts talked about it at length in the unpublished Controversial Discussions of the British Psycho-Analytical Society.

The Controversial Discussions

In the Controversial Discussions psychical reality clearly meant something more, other, than an internalized social reality. It meant this for both sides. Yet as I indicated, they disagreed about how psychical reality should be defined. This is not always clear, as the terms of debate are constantly set up (mainly by the Kleinians) as if it were a debate over psychical and external reality. Ernest Jones, who actively supported Klein in the lead-up to the Discussions, although he was not vocal in the Discussions themselves, wrote:

I think the Viennese would reproach us [the British] with estimating the early phantasy life too highly at the expense of external reality. And we should answer that there is no danger of any analyst neglecting external reality, whereas it is always possible for them to underestimate Freud's doctrine of the importance of psychical reality.[13]

There was certainly some basis for the notion that Anna Freud, and other of Klein's opponents, even some of her qualified supporters, did give more determinant power to external reality. However, on my reading, the argument about psychical reality in the minutes of the Controversial Discussions concerns not only the respective merits of psychical and external reality. It is also about the definition of psychical reality; and it is for this reason that I think the Discussions are useful in pinning down 'psychical reality'. But the fact that the nature of psychical reality was disputed in the Discussions is lost in subsequent published reports of them. For instance it is not mentioned in the most recent account of the Discussions, in Phyllis Grosskurth's biography of Melanie Klein (1986): Grosskurth, like other commentators on the Discussions, writes as if the fight was only about psychical and external reality, and accepts the equation of 'psychical reality' with the 'early phantasy life'.[14]

Anna Freud and her followers did not accept this equation. For them, psychical reality meant something different. To draw out the differences in the Kleinian and Freudian definitions of psychical reality, I shall discuss the Kleinian understanding of unconscious phantasy. It is crucial to the Kleinian view of psychical reality.

Klein argued that unconscious phantasy was present from birth: it was evident in the destructive and idealizing phantasies an infant entertained about the breast, and about the mother it later associated with the breast. There was nothing specifically Oedipal about the earliest unconscious phantasies, although they rapidly became Oedipal or acquired an Oedipal tinge: Klein dated the Oedipus complex considerably earlier than Freud had done. In the first of the five papers presented in the Controversial Discussions, Klein's colleague Susan Isaacs said the primary phantasies are 'representatives of the earliest impulses of desires and aggressiveness'. She stresses, and this is where a certain understanding of psychical reality is important to the Kleinians, that phantasies do not 'take *origin* in articulated knowledge of the external world; their source is internal, in the instinctual impulses'.[15]

The key drives governing the earliest phantasies are the life and death drives. In approximately the first three months of the infant's life, the death drive plays itself out through what Klein came to term the paranoid-schizoid position. By its very existence, the death drive generates anxiety. An infant attempts to relocate the origin of anxiety (a sense of threat, a feeling of badness) outside itself. It *projects* these feelings on to the breast, and imagines that they originate there. In Klein's terminology, the infant fears this bad breast may attack it: it feels persecuted by the threat; and herein lies the origin of paranoia. At the same time, the infant experiences nurture, knows the good breast, feels love for it (something Klein attributed to Eros or the life drive). It splits the bad breast from the good, and in doing so conceals a deeper split. It conceals the origin of the destructiveness embodied in the bad breast phantasy. For by Klein's account, the infant splits good and bad in order to keep the good breast of its imagination safe from its death-drive-derived aggression. In other words, this splitting has two mutually reinforcing aspects: (1) badness is given an external locus, but to keep the locus external, the badness has to be contained, otherwise everything external is potentially bad. So to keep a good breast safe, the infant splits. But (2) the split would be unnecessary if the destructiveness were not split off from oneself, but recognized as 'internal'.[16]

In Klein's theory, the recognition that destructiveness originates internally figures in another phase of psychical life: she called it the depressive position. In it, bad and good are acknowledged to coexist in the same person, the good and bad mother is no longer split, and one feels aggression as one's own. Through the depressive position, the capacity to symbolize comes into being, together with guilt about the damage done in phantasy and the urge to make reparation for it.

At this point enough has been said about Klein to proceed with the discussion of psychical reality, bar one relevant and usually neglected aspect of Kleinian theory. This is the very important idea that the infant not only projects its own aggression on to the 'bad' breast, it also attributes *real bad experiences* to it. By what I think we might regard as an early form of logic, it attributes the origin of its experience of (for example) hunger not to an unsatisfied need, but to a stratagem of the bad breast. The logic here is that the infant does not have a realistic concept of the origin of hunger, but it does have a concept or phantasy about the bad breast. Thus Isaacs argues: 'The hungry or longing or distressed infant feels actual sensations in his mouth or his limbs or his viscera, which mean *to him* that certain things are being done to him . . . he feels as if he were being forcibly and painfully deprived of the breast, or as if *it* were biting *him*'.[17] An infant with a phantasy about the breast has a relation to it as a loved or hated 'part-object'. Later, when the infant has a concept of the mother as a whole object, similar feelings are directed towards her. Klein herself emphasizes how real experiences reinforce the severity of anxiety and feelings of persecution or mitigate them.

Kleinian emphasis on the real object, and the notion that a very young being was capable of object relations, was a significant factor in the formation of psychoanalytic 'object relations' schools. Not all object-relations theorists accepted the notion that drives entered into the course of object relations. One who did not is Michael Balint, who did not accept that the paranoid-schizoid position was an ontological given, but argued that persecutory anxiety could be avoided in a 'good home'. Significantly, Chodorow leans heavily on Balint. Both deny the existence of the psychical reality of the drive-derived phantasy, stressing the formative nature of real social experience in early infancy.

It is important to stress the formative effects of that experience when looking to how psychological changes can be effected through changing social reality. Yet unless something else is at work in the formation of the psyche, there is no accounting for those cases where phantasy does not reflect social reality alone. Balint and Chodorow after him neglect this issue. The Kleinians believe that psychical reality is also formed by pre-given life and death drives which of themselves lead to phantasies and emotions. These have no necessary relation to social reality, and operate from earliest infancy onward. I want to note here that it is one thing to agree that these phantasies are present, and that they cannot be explained by social reality or experience alone, but it is another to say that they can be explained by life and death drives.

Anna Freud flatly disagreed with the Kleinians about infant phantasy, and with the idea that it exemplified a 'psychical reality'. Her disagreements do not emerge in published papers, but in the discussions after the papers. These informal contributions make up some of the most interesting theoretical material of the Discussions. All the published papers are by Kleinians. The debates after the papers, which remain unpublished, show that Anna Freud did not deny psychical reality, but that her psychical reality wasn't theirs:

[Susan Isaacs] gives the impression that only Mrs Klein's theories do full justice to the operative effect of the unconscious as demonstrated by Freud whereas we others have 'an inveterate prejudice in favour of the modes of external reality . . . and of conscious mental processes' and need to be reminded 'that unconscious phantasy is fully active in the normal no less than in the neurotic mind'. I wish to emphasise that this is not a controversial point. Divergence of opinion does not exist between us about the operative effect of unconscious content but about the nature of such content.

(BPS Minutes 1/27/1943)

Anna Freud thought of psychical reality in terms of Oedipal

phantasies, and in terms of psychical organization. Basically, she adhered to Freud's understanding of the Oedipus complex, and to Freud's belief that the infant psyche was governed solely by the pleasure principle. Anna Freud objected that phantasy 'as the imagined corollary of instinct takes the place of the sensorial corollary (pleasure–pain) which, in Freud's view, is the main mental accompaniment of instinctual urges, their satisfaction or frustration'. Isaacs recognizes the sensorial, says Anna Freud, but shifts the emphasis to the imaginal.

In Freud's theory, the pleasure principle only 'gradually' and grudgingly acknowledges reality. Throughout life, the pleasure principle conflicts with the reality principle. Reality governs conscious or 'secondary process' thinking, but the pleasure principle continues to hold sway in the unconscious. In other words the pleasure principle is one of the hallmarks of the 'primary process' thinking that governs the unconscious. In primary-process thinking, pleasurable (and even unpleasurable) wish-fulfilments are hallucinated. Primary-process thinking is also marked by the mechanisms of condensation and displacement; it is timeless, or without a sense of time; contradictory impulses can exist side by side; and negation is absent: there is no 'no' in the unconscious. When Anna Freud refers to psychical reality, she has the pleasure principle in mind. Both pleasure principle and primary process inform her understanding of what constitutes psychical reality.

The notion that the pleasure principle is characterized by the 'sensorial' rather than the 'imaginal' is a little casuistical. Freud thought (and Anna Freud by her own account is defending *Freudian* thought) that the infant hallucinated its pleasurable wish-fulfilments: hallucinations can involve images. Moreover, hallucinatory wish-fulfilment is another primary-process activity.

However, Anna Freud made stronger doctrinal points. Aside from insisting on the sensorial nature of the pleasure principle, she criticized the Kleinians for claiming that the psychical reality they attributed to infancy was the same as the primary process. Anna Freud argued that the Kleinian description of infantile 'psychical reality' confused characteristics of the primary and secondary processes. She discerned certain characteristics of the secondary process in Isaacs's account of 'unconscious phantasy': conflicting impulses do not exist alongside each other; on the contrary, one or other has to be projected out. Also, negation and a rudimentary sense of time seem present. On the other hand, Anna Freud finds characteristics of the primary process in Isaacs's paper: 'hallucinatory wish-fulfilment as the basis of phantasy, disregard of "reality test", displacement and condensation'; these, she says, are implied in Isaacs's description of phantasy and 'also specifically mentioned'.

One of the things that becomes clear through Anna Freud's criticism is that she herself defined psychical reality *as* the primary process: psychical reality escapes the 'reality test'. But Anna Freud also defined psychical reality in terms of *repressed* Oedipal wishes. Unlike Klein, Anna Freud adhered to the classical account of the Oedipus complex. Whereas Klein dated the onset of the Oedipus complex at about six months, Freud located it in the third or fourth year.

It is well known that Freud himself focused more on the boy's Oedipus complex. Here, the boy's desire for his mother and hostility to his father are 'resolved' by the shock of the threat of castration. Crucially, this resolution involves setting up the super-ego as 'heir to the castration complex'. The super-ego is the consequence of an identification with the father, and it represses desire and hostility.

For the girl, things are different. Freud's explanation of why boys and girls follow a different Oedipal course is also well known, but as the subsequent argument will try to look at this difference in a new light, the familiar needs to be repeated. By Freud's account the girl is already castrated, and therefore the threat of castration cannot have the literally shocking effect it has for the boy. Indeed, the course of her Oedipus complex is determined by the notion that she 'already' lacks the penis. Like the boy, she originally desires the mother. But when she 'sees' that she lacks the penis, she has two responses. She envies it in males. She also turns from her mother, blaming the latter for denying her the privileged organ. She turns from her mother to her father. She wants the father to give her a child, which by a 'symbolic psychical equation' she has identified with the penis.

Being 'already castrated', the girl has no motive for setting up a strong super-ego. Nor has she any real motive for giving up the Oedipus complex as such. Freud concluded that in her case the Oedipus complex is only 'gradually' given up, in some cases not at all. He thought too that the absence of a forceful super-ego accounted for characteristics that critics of various epochs had found in women: a weaker sense of justice, and less interest in social concerns.

Given that repression depends on the establishment of the super-ego for its institution, it should follow that repression is different in force in the boy's and girl's Oedipus complex. If the girl has a weaker super-ego, she should be less repressed. Yet Freud was to note that women are more, not less, repressed than men. He does not discuss this repression paradox. But we can note it here as another reason for querying the classic account of the girl's Oedipus complex. Klein however queried that account for different reasons, which emerge in another crucial theoretical disagreement: the question of female sexuality. It was a question discussed at greater length in the lead-up to the Discussions than in the Discussions themselves. Klein, like many others who participated in the psychoanalytic debate on female sexuality of the 1920s and '30s, partly rejected and partly tried to re-situate Freud's phallo-centrism: *contra* Freud, she insisted that knowledge of the vagina was present in early childhood and that it contributed to a receptive attitude to the father.

In some measure, 'the nature of the content' of psychical reality – as Anna Freud put it – is at issue in the Controversial Discussions because she and Melanie Klein held different views on women's sexuality. As noted, Anna Freud accepted her father's view. Accordingly, she accepted a psychical reality populated by phantasies of seduction by the father, along with phantasies of sleeping with one's mother. In some feminist appropriations of psychoanalysis, this view of the formation of femininity is favoured because it describes a 'psychical' reality. Femininity is psychically constructed rather than biologically given. In fact, this distinction is meant to mark the difference between 'feminine sexuality' and 'female sexuality': the 'female' refers to the biological, the 'feminine' to the psychical construction. The female refers to the unchangeable, the feminine to . . . to what? As Freud's theory of a psychically constructed femininity still depends on a biological penis, to stress the psychical specificity of his account only gets it off the im-mutability charge on a technicality: this is something to which I will return.

Anna Freud's recognition of the psychical reality of the classical Oedipus complex and her rejection of the Kleinian psychical reality of infantile unconscious phantasy has another dimension. It focuses on the importance of repression in psychical life. Participants in the Con-troversial Discussions thought that repression had to be taken into account in any discussion of psychical reality. Sylvia Payne, a major contributor to the Discussions, pointed out that psychoanalytically, it is repressed (or fixated) phantasies that maintain their influence. Payne also queried the relation between primitive object relations (those which characterize early infancy) and 'object relations in the genital sense' (BPS Minutes 27/1/1943). These two points seem related. For 'object relations in the genital sense' lie at the heart of the classical Oedipus complex, and are repressed. Primitive object relations are not. The problems the latter pose for the infant are dealt with by splitting. To the extent that repression is tied to the Oedipus complex in Freud's account, it is a very specific defence which comes fairly late into the psychical picture. As Klein noted in a discussion of splitting as a mode of defence, Freud did speculate about earlier defensive modes prior to repression.[18] But repression remains cardinal in his understanding of how forbidden Oedipal wishes are kept outside consciousness.

The problem here is that repression seems to do more than keep Oedipal wishes at bay. It often seems that for Freud, repression is the condition of the separation of the conscious secondary process from the unconscious primary process: his work, and much subsequent psycho-analytic thinking, is ambiguous on this point. A non-aligned participant in the Discussions, Dr Karin Stephen, alludes to this ambiguity when she says of Susan Isaacs's paper: 'it is left uncertain whether this unconscious mental content [phantasy as the psychical representative of instinct] is simply not conscious or is unconscious in the sense of being repressed' (BPS Minutes 17/2/1943).

Isaacs herself noted in anticipation of criticism on this count that she had not discussed repression. For that matter it is generally supposed that the concept does not figure in the Kleinian corpus. However Klein did discuss repression, albeit summarily. She makes it plain that she too regards repression as a more developed and advantageous form of defence, which operates from the second year of life, after the ego 'gradually' acquires more coherence.[19] In the Controversial Discussions Enid Balint says something similar. The 'probable explanation' for why repression is not important in the Kleinian account of the first year of life 'is that the prerequisite of repression is some degree of ego integra-tion' (BPS Minutes 27/1/1943).

The difficulty here is that two accounts of repression are operating. One involves repression by the ego, and depends on ego integration. The other relies on repression by the super-ego, and depends on the (classical) Oedipus complex. One of the things that is not clear in Anna Freud's criticism is the relation of the egoic reality principle to the repressed Oedipal wishes. As noted, psychoanalysis and Freud are ambiguous about repression in its function of defence. However, Freud may have provided the beginnings of a way of clarifying the confusion with a distinction he made between primal repression and repression proper. Primal repression is the precondition of repression proper. While the status of primal repression is a little unclear (it involves a binding of energy; it is not the same thing as a 'gradual' integration of the ego), a point that Freud makes very plain is that repression proper involves language.

At this point I shall break off my account of the Discussions, because from here on, there is little in them that clarifies or reconciles the two forms of psychical reality (Kleinian and Freudian) with which they were concerned. At the same time, there is a lot in Lacan that does. That is to say: if one assumes that both forms of psychical reality exist, the next question concerns the relation between them.

It seems to me that Anna Freud's Oedipally defined psychical reality is consequent on repression proper, while Klein's psychical reality describes the psyche before repression operates. The Freudian psychical reality is a means of organizing the psyche into secondary and primary processes, or thinking and dreaming. But this Oedipal organization depends on a certain relation to castration. This dependent relation is not clear in Anna Freud's account; but it is clear in Lacan's, as I will try to show through a more detailed discussion of the Lacanian feminist arguments for recognizing psychical reality. The irony in all this is that while these arguments do psychoanalysis some service, they leave feminism with the issue of the biological centrality of the penis unresolved. I will return to this matter in concluding, suggesting why Klein is useful to feminism. Let us first consider how Lacan (and the Lacan-influenced feminism that uses his theory) is useful to psychoanalysis.

Lacan and psychical reality in feminist debates

It has been argued by Lacanian feminists that psychical reality is denied and psychoanalysis sociologized if one of two assumptions is made:

First, if it is assumed that gender is socially structured and subsequently internalized, then the psychically formative effects of the classical Oedipus complex are denied. Criticism of this kind has been levelled at Chodorow. It could also be directed at Melanie Klein. For the underlying assumption of this criticism is the Lacanian idea that subjectivity and sexual identity are formed simultaneously through the Oedipus complex. Subjectivity in Lacan's account depends on a relation to language. In the terms I sketched above, it is dependent on repression proper, and the ability to reason in secondary-process terms. It seems to me that through the emphasis on language, Lacan tries to tie the establishment of the secondary process (and its differentiation from the psychical reality of unconscious primary process) to the Freudian Oedipus complex, which of course comes later than the Kleinian version.

Second, psychical reality is denied if it is assumed that there is a direct, one-to-one correspondence between psychical life and social reality. Many feminists have been criticized for this. Interestingly, Anna Freud was criticized, not really deservedly, for something similar. However the criticism is relevant to other participants in the Discussions, like Michael Balint. Moreover, the Lacan-influenced feminist arguments against a one-to-one correspondence are usually directed against theories of the first year of life. While these are highlighted by Lacan's theory, the argument against a one-to-one correspondence is also implicit in the Kleinian insistence that psychical reality has a generic life of its own. Klein attributed this generic life to instincts, Lacan did not; but both see phantasy as something that arises (in part) independently of real social experience.

I suggested at the outset that there is an evident if rough correspondence between the two forms of 'psychical reality' discussed in recent feminist work on psychoanalysis, and the two 'psychical realities' of the Controversial Discussions. As the relevant feminist work is influenced by Lacan, it should follow that both 'psychical realities' are theorized by Lacan. I think he does theorize them, but I suggest that when he does so he re-situates Klein's and (Anna) Freud's psychical realities in terms of his concepts of the imaginary and symbolic registers.

Before discussing what these concepts of the symbolic and imaginary involve, it is worth giving a little more attention to the one-to-one-correspondence criticism: it will bring into focus the need for differentiating the symbolic from the imaginary.

In more detail, the feminist argument against the assumption of a direct correspondence between social or real events and the contents of the unconscious is that such an assumption neglects the significance of phantasy or the inevitability of desire in shaping psychical life. For instance, phantasies of a depriving or cruel mother begin to figure not because the child is (necessarily) deprived in fact, but because it feels deprived through the nature of its own desire. It is easier to find someone to blame than to accept an unpleasant, inevitable verity: namely, the lack or loss at base of all desire.[20] Putting this another way: the child wants everything, and where it senses lack it invents reasons as to why that lack is there. These 'reasons' are phantasies. They are defined as such because in whole or part their relation to reality is distorted, although (I repeat) reality is present, and figures in the child's understanding of what is going on. The thing is, it does so through the lens of the child's own interpretation.

The benefit of this position to feminism is that it relieves the mother of the unremitting responsibility for the child's psychical reality. No matter what she does, there will still be bad mothers in the minds of infants and in the adult unconscious. From the Kleinian perspective, this is a qualified benefit, given that Melanie Klein argued both that phantasies are always with us, and that the action of phantasies was modified or strengthened by external events. Thus difficult weaning increases feelings of anxiety, fears of a bad mother, and aggression towards her. To this extent the mother continues to be held responsible for the final development of her infant. Moreover to assume that phantasies are always there is to place them outside history, beyond mutability. On the other hand, the Kleinian stress on the interplay between phantasy and reality opens out other possibilities. The phantasy of the cruel mother has a real referent in one sense: there is a mother. Its phantasmatic element is the attribution of cruelty. If the real referent affects the force of the phantasy, it makes sense to think about changing the referent, or bringing in an additional referent (the father?).

The problem is that this solution does not prevent the creation of some cruel figure. Nor does it dispel the internal psychical effects of that phantasy, or its projection. At most, this solution represents a change of object. This is very significant, but it does not go to the origins of the phantasy.

It is here that the distinctions between the symbolic and the imaginary are relevant. Lacan's intuition is that phantasies of cruelty – their projection as bad objects, their internal effects – all belong to the imaginary:

when Melanie Klein tells us that objects are constituted through the play of projections, introjections, expulsions, reintrojections of bad objects, and that the subject, having projected his sadism, sees it return to him from these objects . . . don't you feel that we are in the domain of the imaginary?[21]

Lacan also writes that what Klein lacks is a concept of the symbolic. Like many analysts, she relies on a distinction between internal and external reality in understanding subjectivity, and as a criterion for 'mental health'. The difficulty with this distinction is that the imaginary is both internal and external in its effects (projection often leads to action). The judgement of oneself, the relation to others and reality has to involve something more. It has to involve the symbolic.

In sum, the imaginary is the world of psychical closure, fantasy, delusion and illusion. It is the symbolic that 'breaks up' the imaginary.[22] In its best-known, Oedipal form, the symbolic (as the 'symbolic father' and phallus) breaks up the infant's imaginary phantasized union with the mother. By breaking up the imaginary mother/child dyad, this (symbolic) father founds the symbolic order capable of breaking through phantasy. In this more general form, the symbolic is the ability to symbolize, to communicate through language: 'to be understood by others'.[23] In everyday experience, the symbolic is manifest in the logic that brings imaginary fears into perspective. In the analytic, therapeutic situation, its presence is felt through a different chain of reasoning, found in free association.

To suggest simply that the imaginary comes first, the symbolic second, is to give a developmental cast to Lacan's theory which it resists. The two coexist throughout life, the extent to which one dominates over the other fluctuating. Moreover both the symbolic and the imaginary are present from the beginnings of psychical life, a factor which Lacan emphasized in his later work. The symbolic is present as language from the outset. Even though an infant does not speak, language surrounds it, and inflects the imaginary in which it exists. When an infant turns to another to validate its perception of what it sees, it is turning to a point of reference outside itself. This process of referral is a symbolic activity, a 'checking up' against something beyond one's own world of phantasy.

At the same time, there is a sense in which the developmental viewpoint must have its truth. While the infant is born into language,

its position in relation to the symbolic order changes when it speaks as
'I', and of 'he' and 'she'. The 'change' need not be permanent, nor need
it occur at all, and when it does, the imaginary persists. But when the
mother / child dyad is broken up, when the symbolic father intervenes,
the subject takes up a sexual position and, by Lacan's account, assumes
its specifically human nature, its subjectivity.

This brings me back to the first argument for recognizing psychical
reality; to why psychoanalysis cannot make 'a currently popular sociological distinction' between an innate sex and a socially defined
masculinity or feminity.[24] Psychoanalysis cannot make this distinction
because the person acquires the means to function as human when it
enters language and becomes a sexed subject: the two events are one
and the same. Language not only inaugurates the difference between the
sexes. It also divides the mind into the conscious and the unconscious,
for it inaugurates repression.

For Lacan there is no unconscious before repression, and no
repression before language. In this Lacanian symbolic context,
repression, the Oedipus complex and the secondary process are closely
connected. Language and repression together form the basis on which
the subject is able to think its own thoughts from the standpoint of 'I'.
When it represses some ideas it *selects* others. But it can only do this
through the fundamental division established by the phallus. Where the
subject does not accept this division, it lacks the basis for differentiating
and thus the basis for logic. How does the phallus divide? The answer
seems to be: by an analogy, between the visual anatomical difference
between the sexes (penis and 'non-penis') on the one hand, and differentiation in logical terms, such as 'a' and 'not-a', on the other. It is
the *sight* of the mother's non-penis that fixes meaning, or the ability to
differentiate between one thing and another, and brings the anatomical
difference between the sexes and castration into play.

In Lacan's theory, the visual opposition seals off the subject from
psychoses. To be the object of auditory or visual images with no
'meaning' imposed on them by oneself is to be psychotic; and this may
occur when the subject does not take up a place on the basis of visual
opposition. The reason is that it cannot connect itself as a body that
thinks with the oppositions inherent in the language it has to think in.
That is to say, unless it finds an analogy between its body and language
it cannot insert itself into a chain of meaning. As I said, the analogy is
between having and not having a penis, or the visual anatomical
difference between the sexes, and the means to differentiate as such:
'this' and 'not this'. This is one sense in which the phallus is the symbol
of lack: it is the symbol of the 'not': unlike the penis, the phallus
signifies what is not there, as well as what is. As the symbol of lack, it
extracts the child from a free-floating world of signifiers: it enables it

to differentiate itself and to differentiate through language at the same time. It puts it in a position where it is able to assign meanings from its own standpoint, to operate within the symbolic, to make sense.

It seems to me that Lacan's theory is about how the rational secondary process is differentiated from the primary. With this differentiation, the subject passes from a potentially psychotic state to a normal or neurotic one. Thus in one respect Lacan would agree with Klein's critics. The Freudian Oedipus complex constitutes the specific psychical reality of the primary process, and separates it from the secondary. In another respect, Lacan would agree with Klein and the Kleinians. There is a 'psychical reality' that exists 'before' the division into primary and secondary process; an imaginary of aggression and phantasized union.

Lacan's concepts of the symbolic and the imaginary parallel the two 'psychical realities' theorized by Anna Freud and Melanie Klein.[25] There are of course differences, but to me the parallel is striking. Initially, this parallel did not present itself through a study of psychoanalytic arguments: partly because of his practice, Lacan's theory is not taken seriously in British psychoanalytical circles.[26] Rather, the parallel emerged through a discussion of the Lacanian-influenced feminist arguments for recognizing the force of psychical reality. I have tried to show that, seemingly coincidentally, these arguments refer either to the imaginary, or to the symbolic (the Freudian Oedipus complex). Lacan redefines the relation between the two 'psychical realities' by shifting the emphasis from Freud's 'fear of castration at the father's hands' to a symbolic level: he reformulates the Oedipus complex in the context of language, and the separation from the imaginary other in terms of a symbolic castration. To be symbolically castrated is to realize one is not joined with the other, one is not complete, one 'lacks'; it is to relinquish the Kleinian phantasies in which 'lack' is evaded.

I turn now to the question of where this non-sociological account of psychical reality and sexual difference leaves women. To begin, we might ask why feminism turned to this theory in the first place. The theory could of course be true, in which case knowledge about the truths involved is essential to changing anything. However in one way this is incidental to the initial feminist interest in Lacanian psychoanalysis, which seems to contribute more towards reconciling the Controversial Discussions about psychical reality than to feminism's quest for knowledge of the conditions of change. After all, in Lacan's theory, the role of the symbolic and the phallus is not a historically specific one, but a universal, structural condition of sanity. While the early phantasy life and the referents of imaginary phantasies can be modified, the psychical reality of the Freudian / Lacanian Oedipus complex cannot – or rather, it seems it should not. Of itself, this might not matter: if this universal condition of sanity does not entail relations of domination and subor- dination between the sexes, if both sexes have equal access (so to speak) to the symbolic, then the specifically psychical reality of the Freudian / Lacanian unconscious is about something other than sexual domination.

Indeed, if there is a political reason for the feminist interest in Lacan, it is because his was an argument against biological essentialism. In Lacan's theory, femininity is constructed, not biologically given, and sexual difference itself rests on shifting ground. Like Freud, Lacan made the masculine and feminine positions available to both sexes.

The thing is that while the Lacanian rereading of Freud emphasizes non-biological factors in the formation of sexual difference, the penis retains a central role in the theory. Freud construed femininity as woman's reaction to her castration (lack of a penis). While he thought that femininity was an ambisexual psychical state, he identified it in the last resort with the biological woman, in so far as he construed it in terms of what she has not. Lacan puts the emphasis on symbolic castration, and makes this a condition of subjectivity for both sexes. However, the shift in emphasis to symbolic castration retains the phallus as the reference point for sexual identity. Femininity may be *constructed* in relation to it, but it is none the less constructed in relation to a sign that signifies the biological penis, although the phallus signifies more (or less) than that. Again, this might not matter; or rather, it only matters if it has consequences, if it leads to domination. Basically, I do not care if the phallus signifies lack, or if logical differentiation is tied to visual sexual anatomical difference, provided this says nothing about an inequality between women and men. But one Lacanian conclusion is that it does say something about sexual inequality.

This introduces a major tension and debate within and around Lacanian theory.[27] While symbolic castration is a condition of subjectiv- ity, women 'have difficulty' effecting it. The Lacanian analyst Michèle Montrelay sees the difficulty in terms of how women represent lack. Roughly, lack means loss, relinquishing phantasies of union, acknow- ledging separation. Men represent lack with the visually significant penis; women do not have this option.[28] Just why the penis 'lends itself' to the representation of lack is another issue. Lacan's theory ties the ability to make sense to a visual anatomical difference, but it does not follow that the recognition of this difference is easier if one has a penis. The penis is one side of the difference, not the difference itself. Claims about the penis and the representation of lack refer to another psychical process: the process of recognizing separation, in order to recognize difference.

More significantly, there is a very big difference between the 'difficulty' women are supposed to have with symbolic castration and the complete inability to effect it. Strictly, the subject who cannot 'represent lack' is psychotic. Women have difficulty representing it, and are thus, by another Lacanian analyst's account, more likely to be psychotic.[29] Women are more likely to be psychotic, yet all women lack a penis, while the inability to represent lack holds only in some cases. Not all. What are the conditions then, that facilitate the representation of lack in most, but not all? For whatever they are, they must be conditions that operate for most women most of the time, but not for all women. In this regard they must have some variable dimension. Given that all women lack a penis absolutely (one does not have more or less of a penis, provided one is female), the answer cannot lie here.

If we accept the entire psychoanalytic story, the conclusion to which we are forced is that there are two means of elaborating a relation to reality. One relies on representing itself through a bodily organ. In this paper, the existence of the other means is established *in absentia*. If there were no other way than the representative penile one out of psychotic, psychic reality, all women would be mad. The fact is, generally, girls do not stay locked in a psychotic closed space, with no way out of an imaginary unity. Some, most, find a room of their own. They find it through means which are not founded on the possession of a penis. For feminism, the question is, what are those means?

I will conclude this paper with a suggestion as to where to look further. In Klein's theory, the early phantasies and the states they give rise to are resolved – in most cases. Klein's theory also has its psychotic 'before' and its 'normal or neurotic' after; although as with Lacan, there is no necessary sequential transition from the one to the other. The psychotic part of us lives on, although at a certain developmental point it is also dealt with. Not by something termed symbolic castration, but by something termed the depressive position. The depressive position is about other things than the distinction between internal and external reality. It too is a symbolic process. By symbolizing, by creating symbols, the subject makes reparation for, undoes the damage done in phantasy. In doing so, it also identifies with the mother as whole object, at the same time as it differentiates her (and itself) from the phantasies constructed in relation to her. Klein is more concerned with the psychical effects of creative symbolization than with differentiation as such. Yet she is concerned with 'representing lack': the condition and consequence of symbolic reparation is the understanding that the mother is lost, separate.

The relation between Klein's symbolization, her means for 're-presenting lack' and Lacan's is left here on an allusive note. But it seems a note worth striking. While there are major differences between Klein's theory of symbolization and Lacan's symbolic (as Lacan's is restricted to language), access to both the symbolic and the depressive position involves representation or symbolization, and giving something up. If the precondition of the recognition of difference is the understanding that one is separate, then it is important to note that there are different means to separation, as well as symbolization. The hallmarks of the symbolic and the depressive position are 'lack' and 'loss', and they secure some relation to sanity.

In the depressive position, the penis figures as one of many means to reparation. It can be used to repair or restore the phantasized destructive attacks on the mother's body. But the other means to reparation, the creative symbolization of certain forms of labour, play, drawing, writing, are not sexually specific. If explored further, these may help us understand how women represent lack by means other than the penis. For instance, they meet the criterion of variability.

Crucially, symbolization by language, and especially creative symbolization, is something that social circumstances facilitate. If different social realities affect the subject's relation to psychical reality (which is different from saying that the social determines the content of psychical reality), then questions about 'psychical realities' might continue to interest feminism. As I said earlier, the feminist appropriation of Lacan seems to contribute more to reconciling different psychoanalytic understandings of psychical reality than it does to feminist theory, and leaves the penis relatively central in representing lack. By indicating other ways in which the transition from a phantasmatic 'psychical reality' to a symbolized one might be effected, Klein's theory, or a critical appropriation of it, might force us back to more fundamental social questions. Under what circumstances are separation and symbolization, or creative symbolization, effected more or less?

Notes

References in this paper to the Minutes of the British Psycho-Analytical Society are given as 'BPS Minutes', followed by the date of the meeting; the references are all to the minutes of the Society's Scientific Meetings, held to discuss Susan Isaacs's paper on phantasy. I would like to thank Pearl King, the Honorary Archivist, for allowing me to see the Minutes of the Discussions, which she is currently editing for publication. My summary of the background to the Controversial Discussions is in general much indebted to her account of it.

[1] See particularly S. Freud, 'On the History of the Psycho-Analytic Movement' (1914), *SE* xiv. 3–66; also Freud, *Introductory Lectures on Psycho-Analysis* (1916–17), *SE* xvi. 368.

[2] J. Laplanche and J.-B. Pontalis, 'Fantasy and the Origins of Sexuality' (1968), in *Formations of Fantasy*, ed. V. Burgin, J. Donald and C. Kaplan (London 1986), 3–34.

[3] In discussions in and around psychoanalysis, the 'real event' is the now familiar term for seduction as such, rather than phantasies about it. The importance of the 'real

event' and its bearing on Freud's discovery of psychical reality is the subject of a problematic book by J. Masson, *Freud: The Assault on Truth – Freud's Suppression of the Seduction Theory* (Boston and London 1984).

[4] J. Laplanche and J.-B. Pontalis, *The Language of Psycho-Analysis*, trans. D. Nicholson-Smith (London 1973), 363; in *Formations of Fantasy*, 7; *Language of Psycho-Analysis*, 363.

[5] L. Irigaray, *Speculum of the Other Woman*, trans. Gillian C. Gill (Ithaca, N.Y., 1985).

[6] M. Whitford: 'Luce Irigaray and the Female Imaginary: Speaking as a Woman', *Radical Philosophy*, no. 43 (Summer 1986); 'Luce Irigaray's Critique of Rationality', in *Feminist Perspectives in Philosophy*, ed. M. Whitford (forthcoming 1988).

[7] D. Dinnerstein, *The Rocking of the Cradle and the Ruling of the World* (London 1976); J. Mitchell, *Psychoanalysis and Feminism* (Harmondsworth 1974); N. Chodorow, *The Reproduction of Mothering: Psychoanalysis and the Sociology of Gender* (Berkeley, Calif., 1978).

[8] J. Gallop, *Feminism and Psychoanalysis: The Daughter's Seduction* (London 1982).

[9] J. Mitchell: Introduction I to *Feminine Sexuality: Jacques Lacan and the École Freudienne*, ed. J. Mitchell and J. Rose, trans. J. Rose (London 1982); *Women: The Longest Revolution* (London 1984), 221.

[10] J. Rose, Introduction II to *Feminine Sexuality* (1982); P. Adams, 'Mothering', *m/f*, no. 8 (1983), 41–52; J. Sayers, *Sexual Contradictions: Psychology, Psychoanalysis and Feminism* (London 1986).

[11] Chodorow, *Reproduction of Mothering*, 50.

[12] Adams, *m/f* (1983).

[13] E. Jones, 'Early Female Sexuality', in *Papers on Psycho-Analysis* [1935](repr. London 1948), 495.

[14] P. Grosskurth, *Melanie Klein: Her World and Her Work* (London 1986), e.g. p. 320.

[15] S. Isaacs, 'The Nature and Function of Phantasy', in Melanie Klein, *et al.*, *Developments in Psycho-Analysis*, ed. J. Riviere (London 1952), 89, 93. After Susan Isaacs's paper, Ernest Jones gave a good summary of the Kleinian definition of phantasy: '(a) no instinctual urge can operate in the mind without phantasy, (b) that by "phantasy" we indicate a meaningful interpretation of what is being experienced, and (c) that phantasy only arises from somatic excitation, whether this be external (e.g. sensory stimulation), internal (e.g. instinctual needs) or, more usually, both' (BPS Minutes 27/1/1945).

[16] For more details of Klein's views on splitting and phantasy, see esp. her 'Notes on Some Schizoid Mechanisms' (1946), in *Envy and Gratitude: And Other Works 1946–1963* (London 1975), 1–24.

[17] Isaacs in *Developments in Psycho-Analysis*, 92.

[18] M. Klein, 'Some Theoretical Conclusions Regarding the Emotional Life of the Infant' (1952), in *Envy and Gratitude*, 86 n.l.

[19] Ibid., 86–7.

[20] Recent feminist work talks of 'desire' while Klein spoke in terms of phantasy. There is an important conceptual distinction here. The language of 'desire' is more than the lingua franca of the times, although it is certainly that. To emphasize desire is to emphasize the structural formation of what Klein explained instinctually.

[21] J. Lacan, *Le Séminaire livre 1: Les écrits techniques de Freud*, ed. J.-A. Miller (Paris 1975), 88.

[22] Lacan's concepts of the imaginary and the symbolic are more complex than this presentation indicates. For instance, the imaginary is more than a phantasmatic trap: it is also the 'world of images'. In general, my account of Lacan is based on his *Écrits*, especially 'The Signification of the Phallus'. For an exegesis of Lacan's theory, see E. Ragland-Sullivan, *Jacques Lacan and the Philosophy of Psychoanalysis* (London and Canberra 1986).

[23] See J. Lacan and W. Granoff, 'Fetishism' (1956), in *Perversions: Psychodynamics and Therapy*, ed. S. Lorand and M. Balint (London 1965), 268.

[24] Mitchell in *Feminine Sexuality*, 2.

[25] Juliet Mitchell, in the Introduction to her edition of *The Selected Works of Melanie Klein* (Harmondsworth 1986), also draws a distinction between Klein's account and Freud's psychical reality, making the fascinating point that Freud's Oedipus complex establishes the sense of time, while the pre-Oedipal psychical life Klein discusses is marked by spatial relations. Mitchell also argues that Klein's is a theory of a more biological unconscious, while Freud's is a psychical unconscious. My difficulty with this is that the biological unconscious instincts Mitchell discusses in support of this distinction are about attachment (a chick and its mother) while Klein's theory is as much if not more concerned with the death drive, for which biological equivalents are problematic. This is one reason for re-situating the aggressive drives in the context of Lacan's theory of the imaginary, which Mitchell does not mention when discussing Klein, although Mitchell is probably more responsible than any other thinker for introducing Lacan to English-speaking readers.

[26] Lacan's clinical practice included techniques that are incomprehensible to mainstream psychoanalysis: he held short sessions, disregarding the fifty-minute psychoanalytic hour. His violation of established clinical procedure is the main official reason for his expulsion from the International Psycho-Analytical Association. Distress over Lacan's clinical procedure fosters a climate where his theory is under-appreciated.

[27] See particularly S. Heath, 'Difference', *Screen*, xix (1978), no. 3.

[28] On Montrelay, see P. Adams, 'Representation and Sexuality', *m/f*, no. 1 (1978), 65–82.

[29] E. Lemoine-Luccioni, *Partage des femmes* (Paris 1976).

22

Freud's Influence on Other Forms of Psychotherapy

Walter Toman

Philosophy and psychotherapy

Freud's contribution to psychotherapy may well be compared to Socrates' contribution to philosophy. The Socratic technique of philosophizing allowed for a person with a philosophical problem to come to the philosopher. The Socratic philosopher would have the person tell him his problem or often merely his philosophy, and would help him clarify ambiguities of concept and try to resolve inconsistencies among the results of his thinking. There was no teaching of philosophical systems. Instead people were encouraged to develop their own philosophy. The philosopher helped them along as a midwife would.

Freud received people with mental problems that they had encountered in their daily lives. If they were not getting what they longed for from spouses, parents, relatives, friends, children or colleagues, if they could not do their work as they, or others, intended, if they could not relax or sleep, if they were suffering from fits of anger and hatred, of fear and anxiety or of sadness and depression, all of which often they had to hide from others, or if they developed compulsive activities or mysterious physical symptoms, they could come to Freud for his kind of therapy. They could tell him what came into and went through their minds, and he would listen, explore and try to understand what they wanted and what fouled them up. The therapist would ask questions, would comment on or occasionally interpret what he thought his client was trying to attain or to avoid in real life, in memory, phantasy or even dreams, and the client would check whether it fitted. The client was the star witness in the process, and the judge as well. Only he (or she) could tell whether it made sense. Only he could decide whether he should try out any of the insights thus gained or conclusions drawn in his daily life and in his social contacts. In other words, the client or patient of classical or Freudian psychotherapy is being helped to help himself. Here too the therapist is acting like a midwife.

In contrast with philosophers, including Socrates, who tended to view reason as the ultimate source of human activity, Freud postulated emotions and instincts as man's primary motors. They are not in tune with reason at first, but in the course of growing up and gathering experience of his fellow men and the world, a person is likely to move closer to reason. He can never completely reach it, though.[1]

Another contrast to philosophy: Some of these emotions and instincts are, or have become, unconscious. Even so, they are effective in a person's behaviour. Emotions and instincts, including unconscious ones, are the subject of psychotherapeutic or, more specifically, psychoanalytical investigation. Reason is used in the process, as well as it can be, but it is never the whole story. Hence sensing and responding to what truly is on the client's mind in Freudian psychotherapy is a more complex, uncertain and tricky thing than any discourse between a Socratic philosopher and his student or customer.

According to Freud there are other complications in the psychotherapeutic discourse between therapist and client. One is the personal relationship between therapist and patient. It contains emotional and motivational components besides rational and contractual ones, and whenever emotions or wishes or fears emerge in the patient which concern the psychotherapist as a person, the psychotherapist may have to intervene in a special way.

Transference is the process by which a person tends to utilize experience of previous situations to meet a new situation. He views a new situation in the light of the earlier one that most resembles it. How he handles the new situation and what it teaches him is another story, but at first he has only his past experiences to go by. They determine his initial expectation.

Owing to the 'abstinence' of the psychotherapist in Freudian therapy, the classical psychotherapeutic situation is quite different from anything the client is used to. He does not get from the therapist the kind of responses and interaction he can expect from other people in everyday life. The therapist does not tell him anything about himself. He does not help or counteract him. He does not teach him or tell him what to do. That is why the client's transferences from his past on to the therapeutic situation itself and on to the therapist become more clearly apparent than they do in everyday life. The handling of the client's transference behaviour during psychotherapy is among the most delicate and complicated of the skills the psychotherapist is expected to provide.

Still another complication is the client's tendency to resist psychotherapeutic change. He does not like some of the experiences with and insights into his motives and conflicts with important persons in his life, especially the painful or humiliating experiences and insights, nor the wishes that have been permanently thwarted. He can't believe that those wishes were what he wanted nor that he might dare to try for their fulfilment once again. Handling these natural resistances of the client is another important skill for the Freudian psychotherapist. The resistances can't be attacked directly, nor can they be long ignored. As the client senses the therapist's unobtrusive, yet steady tolerance and benevolence and develops more trust in him, his resistances tend to diminish.

Psychoanalysis and psychoanalytically-oriented therapy of people with mental problems is Freud's practical and, in a sense, least disputed contribution to psychology and psychopathology. It has spread all over the world, and psychoanalysts do not seem to run out of patients, at least as long as they offer analytically-oriented therapy as well. The use of psychoanalytic concepts and models to better understand dreams, errors and verbal slips, child and personality development, family relationships and other social systems, as well as literature and art, has become rather ubiquitous too. It won't concern us here.

Psychoanalytic concepts, models and schemas have been more articulate than the concepts, models or schemas of other psychological schools (such as Jung's, Adler's, Schultz-Hencke's or Sullivan's).[2] Unlike other systems, the relationship of psychoanalysis to empirical or even experimental evidence of sorts was good enough to necessitate several conceptual and model changes. In the course of his later work Freud revised his anxiety concept, his instinct or drive theory and his structural model of the mind or psyche,[3] and his disciples added new aspects to his drive theory and to his structural model. Even so, Freud's concepts and models do not have the clarity and precision that you find in physics and chemistry or in mathematics. Even physiology and to an extent biology can do better. Yet the explicitly stated theory is one thing, the theory effective in the psychotherapist's mind another. The theory that Freudian therapists implicitly rely on is better than they can say. And this is true of other depth psychological therapists also.

How can this theory be tested by neutral observers? The answer is to give them records of actual psychotherapy. Let the therapist tell a group of other therapists about his work with a patient or, better still, play an audiotape of the session. It need not be a videotape, which might distract too much from the text of the therapeutic discourse; the text is the number one communication channel. Play the tape and stop it anywhere, perhaps just before the therapist's next intervention. Ask the group of therapists what they have noticed so far and how they understand it. Again and again I have found amazing agreement among different therapists, even among therapists of different schools, regarding the actual conduct of psychotherapy.

A still harder, more objective and more specific test is to let the therapists formulate how each of them would now intervene. A comparison of such interventions proved stunning. They were quite similar, sometimes identical. Trying this method repeatedly within one such therapeutic session showed that the similarities of therapeutic response were not chance hits. Therapists come up with the same answers. They can do it over a series of sessions.

In my visits to other schools of psychotherapy over more than thirty years I have come to feel that a comparative or even literal unanimity is the crucial feature which different psychotherapists and even some of the different schools of psychotherapy have in common. In the conduct of psychotherapy, the variance between good and poor therapists seems to be greater than the variance among some of the major schools of psychotherapy. This holds true, even beyond the depth-psychological schools or camps, for Rogerian therapy and even for some strands of behaviour therapy.

These considerations suggest that we should perhaps focus on the conduct of therapy rather than on theoretical positions, when tracing Freud's influence on other forms of psychotherapy. According to Moritz von Schlick, leader of the Vienna Circle – another group of dedicated people who claimed allegiance to Socrates – and many of his disciples such as Carnap, Neurath, Feigl, Frank, Kraft and others, philosophy has no standing in itself.[4] Rather it is the interpreter of and mediator between the substantive sciences. Philosophy helps them solve their empirical puzzles and conceptual contradictions. It lures the sciences towards a unified science. It matters little that few of the feats of resolving conceptual contradictions have been accomplished by philosophers of science. The scientists have mostly done that themselves, but philosophers of science surely were their enthusiastic collaborators. Their common descent from Socrates ought to make philosophy of science and psychoanalytic therapy siblings. Yet in actuality they have not valued each other very much. While the two still had a common home in Vienna, philosophers of science did not rule out the possibility that psychoanalysis would some day earn better marks in science than it did at the time; and psychoanalysts ordinarily cared little about the philosophers' esoteric discourse even when it bordered on psychology and psychotherapy. The psychoanalysts seemed to want to stay closer to the phenomena of psychological development and inter-action, whereas the philosophers tended to refuse to look at or even discuss a thing until they had clearly defined its concepts, methods and objectives.

Later attempts in exile at bridging the apparent gap between the two did not change much, and regrettably, even now, communication between philosophy of science and psychoanalysis is minimal. I am one of the small number of psychoanalysts who have kept trying, but with only moderate success;[5] Grünbaum is one of the few philosophers and he has had some success, but only among philosophers.[6]

The conduct of classical psychotherapy

Let us now turn to Freud's influence on other forms of psychotherapy, and focus on the conduct of therapy. Looking at it from a bystander's or 'behavioural' viewpoint, we could spell out a few rules that the Freudian or psychoanalytically oriented or classical therapist abides by:

(1) The therapist listens benevolently and attentively to everything the client or patient is expressing. He also looks at him or her for non-verbal cues but, as I have said, the text tends to contain it all. Sooner or later the non-verbal messages also show up in the patient's words. Ordinarily the therapist says something only when the patient pauses.

(2) The therapist does not introduce any topics of his own, but he may take up or come back to something the patient has talked about during the current session. That way the patient can expand on some of his themes. He can give examples of what he means.

(3) In coming back to topics touched on by the patient, the therapist is likely to choose those that (a) go into or reach further back in the patient's past; (b) are affect-laden regardless of whether or not the patient actually shows affect at the time; (c) indicate conflict with others or within the patient himself; (d) involve the therapist as a person (such as when the patient wonders whether the therapist dislikes him, or perhaps how big a family he has). Ordinarily, such questions or references to the therapist as a person are not instigated by anything the therapist has done or feels himself. Hopefully, he bears no enduring grudge against the patient, nor do any members of his family hang around the office.

The routine response to such references is an enquiry into possible reasons for the patient's feeling or his curiosity about the therapist. After these have been cleared up somewhat satisfactorily and the therapist has convinced at least himself that he has not given rise to the patient's feelings by anything he has said or done or omitted, he probes into similar experiences in the patient's past of his feeling disliked or of being curious about other people's families. Obviously, the assumption is that the patient has transferred past experiences into the therapeutic situation. Inadvertently or unconsciously he has viewed something that may have been going on between him and the therapist in the light of similar experiences in his daily life, past or present.

This is only one aspect of transference behaviour, to be sure. Implicitly, much more of this is going on in psychotherapeutic treatment, but the therapist is merely taking note of it. He may have his thoughts about it, but he does not address it. He does so only when there has been prolonged stagnation in the therapeutic process, or when the patient's feelings for and interests in the therapist continue to transcend the therapeutic relationship.

(4) The therapist is also interested in the objective circumstances of his patient's life, past and present. He tries to reconstruct them in his mind so that he may know better when and in response to what the patient's thoughts, feelings, wishes and conflicts originated and developed. In his enquiries, however, he does not violate the other rules of conduct of classical psychotherapy. He does not hunt for objective evidence as a police officer might, but he does take note of clues that emerge in the free-floating therapeutic discourse.

(5) The therapist tries to keep the dialogue going by asking questions and making comments or by encouraging the patient in non-verbal ways to go on. Sometimes the therapist tries to give interpretations. These are comments or statements about affects or wishes or conflicts that seem to underlie longer stretches of the patient's talk, perhaps the entire session so far, occasionally even previous sessions too. Interpretations tend to have greater emotional and/or cognitive value for the patient than mere comments or questions.

(6) The therapist is feeling and thinking with the patient. He keeps checking quietly on how the course of the therapeutic session, its content, the patient's relationships to important persons in his life and to the therapist, and the therapist's interventions all go together. What are the invariances and the connections in the therapeutic exchange? What does the patient want deep down and way up? What does he fear, what does he hate? How do these things fit with previous sessions, how with the patient's life history as far as it has emerged? – Most therapists use ten minutes or so after the session is over and the patient has left to conclude this empathic thinking process. Therapists in training may need up to an hour to do that.

In Freudian and other depth-psychological psychotherapy much depends, of course, on *what* the therapist thinks during and after the therapeutic session, and how sensitive and skilful in a humanistic sense he is in his interventions. But whenever a psychotherapist disregards any one of the above rules, he is no longer doing Freudian or classical psychotherapy.[7]

This may be all right, even for psychoanalysts. Certain types of patients such as those with psychotic disturbances, drug addictions, severe character disorders, low intelligence or early disrupted education may require more guidance, more education, or special organizational arrangements in order to be able to improve psychologically. Freudian and other depth-psychological therapists agree, however, that one cannot reasonably *start* the therapeutic process except in the classical way. It is the 'freedom way', so to speak. The patient can express everything that comes to his mind, and the psychoanalytically oriented therapist is the one who can let him do that best, comparatively speaking. What the therapist does later on and whether he may switch to more supportive therapy or to remedial education, remains to be seen.

These rules apply to individual psychotherapy. That they will need minor modification and a few additional specifications in the case of child therapy, group therapy and family therapy is easy to understand. In a sense the modifications can be derived from the respective context. Children need to play as they talk, and need a few playthings too. In a group every member wants to say whatever comes into his or her mind, and the key difference between group therapy and family therapy is that in the former it is better if members have not known each other before, and even keep apart from each other outside the group, whereas in the latter the members have been living together intimately for a long time. In family therapy it is much harder for the therapist really to get a foot in the door. In all three contexts, child, group and family therapy, the therapist may, eventually, deviate from the classical rules depending on the history of the patients and the severity of their problems.

We can say of most depth-psychological schools of therapy that they heed the classical rules. Different elements may be stressed in the selection of topics the patient brings up. In the eyes of a Freudian, a Jungian therapist may be inclined to over-emphasize artistic and mythological connotations and the work aspects of life, an Adlerian therapist man's social motivation and community feelings. In the eyes of Jungians or Adlerians and some others, the Freudian therapist dwells too much on sexual and genital wishes and fears, comparatively speaking. Yet, if a patient were to switch from one therapist to another who happened to belong to a different school, unless the new therapist wanted to prove to the patient that his former therapist was wrong – a possible counter-transference problem for the new therapist – the course of therapy would still demonstrate that it is the patient who invents the psychotherapeutic process. The patient chooses the themes, consciously and unconsciously, and the therapist merely helps him or her along.

As I have said, the skill of the therapist is more important than the school he belongs to. When there is to be a switch of therapists, for whatever reason, moving from a good therapist to a poorer one within the same school can be worse than moving to a different school. While all the schools claim that they admit only good therapists to the practice of psychotherapy, some differences in quality remain.

Other schools of psychotherapy

There are other schools of psychotherapy that utilize Freudian concepts and Freudian principles for the conduct of psychotherapy, but make a point of expanding on or specializing in some feature. There are neo-Freudians, like Karen Horney, Fromm, Kardiner, and those sticking closer to the classical processes of psychotherapy, like Schultz-Hencke or Sullivan.[8] There are existential analysts (Jaspers, Frankl, von Weizsäcker, Binswanger, Rollo May)[9] and humanistic psychologists (Goldstein, Angyal, Rogers, Maslow, Charlotte Bühler, and others).[10] There is hypnotherapy, psychodrama, gestalt therapy, direct analysis, transaction analysis, primal therapy, body and movement therapy and bioenergetics.[11] Closer to the border of behaviour therapy, yet influenced by Freud and other depth psychologists, are rational-emotive therapy, reality therapy, and something more original and challenging: communication therapy.[12]

Some of the other schools of psychotherapy mentioned above and all of those located closer to the border of behaviour therapy tend to disregard some of the rules of conduct of classical psychotherapy. They may give orders, suggest activities and physical contact. They may lead or join their patients. They may inform them, teach them things, request them to describe their experiences thus induced, and even instruct them how to talk about them.

Behaviour therapy itself is perhaps the only form of therapy that developed in outright opposition to Freud, not realizing that this too might constitute a Freudian influence. Dollard and Miller, and Mowrer, had attempted to translate psychoanalytic concepts into concepts of learning theory.[13] This read and sounded all right as far as it went, but when it came to clinical demonstration, the therapists revealed how far off or how much on the surface, or how absorbed by molecular behaviour and accidental and isolated clinical situations, they had been. One report told how the therapist conditioned a boy not to drop his coat on the floor whenever he entered the house, but to hang it in the closet as his mother had requested.

It was only after Eysenck's somewhat hostile 1953 analysis of the effects of psychotherapy, in particular of psychoanalytically oriented therapy, that behaviour therapy began to stir and eventually emerged.[14] It was a practice of therapeutic intervention where the patient named the symptom or behaviour characteristic that he wanted removed or changed, and the behaviour therapist, on the basis of a few routines such as anxiety-reduction, aversion training and model learning, would do it without asking further questions.

It took until about the middle 1970s before behaviour therapists became aware that there was more to heed and more to enquire about before they could settle for a particular routine of treatment. Increasingly, more than one routine was used. Occasionally talking alone would do. Extensive explorations at the start of treatment began to spread. Cognitive behaviour therapy had come about.[15]

Freud's influence in detail

I would like to demonstrate the kind of influence that Freud exerted posthumously on other forms of psychotherapy with two examples: non-directive or client-centred therapy, developed by Rogers,[16] and behaviour therapy. I hope to show that Rogers's attempt supposedly to humanize psychotherapy and to facilitate the learning of its techniques has led to a reduced scope in the content the patient or client is encouraged to bring up, and to a diminished variety of interventions that the therapist may use. This is not to say that the client will always let the Rogerian therapist get away with such restraints, nor that there are no good Rogerian therapists. There are.

I also hope to show that behaviour therapy, having started as far away from Freud as it did, inadvertently adopted basic Freudian principles as its own before it began eventually to draw closer to the mainstream of classical psychotherapy.

In *client-centred therapy*, according to Rogers, the therapist is to convey to the client his unconditional acceptance of the client (which perhaps is a little more than psychoanalytic benevolence), to listen to what the client expresses here and now and to respond to that client with what the therapist thinks the client has been feeling and saying. To an objective observer, and even to the client himself, this response may sound like a rehash, rephrasing or even a repetition of what has just been said. The therapeutic intervention is a comment, if with a question mark.

However, the Rogerian therapist does not ask outright questions. He does not enquire about anything factual in the present or the past. He concentrates on feelings the client has now and attempts to reflect to the client what they are. Even references of the client to the therapist as a person are merely reflected. The phenomenon of transference is ignored, resistance to change non-existent. The thesis is rather that the client can't but get better.

Thus, in a way, of the six rules of conduct of classical psychotherapy only rule 1 is heeded. It is admittedly the most important one, but the others are no trifles. Rogers, coming from psychoanalytically oriented self-experience and early training,[17] preserved rule 1, but was hoping that, by constant checking with the client as to whether the therapist has listened well and heard the client correctly, he could skirt the other five rules and their implicit complications. What conducting client-centred therapy amounted to was producing verbal reflections of what the client had said and felt. If the therapist could do that well, if the client was satisfied and felt understood, therapy was being accomplished. Change for the better was possible.

One extra thing Rogers started was verbatim documentation of psychotherapy. With the consent of his clients, he and other client-centred therapists made audiotapes of their sessions. They used them in team conferences and supervisions of learning therapists, published them and thus subjected them to discussion with other schools of psychotherapy, including psychoanalysts. This was more than psycho-analysts and other depth psychologists had done thus far. They had published reports of therapies, but those were accounts by the therapists. What they thought had gone on in therapy was put on paper. The reports contained a few highlights of what the patient said, but even those often in the therapist's words. All the rest was therapeutic interpretation, combination, speculation and conclusion. In most instances they sounded good. They probably were good. But for the reader there was no real way of telling.

By his example Rogers promoted research and evaluation of psychotherapy. At the same time he revealed how dull a tool this technique could be in the hands of a less than gifted therapist. Only the very gifted, like Rogers himself, or those who had been exposed in addition to something like classical psychotherapy, seemed to be able to tolerate it without discomfort when the client spoke about the past too, not merely about the present, and about objective aspects of his life as well as the subjective ones. Even the client's transference behaviour was handled properly in such instances, whether inadvertently or with the therapist's awareness. In other words, clients got their needs across and were satisfied in spite of the therapist's limited deployment of therapeutic interest and intervention.

An early forerunner of *behaviour therapy* was J.B. Watson,[18] who had demonstrated how to make an infant either love or fear, say, a furry animal. He presented either a pleasant stimulus or an unpleasant stimulus, e.g. a sudden bang, together with the animal. By the late '60s behaviour therapists had accomplished similar feats of curing symptoms. Some intransigent compulsions had been lifted or at least shifted, phobias reduced, spasms relieved – so much so, in fact, that some classical therapists began sending some of their most difficult patients to behaviour therapists.

I have mentioned three of the routines which behaviour therapists resort to frequently: anxiety reduction, aversion training and model learning. Let me illustrate briefly how they work:

If a young man wants to lose his uncontrollable fear of girls, his behaviour therapist may show him pictures or films of girls and let the young man speak about his feelings, let him rate the intensity of his fear and even stop the performance when it gets too much for him. This arrangement, the presence of the therapist, perhaps his encouragement of the patient to tolerate his fear a little longer, and his praise of him when he does, all tend to reduce the patient's anxiety. In a later session the behaviour therapist may arrange a meeting with a live girl, and between sessions he may give the patient small tasks, such as looking at girls more persistently at his place of work, trying to smile or wink at them, to see what happens and tell the therapist. Again the therapist will laud him, and so on. This is *anxiety reduction.*

It sounds simple, if a bit rigged. It is new, or so behaviour therapists claimed at the time it started. But is it really new? Is there no anxiety reduction in classical psychotherapy? Of course there is. The classical therapist's benevolent presence, the fact that he does not get anxious or angry or depressed when the patient does, that he seems to understand him, his wishes and his interests, sometimes even those that he has not been aware of or admitted to himself, all serve to reduce the patient's various anxieties. However, by letting the patient set the pace, select the themes and develop his relationship with the therapist in any way he wants to, both consciously and unconsciously, the classical therapist keeps the therapeutic process wide open. It may be more difficult for the therapist to handle and keep track of, and it may take longer, but it is not rigged by the therapist. There are no manipulations, no orders, no lessons. The patient does it all himself, and the therapist helps him do it.

Aversion training might be applied, for example, to an alcoholic who does not want to drink, but can't help it, or a child who does not want to wet the bed but does. In one instance of the former, a medication called Antabus was used to scare the alcoholic, while hospitalized, into never touching liquor again. He was taking the medication regularly and kept dry. Then he was asked to take a drink, whereupon he felt physically utterly miserable. That was the effect of Antabus, as previously announced to him. So shocked was the patient, the doctors assumed, that he would never drink again. At least as long as he kept taking Antabus.

A six-year-old bed-wetting boy was prescribed bed-wetters' pants that he had to wear at night. Whenever even a drop of urine reached the pants, an alarm would sound and wake him up. In this example, a young therapist, a woman, and the shy boy, after some exchanges which he seemed to enjoy, agreed upon the training pants, and there was no bed-wetting thereafter. In fact, during the sixth session the therapist wondered whether he could do without the training pants. Sure enough he could.

Psychoanalytically oriented therapy does not resort to aversion training. Forbidding, scaring or shocking the patient – behaviour therapists do it sometimes even with mild electric shocks – goes against the grain of classical psychotherapy. The psychoanalytic assumption is that the patient will give up any dubious or compulsive pleasure all by himself, once he finds out what has kept him from the greater ordinary pleasures that most people are able to enjoy. This would hold even for perversions which, incidentally, behaviour therapists have also tried to cure by aversion training. If the patient had not been crudely discouraged in the past, he or she, the pervert, would enjoy conventional sexual pleasures more than perversion. In classical psychotherapy, relieving the patient gradually and in all the recesses of his mind and past of the fears that have been attached to sexual activity would lead him back to opportunities that he thought were lost to him. He would feel tempted in new ways and begin to try for more ordinary sexual contacts.

One could probably say that wherever aversion training appeared to work it did so because of a love that the patient developed for the therapist or some other person. The alcoholic needs a motherly attendant who will see to it that he always takes Antabus or who wants him in other ways to stay dry. The bed-wetter boy needed the attention of an attractive young woman, the therapist, in order to stop his symptom, and indeed, when the therapist terminated the treatment, he wet the bed again, even with his training pants on.

In *model learning*, the third routine I have mentioned, the behaviour therapist demonstrates to the patient that he can do what he is afraid to do. If he cannot ride elevators, the therapist may show him, take him with him, let him press the buttons himself and one day merely stand by while the patient uses the elevator alone. Fear of dirt may require showing the patient that the therapist can handle dirt. The hope is that sooner or later the patient will follow suit. This routine has also been called identification learning, regrettably without due credit to Freud's concept of identification, an important defence mechanism. Model learning is teaching by showing.

Here too behaviour therapists were likely, at least in their early days, to neglect complexities and implications. What if a male therapist takes his woman patient out into the street to help her cope with her phobia for crowded places, but she does not seem to get any better, whereas a female therapist to whom she eventually switches succeeds within a few trials? It may have something to do with the possibility that it is easier for a woman to identify with or learn from a woman than from a man. Alternatively, it may turn out that moving in the crowd with a supportive man, the therapist, had become an end in itself. The patient did not mind mingling with people when she had male company, but she was afraid of men. Conceivably, that was her problem.

Is there teaching by showing or identification learning in classical psychotherapy? What with all the listening and withholding, and commenting and interpreting, but no telling, no actual helping, the answer seems to be 'No'. Yet there is identification learning. In the course of treatment, the patient gets to know the therapist better and better as a therapist, if not as a person. Sometimes the patient can anticipate some of the responses and interventions he gets from him – increasingly so, as time goes on. The patient learns to deal with his own feelings, wishes and conflicts in ways that he has observed happening with his therapist. He learns to handle himself as the therapist handled him, the patient, and his, the patient's, feelings, wishes and conflicts. He has identified with the therapist in spite of the fact that the therapist has shown nothing, or at least as little as possible, of himself as a person. However, the therapist could not help exposing himself in his conduct of psychotherapy and in his interventions.

When a patient is able to anticipate much or most of what the therapist has to say to his revelations and confessions, the end of therapy may be drawing near. If those anticipations happen rather than seeming forced – that is, if they do not appear to come from a wish to outdo the therapist or to divert attention from a touchy theme, the end *is* drawing near.

When therapy ends, the patient is taking home, among other things, the therapist's benevolent and attentive attitude towards himself, the patient, and some or much of the therapeutic skill of the therapist as it has transpired in his interventions. Hopefully, the patient will use his introjection of the therapist in moments of contemplation and reverie rather than at work or in his dealings with his loved ones. Only if the patient wants to become a therapist himself might he use his introjection of the therapist also at work and with his patients; but even then not with his loved ones, for heaven's sake.

One way of evaluating the quality of services that different schools of psychotherapy or different therapists are offering might be to test how soon a patient can anticipate the therapist's interventions. Providing the therapist is not insisting on a long treatment, and not intentionally or awkwardly confounding the patient, but giving the best he can, those schools of psychotherapy where it takes longest truly to figure out the therapist and his interventions may be the ones that offer the most.

Outlook

Having tried to show that there may be no way around classical psychotherapy, either historically or in actual practice, the question remains: What should be done to make this better known?

My recommendations to other schools of psychotherapy: Get

yourself some good classical psychotherapists for your own team conferences and consultations about your own clinical work. Insist on consultations even if it amounts to what you and others call supervision within your own school or camp. Discontinue the consultations if the consultant is no good for you, something you could hardly do with a supervisor within your own school. Try another consultant. Give him records of your therapies. Ask him for his reasoning on your case, for alternative interpretations, for his diagnostic evaluation. Ask him to conduct a therapeutic interview before your eyes. And pay him a fair price for the time he spends with you.

And my recommendations to classical psychotherapists, especially to Freudians: Leave your closed shop, for such invitations. Concentrate on their cases. Show them in simple terms, in non-argumentative ways, what you can make of a case and how it jells in your mind. Show them how you would conduct a therapeutic interview. And perhaps, on occasion, invite a therapist from another school to tell you what he does in therapy. And perhaps, ask such a person to be your consultant on a particular case. Pay him a fair price too. Or do it on a barter basis, if you want to save on taxes. It is this kind of reciprocal interaction that may open up the most fruitful perspectives for the future.

Notes

[1] S. Freud: *Die Traumdeutung* (1900), *GW* II–III [*The Interpretation of Dreams, SE* IV–V]; *Zür Psychopathologie des Alltagslebens* (1904), *GW* IV [*The Psycho-Pathology of Everyday Life, SE* VI]; *Vorlesungen zur Einfuhrung in die Psychoanalyse* (1916–17), *GW* XI [*Introductory Lectures on Psycho-Analysis, SE* XV–XVI].

[2] C.G. Jung, *Wandlungen und Symbole der Libido* (1912), *Gesammelte Werke* (Olten and Freiburg, 1935–76), V; *Die Struktur des Unbewußten* (1916), ibid., VII. A. Adler: *Über den nervösen Charakter* (1912), 4th edn. (Munich 1928); *Praxis und Theorie der Individualpsychologie* (1920), 3rd edn. (Munich 1927). H. Schultz-Hencke: *Der gehemmte Mensch* (Leipzig 1940); *Lehrbuch der analytischen Psychotherapie* (Stuttgart 1951). H.S. Sullivan: *Conception of Modern Psychiatry* (Washington, D.C., 1947): *The Interpersonal Theory of Psychiatry* (New York 1953).

[3] S. Freud: *Jenseits des Lustprinzips* (1920), *GW* XIII [*Beyond the Pleasure Principle, SE* XVIII]; *Das Ich und das Es* (1923), *GW* XIII [*The Ego and the Id, SE* XIX]; *Hemmung, Symptom und Angst* (1926), *GW* XIV [*Inhibitions, Symptoms and Anxiety, SE* XX].

[4] M. von Schlick, *Gesammelte Aufsätze* (Vienna 1938).

[5] H. Hartmann, *Die Grundlagen der Psychoanalyse* (Leipzig 1927); L.S. Kubie, *Practical and Theoretical Aspects of Psychoanalysis* (New York 1950); T.M. French, *The Integration of Behavior* (Chicago 1952–8), vol. I: *Basic Postulates*; W. Toman, *Introduction to Psychoanalytic Theory of Motivation* (London and New York 1960); E. Prelinger and C.N. Zimet, *An Ego-Psychological Approach to Character Assessment* (Glencoe, Ill., and London 1964); G.S. Klein, *Psychoanalytic Theory* (New York 1976); R. Schafer, *A New Language for Psychoanalysis* (New Haven, Conn., 1976).

[6] A. Grünbaum, *The Foundations of Psychoanalysis* (Berkeley, Calif., Los Angeles and London 1984).

[7] See also Toman, *Introduction to Theory of Motivation*, and *Motivation, Persönlichkeit,*

Umwelt (Göttingen 1968); *Tiefenpsychologie* (Stuttgart 1978); *Familientherapie* (Darmstadt 1979).

[8] K. Horney, *New Ways in Psychoanalysis* (New York 1939); E. Fromm, *Escape from Freedom* (New York 1941); S.A. Kardiner, *The Psychological Frontiers of Man* (New York 1945); and see n. 2.

[9] K. Jaspers, *Psychologie der Weltanschauungen*, 4th edn. (Berlin 1954). V.E. Frankl, *Die Existenzanalyse und die Probleme der Zeit* (Vienna 1947); V. von Weizsäcker, *Der Gestaltkreis* (Stuttgart 1947); L. Binswanger, *Grundformen und Erkenntnis menschlichen Daseins* (Zürich 1953); R. May, *Existential Psychology* (New York 1961).

[10] A. Angyal, *Foundations for a Science of Personality* (New York 1941). C.R. Rogers: *Counselling and Psychotherapy* (Boston and New York 1942; in German, Munich 1972); *Client-Centered Therapy* (Boston and New York 1951). A.H. Maslow: *Motivation and Personality* (New York 1954); *Toward a Psychology of Being* (Princeton, N.J., 1962). *The Course of Human Life*, ed. C. Bühler and K. Massarik (New York 1968; in German, Stuttgart 1969).

[11] HYPNOTHERAPY: L.R. Wolberg, *Medical Hypnosis*, 2 vols. (New York 1948); M.H. Erickson, *Advanced Techniques of Hypnosis and Therapy*, ed. J. Haley (New York and London 1967). PSYCHODRAMA: J.L. Moreno, *Psychodrama* (New York 1946). GESTALT THERAPY: F. Perls, R. Hefferline and P. Goodman, *Gestalt Therapy* (New York 1951). DIRECT ANALYSIS: J.N. Rosen, *Direct Analysis* (New York 1953). TRANSACTION ANALYSIS: Eric Berne, *Games People Play* (New York 1964; in German, Hamburg 1967). PRIMAL THERAPY: A. Janov, *The Primal Scream* (New York 1970; in German, Frankfurt 1973). BODY AND MOVEMENT THERAPY: H.G. Petzold: *Psychotherapie und Körperdynamik* (Paderborn 1974); *Die neuen Körpertherapien* (Paderborn 1977). BIOENERGETICS: A. Lowen, *Bioenergetics* (New York 1975), based on W. Reich, *Charakteranalyse* (Copenhagen 1933; in English, *Character Analysis*, 2nd edn., Los Angeles 1945).

[12] RATIONAL-EMOTIVE THERAPY: A. Ellis, *An Introduction to the Principles of Scientific Psychoanalysis* (Provincetown, Mass., 1950). REALITY THERAPY: W. Glasser, *Reality Therapy* (New York 1965; in German, Weinheim, Basel 1972). COMMUNICATION THERAPY: G. Bateson *et al.*, 'Toward a Theory of Schizophrenia', *Behavioral Science*, 1956, no. 1, 251–64; R.D. Laing, H. Philippson and L. Russell, *Interpersonal Perception* (London 1966); P. Watzlawik, J.H. Beavin and D.D. Jackson, *Pragmatics of Human Communication. A Study of Interactional Patterns, Pathologies and Paradoxes* (New York 1967; in German, Bern 1969).

[13] J. Dollard and N.E. Miller, *Personality and Psychotherapy* (New York and London 1950).

[14] H.J. Eysenck, *The Structure of Personality* (New York 1953; in German, 1959). J. Wolpe, *Psychotherapy by Reciprocal Inhibition* (Stanford, Calif., 1958); H.J. Eysenck, *Experiments in Behavior Therapy* (London and New York 1964); V. Meyer and E.S. Chesser, *Behavior Therapy in Clinical Psychiatry* (Harmondsworth 1970; in German, Stuttgart 1971); and others.

[15] M. Mahoney, *Cognition and Behavior Modification* (Cambridge, Mass., 1974); D. Meichenbaum, *Cognitive Behavior Modification: An Integrative Approach* (New York 1977).

[16] Rogers, *Counselling and Psychotherapy* and *Client-Centered Therapy*.

[17] See Rogers, *Counselling and Psychotherapy*.

[18] J.B. Watson, *Psychology from the Standpoint of a Behaviorist* (Philadelphia 1919).

23

The Significance of the Freud Museum

David Newlands

A living museum

At a symposium organized to celebrate the opening of the Freud Museum in July 1986, the historian Peter Gay offered salutary words of warning: 'A museum is a danger as well as an opportunity. The term invites thoughts of immobility, of things done with and put under glass. It would be unfortunate, nor is it necessary, for the Freud Museum to become such an institution'.[1] Many people would welcome a static museum in London to venerate Freud, to provide a shrine to the man whose genius created a profession and changed the way we see ourselves and those with whom we come in contact. To create such an edifice would be a danger and of little benefit to the psychoanalytic profession or to Freudian scholarship. Instead, the Freud Museum is being developed as a forum for the presentation, discussion and interpretation of Freud's life and work, a museum that absorbs new ideas, evaluates new insights and offers a place where those interested in mental health knowledge can meet. I believe Freud would have welcomed such a dynamic approach to a museum, as he did not develop a fixed body of observations, but a set of insights, which he continually refined, as he studied the functioning of the human mind.

Not all visitors come to learn about Freud and his work; some are merely curious to see the couch on which his now famous patients recalled their past experiences, others to heap scorn on a man whose contributions they do not accept or understand. The Museum must provide an opportunity for these visitors to re-examine their views about Freud and his work. This can only be done if the Museum is a 'living' place, rather than, as Professor Gay warns, an institution that 'invites thoughts of immobility, of things done with and put under glass'.

The presentation of Freud and his work

Before the Museum opened, much of what was in the Freud family home was seen only by those personally admitted by Miss Freud.

During the last two decades of her life, Anna Freud, with the collaboration of Dr Muriel Gardiner, through Dr Gardiner's New-Land Foundation, made arrangements for her home to become a public museum. The centre-piece of the Museum is Sigmund Freud's study and library, with his couch, books and antiquities, brought from his Vienna home and working place and kept intact by Anna Freud to show the environment in which Freud worked during his life in London.

But the Museum will have missed an opportunity to be an educational institution if it provides only restored rooms. The major significance of the Museum will be its active encouragement of dialogue on Freud's contributions to mental health, social studies and the humanities, through the development of exhibits, research, publications and public programmes.

The exhibits are to be developed on the assumption that visitors may have little specific knowledge about Freud. The aim is also to enlighten the curious and interested lay person as well as to correct misunderstandings propagated by the misinformed. Therefore, the exhibits will attempt to communicate Freud's ideas in non-technical language, and at a level of complexity that will be easily comprehensible to the majority of the visitors.

There is no doubt that by presenting exhibits and public programmes the Museum may at times appear controversial, even if it avoids the pitfalls of being provocative or superficial. Currently in preparation are two exhibits on major subjects from the work of Freud, applying some of the techniques pioneered by the British Museum (Natural History), which has for many years experimented with improved methods of communicating abstract ideas through exhibition texts and graphics.

The Museum has limited physical and financial resources and plans to co-operate with other organizations in the mental health professions, universities, and public museums in order to offer lectures, seminars and workshops. Touring exhibits and the loan of objects from the collection for a short term are also being planned. The symposium on 'Freud in London' is an example of the deep interest of the Museum in collaboration and co-operation.

An active research programme

The Museum, if it is to be 'alive', must have a research programme to give authority to its interpretation and presentation of Freud's life and work. Research is not restricted to citing what has already been published by others, but should contribute new insights, using unpublished sources and the Museum's collection.

Many documents, numbering in the thousands, were kept in the house during Miss Freud's lifetime. It was her wish that these be placed

20 and 21. The Freud Museum, London: books and antiquities, and (*below*) the couch.

together with others of her father's papers which had been collected by the Sigmund Freud Archives Inc. of New York, and deposited in the Library of Congress in Washington, D.C. To this end Miss Freud made arrangements in 1976 for all the original manuscripts of Freud's published works to go to the Library of Congress after her death.[2]

There remains at the Museum a collection of about 2,000 documents. These comprise:

letters of Lou Andreas-Salomé to Freud, covering the years 1912–32, approximately 150 documents;

letters between Sigmund Freud and Oscar Pfister, covering the years 1909–37, approximately 134 documents;

letters from Anna Freud to Sigmund Freud, 1910–30, a total of 139 documents;

letters from Lou Andreas-Salomé to Anna Freud, *c.* 1921–30, numbering 217;

letters between Freud and Abraham, Ferenczi, Jones, Jung, Putnam, Rank, Marie Bonaparte and other persons, number several hundreds;

letters to Freud from well-known persons such as Einstein, Thomas Mann, Charcot, Breuer, Stefan Zweig, Fliess;

letters from Sigmund Freud to Martha, Minna, and other members of his family, about 500 items;

Freud's concise chronicle, 1929–39;

his list of correspondence during his life in London and his address book;

exit permits for the family to leave Vienna, notification of emigration tax owed by the Freuds, and a considerable body of other material which is in the process of being catalogued.

The archive at the Museum is five-sixths owned by the Sigmund Freud Archives Inc. of New York, through gifts made by the beneficiaries of Sigmund Freud's estate. Anna Freud's one-sixth share in the material was bequeathed to the English Charitable Trust formed at her death. It is the intention of the Trustees of the charity, a number of whom are also trustees of the Sigmund Freud Archives Inc. of New York, that all this material should eventually be sent to the Library of Congress. The removal of the documentary material to the USA will not limit the value of the museum as a centre for research, because copies of the material will be available for public use in London.

At a press conference on 25 July 1986, shortly before the opening of the Museum, the Trustees announced that documentary material in London and the USA would be available to researchers as soon as possible. It would be necessary to withhold only those documents which, if released, would be a breach of medical confidentiality. The decision as to what will be released will be made by the Sigmund Freud Archives Inc. of New York.

Anna Freud gave her Trustees the absolute power to dispose of her correspondence and other records. Most of her papers and photographs which were in the house have been sent, or are being sent, to the Library of Congress. It is hoped the return of all the items related to Miss Freud's life and work can eventually be negotiated, in order to establish an Anna Freud Archive. Many of Miss Freud's colleagues, still active in the psychoanalytical profession in Britain and the USA, would value such an archive, and it is hoped that the prospect of proper care and handling of material related to Miss Freud will mean that the documents can be given to the Museum.

Freud's library of 2,500 volumes will remain in London. The Museum staff have identified at least 120 books with Freud's markings or annotations, which can now be consulted by researchers, but under conditions that will protect these fragile volumes from damage.

In the 1970s two colleagues of Miss Freud's catalogued the books in the library. In March 1986 the Museum staff made an inventory of these books as they were unpacked from boxes in which they had been stored during renovations of the house. A comparison of that inventory with the previous records revealed that some books are missing. It is likely that in the last few years of her life Miss Freud lent books, which for some reason were never returned. A list of missing books is being compiled, in the hope that some may find their way back to the Museum.

A complete bibliographic catalogue of the library, prepared according to Library of Congress standards, should be completed shortly. This catalogue of the books, and of Freud's antiquities, will be published in both microform and book form.

The Museum's collection, apart from the books, consists of approximately 75 pieces of furniture, 1,800 antiquities, 100 paintings, prints or etchings, 20 Oriental carpets, and 3,500 photographs (1,500 pre-1939 and 2,000 post-1939). Many of the objects in the Museum are significant in themselves, beyond the part they played in forming the environment in which Freud lived and worked. Now for the first time these are available for viewing, and, under certain conditions, for detailed examination. Access to this material has been given to a number of scholars so they can publish reports of the collection in the relevant scholarly journals.

A public museum of high standard

The Museum does not receive a guaranteed annual income from any source. It depends on admission fees, earnings from its non-Museum assets, the financial support of the Friends of the Freud Museum, grants from foundations such as the New-Land Foundation, donations from individuals, and the profits, if any, from sales.

Opening the Museum to the public has meant that some rooms could not be kept as they were during Miss Freud's lifetime. For example, to have made a completely accurate replica of the study / library would have meant keeping only the two globe lights that were there when Freud used the rooms. But obviously visitors require more light to view adequately the antiquities and furnishings; even with additional lighting, some visitors have complained of inadequate illumination.

Freud's Oriental carpets have been put back on the floors, but 25,000 pairs of feet walking over them each year would soon destroy these valuable coverings. The carpets cannot be allowed to wear away, but if the Museum were to purchase replacements, it would be criticized for being inauthentic or for desecrating Freud's home. So areas of wear have been covered with runners. Compromises are necessary, but may upset those who would prefer accuracy of restoration to public accessibility and safety.

Modern museums are also required, often by statute, to provide public amenities such as toilets, rest areas, fire extinguishers, exit signs, security equipment (including exterior lighting). Not to provide these would either be a violation of the law, or would seriously restrict the Freud Museum's ability to function as a public institution. A museum that responds to the interest and need of the public has to resolve many conflicting demands; for example, protection of the collection versus its accessibility to the public; or the safety of visitors and accuracy of restoration.

Should a sales area be included in the Museum? Some believe it should, offering for sale items that are educational, as an extension of the Museum's education programme. Visitors can purchase books and other material that will not only further their knowledge of Freud but will also be a memento of their visit.

A tale of two museums

In 1969, when the Freud Society was being established, with one of its aims being to create a museum to Freud in Vienna, at Berggasse 19, an approach was made to Anna Freud by B'nai B'rith of Europe. Through B'nai B'rith of the United Kingdom, Miss Freud was asked to give her approval to the museum project and to agree to the return of Freud's furniture, books, antiquities, etc. to Vienna. A London businessman was asked to act as intermediary in any negotiations. B'nai B'rith was seen as an appropriate channel through which to approach Miss Freud because of her father's lifetime interest in that organization.[3]

It was at this point that news reports in the *Jewish Chronicle* and the London *Daily Express* in England and reports in Austrian newspapers began a round of speculation and false hopes. While the British papers reported Miss Freud as saying that the items would not go back to

page from Freud's autograph chronicle for 1938; the first entry, for Friday 15 July,
the sale of the U.S. rights of *Moses and Monotheism*.

Vienna, the Austrian newspapers gave a different story. The British newspaper reports prompted a letter from the B'nai B'rith intermediary in London to Anna Freud:

May I express my personal admiration and thanks to you for making a stand in maintaining Freud's home as it is, and resisting any attempts to remove 'souvenirs' to Vienna. I am quite sure that [as] London was his last refuge and resting place . . . he would not have wished any of his precious possessions to be returned to Austria, which up to 1969 took very little interest in preserving the dignity of his last residence. Quite apart from this, it is only right that his possessions should share the fate of the great man himself and should find [a] final resting place here in London.

On 3 October 1969 Miss Freud responded, 'Thank you very much for your nice letter. I do wish the Viennese would not make so much undignified noise now and print all the most untrue items. I must say that I preferred the quiet and neglect that preceded it. I am glad that you understand.'[4]

A decade later, in response to a letter from the former intermediary, Miss Freud wrote to say, 'As regards your question about the future of my father's library, antique collection, etc., this is not difficult to answer. Fortunately enough, an American foundation is ready to acquire my house here either before or after my death and keep my father's rooms intact as a Freud museum. I am very happy about that solution . . .'.[5] Herein lies the tale of two museums.

The existence of two museums devoted to Freud, one in Vienna and one in London, is a physical reminder of the historical events which forced the Freud family to flee Austria for sanctuary in England. The Freuds were able to come to England and establish a new home at 20 Maresfield Gardens through the help and support of psychoanalysts, the British Government, and Jews throughout the world. Now, almost fifty years later, the house has been restored as a museum thanks to the generosity of these same groups.

The Museum is a memorial to the Jews who had found refuge in England, and those who lost their lives in the Holocaust. Freud suffered all his life from anti-Semitism, and the Museum is a reminder to many visitors of the awful consequences of anti-Semitism in the loss of countless lives and the destruction of a major part of the intellectual life of European society. Perhaps the most eloquent statement we have about the relationship of the Museum to the Jewish community is a single sheet among the collection of greetings sent to Freud on his eightieth birthday, which reads, 'To the greatest contributor of modern times to the self-respect of the Jews'.

A museum to Freud in London must reflect the unique contribution of Freud to our culture, the complex development of the profession he founded, the continuing debate about Freud's central ideas, and the public interest in a man whose name so many have heard, but whose contributions so few have understood.

Freud in London should not be a copy of Freud in Vienna; Freud's legacy is woven into the cloth of time and the history of the Western world. I can only hope that the Freud Museum in London will in years to come present as clearly as possible the life and work of Freud to those of us who are his beneficiaries.

1 November 1986

Notes

[1] From p. 1 of the TS of the lecture by Peter Gay, delivered on 28 July 1986 to mark the opening of the Freud Museum. (Copies of this typescript, and of the other documents and letters referred to in these notes, are in the archives of the Museum.)

[2] 'Instrument of Gift', signed by Anna Freud, 19 May 1976.

[3] See the correspondence in the spring of 1969 between Georges M. Bloch, Fred Worms, Arnold Horwell, E.L. Ehrlich and Anna Freud.

[4] Letter of 1 Oct 1969 from Arnold Horwell to Anna Freud; letter of 3 Oct 1969 from Anna Freud to Arnold Horwell.

[5] Letter of 26 Nov 1979 from Anna Freud to Arnold Horwell.

Notes on Contributors

STEPHEN BANN read history at the University of Cambridge, and in 1967 joined the staff of the University of Kent, where he is at present chairman of the Board of Studies in History and Theory of Art, and Reader in Modern Cultural Studies. His publications include two studies of the twentieth-century avant-garde, *Experimental Painting* (1970) and *The Tradition of Constructivism* (1974), as well as a work on the representation of history in visual and verbal forms, *The Clothing of Clio* (1984). He edited a special supplement on Adrian Stokes for *PN Review* (no. 15, 1980), and helped to compile the documentary section of the 1982 Stokes retrospective exhibition at the Serpentine Gallery, London.

JOHN BOWLBY read natural sciences and psychology at Cambridge, qualified in medicine in 1933 and in psychoanalysis in 1937, and specialized thereafter in child psychiatry. After five years as an army psychiatrist, he joined the Tavistock Clinic in 1946 as chairman of the Department for Children and Parents. Since his retirement in 1972, he has continued to work at the Clinic in an honorary capacity. His publications include *Forty-four Juvenile Thieves* (1946), *Maternal Care and Mental Health* (1951), *Attachment and Loss* (3 vols., 1969, 1973, 1980) and *The Making and Breaking of Affectional Bonds* (1979).

TERESA BRENNAN studied political philosophy and social psychology at the Universities of Melbourne and Sydney (Australia) and Cambridge (England), and psychoanalysis at the Tavistock Clinic in London. She is the author of *Bending the Stick*, a study of feminism and the feminine (forthcoming), and editor of another book, *New Directions in Psychoanalysis and Feminism* (forthcoming in 1988).

ERNST FEDERN was born in 1914 in Vienna, and studied law, social sciences and history at the University of Vienna. Imprisoned in the 1930s for his part in the anti-fascist resistance, he spent seven years in the concentration camps of Dachau and Buchenwald, before being liberated by the US Army. In 1948 he joined his family in New York City, where he took a degree at Columbia

University in 1951. He worked as a therapist and supervisor of social work in New York and Cleveland, Ohio, until 1972, when he returned to Austria to become a psycho-social consultant and therapist in the reformed state correctional system. Editor, with Herman Nunberg, of the four-volume *Minutes of the Vienna Psychoanalytic Society, 1908–1918* (1962–75), and co-editor of the *Collected Papers* of his father, Paul Federn (1952), he is also the author of more than 70 papers on psychoanalysis and its applications.

ERNEST GELLNER, born in Paris in 1925, was educated in Prague and in England, at Balliol College, Oxford, and the University of London (Ph.D. in Social Anthropology, 1961). He was on the staff of the London School of Economics, 1949–84 (as Professor after 1962); in 1984 he became William Wyse Professor of Social Anthropology in the University of Cambridge, where he is a Fellow of King's College. His principal publications are *Words and Things* (1959); *Nations and Nationalism* (1983); *The Psychoanalytic Movement* (1985); *Culture, Identity and Politics* (1987).

SANDER L. GILMAN is Professor of Humane Studies in the College of Arts and Sciences, Cornell University, and Professor of Psychiatry (History), Cornell Medical College, Ithaca, N.Y. He is the author of more than 20 books, the most recent being *Jewish Self-Hatred* (1986).

MURRAY G. HALL was born in 1947 in Winnipeg, Manitoba, Canada, and attended elementary and secondary schools in Manitoba, Ontario and West Germany. He holds degrees in French and German from Queen's University, Kingston, Ontario, and from the University of Vienna (Dr. phil. 1975, with a thesis on Robert Musil; Dr. phil. habil. 1987), and is now *Dozent* at the Institut für Germanistik in Vienna. He has worked on various editions of Musil's writings, and is co-editor of the 2 vol. *Briefe 1901–1942* (1981). His publications on Austrian literature and the publishing trade in the interwar years include *Der Fall Bettauer* (Vienna 1978) and *Österreichische Verlagsgeschichte 1918–1938* (2 vols., Vienna 1985).

ALEX HOLDER, Dr. phil., was born in 1931 in Basel, Switzerland, and studied English, German and history at the University of Basel. Later he studied psychology at University College, London, and trained as a psychoanalyst for children at the Anna Freud Centre in Hampstead, and as a psychoanalyst for adults at the British Institute for Psycho-Analysis. Since 1983 he has been head of the Department of Child and Adolescent Psychotherapy at the Michael Balint Institut in Hamburg, West Germany. He is a training analyst and supervisor in the German Psycho-Analytical Association.

HELMUT JUNKER, born in 1934, teaches psychoanalysis at the University of Kassel in West Germany. He is a member, through the German Association, of the International Psycho-Analytic Association and has published widely in the fields of psychoanalysis and psychotherapy. He is also the author, or co-author, of a number of novels.

PEARL H.M. KING, B.A. Hons. in Psychology, worked in industry doing social research with the Medical Research Council and the Tavistock Institute of Human Relations, before qualifying as a psychoanalyst in 1950. She has been a training analyst since 1955, and has published a number of clinical and historical papers. She has held many administrative posts in psychoanalytic organizations, including those of secretary, vice-president, and president of the British Psycho-Analytical Society; she was secretary of the International Psycho-Analytical Association from 1957 to 1961. As Honorary Archivist of the British Society, she is currently engaged in reorganizing the Society's archives and, with the help of others, entering the contents on a computer data base in order to index them.

DAVID L. NEWLANDS, first Curator of the Freud Museum in London, is now Executive Director of the Ontario Museum Association, Toronto. He holds B.A. and M.A. degrees in Near Eastern Studies from Wilfred Laurier University, Waterloo, Ontario, and in the 1970s worked in the Canadiana Department of the Royal Ontario Museum, Toronto, and later as coordinator of the M.A. programme in Museum Studies at the University of Toronto. From 1982 he was Principal Curator of the Museums of Malawi, East Africa, before being given responsibility for establishing the Freud Museum in London. He has published extensively in historical archaeology and museology, as well as in his field of special interest, Canadian potteries.

DARIUS GRAY ORNSTON, JR., MD, a psychiatrist, has published a series of studies on the problems of translating Freud. His articles on the Standard Edition have been widely circulated and translated into several languages. After 25 years of private practice and teaching at Yale University, he has recently moved to Greenville, S. Car., where he is practicing general psychiatry and continuing his research into Freud's sources and style.

IVAR OXAAL, of Norwegian descent, was born in Oak Park, Ill., in 1931, but spent his childhood in Norway. Educated at schools and universities in Ohio, he worked as a newspaper reporter and at other jobs before completing a Ph.D. in Political Sociology at UCLA in 1964. For some years he conducted research in the Caribbean area, and was Foundation Professor of Sociology at the University of Guyana, where he headed a commission of enquiry into industrial relations in the Guyanese bauxite industry. His interest in Freud and

Vienna stems from a convergence in his research on intellectual history and race relations; his publications include *Black Intellectuals: Dilemmas of Race and Class in Trinidad* (repr. 1982), and (as editor and contributor) *Jews, Antisemitism and Culture in Vienna* (1987). He is now Honorary Research Fellow in the Department of European and Modern Dutch Studies at the University of Hull.

R. ANDREW PASKAUSKAS holds M.A. and Ph.D. degrees in the History and Philosophy of Science from the University of Toronto. He was a Research Fellow at the Wellcome Institute for the History of Medicine (1985–7), and a Freud Fellow at the Freud Museum (1986–7). He is currently a member of the Faculty of Medicine, Department of Humanities and Social Studies in Medicine, at McGill University in Montreal, where he is working on a book-length study of Freud's Secret Committee. His edition of *The Freud/Jones Correspondence, 1908–1939* is forthcoming.

UWE HENRIK PETERS, born in 1930 at Kiel (Holstein), Germany, attended the medical schools of Freiburg/Br., Heidelberg and Kiel Universities, and served his internship in Strasbourg. He qualified as an MD in 1957, and from 1959 worked in the Department of Nervous and Mental Diseases at Christian Albrecht University, Kiel, after 1965 as lecturer in neurology and psychiatry. In 1969 he went to Johannes Gutenberg University in Mainz as Professor of Neuro-psychiatry; since 1979 he has been Professor of Neurology and Psychiatry in the University of Cologne. In 1981 he was Adjunct Professor of German Literature at Cornell University, Ithaca, N.Y. His main fields of interest are disturbances of texts and language in the mentally ill, and the history of psychiatry; among the 29 books of which he is author or editor are *Wörterbuch der Psychiatrie u nd medizinischen Psychologie* (Munich 1971, 4th edn. 1988); *Anna Freud. Ein Leben für das Kind* (Munich 1979), translated into both English (1985) and French (1987); and *Hölderlin – Wider die These vom edlen Simulanten* (Reinbek b. Hamburg 1982).

MALCOLM PINES, MB, ChB (Cantab), FRCP, FRCPsych, DPM (Distinction), is a full member of the British Psycho-Analytical Society, and a founder member of the Institute of Group Analysis, London. He has been a consultant psychotherapist at the Tavistock Clinic and the Maudsley Hospital, Senior Lecturer in Psychotherapy at St. George's Hospital, and consultant psycho-therapist at the Cassel Hospital, Richmond, Surrey. A former president of the Psychiatry Section, Royal Society of Medicine, and past president of the International Association of Group Psychotherapy, he is the editor of the International Library of Group Psychotherapy and Process, and editor of the journal *Group Analysis*. He is the editor of two books, *The Evolution of Group Analysis* (1983) and *Bion and Group Psychotherapy* (1985), and the author of numerous articles on related subjects.

RITCHIE ROBERTSON is Fellow in German at Downing College, Cambridge. He is the author of *Kafka: Judaism, Politics, and Literature* (1985) and *Heine* (1988), as well as many articles on German and comparative literature.

NAOMI SEGAL is a Fellow of St. John's College, Cambridge, where she teaches French, German, and comparative literature. In addition to articles and reviews, her publications include *The Banal Object: Theme and Thematics in Proust, Rilke, Hofmannsthal and Sartre* (1981), *The Unintended Reader: Feminism and 'Manon Lescaut'* (1986) and *Narcissus and Echo: Women in the French* récit (forthcoming 1988). She is currently working on a study of mother–infant relations in literature and feminist–psychoanalytic theory, to be published under the title *Mothers and Daughters and Sons*.

MARTIN STANTON was educated at the University of Sussex, the Ecole Normale Supérieure in Paris, and at St. Antony's College, Oxford, where he obtained a doctorate in Modern History in 1975. He has published a number of articles, as well as poems and reviews, in journals including the *London Magazine, PN Review*, the *TLS*, the *Journal of Modern History, History Today* and *Government and Opposition*. His first book, *Outside the Dream: Lacan and French Styles of Psychoanalysis*, appeared in 1983, and has since been translated into French and Japanese. He is working on a history of European intellectuals, politics and the media, 1860–1968, and is finishing a novel. He is presently a Lecturer and Director of Graduate Studies in European Studies at the University of Kent.

RICCARDO STEINER, a full member of the British Psycho-Analytical Society, has studied linguistics, philosophy, history of ideas and psychology. He has published several papers, a number of which have been translated into Spanish, Italian and French, and a book on *The Process of Symbolisation in the Work of Melanie Klein* (published in Italian, 1975). He is at present researching the history of Freud translation in England, and is preparing his papers on the early Freud for publication.

EDWARD TIMMS is Lecturer in German at the University of Cambridge and Fellow of Gonville and Caius College. His interest in psychoanalysis originated from his study of Austrian culture and politics of the early twentieth century, the subject of his book *Karl Kraus – Apocalyptic Satirist: Culture and Catastrophe in Habsburg Vienna* (1986). He is joint editor of two collections of essays on comparative literature: *Unreal City: Urban Experience in Modern European Literature and Art* (1985) and *Visions and Blueprints: Avant-Garde Culture and Radical Politics in Early Twentieth-Century Europe* (1988). He is currently writing a book about the impact of psychoanalysis on literary form in the work of twentieth-century novelists.

WALTER TOMAN, born in 1920 in Vienna, received his Ph.D. in Psychology from the University of Vienna and his psychoanalytic training at the Vienna Psychoanalytic Institute. A lecturer at Vienna University until 1951, he lectured at Harvard University 1951–4, was Professor of Psychology at Brandeis University, Boston, 1954–64, and since 1964 has been Professor of Psychology at the University of Erlangen-Nürnberg, West Germany. He has been back to the USA on lecture tours almost every year. The focus of his teaching and research has been clinical psychology, the practice, training and evaluation of psychotherapy, and family structures and social contexts. He is the author of 10 books, published in both German and English, the best-known being *Family Constellation* (3rd edn. 1976), and the most recent *Tiefen-psychologie* [Depth Psychology] (1978) and *Familientherapie* [Family Therapy] (1979).

FREDERICK WYATT, born in Vienna in 1911, studied philosophy, psychology and literature at the University of Vienna, from which he received a Ph.D. in 1936. He left Austria in March 1938, and took up residence in the United States in December of that year, becoming an American citizen in 1944. He did postgraduate work at the University of London and at Columbia University, and continued his psychoanalytic training, begun in Vienna in 1933, in Boston, especially with Dr Hanns Sachs. From 1939 onwards he taught at American universities, including Ohio State, Harvard (and the Harvard Medical School) and Clark, and worked in a Veterans' Administration hospital. In 1952 he became director of the Psychological Clinic, and from 1956 to 1979 was Professor of Psychology, at the University of Michigan. He was Guest Professor at Freiburg University in West Germany, 1974–6, and has been Professor h.c. there since 1981. A training and supervising analyst in the German Psycho-Analytical Association, he has done research on the uses of phantasy, the structure and function of ideology, problems of training in psychoanalysis, and the history of the psychoanalytic movement, and has published widely on these and related subjects.

Index of Names